Regulating Competition

Cartels, trusts and agreements to reduce competition between firms have existed for centuries, but became particularly prevalent towards the end of the nineteenth century. In the mid-twentieth century governments began to use so called 'cartel registers' to monitor and regulate their behaviour. This book provides cases studies from more than a dozen countries to examine the emergence, application and eventual decline of this form of regulation.

Beginning with a comparison of the attitudes to regulation that led to monitoring, rather than prohibiting cartels, this book examines the international studies on cartels undertaken by the League of Nations before the Second World War. This is followed by a series of studies on the context of the registers, including the international context of the European Union, and the importance of lobby groups in shaping regulatory outcomes, using Finland as an example. Part II provides a broad international comparison of several countries' registers, with individual studies on Norway, Australia, Japan, Germany, Sweden and the Netherlands. After examining the impact of registration on business behaviour in the insurance industry, this book concludes with an overview of the lessons to be learned from twentieth-century efforts to regulate competition.

With a foreword by Harm G. Schröter, this book outlines the rise and fall of a system that allowed nations to tailor their approach to regulating competition to their individual circumstances while also responding to the pressures of globalisation that emerged after the Second World War. This book is suitable for those who are interested in and study economic history, international economics and business history.

Susanna Fellman is Professor of Business History at the School of Business Economics and Law, University of Gothenburg, Sweden.

Martin Shanahan is Professor of Economic and Business History at the School of Business, University of South Australia.

Routledge Explorations in Economic History
Edited by Lars Magnusson
Uppsala University, Sweden

For a complete list of titles in this series, please visit www.routledge.com.

48 **The International Tin Cartel**
   John Hillman

49 **The South Sea Bubble**
   Helen J. Paul

50 **Ideas and Economic Crises in Britain from Attlee to Blair (1945–2005)**
   Matthias Matthijs

51 **Bengal Industries and the British Industrial Revolution (1757–1857)**
   Indrajit Ray

52 **The Evolving Structure of the East Asian Economic System since 1700**
   Edited by A. J. H. Latham and Heita Kawakatsu

53 **German Immigration and Servitude in America, 1709–1920**
   Farley Grubb

54 **The Rise of Planning in Industrial America, 1865–1914**
   Richard Adelstein

55 **An Economic History of Modern Sweden**
   Lennart Schön

56 **The Standard of Living and Revolutions in Russia, 1700–1917**
   Boris Mironov (edited by Gregory L. Freeze)

57 **Europe's Green Revolution and Others Since**
   The rise and fall of peasant-friendly plant breeding
   Jonathan Harwood

58 **Economic Analysis of Institutional Change in Ancient Greece**
   Carl Hampus-Lyttkens

59 **Labour-Intensive Industrialization in Global History**
   Edited by Gareth Austin and Kaoru Sugihara

60 **The History of Bankruptcy**
   Economic, social and cultural implications in early modern Europe
   Edited by Thomas Max Safley

61 **The Political Economy of Disaster**
Destitution, plunder and earthquake in Haiti
Mats Lundahl

62 **Nationalism and Economic Development in Modern Eurasia**
Carl Mosk

63 **Agricultural Transformation in a Global History Perspective**
Edited by Ellen Hillbom and Patrick Svensson

64 **Colonial Exploitation and Economic Development**
The Belgian Congo and the Netherlands Indies compared
Edited by Ewout Frankema and Frans Buelens

65 **The State and Business in the Major Powers**
An economic history 1815–1939
Robert Millward

66 **Privatization and Transition in Russia in the Early 1990s**
Carol Scott Leonard and David Pitt-Watson

67 **Large Databases in Economic History**
Research methods and case studies
Edited by Mark Casson and Nigar Hashimzade

68 **A History of Market Performance**
From ancient Babylonia to the modern world
Edited by R. J. van der Spek, Jan Luiten van Zanden and Bas van Leeuwen

69 **Central Banking in a Democracy**
The Federal Reserve and its alternatives
John H. Wood

70 **The History of Migration in Europe**
Perspectives from economics, politics and sociology
Edited by Francesca Fauri

71 **Famines in European Economic History**
The last great European famines reconsidered
Edited by Declan Curran, Lubomyr Luciuk and Andrew Newby

72 **Natural Resources and Economic Growth**
Learning from history
Edited by Marc Badia-Miró, Vicente Pinilla and Henry Willebald

73 **The Political Economy of Mercantilism**
Lars Magnusson

74 **Innovation and Technological Diffusion**
An economic history of early steam engines
Harry Kitsikopoulos

75 **Regulating Competition**
Cartel registers in the twentieth-century world
Edited by Susanna Fellman and Martin Shanahan

Regulating Competition
Cartel registers in the twentieth-century world

**Edited by
Susanna Fellman and Martin Shanahan**

LONDON AND NEW YORK

First published 2016
by Routledge
2 Park Square, Milton Park, Abingdon, Oxon OX14 4RN

and by Routledge
711 Third Avenue, New York, NY 10017

Routledge is an imprint of the Taylor & Francis Group, an informa business

© 2016 selection and editorial material, Susanna Fellman and Martin Shanahan; individual chapters, the contributors

The right of the editors to be identified as the author of the editorial material, and of the authors for their individual chapters, has been asserted in accordance with sections 77 and 78 of the Copyright, Designs and Patents Act 1988.

All rights reserved. No part of this book may be reprinted or reproduced or utilised in any form or by any electronic, mechanical, or other means, now known or hereafter invented, including photocopying and recording, or in any information storage or retrieval system, without permission in writing from the publishers.

Trademark notice: Product or corporate names may be trademarks or registered trademarks, and are used only for identification and explanation without intent to infringe.

British Library Cataloguing in Publication Data
A catalogue record for this book is available from the British Library

Library of Congress Cataloging in Publication Data
Regulating competition : cartel registers in the twentieth century world / edited by Susanna Fellman and Martin Shanahan.
pages cm
Includes bibliographical references and index.
1. Cartels—History—20th century. 2. Competition—History—20th century. I. Fellman, Susanna, editor. II. Shanahan, Martin (Martin P.), editor.
HD2757.5.R44 2016
338.8'2—dc23
2015026657

ISBN: 978-1-138-02164-8 (hbk)
ISBN: 978-1-315-77761-0 (ebk)

Typeset in Times New Roman
by FiSH Books Ltd, Enfield

Contents

List of figures	x
List of tables	xi
List of contributors	xii
Foreword by Harm G. Schröter	xvi
Acknowledgements	xix

1 **Introduction: regulating capitalism – the rise and fall of 'cartel registers' in the twentieth-century world**   1
   MARTIN SHANAHAN AND SUSANNA FELLMAN

PART I
Context of cartel registers   15

2 **Publish or be damned? Early cartel legislation in USA, Germany and Norway, 1890–1940**   17
   ESPEN STORLI AND ANDREAS NYBØ

3 **Legitimising Cartels: the joint roles of the League of Nations and of the International Chamber of Commerce**   30
   MARCO BERTILORENZI

4 **Competition policy in the European Economic Community, 1957–1992: the curse of compulsory registration?**   48
   LAURENT WARLOUZET

5 **How the tortoise became a hare: on the initial sclerosis and ultimate modernisation of Dutch competition policy**   66
   LILIAN T. D. PETIT, JARIG VAN SINDEREN AND PETER A. G. VAN BERGEIJK

viii *Contents*

6   Creating the 1957 cartel law: the role of pressure groups on
    Finland's competition policy and cartel registration   88
    SUSANNA FELLMAN

PART II
Registers in different countries   111

7   Cartel registers around the world   113
    MARTIN SHANAHAN AND SUSANNA FELLMAN

8   Transparency of cartels and cartel registers: a regulatory
    innovation from Norway?   133
    HARALD ESPELI

9   The secret register and its impact in advancing competition
    in Australia, 1900–2010   152
    MARTIN SHANAHAN

10 Policy transfer and its limits: authorised cartels in
    twentieth-century Japan   169
    TAKAHIRO OHATA AND TAKAFUMI KUROSAWA

11 Cartel law and the cartel register in German twentieth-century
    history   191
    JAN-OTMAR HESSE AND EVA-MARIA ROELEVINK

12 Cartel registration in Sweden in the post-war period   208
    PETER SANDBERG

13 The Dutch cartel collection in the twentieth century:
    facts and figures   227
    LILIAN T. D. PETIT

14 Regulating competition of the Swedish insurance business:
    the role of the insurance cartel registry   248
    MATS LARSSON AND MIKAEL LÖNNBORG

PART III
Conclusion 269

15 **Conclusion** 271
   SUSANNA FELLMAN AND MARTIN SHANAHAN

   References 277
   Index 303

Figures

5.1	Timeline of the different competition acts in the Netherlands	67
10.1	Swing, continuity and discontinuity in Japan's cartel policy, 1884–2000	171
10.2	'Exempted cartels' in Japan (registered Type A and Type B cartels)	185
12.1	Cartelisation groups, 1920–1939	209
12.2	Cartelisation groups, 1950–1990	210
12.3	Lines of business with more than 100 cartel agreements registered in the Swedish cartel register, 1947–1988	220
12.4	Number of new registrations in the Swedish cartel register, 1947–1988	221
12.5	Types of contracts in the Swedish cartel register, 1947–1988	223
13.1	Number of active agreements reported in the cartel register	236
13.2	Entry and exit of agreements	236
13.3	Frequency of restrictive elements by type, 1961–1981	238
13.4	Frequency of restrictive elements by type, 1980–1998	239
14.1	Swedish cartels by insurance type, 1873–1980	259
14.2	Cartel agreements by objectives and year of establishment	260
14.3	Cartel agreements by objective, valid and cancelled, 1947–1980	261

Tables

6.1	Composition of the 1948 Cartel Committee	89
6.2	Registrations, inquiries and investigations by the Cartel Bureau/Bureau for Freedom of Commerce, 1958–1966	102
7.1	Countries with cartel registers in the twentieth century	117
7.2	Selected contents of agreement registers, 1961–1970	121
7.3	Selected contents of agreement registers, 1971–1980	123
7.4	The year selected registers closed	129
9.1	Cartels and industries involved in restrictive practices, 1901–1939 and to the 1960s	160
9.2	Cartels present throughout the twentieth century	166
10.1	Legal bases of 'exempted cartels' (Type B)	180
13.1	International cartels including the Netherlands during the inter-war period	229
13.2	Dutch registered cartels classified by industry (1961, 1971, 1981) and two most common restrictive elements	241
13.3	Dutch registered cartels classified by NACE industry, 1980–1998	243

List of contributors

Dr Peter A. G. van Bergeijk is tenured professor of International Economics and Macroeconomics at the International Institute of Social Studies of Erasmus University in the Netherlands. He is also research programme leader of the Economics of Development and Emerging Markets (EDEM) project. He received his PhD titled 'Economic Diplomacy, Trade and Commercial Policy', in 1990 from Groningen University. Van Bergeijk has also held different management positions in the public sector.

Dr Marco Bertilorenzi is research fellow at the Ecole de Mines de Saint-Etienne and at Université Paris-Sorbonne. He obtained a double PhD in Economic History from University of Florence and in History from Université Paris-Sorbonne in 2010. His research interests focus on business and economic history, with particular attention to international cartels and other forms of business cooperation, business-governments relationships, foreign investments and multinationals and technological innovation. His current project is on the French engineers and economic elites during the twentieth century.

Dr Harald Espeli is a senior researcher at BI Norwegian Business School. He has a doctorate in agriculture and economic history from the Norwegian Agricultural University. He has written a number of commissioned works, including the second volume of the history of Norwegian telecommunications between 1920 and 1970 (2005). He has published extensively on Norway's economic and political history in the twentieth century. Competition policy and various forms of cartelisation in Norwegian business has been a long term interest.

Dr Susanna Fellman is professor of business history at the School of Business Economics and Law at the University of Gothenburg. She received her PhD at the University of Helsinki in 2001 where she also worked until 2011 when she moved to Gothenburg. Her research interests are professionalisation and modernisation of management and competition policy and cartels in a historical perspective. She has also carried out research on family business and labour market issues.

Dr Jan-Otmar Hesse is a professor of economic and social history at the University of Bayreuth. He studied history and economics in Bochum, where he earned his Ph.D. He has occupied positions at the universities of Frankfurt, Goettingen and Bielefeld and has been research fellow at the Historisches Kolleg, Munich, and at the Harvard Business School in Cambridge, Massachusetts. His research encompasses German business and economic history of the nineteenth and twentieth centuries, as well as history of twentieth-century economics. His current work is on structural change of global value chains using the example of the German textile industry.

Dr Takafumi Kurosawa is professor in the Graduate School of Economics at Kyoto University, where he received his PhD in 2001. His dissertation analysed the Swiss economy and the formation of the cross-border economic region in the nineteenth century. His publications in English deal with multinational enterprise and political risk, industrial clusters, the paper and pulp industry, and industrial policy. His works examine both European and Japanese cases. Since 2012, he has been managing a large-scale international project on the competitiveness of regions, especially focusing on industrial history.

Dr Mats Larsson is professor at the University of Uppsala, Department of Economic History and head of the Uppsala Centre for Business History (UCBH). His current research interest concerns big business in Sweden, mutual insurance, the Stockholm Stock Exchange, financial crises and the Swedish cinema industry.

Dr Mikael Lönnborg is associate professor at Södertörn University, Department of Social Sciences, School of Business Studies, EnterForum, Stockholm, Sweden and the BI Norwegian Business School, Oslo, Norway. His current research interests concerns insurance and corporate forms, privatisation, financial markets in transition countries, institutional ownership strategies, business history and internationalisation.

Andreas Nybø MA works as a publishing editor at Fagbokforlaget V&B (in Trondheim, Norway). He is currently also a PhD candidate in history at the University of Oslo. His main research interests include the globalisation of trade and trade policies, cartels and cartel policies, shipping and business–government relations.

Dr Takahiro Ohata is assistant professor (with tenure, *Sennin koushi*) at the Graduate School of Social Science at Hiroshima University. He received his PhD from Kyoto University. His main interest is research into Japanese economic history and especially the period of American occupation (about 1945–1952). Ohata focuses especially on the General Headquarters of the Supreme Commander for the Allied Powers (GHQ/SCAP) as one of the main factors of Japan's economic recovery and development.

Lilian T. D. Petit MSc is economist at the Competition Department of the Authority for Consumers and Markets and its predecessor, the Netherlands Competition Authority since 2009. Her primary research topic is economic cartel detection. Lilian achieved her master's degree in Organization Economics at the University of Amsterdam in 2009.

Dr Eva-Maria Roelevink is assistant to the chair of Economic and Business History at the Ruhr-University Bochum. Her thesis dealt with the Rhenish-Westphalian Coal Syndicate, the most important German cartel until 1945, and its internal organisation after the outbreak of the First World War (published as *Organisierte Intransparenz: Das Kohlensyndikat und der niederländische Markt, 1915–1932* by C. H. Beck, 2015). Her research interests are cartelisation, economic order, mining history and industrialisation.

Dr Peter Sandberg is a researcher at the Municipality of Kungälv, Sweden. He received his PhD in economic history at the School of Business, Economics and Law at the University of Gothenburg in 2006, where he also worked as a researcher for several years. His main research interests have been issues in relation to business organisation and competition policies

Dr Martin Shanahan is professor of economic and business history at the University of South Australia. He received his PhD from the Flinders University of South Australia and is currently president of the Australian and New Zealand Economic History Society. He has worked on Australian cartels for a number of years. His most recent publication is *From Protection to Competition: The Politics of Trade Practices Reform in Australia.*

Dr Jarig van Sinderen is chief economist at the Authority for Consumers and Markets in the Netherlands and part-time professor of economic policy at the Erasmus School of Economics where he also received his PhD in 1990. Van Sinderen has also held different management positions, among others at the Statistics Netherlands and the Ministry of Economic affairs, where his work has a focus on translating academic insight into policy advises.

Dr Espen Storli is associate professor in the Department of Historical Studies at the Norwegian University of Science and Technology (NTNU), Trondheim, where he also received his PhD. His main research interests lies at the intersection between business and politics, including the history of cartels, regulation of natural resources and the history of international trade in raw materials.

Dr Laurent Warlouzet is associate professor at the University of Artois (France). He was a postdoctoral fellow at the European University Institute (EUI) and at the London School of Economics (LSE). His main interests lie in the history of European integration from the perspective of economics and institutions. After a PhD on France and European Economic Integration from 1955 to 1969, he has worked on the Europeanisation of economic policies in Western Europe (UK, France, West Germany) from 1973 to 1985.

Foreword

Welcome to a new field of research on co-operative behaviour: cartel registers

Harm G. Schröter

'Eni calls for OPEC and rivals to join forces – Italian energy group's chief says teamwork could help fend off swings in crude price.' This was the headline and subtitle of the *Financial Times* on 20 April 2015. The CEO of Eni, a company in the Dow Jones Global Titans 50 Index, was openly demanding enlargement of the OPEC world oil cartel, because 'for the industry we need stability and stability means guidance'. Economic reality repeatedly calls our attention towards the existence and power of cartels. Similarly, business historians regularly reveal their impact in society. Marco Bertilorenzi's contribution on the aluminium cartels in *Business History* was the most read article of the journal in 2014. At this particular moment, therefore, a volume on the state registers of cartels is most welcome.

I want to congratulate the editors for their masterly organisation of so many contributions on cartel registers. Analysis of nine separate registers, the legislation in over a dozen countries, together with international debates and regulations from the League of Nations, to the European Union, and the interaction between registers and individual firms, associations and lobby groups in several national case studies, provides a multi-tiered and comprehensive contribution to our knowledge of cartel registers. Even so, not every country that had a register is included here; that would have required a much larger book and many more years to complete. While in some cases information about the registers and their contents no longer exists, the range and number of countries and cases included here is impressive.

The very creation of such registers was, of course, an act of state intervention; a tendency enterprise usually argues against. The earliest register in this volume was in Norway. It originated in 1920, and monitored all economic concentration, something not all later registers achieved. Behind this register is the intriguing story of key personnel and the political environment. Wilhelm Thagaard, the Norwegian general director of the register, actually helped some industries to become cartelised, while the Norwegian register was hardly ever consulted even by its own government. Even for a single country, the gap between stated aims and practical reality reveal how difficult it is to assemble the wide variety of information provided by multiple national registers into a single coherent whole. The editors, in their introduction, however masterfully demonstrate what can be done in comparing and assessing these difficult data.

Interestingly, the life-span of the majority of these registers cluster around the three decades between 1950 and 1980. Is this an accident or can we identify an explanation? Concurrent with these years was the so-called Golden Age of economic growth, (1949–1973/4) and the subsequent efforts to revive it. It was the period of the rise and fall of Keynesianism and widespread trust in state regulation. During the 1930s, the peak time of cartelisation, many governments thought registers unnecessary or even unwise, as they might alienate enterprises and consequently undermine national strength. The pro-cartel attitude diminished after 1945 but it was not terminated. In this respect a great difference emerged between the USA and in Europe. The contrast even included the former Allied member nations of UK and France. Both countries wanted not only to keep their own national cartels but also to restart international cartelisation in their zones of occupation in Germany and Austria. The US government had no real sovereignty in the two countries, but was able to stop any such attempts in all of the Western occupation zones. Thereafter cartels were interdicted in Austria and Germany; very much in contradiction to the intentions of the indigenous economic actors. After 1945 few Europeans considered abandoning cartels, but the American superiority made itself felt. The Marshall Plan triggered an economic upswing previously unexperienced in breadth and length. It was followed by the 'Productivity Mission' during which thousands of European experts and decision-makers travelled to the United States, at that time the obvious country of reference, to understand why that country was so much ahead of all others. The idea was, in general terms, to learn the obviously superior American way, and more concretely, how proceedings were carried out there. In many countries the traditional curriculum in economics at universities and high schools was exchanged for an American version. Students of economics, that is future economic decision-makers, were taught the American way of understanding the paradigm of competition. As a consequence the perception of cartels gradually changed from 'useful', to 'questionable', to 'harmful' instruments. At the end of this change stood the prohibition of cartels, a fact which ultimately made the process of registration redundant. It is interesting to compare the shift in paradigm of which the registers are an indicator. While the starting date of registration varies greatly between nations, nearly all the registers were terminated during the 1980s (see Table 7.4, page 129). It seems that international politics, as well as economics, converged during the latter half of the twentieth century. One single country stands out. Switzerland terminated its register about a decade later than the rest, a fact which added to the perception of that country being the world champion of cartelisation.

Where does this book figure in the line of today's research on cartels? In 2013 a special edition of the French journal *Revue Économique* (no. 6) suggested fourteen fields of new research on cartels, but omitted examining registers. There is, however, considerable overlap between the research on registers and the fields mentioned; for instance, questions on definition, and the extent and limits of collusion. If a common definition of cartels was applied, such as cartels are arrangements between independent organisations of the same industry that aim to influence the conditions of their own business and/or market environments to their advantage, many institutions would be targeted; for instance, chambers of commerce, co-operatives, or economic pressure groups which lobby during the process of law-making. Of course, the registers did not include these organisations, but some did include not only cartels but also firms with dominant market positions. As the editors explain, some registers adopted a broad approach and included firms exhibiting uncompetitive behaviour, while others did not even provide a comprehensive list of cartels. Excluded from most registers were, for instance, export cartels, banks and insurance companies and agricultural producers, or even inter-firm co-operation which was considered an advantage for the respective country. In other words the registers were not designed according to an economic paradigm or scholarly insight but rather, were based on political considerations and compromise. The variety of registration processes reflects very well the recent research which examines the limits of cartelisation. The traditional approach of a clear division between 'bad' collusion on the one hand and 'good' cooperation on the other, seems more and more blurred.

The problem of definition leads to new paths of research which the work in this book opens up. The difference in national ideas about what should be excluded and included in the registers, reveals substantial variation in the views of what is more or less important in identifying anti-competitive behaviour. For researchers the book thus provides case studies on which to assess the issue of the continuum between devilish collusion and heavenly cooperation.

Another avenue opened by the book addresses one of the oldest questions on cartelisation, but now with much better quantitative evidence. The first ever publication on cartels by Kleinwächter in 1883 suggested these organisations were 'children of need', born more or less undesired as a solution of last resort during phases of recession. (The opening quoted demand of Eni's CEO could serve as a similar recent example). Kleinwächter's thesis was discussed several times but rarely tested quantitatively. The editors point out good reasons why the data in the registers examined here cannot be simply assembled into a single body. Nonetheless researchers who apply the necessary methodological care might now try to relate cartelisation to the economic swings in single countries. Since independent states vary in their economic cycles, both from each other and from general worldwide swings, the results may be more accurate than any aggregated international comparison. If the research revealed that in most countries economic contraction stimulated cooperation, it would support Kleinwächter's thesis.

Finally, this volume opens a political question; why do we still tolerate the exemption of collusive behaviour in some sectors of the economy? Perhaps government-run registers of collusive behaviour in the national and international banking sector, insurance and agriculture may be a first step into enhancing competition in these fields – as was achieved by the historical registers this volume discusses.

Acknowledgments

Any enterprise that involves 18 authors, at least three conferences and multiple scholars will always be the work of a team of committed individuals assisted by many less prominent but important contributors. This book is no different.

We would like to thank all the authors who worked hard at shaping their contributions to fit our design. Multiple drafts were always completed with good grace and (mostly) on time. Without their contributions this book could not have been completed.

The authors too were supported by archivists, librarians and many others who provided information, tracked down reports and otherwise ensured the accuracy of our work. All errors remain, naturally, our responsibility, but to everyone who helped us, we say thank you.

We would also like to acknowledge particular individuals who have helped shape this book. Harm Schröter has done us the honour of writing a foreword, agreeing even before he knew whether we could deliver a manuscript. Harm has been a leading figure in research into cartels for many years, and we are deeply appreciative of his support.

Otto Toivanen and Ari Hyytinen initiated the historical cartel register research in Finland in 2006 and enabled Susanna Fellman access to the Finnish cartel register. Their continuous support and readiness to discuss cartels and cartel behaviour have been valuable at all stages. David and Kerry Round helped access the register in Australia – a register that otherwise still remains confidential. Several of the authors Takafumi Kurosawa and Takahiro Ohata (Japan), Peter van Bergeijk, Lilian Petit and Jarig van Sinderen (the Netherlands) and Jan-Otmar Hesse and Eva-Maria Roelevink (Germany) initiated new research in their countries' registers in response to our requests for wider coverage of registers and more in-depth analysis.

The comments of multiple scholars at various workshops and conferences have provided critical but supportive feedback to numerous papers. In particular Bram Bouwens, Joost Dankers, Dominique Barjot, Bernardo Batiz-Lazo, Niklas Jensen-Eriksen, Maggie Levenstein, Christopher Lloyd, Peter Sandberg, the participants at sessions at the Global History Conference in London, the European Historical Economics Society Conference in Dublin 2011, and the EBHA conference in Utrecht 2014 made valuable comments at various stages of the process. We would make particular mention of Professor Hans Schenk, who commented on one of the sessions in Utrecht in which drafts of these chapters were made. His comments greatly improved our thinking on the importance for a wider audience. All have made important contributions to chapters that constitute the final components of this manuscript.

Colleagues at the unit for economic history at School of Business, Economics and Law at Gothenburg University played an invaluable role in their ongoing support and collegiality for Susanna Fellman and their hospitality and generosity when Martin Shanahan visited in May 2015. Similarly Martin thanks colleagues in Aachen at the university RWTH for providing the space and opportunity to work in their business history research institute (Wisotech). Without all their support this book would still be in draft form. Martin would also like to thank the Business School at the University of South Australia. Without the School's financial support, and the support of colleagues in Commerce, the time and opportunity to finish this book would have not been possible.

We would also like to thank all the scholars interested in the history of cartels and competition policies who have contacted us over the past few years and the two anonymous referees for their important feedback on the original book proposal.

Laura Johnson at Routledge showed great patience and generosity as we missed several deadlines for this book, and yet never wavered in her support of us or the project. Laura Ekholm and Janne Itkonen provided critical research assistance in the Finnish project on cartel register and competition policy all since 2006.

Susanna Fellman's work in this project was funded by Academy of Finland, within the Academy Research Fellow project 'Beyond "from Cartelisation to Decartelisation" – Competition Policies, Cartel Behaviour and Internal Cartel Dynamics, 1930–2000'.

Finally our greatest debt is to our families. Writing this book took us away from them too much. Susanna dedicates this book to Risto, Oskar and Sofia, and Martin to Fiona, Brendan and Katherine.

1 Introduction

Regulating competition – the rise and fall of 'cartel registers' in the twentieth-century world

Martin Shanahan and Susanna Fellman

> ... trade is a social act. Whoever undertakes to sell any description of goods to the public, does what affects the interest of other persons, and of society in general; and thus his conduct, in principle, comes within the jurisdiction of society ... both the cheapness and the good quality of commodities are most effectually provided for by leaving the producers and sellers perfectly free, under the sole check of equal freedom to the buyers for supplying themselves elsewhere. ... Restrictions on trade, or on production for purposes of trade, are indeed restraints; and all restraint, *qûa* restraint, is an evil: but the restraints in question affect only that part of conduct which society is competent to restrain ... As the principle of individual liberty is not involved in the doctrine of Free Trade, so neither is it in most of the questions which arise respecting the limits of that doctrine: ... Such questions involve considerations of liberty, only in so far as leaving people to themselves is always better, *cæteris paribus*, than controlling them: but that they may be legitimately controlled for these ends, is in principle undeniable.
>
> (John Stuart Mill, *On Liberty* ch. 5, 1859)

Introduction

Balancing producers' freedom of contract and right to trade against consumer sovereignty and their right to free choice has long been a difficult task for regulators. The pendulum has swung in favour of one side or the other several times. In the area of preventing restrictive trade practices, authorities have swung between *laissez-faire* to prohibition depending on the prevailing views. This book is about one form of instrument used to regulate anti-competitive behaviour by firms, registers of restrictive trade practices (sometimes called cartel registers). Our focus covers a period, mostly in the middle of the twentieth century, when many government authorities around the world attempted to steer a middle course; one built on observation and negotiation; and one that frequently left contemporary records of the number and type of private sector restrictive trade practices in the official government registers. The contributors to this book look at a number of these registers and the legislation that created them, identifying their aims, methods and ultimately, their effectiveness. In the process we gain important insights into the issues facing the regulators of capitalism in many fields today.

For our purposes, a register of restrictive trade practices is a regulatory instrument, used by authorities to further the government's efforts to regulate anticompetitive practices and achieve their competition policy. The register itself, therefore, forms a central part of the policy to improve competition. In this sense, the 'cartel' register; 'restrictive practices register' or related instrument, differs from the incidental, or procedural documents of tribunals, committees and courts, which were also kept as records, but which are sometimes also referred to as registers. While these later records are frequently public documents, they are not used by competition authorities as a direct mechanism to alter the behaviour of firms, make an example of their behaviour or otherwise alter the activities of others.

Today, regulating markets to control individual excesses, is again a topic of interest. After recent financial crises in Asia in the 1990s and globally in 2007, many are looking at the rules that regulate markets, firms and individuals (Eatwell and Taylor 2000; Goodhart 2008; Levine 2012). The consequences of the financial crisis reminded many of what can occur when regulators do not fulfil their obligations, and businesses, their owners and their employees conspire to increases profits and lessen competition.

The decline in the use of registers occurred in the late 1980s; around the same time the dominate view of the role of government began to change. As the post-war golden age of economic growth slowed in the late 1970s, there was a general questioning of state ownership of enterprise, government intervention in the market and the role of fiscal and monetary policy. Contemporaneously the planned economic systems in Eastern Europe began to unravel. With increasing globalisation the dominant and generally accepted view became one of governments not 'interfering' in markets (Prasad 2006). By 2002, however, the Sarbanes–Oxley Act in the United States was a clear indication that the pendulum had begun to swing back. Corporate scandals, together with international financial crises in Asia and more recent banking and global financial distress brought the role of the state in the economy back to centre-stage. This does not mean a return to earlier models, but rather that regulation and state involvement was again seen as a viable response to market problems. How and to what extent should and can markets be controlled and regulated? What is the role of the state in securing the stability of the market economy? Who can influence regulative models? These remain important theoretical and practical questions.

Competition policy is only occasionally a major topic of public debate; and usually only after a spectacular corporate collapse. Among academics, politicians, civil servants and representatives of various interest groups, however, it is a regularly contested field. Indeed competition policy is often perceived publicly as quite depoliticised or as quite technical and an issue for specialists. (McGowan 2010: 2–3; Fellman and Sandberg 2015). Pushed to the side-lines, the general public (often the consumers whose rights are most affected) are often seen as unwilling or unable to engage with these debates. As the chapters here show, however, interest groups know exactly how important these policies are and will use an array of arguments to achieve their desired outcomes. One of the more self-serving arguments for a secret register, for example, was that transparency was not in the public's interest as they would not be able judge the information correctly.

As chapters in this book reveal, ignorance of the issues has not always prevailed. The use of registers of restrictive practices also involved a process of education; potentially for the citizens most impacted, but also for the public authorities charged with administering the process, and industry representatives. In many countries the main contents of the registers were open to the public. This revealed to consumers and competitors what agreements existed in the market; to firms in the private sector what was acceptable behaviour; and to the authorities, the numerous variations and forms of harmful behaviour that needed to be addressed.

Cartel registers: a brief history

The pinnacle of *laissez-faire* and freedom of contract is often described as occurring in the nineteenth century (Atiyah 1985). Towards the end of that century, however, American federal lawmakers, concerned at the anticompetitive behaviour of giant corporations in steel, railways and oil initiated a series of statues aimed at increasing competition and preventing harmful mergers. The Sherman Act of 1890 and Clayton Act of 1914, are regularly depicted as embodying America's vigorous pro-competition approach to regulation; an attitude that is encapsulated as 'anti-trust'.

In the field of competition regulation, this uncompromising approach is regularly contrasted with the 'European' approach, which until the late twentieth century was considered more lenient; where policies were more pragmatic and the agnostic attitude to restrictive practices resulted in a focus on the effects of restrictive practices, rather than on the agreements themselves (Harding and Joshua 2010: 40).

The regulatory approaches in Europe often meant balancing the pros and cons of cartels via market examination and market analyses, often on a case-by-case basis (ibid.: 44). The effects of firms' agreements were often assessed from a public interest perspective, weighing business interest against consumers, and often taking into consideration economic and political goals such as growth, inflation, or rationalisation (Thorelli 1959; Timberg 1953). According to Harding and Joshua, the American's uncompromising stance was likely because the concentration of economic power was as much a political principle as an economic question (Harding and Joshua 2010: 47). Even in the US however, attitudes have varied over time. It has been noted for example, that during the inter-war period and up until 1935, US authorities were more tolerant of trusts and the Supreme Court often adopted a 'rule of reason' (only unreasonable restraints of trade were prohibited) in its decisions (Kovacic and Shapiro 2000). Some US firms also looked longingly to the more lenient attitude of the European regulations (McGowan 2010: 64). Until the more recent EU policies were adopted in Europe (post-1993) the

American approach was also considered more legalistic, and the European approach more administrative.

If the high point for trusts in America was the 1890s, the inter-war period is usually seen as a highpoint for cartels in Europe and countries outside the American sphere of influence. The rise of big business globally in the second half of the nineteenth century and the issues governments had in dealing with it became a growing concern for many European states. Governments grappled with the problem of controlling ever larger corporations, or defending their country against 'outside' monopolies, trusts and combines. The result was rising tension between free market capitalism and national sovereignty. In the 1920s and 1930s discussions about the cartels, monopolies and trusts increased and concern about their detrimental effects came onto the agenda in Europe (McGowan 2010: 60–63). The possible problems and negative effects from anti-competitive behaviour and the power of big cartels were recognised. For example, Austria had legislative initiatives combatting their effects as early in the 1890s; Norway in 1920. Bulgaria, Czechoslovakia, Hungary, Poland, Rumania and Yugoslavia also introduced registration legislation before the Second World War. It was noted by many that cartels, monopolies and anti-competitive practices raised prices and could be detrimental to consumers. Competitors could be excluded from the markets. After the First World War it was feared they would hinder a return to free trade.

At least one important reason for this tolerance for local cartels in countries outside the United States may have been the existence of the Webb–Pomerene Act in the US (Amacher, Sweeny and Tollinson 1978). This statute, passed in 1918, allowed US firms to form their own cartels if they were trading internationally, where it was argued, such arrangements would enable them to compete. Smaller and industrially less-developed countries would have been very aware of the size and economic power of American firms, and how difficult it was for their own local companies to compete.

The League of Nations addressed the issue of trusts, combines and cartels on several occasions; especially in Geneva in 1927. Although it was stressed that cooperation between firms could have advantages, primarily in the form of technological advancement and rationalisation, many concerns were raised that they also had detrimental effects. In the League of Nations' discussions, the big international cartels were seen as problematic for the abolishing of trade barriers.[1] The 1927 Conference did not, however, recommend member countries ban, or even restrict, the cartels or big combinations by legislation, but suggested that instead individual countries might adopt legislation which controlled them. The opposition towards any kind of regulation was strong, but the meeting urged the international community and independent countries to at least follow their activities closely (League of Nations 1927). It was also suggested that the League of Nations could establish a general observation position for evaluating restrictive agreements, publish reports on their investigation and give decisions in the forms of reports or memorandum, in response to request from various parties in these issues.

The European consumer cooperatives formed a group that regularly returned to these issues (Suortti 1927: 140–156). During the 1930s depression some countries accepted cartels as a reasonable response to the economic situation. The autocratic regimes often organised business in 'new ways' so as to control and direct production. For example, in Germany before the Nazi regime 'uneconomic' price fixing was illegal, but during the Nazi regime cartels became not only compulsory, but quasi-public bodies. This also applied in Fascist Italy (Wise 2005; McGowan 2010: 63). Occasionally international cartels were seen as able to release international tension. In the 1930s for example, coal and steel cartels were connected to appeasement policies (McGowan 2010: 67.) Even though the international cartels could not prevent military war, they might have prevented the outbreak of trade wars (Freyer 2006).

The Inter Parliamentary Union IPU of 1930 and 1931 adopted a harsher view on cartels, trusts and monopolies than the League of Nation. While the London delegates recognised cartels and trusts as producing some benefits, because they also had harmful effects, the final view was that they should be controlled. The London resolution suggested control based on the principle of 'publicity'; a system of notification and registration of agreements, making them public, and so restraining firms' anticompetitive behaviour (Boje and Kallestrup 2004; McGowan 2010: 64).

Post-Second World War: changing attitudes towards restrictive agreements

After World War Two, any lingering ambivalence towards restrictive practices began to evaporate. National Socialism and Fascism had demonstrated the dangers that might result from an extreme combination of government intervention and business cartels, while the material strength of the American economy and post-war political dominance provided evidence of the success of strong competition.

Concurrent with a rise in household consumption, stronger consumer interest groups and the need to rebuild economies, governments began to question (and seek answers) about the size and extent of anti-competitive arrangements. The result was that several European countries adopted some form of 'competition legislation'. It was not really 'anti-trust legislation' of the type known to the Americans; rather it was legislation designed to monitor, assess and sometimes restrain, restrictive trade practices. The gradual shift towards a more hostile attitude towards restrictive business practices has frequently been portrayed as the result of outside (read, American) pressure, which often was an outcome of American and European policy networks (Schröter 2010; Djelic 2002, 2005; Leucht 2009; Edwards 1967). While the 'register' system of regulation has often been interpreted as a first step towards controlling anti-competitive behaviour, and 'inevitably' harsher anti-cartel positions, in reality the legislation was more a function of the national context. The various pressure group activities; particular historical and political situations; individual countries' economic and industrial structure; the business cycle; the legal context and awareness of developments in neighbouring or trading partner countries all shaped the final outcomes. The number of possible factors influencing a country's regulatory policies helps explain the many different types of regulatory policy that emerged, and the many slightly different 'cartel registers' that were created.

As the chapters in this volume show, the spectrum of outcomes was large. Some legislation appeared quite strict, but the competition authorities were granted so little jurisdiction that, 'the watchdogs were efficiently kept on their chains' (Dumez and Jeunemaître 1996). At the opposite end of the scale, the legislation might have appeared rather 'open' and conciliatory, but the regulatory authorities were granted considerable power and enough resources to interpret the legislation and act. The combined final outcome of both the formal legislation and the actual practices employed to enforce them were often a balancing act between strong business interest groups, the legislators, the competition authorities, and occasionally, unions and consumers.

An important driver of change was increasing trade liberalisation after the Second World War. Many countries needed to improve the capacity of their economies to respond to transformations in world markets. Earlier 'private' arrangements, which had been designed to assist internal markets and local interests, were increasingly perceived as imposing costs on others inside the economy. Restrictive trade practices also made it harder for 'outsiders' to enter markets and compete, thereby thwarting government efforts to grow economies and raise citizens' standard of living. The emergence and growth of international free trade agreements changed the regulatory environment up to the border. This needed to be matched by regulatory change 'inside' the border. Registers helped this process.

The international community also turned their gaze to national regulation of non-competitive practices as a necessary component for promoting international free trade. National legislation was often in conflict with the goals of the free flow of goods. For example the European Free Trade Agreement's (EFTA) articles 14 and 15 were explicitly designed to ensure that private and government actions would not frustrate the benefits derived from the removal of trade barriers (Szokolóczy-Syllaba 1975: 15).[2] While EFTA regulations remained dormant, and in practice had little effect, the international promotion of free trade carried with it expectations of competitive markets. In many countries, policies to control and gradually remove harmful anticompetitive behaviour evolved as a result of both demands at the domestic level and participation in international agreements. The restrictive trade agreement registers can thus be seen as important transition instruments as regulatory frameworks shifted from a focus that was internal and protective to one that was more open and competitive in outlook.

By the late 1970s and early 1980s, as the pace of globalisation increased further, the virtues of competitive markets came to dominate political and economic debate. Internationally there was a shift to a more private, competitive market focus for many developed and developing countries. International coordination of markets and trade regulation best exemplified by the EU and its supranational policies that required individual member nations to tackle non-competitive agreements within their own boarders and gradually harmonise their competition legislation according to the EU's common policy. Although the USA had lead the way, Europe followed with a growing consensus that competition was a driving force behind enhanced economic efficiency and welfare. The member countries either adopted the policies voluntarily or were gradually pressured towards harmonisation (McGowan 2010: 1–2; Vives 2009). By the last two decades of the twentieth century anticompetitive market structures, both in the private sector and in some countries in the public sector, were treated with open hostility. At the international level, serious cartel conduct became an offence with criminal sanctions. While the pace of change varied between different countries, the 'wait and see' or 'gather more information' or 'quiet negotiation' methods often embodied in the restrictive trade practices register was no longer acceptable, and became obsolete. Within the space of twenty years the registers that did exist were swept away by legislation that dealt harshly with intra-firm cooperation.

The aims of this book

Registers of restrictive trade practices were kept in many countries by the competition authorities, and used to record anti-competitive agreements made by firms. This book examines the context in which the registers were negotiated and implemented, their design and their impact on anti-competitive behaviour. The registers emerged in several countries around the same period – primarily in the mid-twentieth century – and were eventually progressively abolished starting in the 1970s and ending in the early 1990s (apart from a few short-lived exceptions), when they were phased out and replaced by other forms of regulation. From today's perspective the cartel registration system might be considered an outdated form of regulation with little bearing on current debates, or even a curiosity, but it was not like that at the time. Similar systems existed in many countries and in some cases, for decades.

The legislation appeared mostly in economies where earlier in the century governments had either ignored or been apathetic toward, and sometimes even supportive of, non-competitive agreements between firms (Schröter 1996; Freyer 1992). Nevertheless, governments gradually sought to identify non-competitive business arrangements. Rather than prohibit such behaviour, the legislation often aimed to bring anticompetitive business practices to the surface and so allow authorities to monitor firms' behaviour. In some cases the agreements were made public, to alert consumers and possible competitors, and to have a deterrent effect. In other countries the registers were confidential, and only market regulators could access them. The information gathered in these cases formed a basis for administrative work. Interestingly, registers existed in countries with diverse legal and institutional traditions, suggesting this practice was a time-specific phenomenon rather than one shaped by common or civil law systems. Although fully established cartel registers seem to be a particular occurrence stemming from northern Europe (Norway, Sweden, Finland, Denmark) and European countries more generally (Germany, Austria, Denmark, Spain, the UK, the Netherlands), they also existed in Australia, New Zealand, Israel, India, Japan, South Korea and Pakistan. They could also be transnational. The Webb–Pomerene statute established a register for

US companies operating externally to that country (Evenett, Levenstein and Suslow 1997). The EEC had a register that included agreements affecting trade between member states (OECD 1978b; Warlouzet 2010). The registers were a widely used tool of emerging competition regulators.

These registers are an under-researched instrument, although they formed an important policy tool during several decades around the globe. Moreover, the registers and their content can provide interesting insights into several broader topics. They form, for instance, a good 'window' through which to assess governments' attitudes to market liberalisation and the extent of national firm competition in particular economies. They can provide an insight into a particular period of important change to national markets in the twentieth century and while revealing different 'gradualist' approaches; they also have the potential to provide important evidence on the behaviour of the private sector. Thus, this book examines a specific aspect of regulatory change and uses alterations to this institution to trace shifts in individual county's attitudes towards internal competitive reform and preparedness to engage with global markets.

Our aim has been to acquire a broad overview of the registers in different modes of capitalism. This book provides detailed evidence on eight registers. We have not been able to include chapters on all countries with a register. Our most important criterion has been countries which had registers that operated for sufficient time to impact on businesses. We have also aimed to focus on countries that have not been dealt with in previous literature to any great extent such as the Nordic countries, Australia, Japan, and the Netherlands. Overall, the cartel literature tends to discuss dominant countries like the US or UK, and it is not uncommon that the European practice is perceived as simply 'equivalent' to the German case, especially for the period before common European policies. While the US had no internal register, the UK did adopt this form of regulation. While referenced frequently through the book, there is no separate chapter devoted its restrictive trade practices legislation and register. Interested readers are directed to the existing works of Mercer (1995), Wilks (1996), Symenoidis (2002) and Rollings (2007). We focus here on countries that had a register during the high-point of this form of regulation – the 1950s and 1960s; 'late-comers' such as South Korea, Pakistan and India do not have chapters of their own.

By looking at our comparatively under-researched set of countries, different aspects have been revealed. For example, the chapters show the great variation in approaches to restrictive practices in different contexts, the different strategies used to curb anti-competitive behaviour, whether publicity or secrecy was deemed the most suitable approach and what behaviours were considered a priority to control or ban.[3] This volume reveals the variety not just within Europe, but also in countries in other parts of the world, like Japan and Australia whose registers had some noteworthy differences.

It is also obvious that it has occasionally been difficult to acquire information about the registers in some countries. This is especially the case for those Eastern and Central European Countries which after the Second World War became part of the socialist bloc. Other registers only existed for a very short period of time; such as New Zealand where their register was active for only about three years. In Italy the Fascist origins of the register and in Spain the post-Franco origins of their regulations make them almost incomparable with those in other parts of the world. Along with the register established in Nazi Germany (the purpose of which later changed) all three were designed as exercises in state-business networking and economy building, rather than advancing competition. Thus Spain and Italy's registers are not included here.

Despite the limited number of countries considered, in this book we take a comparative and transnational perspective. The availability of data and the fundamental principle of public access to information that underpins many Northern European countries' government sector means that this region is over-represented here. While the result is a somewhat 'western' bias, these countries, together with others in Europe, also represent some of the first countries that experienced American attitudes to competition after the Second World War. As the chapter on Japan shows, this influence was not only a European concern, and remains relevant today. Competition legislation that is not tolerant of anticompetitive behaviour has, in recent decades, been introduced in areas, which have not had such laws before; for example Latin America, Southeast Asia and the Middle East. The question of a global convergence in competition policies, or even a 'global competition law' is being debated in many parts of the world (Dabbah 2011; Dowdle *et al.* 2013). As Dowdle emphasises, however, a regional approach to studying competition policy developments can enable a deeper understanding of how competition policies and anti-trust regimes have spread (Dowdle 2013: 11–12). Although this book primarily takes a national approach, many of the individual chapters also shed light on how specific models travelled around the globe.

The research in this book suggests that despite the sometimes tortured path needed to pass the underlying anti-competitive regulations, the many variations between jurisdictions and the registers' ultimate demise, they played an important role in changing business attitudes to competition. They educated administrators about competition and its forms and enhanced their skills in balancing the rights of consumers with the rights of business owners. They also played an important role in advancing international trade by developing competition in national markets. They thus deserve more attention than they have previously received. This book is a start.

The content of the book

The chapters in Part I show how, initially, policy makers viewed cartels rather equivocally, recognising their advantages in stabilising markets in some circumstances while fearful of the consequences of unconstrained price manipulation in others.

In Chapter 2, Espen Storli and Andreas Nybø compare the debates surrounding the early legislation that emerged in the USA, Germany and Norway, in the fifty years preceding the Second World War. They highlight how the attitudes held before a country's legislation was created were critical to the final regulatory outcomes; the Americans were generally sceptical towards combines, while the Germans saw cartels as useful tools for industrial progress. The Norwegian position was more ambiguous, given they both feared large foreign cartels while also believing domestic businesses could use cartels to benefit the national economy. The result was three very different types of legislation. Despite these differences, however, transparency and public scrutiny were seen as important components of regulations to remove restrictive practices. They also show how the emphasis on publicity in combating 'harmful' restrictive practices, and often considered a European feature, also penetrated the debate in the US (see also Thorelli 1959).

Marco Bertilorenzi shows in Chapter 3 that the view that cartels could contribute to public welfare emerged from the findings of the International Industrial Cartel Committee, established by the League of Nations in the interwar period. Importantly, he documents how pro-business and pro-cartel interests dominated these groups, and so ensured a narrative that was positive towards the activities of cartels, trusts and monopolies at this time. This work also highlights the importance of lobby groups and proactive individuals in shaping public discourse, in a way that uses economic arguments to achieve political outcomes.

Chapter 4, by Laurent Warlouzet, on competition policy in the European Economic Community, highlights one of the real dilemmas facing any form of regulation: process. In the case of the EEC, the cartel assessment procedures established in the early 1960s became a curse, as administrators drowned under the number of notifications they received and the steps needed to investigate each. One factor leading to abolition of the registration policy in 2003 was the unmanageable processes that had been adopted.

Petit, van Sinderen and van Bergeijk in Chapter 5 move the focus from the whole of Europe to the specific example of Holland. They argue that the 'polder model' of consensus politics played a large part in allowing cartels to continue in Holland long after other European countries had moved to curb restrictive trade practices. Tolerance of cartels, so long as they did not abuse their position, combined with cooperative policy building was only challenged after the cost of restrictive trade practices was made clear. Later than many neighbouring countries, it was not until the 1990s that the cartel paradise of Holland fully moved away from tolerating restrictive practices and adopted the EU principles.

Susanna Fellman (Chapter 6), writing about the processes involved in creating Finland's 1957 cartel law, also highlights the importance of lobby groups in shaping the strength and vigour of the final legal and administrative outcomes. Finland too had a neo-corporatist approach to policy making, but in contrast to the almost complete deadlock occurring in the Netherlands, Finnish law was influenced both by their Swedish cousins' lead, and particular lobby group representatives who sought to create a workable competition law. Ultimately quite tolerant of restrictive practices, the 1957 legislation did establish basic principles that endured for the next 35 years.

Collectively these chapters highlight some of the major difficulties in establishing competition policy. Achieving a balance between different interest groups' views without succumbing to one group's dominant interest; creating an administrative process that is sustainable and effective; and finally, enhancing welfare by curbing restrictive trade practices is a difficult outcome that was not always achieved. Only when international considerations overcame the power of local vested interests did some countries achieve effective competition policy.

Part II presents studies of individual countries' paths to competition policy and highlights the many variations that occurred. To begin this part, Susanna Fellman and Martin Shanahan (Chapter 7) provide a broad overview of the registers in 14 countries around the world – especially those existing in the 1950s and 1960s – the highpoint of this form of regulation. It is clear that countries varied in their reasons for creating a register, and that the path to implementation varied greatly between jurisdictions. Although special interest groups heavily shaped policy, there were significant differences in the form and content of each county's register. For researchers, this makes the records unreliable sources of comparative information on the extent of cartels in each country. They do, however, provide useful insights into individual countries' attitudes to competition. Cartel registers ultimately fell from favour as international agreements and reduced tolerance to anticompetitive behaviour saw registers superseded by laws banning outright activities that had previously been tolerated.

In Chapter 8, Harald Espeli writes on the origins of Europe's first 'real' competition law; originating in 1920, the 1926 Norwegian Act on the Control of Restraints of Competition and Price Abuse. Norway was the first European country to implement specific legislation to regulate competition, including intervention against abuse of restraints on competition and compulsory notification and registration of restrictive business arrangements. Their regulations also covered subsidiaries of foreign multinational companies. Their public cartel register existed from 1920 to 1993 and unlike the registers in several other countries, it did produce a correct impression of existing restrictive business arrangements.

Martin Shanahan in Chapter 9 focuses on Australia's secret cartel register that was not introduced until the late 1960s. Despite having antitrust legislation early in the century because of a fear of international combines, little action was taken against anti-competitive behaviour for 50 years. As a consequence, by the end of the Second World War, the economy was rife with trade associations, cartels and restrictive practices. The creation of a secret register, ultimately through the efforts of a few key supporters began a significant change to business attitudes which had accepted anticompetitive behaviour as the norm. By the end of the century, Australia had a modern competition policy, on a par with comparable nations, which promoted competitive markets and criminalised serious cartel conduct.

Japan's register of anti-competitive practices differed radically from many of the others in this volume, being imposed by the Americans after the Second World War. Takahiro Ohata and Takafumi Kurosawa (Chapter 10) show that the scope of the reporting requirements in Japan was among the widest in the world in the 1950s and 1960s. They also discuss the many significant changes in policy towards restrictive trade practices that occurred in Japan. Of special mention was the initially harsh, but quickly ameliorated American anti-trust type policies after the

Second World War. Despite Japan's reputation for integrated business interests (*Zaibatsu* and *Keiretsu*), the register and its contents has barely been researched either inside or outside Japan. This chapter fills an important gap in understanding the role and content of their register.

In Chapter 11, Jan-Otmar Hesse and Eva-Maria Roelevink reveal how complex and volatile Germany's cartel law had been in the twentieth century. In a paradoxical situation, while the discussions about registration processes in interwar Germany were fierce, appearing in the press, science and parliament, the reality was that actual cartel registration was of only marginal importance in shaping business practices. It was not until 1936 that the National Socialists made registration a legal requirement. This was only one step in an evolution of the register and its administration. From a milieu that was initially tolerant of cartels, though a period of case-by-case analysis (and with some cartels as significant exemptions), restrictive trade practices legislation ultimately attempted to prohibit cartels and cartel-like behaviour. The German situation therefore provides a classic case study of how administrative processes and attitudes can change over time.

Peter Sandberg (Chapter 12) addresses cartel registration, and examines Sweden's reputation as a leader in tackling restrictive trade practices. He finds little evidence for this claim. His chapter thus illustrates well the care that needs to be taken in separating 'fact' from 'fiction' in the area of regulation. For most of the post-war period their approach was consistent with a policy of regulation by supervision, looking to prevent abuses caused by restrictive trade practices. The aim was not to prohibit cartels but to prevent negative economic effects. He finds too that the participation of business interests and trade unions in key tribunals slowed the implementation of stricter competition policies. Rather than demonstrating the vigour of Sweden's approach to tackling restrictive trade practices, the register is better described as a first step towards the post-1992 policy that does aim to stop cartels.

In Chapter 13, Lilian Petit examines the Dutch approach to regulating cartels; a case all the more important given their reputation as a cartel paradise. She provides quantitative evidence by accessing records from the register itself. She relates the history of policies that were highly tolerant of restrictive practices and reluctance to change. Nonetheless, and contrary to others, she finds a decrease in cartels which began in the 1990s, before the introduction of legislation prohibiting cartels outright. Her closely researched work not only illustrates what might be learnt in other countries if the registers were accessed, but also that businesses usually respond in anticipation of change, rather than after the event. This often makes establishing effective regulatory frameworks all the more difficult.

Concluding Part II, Mats Larsson and Mikael Lönnborg (Chapter 14) present an important case study on the developments in a single industry in Sweden – insurance – and the interplay of restrictive practices, the register and regulation. Originally collusion was viewed as necessary to stabilise the industry and give confidence to consumers that their purchases of insurance would be honoured. This advanced the reputation of the industry and gave its members expert status when regulations were being designed. The cartel registry allowed outsiders to scrutinise formal agreements, but overlooked the gentlemen agreements and other less visible forms of collaboration. The agreements were undermined by the merger waves of the 1960s and 1970s as globalisation increased competition and the cartel agreements were dismantled. As occurred in other countries, the legacy of nineteenth-century cooperation to avoid 'ruinous competition' was felt deep into the twentieth century, again demonstrating the importance of history in shaping outcomes.

Taken together, these case studies show how carefully different jurisdictions attempted to address the issue of restrictive trade practices. Aims, methods and outcomes varied, but in each case, ultimately, behaviours changed. The Dutch, for example, moved slowly, but finally did adopt EU policy; the Norwegians adopted a registration process quite early; many countries learnt from observing the processes in neighbouring countries or from further afield. Chapters 13 and 14 present insightful details about how the registers were used, and how members of the industry responded to regulation. This highlights the insights that can be derived from studying the content of particular registers in more detail. In Part III (Chapter 15), we provide some conclusions to be drawn from the preceding chapters.

As John Stuart Mill stated, trade is a social act. Competitive markets too involve social acts. The need to legitimately regulate against restrictive trade practices, and so maintain the liberty created by competition, on and on behalf of, businesses and consumers is, we believe, undeniable.

Notes

1 In the Geneva meeting, three experts were asked to report on the international combines. One was a professor of economics in Berlin, Julius Hirsch. In a 1926 report for the Preparatory Committee of the conference, Hirsch concluded that international cartels 'are a new impediment to commerce which must, in the long run, have effects more harmful than those which free competition has on the organisation of the world's trade and industry' (Hirsch 1926: 18–19, 24). In 1929 the Economic Committee concluded that special attention be paid to the effects of international combinations on global trade (Société des Nations, Comité Économique 1929: 9).
2 The EFTA consisted until 1972 of Austria, Denmark, Finland (associate member), Iceland, Norway, Portugal, Sweden, Switzerland and UK.
3 Already Thorelli (1959) and Timberg (1953) emphasised these variations as important.

Part I
Context of cartel registers

2 Publish or be damned?

Early cartel legislation in USA, Germany and Norway, 1890–1940

Espen Storli and Andreas Nybø

Introduction

In the second half of the nineteenth century, cartels became increasingly important. Cooperation between businessmen was obviously not a new thing, but in this period they found new ways of organising such collaborations, and thereby extending the scale and scope of their cooperative practices. These cooperative capitalist entities were known by many names: cartels, trusts or syndicates, to name a few. The arrangements ranged from gentlemens' agreements on geographic market sharing, to complex agreements consisting of hundreds of pages, regulating prices, markets, output quotas, quality, marketing, sales, distribution, agents and pretty much any other aspect of business. Many cartels had organisations set up to monitor the behaviour of both member companies and outsiders, and sales and marketing departments. To some, these new entities were perceived as useful tools to prevent destructive competition; to others, they represented predatory business practices aimed at monopolising markets.

The aim of this chapter is to analyse how lawmakers first approached the cartel question, and in turn, to discuss how the issues of state investigation, publication and cartel registers fit in to that general story. Towards the end of the nineteenth century it became increasingly clear to most states that, one way or another, cartels and intra-firm cooperative practices had to be regulated. As the existing literature has argued, before 1940, there were two basic and opposing ways of dealing with the issue. In the US, cartels were made illegal through the Sherman Act of 1890, and the Clayton Act of 1914 increased the scope of the legal framework. In Germany, on the other hand, cartels were accepted as a valid economic instrument that could ensure better coordination and higher economic efficiency and from the late 1890s and onwards cartel agreements were even protected by courts of law. Most other industrialised countries chose a path somewhere between that of the US and Germany.

However, there was also a third way. Germany and the US were large states where the authorities were predominantly concerned with the possible abuses of market power by domestically-based companies and cartels, and the legislation was thus mostly aimed at national companies. In smaller economies the lawmakers worried more about powerful foreign combines. When smaller states regulated cartels, they therefore also had to take into account the operations of international cartels. Norway is the most prominent example of how a small country tried to deal with this issue in the pre-Second World War world. In 1926 the country adopted a competition policy, which although inspired by the existing German and US legislation, differed substantially from its inspirational sources. Unlike the United States, Norway allowed cartels, and unlike Germany, the cartels were much more strictly monitored and regulated. A central tenet in the new Norwegian legislative system was the need for public supervision of agreements regulating competition, and the main pillar of the system was a cartel register, a record of all such agreements.

The main research question of the chapter is: How did different countries decide on what was legal and what was illegal when it came to intra-firm cooperation? Why did the countries in this study end up with quite different legislative solutions to seemingly similar challenges? We will focus on the birth and early development of the US, the German and the Norwegian regulatory regimes, and highlight similarities and differences in their approaches to cartel legislation. By comparing and contrasting these countries we will gain new insights into how different states developed distinctive answers to the question of cartelisation.

'... a remedy for the evils under which the country is now suffering': the US and the birth of modern antitrust law

> People of the same trade seldom meet together, even for merriment and diversion, but the conversation ends in a conspiracy against the public, or in some contrivance to raise prices. It is impossible indeed to prevent such meetings, by any law which either could be executed, or would be consistent with liberty and justice. But though the law cannot hinder people of the same trade from sometimes assembling together, it ought to do nothing to facilitate such assemblies; much less to render them necessary.
>
> (Smith 1776: 82)

Although the term 'cartel' first got its modern meaning towards the end of the nineteenth century, the activity that it describes was not invented then. A century earlier, Adam Smith had already pointed out how businessmen had an almost innate desire to regulate through intra-firm cooperation the markets in which they operated. Although this behaviour was seen as disagreeable he found it difficult to suggest effective legislation against it.

A century later, the practice that had troubled Smith had only become more widespread. All over the western world the public awoke to the reality that combines, syndicates, trusts, associations, pools and cartels were becoming increasingly important, and that these entities in some instances were wielding significant economic power affecting the development of industry and society alike. Although cooperation between firms took many forms, it was obvious to many that the combined effect of the cartels and their like were altering the way markets functioned. Critics were soon complaining that some of these entities had grown large enough to monopolise whole industries; in the process ruthlessly destroying competitors standing in their way and earning exorbitant profits by charging the consumers inflated prices for their products and services. Proponents of the combinations argued that the cartels were defensive mechanisms established to lessen the evils of cutthroat competition and thereby instruments of stabilisation and order which ultimately benefitted society at large.

The perceived evils of cartels gradually made many question Adam Smith's conclusion that this form of cooperation should not be legislated against. From the 1880s onwards public debate about the rise of cooperative practices in industry only grew in strength. Half a century later, most countries in the western world had established legal frameworks for dealing with this phenomenon. Through specialised laws, different states found different solutions to the issue. One of the first countries to act was the United States.

It is easy to understand why the United States would become among the first countries to effectively institute laws dealing with anti-competitive practices. The rise of cartelisation was intimately connected with the Second Industrial Revolution, a process in which the country took the lead. Through advances in production, information, and transportation technology, firms could produce more and sell their products in ever increasing geographical markets. A natural consequence was the growth of big business, and in many industries, the leading US firms became bigger than anywhere else in the world, be it through natural growth, mergers or acquisitions. The end result was that from the 1880s many sectors in the US economy were dominated by a small number of large companies. These companies often cooperated in regulating their markets in ways ranging from loosely coordinated gentlemen's agreements and selling pools, through formal cartels, to tight combinations like the trusts. In the US, the word 'trust' was used in public debate as a generic term that covered more than what was technically speaking a trust. A 'trust' came to signify any form of cartel organisation or combination of big businesses (Freyer 1992: 86; Thorelli 1954: 84).

The behaviour and power of some of these combinations created mistrust and soon generated significant publicity. Perhaps most notorious in the public debate were the business methods of the Standard Oil Trust (founded 1882). Leading capitalists were increasingly targeted by the press and progressive politicians as 'robber barons' – although not all were rightfully accused. The anti-trust movement in the US was a response to the rapid changes brought on by the second industrial revolution and the emergence of big business. By the time of the presidential election of 1888, the question of what to do with 'combinations of capital' was an unavoidable issue and both the Democrat Grover Cleveland and the Republican Benjamin Harrison adopted antitrust planks in their election campaigns (Peritz 1996: 13). The future President Benjamin Harrison, when accepting his party's nomination, warned that 'the legislative authority should and will find a method of dealing fairly and effectively' with trusts who abused their market power (Harrison 1893: 6).

Yet, the first development did not take place at the Federal level. Some individual states in 1887–1890 actively started to regulate trusts. For instance, in

Louisiana, Ohio, and New York trusts were prosecuted for exceeding the privileges granted under the incorporation statutes, while Kansas and Missouri passed anti-monopoly legislation. By contrast, in other states new laws, like the incorporation legislation in New Jersey and Delaware, specifically allowed for holding companies and trusts. By reorganising their business, the combines could easily escape prosecution (Peritz 1996: 10; Thorelli 1954: 79–84). The experience made it obvious that any durable solution would have to be found at the Federal level.

From the autumn of 1888 until 1890, Congress worked on several different antitrust bills. It also heard a number of petitions for action against the trusts from different constituents. In the summer of 1890 the Sherman Antitrust Act, named after Senator John Sherman, was finally passed. With the new law, the US lawmakers took a step into unknown territory. Even though Canada had in fact implemented anti-combine legislation a year earlier, the Canadian legislation was a mere watered down version of a private bill from New York State. The Canadian law later proved to be inadequate, as it did not contribute to breaking up a single combine (Bliss 1973: 177–188).

The Sherman Act was couched in terms from the English common law tradition, where there was a traditional dislike of monopoly and contracts in restraint of trade. To deal with the new reality of cartels and trusts, however, the new law introduced aspects that were alien to common law (Ræstad 1916: 131–132; Peritz 1996: 10). The feeling that many of the legislators had towards the new Bill was summarised by Senator Rogers in the House Debate; he was filled with doubt towards the effectiveness of the new legislation, but the emergency of the situation made him accept that this was the best that could be done to find a 'remedy for the evils under which the country is now suffering' (Thorelli 1954: 205).

The act in eight short sections tried to draw the line between lawful and unlawful combinations. The central part of the Act, section 1, stated that 'Every contract, combination in the form of trust or otherwise, or conspiracy, in restraint of trade or commerce', interstate or foreign, was illegal. To underline how serious Congress found this new felony, a corporation found guilty of breaking the law could be awarded fines of up to 10 million dollars, and a person found guilty could receive a hefty fine and up to three years in jail. Section 2 was directed against monopolies. In section 7, it was established that any person who was 'injured in his business or property' by someone breaking the Sherman Act, could be awarded up to threefold damages.[1]

The aim of the new law was clear, to regulate against monopolies and combinations operating to restrain trade, and the experience with the trusts in the 1880s had shown that this was an area where the public needed protection. During its first decade of operation, however, the effect of the Sherman Act proved to be decidedly underwhelming. Two important aspects stand out. First, in interpreting the Act, the courts distinguished legal and illegal cooperatives by differentiating between 'loose combinations' and 'tight combinations'. Loose combinations – pools, syndicates and cartels – where the participants retained their legal independence and freedom of action were clearly covered by the Sherman Act and were unlawful. Tight combinations – merged companies and the trusts – where several firms were united under joint management were more problematic for the courts. When examining tight combinations, a key problem for the courts was the difficulty in distinguishing between organisational structures designed to manipulate markets from those designed to increase business efficiency (for the definition of tight and loose combinations, see Thorelli 1954: 1–2).

In the narrowest sense, trusts now became illegal. It was therefore now not possible to use the trustee device to control a number of different companies in the way that Standard Oil had done. Yet, from a business perspective, it was possible to achieve the same degree of control through the use of holding companies or through mergers between firms, so the entities previously set up as trusts, could instead reorganise. After 1890, the traditional trusts disappeared, only to be reborn as enterprises controlled through holding companies or mergers. In the years between 1895 and 1904 the merger movement washed over the American economy, and more than 1,800 firms disappeared into consolidation (Lamoreaux 1985: 1–2). So while the Sherman Act had an immediate effect on the number of cartels and pooling agreements in the country, it did not necessarily put an end to restrictive practices. Instead of cooperating in the form of cartels, companies continued their practices through mergers, in turn creating still larger companies with more extensive market control than before.

Second, Congress seemingly did not give much thought into how the Act should be implemented. By inserting provisions that allowed for triple damages to private parties injured by breaches of the Sherman Act, the legislators hoped the law would have capacity for self-enforcement. Yet, as it turned out, private parties did not contribute substantially to the enforcement of the law. At a Federal level, the administration of the law was given to the Attorney General, but Congress did not allocate any extra funding for antitrust investigations (Thorelli 1954: 369–370). With few resources, and with Presidents in power that had little interest in antitrust matters, the Sherman Act was not heavily used. From 1890 until 1901 an average of only 1.5 cases were prosecuted each year; of these, more than a quarter were against labour unions (see Cheffins 1989: 457). As one of the leading students of the Sherman Act drily summarised: 'to legislate against monopolies and restraints of trade may not necessarily be the same as to enforce, or maintain, free competition' (Thorelli 1954: 210).

While the Sherman Act languished, public concern about the power of trusts only grew in strength. The merger movement created numerous combinations so large that they could be labelled monopolies. President Theodore Roosevelt acknowledged the need to do something about these combinations in his end of year messages to Congress both in 1901 and in 1902. In both cases he called for more publicity; to make information about large corporations publicly available. To that end, in 1903, a new Bureau of Corporations was established as part of the new Department of Commerce and Labor. The Bureau soon staffed with more than 100 employees, published reports on a number of industries that revealed corporate abuse. The reports in some cases led to changes in business practices, in others, to prosecutions by the Attorney General (Johnson 1959; Knauth 1914).

The most important example was the Standard Oil case. Since the 1880s Standard Oil had been the most publicly contested of all the trusts, and for critics it was a glaring symbol of everything that was wrong with giant combines. The Bureau of Corporations started to investigate the oil industry early in 1905, and after it published a report a year later, the Attorney General in 1906 initiated a prosecution against Standard Oil for violation of the Sherman Act (Johnson 1959: 583–588). Federal prosecution was now more effective than it had been in the first decade of the Act. This was especially the case after 1903, when Congress for the first time made available special funds for antitrust enforcement. The Attorney General could now move more forcefully against companies that were prosecuted (Thorelli 1954: 561).

The Standard Oil case was finally decided by the Supreme Court in 1911 and the verdict significantly altered the way the courts implemented the Sherman Act. The company was found to have violated the antitrust act by monopolising the oil industry through abusive and anticompetitive actions, and the judges ordered it broken up into several different firms. The same day, in a similar case, the American Tobacco Company received a similar verdict. Both verdicts were based on the legal principle of the rule of reason. Earlier verdicts in Sherman Act cases had made loose combinations illegal since they were found by their nature to be aimed at restraining trade, while mergers remained legal. Now, however, large combines established through mergers could be declared in breach of the law if the 'evident purpose' of the combination was to restrain trade. As a consequence, cartels were still illegal *per se*, while a combination was deemed unlawful when it engaged in conduct seen as unfair to competition (Lamoreaux 1985: 174; Peritz 1996: 52). The Sherman Act could now be successfully used to prosecute 'bad trusts', while 'good trusts' would still be safe.

The trust issue, which had originally surfaced in the 1880s, climaxed as a politically burning question in the United States in 1914 with the adoption of the Clayton Act and the creation of the Federal Trade Commission. The Clayton Act supplemented the Sherman Act by prohibiting four specific types of monopolistic practices: price discrimination, exclusive-dealings contracts, the acquisition of competing companies (through stock purchases), and interlocking directorates among companies within the same industry (Ramírez and Eigen-Zucchi 2001: 159). The Federal Trade Commission took over from the Bureau of Corporations, whose employees were transferred to the new organisation. The Federal Trade Commission had two main missions. First, to investigate and publish reports on different parts of the economy, which was done by the Commission's Economic Division. Second, the other principal branch of the organisation, the Legal Division, could challenge 'unfair methods of competition' and bring administrative cases against corporations. It could also enforce the Clayton Act's specific prohibitions against monopolistic practices (Watkins 1926).

After 1914, the trust issue receded into the political and economic background. The legal framework established by the Sherman Act, as slowly defined by the courts and supplemented by the Clayton Act and the Federal Trade Commission, continues to this day to direct how the United States government handles anticompetitive practices. The Sherman Act was immediately effective in regulating loose combinations in the form of traditional cartels by making them illegal, but it proved more difficult to find a satisfying way to deal with tighter combinations. As it turned out, the Sherman Act had a number of anticompetitive consequences. Activities considered illegal if undertaken by several firms acting together might be considered legal if done by a single corporation, as long as it was not possible to prove that the intention were to secure monopoly power through the actions (Lamoreaux 1985: 179). The US antitrust regime thus indirectly, and unintentionally, encouraged the combination of several firms into one, instead of promoting competition between several different legal entities. Yet, by being a pioneer in tackling the issue, the United States became a point of reference to other countries that also had to decide what to do with the growing power of cartels. The importance of publicity, as witnessed in the actions of the Bureau of Corporations and the Federal Trade Commission, would also have important influence.

The land of cartels? Germany and cartel regulation

Despite having a large number of cartels and combines, the first German law regulating competition between corporations was established more than 30 years after the Sherman Act. As Germany rapidly industrialised from the 1850s, corporations invested heavily in production facilities. Instead of unbridled competition, with the risk of incurring huge losses, firms in many industries decided to share markets through cartel agreements. So widespread did cartels become in Germany that the country received the designation as the 'land of cartels' (Gerber 1998: 74–75; see also Chapter 11 in this volume).

While the trust issue became well established in the US political debate in the 1880s, in Germany it took until the 1890s before public discussion of cartels really began. But the German debate never reached the polemical heights of the United States. The general perception of cartels was predominantly positive; a view that was reinforced by German economists' analysis of cartels as natural and appropriate institutional responses to economic crises. In this prevailing interpretation, cartels were seen as instruments that reduced overproduction and provided employment stability. In the swelling German economic literature on the subject, the benign German cartels were often contrasted with the American trusts, which were depicted as only concerned with maximising profits and without concern for consumers, competitors or the society at large (Gerber 1998: 86–88).

In the United States, politicians eventually took the initiative to regulate trusts; in Germany that role fell to the courts. Cartel cases began to appear in the court system during the 1880s, mostly concerning litigation between cartel members or between cartels and former members. The issue that the courts had to confront was whether or not a cartel contract should be enforceable. If a company had entered into a cartel, would they be legally bound to uphold that contract? Two different legal principles clashed on the matter. According to the principle of contractual freedom (*vertragsfreiheit*), cartel contracts should be viewed as any other contract, and thus be enforceable by the courts. On the other hand, according to the principle of business freedom (*gewerbefreiheit*), private companies had the right to decide freely how they should conduct their business. Companies that wanted to leave cartel agreements often argued that the cartels interfered with their decision-making, and so violated their business freedom (Øvergaard 1919: 89–90).

The issue was resolved in 1897, when the German Imperial Court (the *Reichsgericht*) decided the Saxon Wood Pulp case. The case concerned a cartel agreement between a group of wood pulp producers in Saxony. In its ground-breaking verdict, the court argued that if prices dropped too low, the economic crisis that followed did not only harm the individual producers, but also society at large. It was therefore in the interest of society to avoid too many price falls. The verdict then made reference to how the German state had attempted to raise the prices of several products through establishing a protective tariff. The court concluded that if firms joined together in a cartel to prevent or moderate undercutting, this could not automatically be said to be against the public welfare. When prices fell so low that they threatened the producers with economic ruin, association with a cartel should be interpreted not only as a valid expression of self-preservation, but also as a precaution that served the common good. The court therefore resolved that cartels or syndicates could only be attacked if they aimed at creating a monopoly or to exploit consumers usuriously; or if this was the effect of the actions of the cartel (Fear 1997: 148–150). The ruling made cartel agreements valid and enforceable under German law and also established that the principle of business freedom could not be used against a cartel.

The verdict of the German Imperial Court cemented the country's reputation as the centre of the cartel movement, and in the coming years the courts intervened against cartels only in exceptional circumstances. The most prominent example was a case in the petroleum industry. In 1907, a German subsidiary of the US Standard Oil company entered into a cartel agreement with its largest German competitor, Deutsche Petroleum-Verkaufsgesellschaft. The two companies allocated the market between them, the 80–20 division in favour of Standard Oil revealing the difference in economic power between the former competitors. In addition, the German company had to cede control over pricing to Standard Oil, which was also given the right to hire or fire any of the accountants or the sales personnel in the German company. Standard Oil was also entitled to purchase all of the German company's production facilities, at book value, after five years, a value that would be decided in tandem by the two companies. In 1912, just before the stipulated five years had elapsed, the German company went to the court to have the agreement annulled, arguing that it had been pressured into accepting the cartel contract. The Imperial Court agreed with the German company, and declared the contract to be void as it was against good business practice. The court argued that for one company to gag another to such a degree was against the governing German interpretation of good practice (Øvergaard 1919: 53–54). Deutsche Petroleum-Verkaufsgesellschaft was allowed to exit from the cartel, without having to pay Standard Oil the fine stipulated in the original contract.

The case illustrates that cartels could be found illegal, but it probably helped that the culprit in this instance was a large foreign trust notorious for its behaviour against competitors. More than an indictment against cartels in general, the verdict must be interpreted as a confirmation that American trusts were bad and were placed in a completely different category from the more wholesome German cartels.

This is not to say that cartels were universally applauded in Germany. The growing importance of cartels in the economy led to some public concern. In the German Parliament voices could be heard calling for cartel legislation. The Imperial bureaucracy responded by carrying out a public investigation of cartelisation in the German economy, the Kartell-Enquête between 1902 and 1905. The investigation studied a number of different important industries, the findings of which were published in several volumes (Walker 1912: 188). Between 1905 and 1908 the German Chancellor presented the Parliament with an account of cartelisation in the country in four volumes. The published volumes, the Kartell-Denkschrift, gave an overview over the existing cartels in Germany with their association statutes, in addition to an outline of domestic and foreign cartel laws (Øvergaard 1919: 59; Schröder 1988: 164–165).

The government's publishing efforts were spurred on by political initiatives in the Parliament for the State to build the administrative capacity to monitor and regulate cartels. The influential German economist Gustav Schmoller in 1905 proposed the idea of setting up a cartel office to supervise cartel activities. Schmoller, who seemed to be influenced by the US Bureau of Corporations established two years earlier, wanted a central office that could gather information on cartels and to enforce general norms for cartel activity. Schmoller's idea was gradually taken up by Parliament, where in 1908 a large majority of the representatives supported a proposal to establish a cartel office. The chancellor first simply ignored the request, but when Parliament persisted, he eventually complied. Before the Cartel Office could become fully operational, however, the First World War broke out, and the establishment of the office slipped down the priority list (Gerber 1998: 97, 109).

By the end of the war, Imperial Germany had broken down and was replaced by a new Germany; the Weimar Republic. Although the old German affinity for cartels survived the war, the post-war inflation period from 1919 to 1923 did much to change public perceptions of cartels. As the German economy went from bad to horrible and succumbed to hyperinflation, many blamed cartels for contributing to inflation and for shifting the adjustment burden to consumers. The cry for regulation of cartels increased, and in October 1923 the newly appointed chancellor Gustav Streseman launched emergency legislation aimed at controlling the activities of cartels. The decree was enacted under special constitutional authority given to the chancellor due to the crisis. As a consequence it was not debated by parliament, and lacked democratic legitimation (Kessler 1936: 681–682; Gerber 1998: 120–123).

The decree made it mandatory for all intra-firm agreements that regulated markets, whether they concerned pricing, market allocation, production restrictions or the like, to be in writing. Unwritten gentlemen's agreements were invalid. To initiate any form of boycott action, a cartel first had to get consent from the cartel court. This special court was established by the new decree and was placed within the administrative system rather than being part of the traditional judiciary. The primary function of the court was to hear appeals from administrative actions taken under the decree. The decree gave wide discretionary powers to the Minister of Economics. He could order a cartel to disband, could demand that all cartel measures be first submitted to him before becoming effective, and he could ask the cartel court to declare a cartel agreement void. These administrative actions could only be carried out if the cartel in question was deemed to be dangerous to the public interest (Brinch 1935: 81–85; Kessler 1936: 681–683; Gerber 1998: 125–129). The decree lost its importance after the Nazis came to power in 1933 and turned cartel legislation on its head (Kessler 1934).

The German cartel law, was in reality a decree issued under emergency circumstances. It established an enlarged administrative framework for regulating cartels and gave the Minister of Economics significant powers in dealing with cartels. Although the decree made written contracts mandatory and the Minister of Economics could demand information about the activities of cartels from the participant, it did not create an outlet for making information publicly available, as the US legislation did with the Federal Trade Commission. Information was made available to the public through the verdicts of the cartel court, but not in a general way as in the US, or as comprehensively as in Norway, as we shall see.

The first real European competition law? The Norwegian Trust Act and the birth of the cartel register

In 1926, the Norwegian parliament finally decided to adopt legislation regulating cartels and other agreements limiting competition. The issue had been vigorously debated for at least a decade. The new law, the Trust Act (*trustloven*), was heavily influenced by the American and German experiences in dealing with trusts and cartels. The parliamentary debate, as well as the numerous proposals and official investigations into the issue, was littered with references to American trusts, to the effects of the Sherman Act, and to the German way of dealing with cartels. Yet, the new Norwegian law differed significantly from what could be found in the two bigger countries. The foreign legal practice was used as a point of reference for discussion and analysis, but the final outcome in Norway was decidedly different. According to the Swedish legal historian Ulf Bernitz, the final result was an Act that touched on all the important forms of restraints on competition and for this reason he characterises it as the first European competition law in its real sense: 'Europas första konkurrensbegränsningslag i egentlig mening' (Bernitz 1969: 394). It was also the first law to establish a permanent cartel register. This subject is dealt with in detail by Harald Espeli in Chapter 8 of this volume.

The question of the public regulation of cartels and trusts was first introduced into parliament in 1909. In a parliamentary debate on the Concession laws (*konsesjonslovene*), the regulatory regime regulating ownership of natural resources in Norway, the Minister of Justice explicitly warned that foreign trusts and monopolies might come to dominate crucial parts of Norwegian business life if allowed to operate unchecked in the country. His view was influenced by the developments in the United States, which he used as a cautionary tale (Haaland 1992).

By 1913, the fear of foreign monopolies and cartels compelled the Department of Justice to start preparing cartel legislation. To motivate the initiative, the Department pointed to the economic abuses of the trusts in the United States, and the fact that some foreign combinations had acted in ways that indicated that they aimed at taking control over parts of the Norwegian business life (Epland 2012: 20–21). Even though the Department proposed to set aside funds to establish a commission to consider competition laws, as in Germany with the Cartel Office, the outbreak of the First World War meant that the initiative was put on the backburner. The idea was not restarted before 1916 when parliament appointed a trust commission with the mandate to investigate and present legislation on the issue. The commission was never known as fast working, but in 1921 it delivered three proposals; as the members could not agree to a single joint proposal. The majority proposal made it clear that the US antitrust laws had proved that making cartels outright illegal was impractical. In contrast, the proposal argued that increased cooperation in the domestic economy was rational and that more cartel agreements would mean that fewer resources were wasted in destructive competition. Cooperation should be allowed to continue, and politicians should only try to minimise the societal problems that cartels and trusts had been proven to create (Haaland 1994: 46–50).

Although a comprehensive competition law based on the 1921 proposal was not passed before 1926, the matter was deemed so important that parliament had in 1920, already passed a provisional law on price regulation. The provisional law, which built on the price regulation laws enacted during the First World War, included measures to control cartels, market-dominant companies and monopolies. As Harald Espeli shows in Chapter 8 of this volume, the provisional law was the first time that a state demanded that corporations should notify the authorities about all arrangements aimed at reducing free competition. In fact, the notification system had been used previously in 1919, in a limited test for a temporary law which made it mandatory to give information to the working Trust Commission (Haaland 1994: 174–177).

The reason it took five years from the time the Trust Commission proposals were first presented until a Trust Act was finally passed, was of course that the issue was highly politically sensitive. The business community was generally sceptical of an act that gave the state significantly increased powers over the economy, as well as providing the public with better insights into what kind of market regulating agreements actually existed. It is easy to understand the disquiet since the act went further than any other existing framework regulating cartels in other countries. Yet the act was successfully guided through parliament by the ruling liberal party in 1926. During the interwar years, the Norwegian system served as an example to many of the smaller economies in Europe as to just how far the state could intervene in cartel matters. Although few other states were prepared to venture as far, the Norwegian model played an important role in discussions in countries like Denmark, Sweden, Poland and Czechoslovakia.

Conclusion: cartels, trusts, and the idea of publicity

When Adam Smith wrote his famous treatise in the 1770s he worried about conspiracies between businessmen. To him, however, legislation was not the way to stop these deplorable activities. Instead, he argued that public regulation advanced these cartel meetings; when all those in the same trade in a particular town were obliged to enter their names and places of abode in a public register, it only facilitated assemblies where the businessmen could conspire. Regulation through publicity was seen as ill-advised. In *Wealth of Nations*, in the paragraph were he described the tendency of businessmen to conspire against the public, Smith also wrote: 'A regulation which obliges all those of the same trade in a particular town to enter their names and places of abode in a public register, facilitates such assemblies' (Smith 1776: 82).

By the end of the nineteenth century, feelings about state regulation were starting to change, and by the dawn of the Second World War all countries in the western hemisphere had enacted a competition law in one form or another. In doing so, the states could study the US, German and Norwegian legislative frameworks to search for inspiration. As all state legislators realised, there were significant differences in how these three countries had gone about the business.

In the United States, the antitrust legislation was the outcome of a political debate essentially about how domestic companies abused their market power in the domestic market. Protected by high tariffs, American business developed into big business during the second industrial revolution, and they could operate in their home markets without accounting for foreign competitors. For the American legislators the question was therefore essentially a domestic issue.

In Germany, the second industrial revolution also lead to the dramatic growth of big business, and just like the US, these companies were protected in their domestic markets by high tariffs. In Germany, however, the biggest and most influential cartels were found in industries that were export orientated. The success of these companies on foreign markets was instrumental in maintaining employment and in developing the economy. German companies could therefore respond to any initiatives to regulate them by claiming that it would hurt them in foreign markets, and so regulation would indirectly harm German society. Only in the economic crisis brought on by hyperinflation after the First World War was this argument weakened enough to allow for the introduction of legislation.

In Norway, things were different. As a small, open economy, the Norwegian public was more afraid of big foreign trusts and cartels than abuses by local businessmen. The country therefore adopted a cartel law that tried to cover both the local cartels and large foreign concerns. The legislation aimed at protecting the country against bad, foreign trusts and at the same time to induce the domestic corporations to become more effective and coordinated.

Although the debates in the three countries had very different starting points, and as a result the outcomes were very different, it is evident that the debates on cartels and the legislative solutions in all three countries were heavily influenced by pragmatic adaptions to economic realities. In the United States, the main problem was that domestic trusts would gain too much market power. In Germany, on the other hand, the primary challenge was to keep the cartels strong enough to be able to compete in foreign markets. Neither in the United States nor in Germany, did the role of foreign cartels seem to play a decisive role in the development of legislation. In Norway, by contrast, the fear of foreign trusts was substantial. The perception of 'the cartel problem' and the three different legislative paths chosen by the United States, Germany and Norway was thus deeply rooted in the nature of their different national political economies.

In all three countries, however, the question of public access to information came to be a part of the solution. In the United States, President Theodore Roosevelt was not alone in arguing that more publicity, more knowledge about how the big combines actually worked, was essential for the antitrust policy to work properly. The establishment of first, the Bureau of Corporations and then the Federal Trade Commission, ensured that the public received what was considered to be relevant information. In Germany, the cartel office was meant to fulfil much the same role, but this administrative reform was cut short by the outbreak of the First World War. The cartel decree of 1923 was also established on the principle of the need for information, but in this instance the information about cartel operations were to be made available to the Minister of Economics, and not necessarily the public. The Norwegian legislation took the policy of providing information further. First, the Norwegian state demanded that all contracts restricting competition be filed with the new Trust Control in a central cartel register. Second, the register was made accessible to the public, both through information published in a special journal from the Trust Control, and through the accessibility of the full register to the public in the offices of the administration. The Norwegian legislators determined that the best way to control cartels was through the means of a central cartel registry, an idea that later would be taken up by a host of other countries.

Note

1   For the full text of the Sherman Act, see www.ourdocuments.gov/doc.php?flash=true&doc=51.

3 Legitimising Cartels

The joint roles of the League of Nations and of the International Chamber of Commerce

Marco Bertilorenzi

> It is certainly and conceivable that an all-pervading cartel system might sabotage all progress, as it might realise, with smaller social and private costs, all that perfect competition is supposed to realise.
>
> (Schumpeter 1942: 91)

The interwar period is often considered the 'golden age' of international cartels. Both general investigations about cartels (Barjot 1994; Kudo 1993; Schröter 1996; Fear 2008) and empirical case studies (Barbezat 1989; Wurm 1988; Schröter 1993; Gupta 2005; Cerretano 2011; Bertilorenzi 2014) find them pervasive between the wars. Yet this does not mean that cartels were either dismissed afterward or that they were insubstantial before 1914. Internationally, in the 1920s and the 1930s, they had great credibility as tools for economic and political governance. On the one hand, many governments endorsed their nation's firms participating in international cartels. On the other hand, managers from various industries believed cartels were powerful tools to manage their industries. Between the wars, cartels were part of the 'business philosophy' (Hannah 1976) of policy makers, businessmen and administrators whereby the international cooperation of private business actors were viewed as supporting public policies and international political actions.

This chapter focuses on the process of legitimisation of cartels. Two important issues are linked to this process. The first is that cartels became part of a specific narrative concerning their desirability for international economic governance. The second is that this narrative opposed the creation of an official international register. As Hansen (2014: 608) has recently pointed out, 'the interesting thing about narratives ... is that they are performative. This means that narratives co-construct and legitimise social reality.' This vision perfectly fits with the narrative about cartels in the inter-war period. Not only was it performative for the business community, it also shaped the way in which cartels were tackled by governments and international organisations. In spite of the constant diffusion of information between national governments and international organisations, the creation of an international register to survey the activity of international cartels was hampered throughout the whole interwar period. As we will show, a type of register was formed at the end of the 1930s, but it aimed neither to control cartels nor to survey their activities. The International Industrial Cartel Committee, or Comité des ententes industriels internationaux (hereafter CEII), which was a joint observatory of the League of Nations (hereafter LoN) and the International Chamber of Commerce (hereafter ICC), undertook to study cartels and to gather information about then. Their 'register' was designed only to promote a positive attitude towards cartels. The CEII is almost forgotten today, despite the important role it played in the dissemination of a specific narrative about cartels during the interwar period. Cartels achieved their general acceptance thanks mainly to the CEII's efforts, which was diffused through both economic practitioners and public servants.

Even if the CEII has not been examined by international scholarship, historians have explored the LoN and its cartel policies during 1920s, often focusing their attention on the Economic Conference of 1927. These studies typically agree that cartels emerged as tools of international governance in the LoN. For instance, Terushi Hara (1994) examined how the Economic Conference members started to consider cartelisation as a way to promote the recovery of European economy after the Great War. Recently, Dominique Barjot (2013) provided new materials about the birth of this discussion in the LoN, retracing Loucheur's proposal to place cartels on the international economic agenda. In 1925 the French manager and politician Louis Loucheur proposed that cartels be used to promote European economic integration. Eric Bussière (1994) showed that the cartel debate was linked with the proposal to reduce barriers and to promote effective market integration in Europe till the early 1930s. Michele D'Alessandro (2007) has also reviewed the impact of the LoN economic committee on public opinion during 1920s, exploring in detail how it worked as a 'consultative body' from 1925 to 1929. Focusing on the place of Italy in the LoN's cartel debates, Barbara Curli (1990) claimed that in the 1920s cartels were considered a specific European form of business organisation, alternate to the American firm model. These studies found that the 1920s arguments for cartels progressively lost their attraction after the failure of the LoN to use cartels to reduce trade barriers and promote economic integration in the early 1930s.

Two aspects, however, were overlooked in these former researches. First, the cartel debates continued in the following decade, obtaining international political endorsement. Second, the LoN did not stop studying cartels; rather it continued to work in strong collaboration with the ICC, creating the CEII, the joint-committee on cartels. This chapter argues that the narrative of the benefits of cartels was disseminated with much efficacy by the official adoption of the idea that cartels were an optimal solution for the problem of international economic governance. The role of a specific organisation in this process was critical because 'experts' from cartelised industries were called to serve among scholars and policy makers in the CEII, which acted as an international technocracy. The quality of this joint-committee, situated between two of the main international organisations of the interwar era, was able to play a semi-official level role in linking businessmen to civil servants in both national and international organisations. It worked actively between the wars to argue for the utility of cartels and preserve them from public control. This chapter examines this 'positive attitude' toward cartels as it was settled within the joint-study group of the LoN and the ICC, focusing also on the interplay of these two institutions and on the role of their members.

The ICC was not a political body. Its members were mainly entrepreneurs who joined the Chamber as individuals, and its focus was on economic issues. The main role of the ICC was, and is still, to define the international rules of commercial arbitrage. Arbitrage is a key tool to resolve contractual conflicts in matters related to trade. Yet, during interwar period the ICC also played a less defined political role. Similarly to the LoN, the ICC was an international organisation created to recast peaceful international relationships after the First World War. Since its creation in 1919, it had two main differences from the LoN. First, the ICC had a personal membership. Even though it was organised into national committees during the early 1920s, the ICC was relatively independent from public authorities and was not representative of national interests. Its main purpose was to gather businessmen together to coordinate their actions. Second, the ICC welcomed American businessmen. Its foundation meeting was in Atlantic City in 1919 and while US membership to the LoN was not ratified by the American Congress, ICC membership did not need ratification and it was a truly global institution (Ridgeway 1938).

The nature of the ICC and its ability to gather businessmen from all countries made this institution a key partner in the economic section of the LoN when it studied the cartel problem. The involvement of the ICC highlights some commonly overlooked issues: the first was the global nature of cartels. Often believed to be merely European institutions, cartels frequently involved American firms. This participation could be either legal, thanks to the Webb–Pomerene Act, or less legal, if done by other means. How much of the claimed 'European' nature of cartels was the result of rhetorical argument from the Cartel Committee remains an open question. The second issue is related to the links between public authorities and private business and their changing relationship. While during the 1920s cartels were viewed as private mechanisms to integrate markets, during the 1930s the involvement of governments in the establishment and administration of cartels swiftly changed their scope and working methods. This change emerged, in part, from the debates held in the Cartel Committee, which themselves can be used to explore the Great Transformation (Polanyi 1944) of the capitalistic economy during the 1930s.

Legitimisation of the international cartel movement, the 1927 League of Nations economic conference.

The original Loucheur's proposal, which called on cartels to play a role of public utility, was launched in the context of the return to economic normalcy after the shock of the Great War. After the progressive political rehabilitation of Germany, following the Locarno Agreement, and the rebuilding of an international payments system, (especially through the Dawes Plan and the restoration of British Pound convertibility to gold), the role of the state in the economy progressively faded. For example, until the mid 1920s many governments still exercised control over international trade with licenses and high tariffs, while after 1925 a general appeasement started. This did not mean that a free-trade system suddenly reappeared, but rather, tariffs continued to hamper the development of freer international trade. There was much political resistance to change. Yet the general trend was toward a reopening of capitals flows and commodities (Svennilson 1954; Aldcroft 1977; Liepmann 1938). From the mid-1920s the actions of the LoN and the ICC aimed to encourage the return to freer trade.

The Loucheur's proposal sought to use cartels to overcome the political reluctance to open markets. The core of this proposal was to use cartels to achieve political goals that policy makers were not able to carry out freely (Hara 1994; D'Alessandro 2007). The 1924 French–German potash agreement to share quotas in the American market, and the 1926 formation of a full cartel are considered to be decisive in the recasting of normal economic and political relationships between France and Germany (Schröter 1993). At the same time, many other cartels were settled in this period. In 1924 the international calcium carbide cartel was formed; in 1925 the international cartel of the electric lamps, the 'Phoebus' was settled, and a year later the Entente International de l'Acier together with a series of agreements in the iron and steel industries were achieved. In 1926 the Aluminium Association and the Copper Exporters Incorporation were formed. Before 1929 many other agreements, in the chemical industry, and in almost all the raw and industrial materials sectors were also signed (Conte 1928; Domeratzky 1928; Ballande 1937; Hexner 1946; Mason 1946).

Almost all these cartels involved German producers. American firms did not figure in the list of the participants, in spite of the connexions that they often had with these cartels. The Americans only openly entered into the agreements foreseen by the Webb–Pomerene Act, which granted special immunities to participate in particular cartels, such as in copper. The new institutional features brought by American participation in international cartels meant a rupture of the anti-trust attitude prevalent before the First World War and could be considered a consequence of President Wilson's subsequent policies following the end of the war (Eddy 1912; Notz 1918; Cuff 1973). It is not surprising that many observers characterised the cartels of the 1920s, especially the ones in the chemical, iron and steel industries with two main features: 'European', on the one hand, and 'private', on the other hand. These qualities were intrinsically linked: over-investment in these industries created by military demand and political decisions during the Great War had left the international balance between demand and production in many industries deeply altered. Subsequent monetary policies and inflation made the rapid transition to more competitive markets troublesome. The international cartels represented the success of private producers, without the help of national governments, in coping with this difficult environment. The chief of regional information of the US Department of Commerce, Louis Domeratzky, wrote of the cartel movement:

> While before the war it was essentially an economic movement ... in its postwar phase it is looked by its chief exponents as a means for readjusting the whole economic structure of Europe ... The postwar international cartel movement is taken much more seriously and had more political attributes than its predecessor before the war.
>
> (Domeratzky 1928: 38)

The ICC was an advocate of the debate about cartels as political tools. During 1925, as a consequence of the Locarno Agreement, the first German delegates were welcomed in the Chamber. Their inclusion gave the impetus for a special committee on the *Restauration économique*, whose works were divided among three sub-committees: one on international payments, one on trade barriers and a third on international cooperation. Their goal was to help the LoN organise a conference to study the difficulties of the international economy. During a meeting on trade barriers, Etienne Clementel, *président-fondateur* of the ICC and former minister in France during the First World War mobilisation (Kuisel 1981; Godfrey 1987; Rousseau 1998), declared that the tariff question has to be analysed from the standpoint of international cartels, recommending them as a way to avoid excess in tariffs.[1] During 1926, a *comité de liaison* between the ICC and the LoN helped the organisation of the International Economic Conference; and cartels were presented as possible tools to open up international trade and to rationalise world industrial production (International Chamber of Commerce 1926). The ICC, moreover, charged Roger Conte, who was coordinating a special ICC group on trade barriers, to prepare a specific publication to support these ideas.

When the International Economic Conference of the LoN began in 1927, the cartel movement was at its apogee. Scholarly accounts of the LoN conference claim it failed to give a clear message on cartels (Hara 1994; D'Alessandro 2007). It can be argued, however, that the Conference provided the first institutional legitimisation of international cartelisation because it aimed to seize the role of the cartels in the process of rehabilitation of European economy. Many publications that went along with the preparation of the conference underpinned this point, sharing two common threads (De Rousiers 1927; MacGregor 1927; Wiedenfeld 1927; Conte 1928; Oualid 1926; Person 1927; Spitzer 1927; Hirsch 1927). First, they rejected the idea that cartels were intrinsically negative; any judgement on their value depended on the specific case. Second, they argued that additional studies on the actual working of cartels were necessary to provide a judgement about the impact of cartels on the European recovery. In a few cases, they raised second-order criticisms of the cartel movement. Oualid (1926), for instance, emphasised the anti-syndicalism activity of many cartels. Hirsch (1927) drew attention to the potentially negative outcome that some cartels could have on the free circulation of goods, claiming that cartels could work as indirect forms of protectionism. MacGregor (1927) pointed out that national cartels were less efficient than trusts to rationalise outputs and that a mismatch could exist between the strategies of cartels and national policies. Only the study of Gustav Cassel (1927) in this group of LoN's publications showed cartels as harmful to the general welfare.

The second thread in these publications deserves particular attention. Emerging from the conference, the call for further studies and information about cartels represented a potential threat for the cartel movement. A formal request for more information from the international organisations could have led to more extensive measures to control cartels, or at least to monitor their activities. Hypothetically, this need for more information could have led national powers and international organisations to agree to an international register of cartels. During the conference this risk was countered by the claim that cartel agreements were essentially 'private' and that they should remain autonomous and as independent as possible from both political powers and international organisations.[2] As a consequence the study of the cartel problem never resulted in the view that their operations should be monitored through a specific register. Instead, a study group of businessmen from cartelised industries was formed to investigate 'the cartel problem'. Soon, this group became the principal vehicle for the legitimisation of the international cartel movement.

The aftermath of the LoN conference: the creation of the CEII, the international cartels study group

After the conference, the ICC continued to cooperate with the LoN to study international cartelisation avoiding any activity could have be turned into a public survey. In particular, they studied whether cartels were helping rehabilitate economic conditions and reduce tariffs. During 1928 a special joint-committee of the LoN and ICC created the CEII to undertake this work. It was committed to gathering as much information as possible about cartels. The ICC members were actively involved in the work which ultimately settled the 'discourse' concerning cartels. In the first meeting, Paul de Rousiers, who also worked at the LoN and was as a great supporter of the cartel movement (de Rousiers 1901; Savoye 1988), was appointed as the ICC expert. He argued the work of the CEII should be a simple economic survey, and to avoid any international regulation of cartels, baffling the risk to creating special international sanctions. In his opinion, national sanctions were sufficient to preserve the public order and, moreover, he argued that the choice of the Economic Conference of Geneva underpinned the refusal of any study that could have led to an international regulation of cartels.[3]

The CEII adopted and disseminated this liberal position toward cartels. All the officers and experts involved in the CEII shared the same opinion that theoretically justified cartels: as cartels were similar to other forms of industrial activity they needed the freedom to set agreements without any regulatory controls. Cartels were not evil *per se* for the public welfare, and so no particular deterrent or control was required. Even registering cartel activity was always viewed as impacting negatively on their ability to rationalise industrial production. Cartels were 'voluntary' institutions merely responding to economic issues. Thus any mandatory involvement by political powers in national or international cartels had a negative influence on the rationalisation of industry. This opinion was publically defended by some famous managers of the time, such as Alfred Mond (1927), chairman of the Imperial Chemical Industries (and formerly managing director of Mond, Bruner and Co.). The business philosophy of the CEII epitomises Fear's insights, according to which cartels were 'not necessarily the opposite of liberalism and competition, but a variation on them' (Fear 2006: 3).

In 1929, this opinion became the intellectual backbone of the CEII because the members of the ICC were able to modify the methods with which the LoN began the study of cartels. The Economic Secretariat of the LoN started to prepare tables, to describe the general reach of the international cartel movement and to provide material to the CEII. The aim was to collect data on existing cartels, such as date of foundation, duration, members, headquarter, and scope. Individual firms were not identified as members, but their nationality was recorded to measure the geographical extent of agreements. The indication of a headquarter, when it existed, also served to reveal if the agreements were only verbal or if they involved contractual enforcements or specific organisations. The addition of few lines to describe a cartel's scope allowed a general taxonomy of cartels (quotas, prices, territorial divisions, and so on) to be created. Data were gathered into specialised economic publications. The LoN then sent this to each government for feedback and to complete or modify the information.[4] Even though this process did not rely on information coming from the cartels but only from the economic press, Pietro Stoppani, the secretary of the Economic Section of the LoN who organised the CEII in Geneva, claimed to the officials of the Board of Trade that it was 'the most complete inventory concerning international cartels'.[5]

The ICC did not appreciate this work by the LoN. In several meetings the ICC argued the LoN should have taken a deeper economic analysis of the specific working of cartels, instead of relying on information from the press. To achieve this the CEII sought to involve businessmen directly to work as 'experts'. This was not motivated by the desire to survey cartels activities, but to promote cartels through a wider circulation of their work. Even though the specialised press contained much information on cartels, it did not describe the internal workings of such organisations. The decision to involve some managers of cartelised industries was intended to disclose information about the internal working of cartels and to diffuse it publically. It also gave businessmen the opportunity to establish a consultative chamber and share opinions on improving their organisations.[6] The LoN endorsed the ICC's outlook because it considered it useful to gather more information about the cartel movement instead of expressing general assertions. In this way, the CEII also acknowledged the need to accumulate information about the cartel movement, so as to assist governments legislating on cartels. The LoN formed two groups of experts: the first examining the nature of cartels, the second the different national legislation.[7]

In December 1929, thanks to the intermediation of the ICC, the CEII invited several prestigious industrialists from cartelised industries to undertake the first task. Aloys Meyer was invited because of his chairmanship of the Entente Internationale de l'Acier. Louis Marlio as chairman of the Aluminium Association, the international aluminium cartel, was also involved. Harry McGowan, chairman of Imperial Chemical Industries and board member of many cartels in the chemical industry, replaced Alfred Mond on the CEII and the ICI after his death.[8] Among these businessmen, Marlio was most influential because as well as being a prominent businessman he was a member of the French academy. Marlio was also a professor of international economics in some Parisian business schools and the successor of the eminent French liberal economist Clément Colson. Having been a French civil servant before and during the Great War, he became the chairman of Pechiney, the leading French aluminium and chemical producer of the 1920s (Morsel 1997). Gino Olivetti, who was a preeminent Italian industrialist and president of the ICC, also served as an expert in this committee as did Clemens Lammers and Antonio Stefano Benni. Both already worked in several committees at the LoN economic conference (Curli 1990; D'Alessandro 2007). They were selected for the CEII because both Lammers and Benni were representative of industrial organisations: the first was a leading member of the German Reichsverband der deutschen Industrie, and the latter was the president of the Confederazione Generale Fascista dell'Industria Italiana.[9]

For the second task, the study of cartel legislation, the LoN invited in other experts. Even here, the leading experts were directly linked with the cartel movement. Among them, was Siegfried Tschierschky, a reputed German legal expert, and also director of the Kartellrundschau. This was the official publication of the Kartellamt, the German government's office of cartels. The Kartellrunschau was not simply a legal review. Since its foundation in 1924, it published information about the formation and modification of cartel agreements that involved German enterprises. Its creation followed the enactment of the Kartellamt, which also served to register cartels. Tschierschky's ideas about cartelisation had already been published in 1911, 1927 and 1930 when he joined the cartel study group. He had a positive attitude toward cartelisation, which aligned with German legislation of that time. The ICC also included other two scholars in this project; Robert E. Oldset, who was a member of the American delegation, and Henry Decugis, a preeminent French expert in commercial law and incorporation, who worked as a legal consultant for many French enterprises.[10]

During 1930 and 1931, the CEII organised four conferences to study the problem of cartels, the outcome of which was the publication of three reports. Edited by the LoN, these included one with specific case studies, called *Etude* (Benni *et al.* 1931a); one on the general nature of cartels, called *Rapport Général* (Benni *et al.* 1931b); and one on national cartel legislation (Decugis *et al.* 1930).[11] This last study provided a review of all national cartel legislation, but without expressing any views on future policies. The central idea of this report was that national legislation, following the German example, should neither hamper the participation of firms in cartels, nor scrutinise their behaviour. In other words, they claimed that, even if control over cartels was established, this should be done *ex-post*, and without any *ex ante* control.[12] The group of experts made more detailed descriptions of some leading cartels, claiming to present cartels from an objective viewpoint. It was argued that the experts' reputation, along with their internal knowledge of cartels, guaranteed the quality of the provided information. At the same time, these experts were able to define what could be released to the public and what had to be kept confidential.[13]

The initial choice of industries could have included: steel, aluminium, rail materials, linoleum, rayon, bone glue, zinc, copper, tin, lead, mercury, potash, dyestuffs, electric lamps, matches, glass, bottles, banks and petroleum. The study aimed to include those industries that either experienced effective cartelisation (steel, aluminium, glass, potash, mercury, copper, zinc, tin, and rail materials) or were examples of international trusts (matches, linoleum, bottles[14] and SOFINA, the Belgian bank trust). The aim was not to limit studies to pure cartels, but also to include other forms of industrial organisation with a comparative goal. The Committee sought to use Marlio's 1930 article, which had a positive view about the desirability of cartels for the rationalisation of the European economy, on these studies and so serve as the basis for further analysis.[15] The final choice of case studies, however, was limited to an arbitrary potpourri that only included the sectors directly under the experts' control: steel, rails, aluminium, zinc, copper, tin, lead, lamps, rayon, mercury, linoleum, potash and dyestuff (Benni *et al.* 1931a).

The information gathered on these specific cartels were prepared by one expert and commented on by the others. Lammers prepared the studies on rayon, linoleum and potash, and these were commented on by Marlio, Benni, Meyer and McGowan. Originally Marlio was to write about the European aluminium cartel, electric lamps, SOFINA and the metals industries during 1929, but he ultimately only prepared one on aluminium and served as a referee for others.[16] Benni prepared the study on mercury and Meyer authored the one on steel. The CEII then argued these studies provided evidence that cartels were not only a private form of rationalisation of international business, but that they also served to reduce costs, stabilise prices and help balance demand and supply. For instance, in this study, the definition of a cartel was 'les cartels sont des associations entre des entreprises indépendantes de la même branche ou de branche analogues, crées en vue d'une amélioration des conditions de la production ou de la vente' (Benni *et al.* 1931b: 8).[17] Cartels were thus a tool of the economic 'rationalisation' in vogue during the 1920s. Cartels were also beneficial to public welfare because they sought to 'éviter les conséquences désastreuses de la concurrence déréglée entre de très grandes usines qui, dan les périodes de dépression économique ou en cas de surproduction, ne peuvent plus marcher qu'à allure réduite' (Benni *et al.* 1931b: 36–37).[18]

Thanks to the work of the CEII, between 1925 and 1930 cartels changed from being obscure and almost secret organisations to being displayed publically as 'common actions in the international field', and part of the international economic and political debate about the organisation of the international business.[19] The views of the group of experts concerning 'their' cartels received the imprimatur of the LoN. It was a mutually beneficial process: on the one hand, the expert members gave the LoN authority in the debate about international cartels; on the other hand, the official publications of the LoN served to give objectivity to the personal views of the industrial and legal experts. Thus individual opinions of the Committee members such as Benni, Marlio, Meyer, Mond and Tschierschky received official endorsement. This was the main public relations outcome from the committee of experts. This confirms earlier research that the LoN served as an international technocracy in the public debate on the economic situation and legal regulation

(D'Alessandro 2007; Thiery 1998; Bussière 1997; Clavin and Wessels 2005; Berger 2006). The important novelty is the link between the LoN and the ICC, which enabled the settlement of this specific technocracy, through the businessman who served as experts in the public debate.

The internal debate of the CEII during the Great Depression: the first 'private' international register

During the 1930s, the ICC gave new tasks to the CEII, beyond those of its original role as a consultative board. The international crisis again reshaped the committee's view on cartels. Many members of the CEII sought to do more than the simple consultative task decided after the LoN conference. Since the study group members were convinced that cartels were useful in balancing demand and supply at less social cost than free competition, cartels became an issue in debates during the Great Depression. One of main arguments of cartel supporters was that these institutions were useful both to prevent over-production and to cope with it once it appeared. These ideas emerged in the board of the CEII at the end of the 1920s and, after a few modifications, were put forward during the following decade. External change and, especially, the emergence of governments as possible regulators of the economy during the international economic crisis had challenged the core belief that cartels as private business organisations could operate without political controls (Staley 1937; Davis 1946; Mason 1946).

The reconfiguration of the study group's action plan acknowledged the lack of effectiveness that cartels had in opening up trade in the real economy. According to Bussière (1994), in spite of the great expectations that emerged after the conference of 1927, the LoN achieved only minimal reductions to trade barriers. The Great Depression played an important role in delaying this project and international organisations were not able to achieve free-trade policies in a period of rising economic nationalism (James 2001; Clavin 2013; Decorzant 2011). After October 1931, the CEII initiated a broad discussion into the failure of policies to eliminate trade barriers, and the role of cartels were again considered as effective tools to achieve these aims. Rather than re-think the desirability of cartels, efforts were made to modify the *modus operandi* of the study group. Several members of the CEII considered that they had little impact on the action of governments, and that to act as a simple consultative board was not sufficient. Both the LoN and the ICC were considered ineffective in proposing policies to national governments, and the CEII sought a more active role for these organisations for the future.[20]

The international economic crisis gave new weight to the idea, already expressed in the 1920s, that cartels were more effective than public policies and diplomatic channels in coping with economic difficulties. The CEII tried to play a more decisive role once again calling on cartels to promote international trade interconnexions. In its lexicon, cartels represented a 'trilateral' (or more generally multilateral) approach to international trade, as opposed to the 'bilateral agreements' between governments that were reshaping international economic relationships. Unlike the 1920s, several members of the ICC and the CEII aimed to transform their study group into a consultative board, to assist the formation of new cartels directly, rather than simply study them. The direct connection between the most influential cartels and the CEII supplied important intelligence to distribute to non-cartelised industries. This view was expressed during the October 1931 council of the ICC, which discussed the proposal to re-cast the study group into a consultative board for the settlement and administration of cartels. René Duchemin, Vice-President of the ICC and the president of the French employers association (Fraboulet 2007) endorsed the CEII proposal, claiming

> La Chambre de Commerce Internationale exprime l'opinion que les ententes industrielles internationales, bien conçues et soucieuses des intérêts des consommateurs des différents pays, peuvent avoir des résultats hautement bienfaisants et que leur extension pourrait contribuer sensiblement à une amélioration de l'organisation de la production. ... Le Conseil de la Chambre du Commerce Internationale estimant au surplus que l'extension du principe des cartels à branches d'industries non touchées jusqu'ici peut conduire à des nouveaux rapprochements internationaux, charge le Secrétariat Général de poursuivre l'étude de la question des cartels et, le cas échéant, d'offrir de se mettre à la disposition des industries privées, si elles désirent se réunir sur un terrain neutre, afin d'examiner les moyen de réaliser une amélioration de la coopération internationale.[21]

The language of the debates reveals it was considered obvious that the crisis imposed new responsibilities on the CEII. The failure of the international economy to achieve more open trade was considered to be the result of the 'moderation' of CEII delegates. As a consequence, a more radical approach was demanded; one which promoted the formation of cartels and created an office to provide the legal and economic knowhow needed for their formation.[22] The American members, who could not endorse this scheme because of the American law against cartels, opposed the specific proposal on cartels. After discussion, a compromise was reached and the committee agreed to a partial endorsement of this new objective. Only Europe was to be involved with these actions and they would not apply to the American economy or to American firms. Despite the participation of American firms in international cartels, they were presented as a specific form of European business organisation. The divide between Europe, as the land of cartels, and the United States as the land of trusts, was a rhetorical construction to create agreement among the experts of the committee.[23]

After this resolution, the ICC started to explore how to create the bureau of cartels that Duchemin sought to build. Lammers suddenly undertook its formalisation, as chief expert in the ICC on cartel matters. The problem was to form a register of all existing cartels without putting them under the control of a public authority. Lammers and Duchemin wished to avoid a public register; they preferred a private register located in the ICC rather than in the LoN, to keep confidential the information that cartels would have shared with this bureau. While claiming cartels useful to cope with the international depression, the ICC was convinced that the solutions adopted in various cartels could be harmonised to create a common strategy for the whole industrial world. To achieve this, the CEII had to be less consultative than before, acting as a general director of international cartelisation. The formation of an observatory of experts would have been a way to use cartels for political purposes. For example, they could fight inflation, through the stabilisation of commodity prices, and restrain the adoption of trade barriers and bi-lateral agreements. Lammers, Marlio and Duchemin recognised that the ICC was also attractive for the businessmen of cartelised industries. The problem of cheating, which was later defined theoretically (Stigler 1964; Suslow and Levenstein 2006), was already a practical issue at that time. The existence of a cartel bureau could reduce these problems through a special arbitrage process for cartel contracts, and the harmonisation of fines and rules.[24]

The establishment of such an organisation, however, appeared unworkable. A consultative board required numerous legal experts with comparative knowledge of the different laws on cartels. It also required economic and statistical experts able to enter into the mechanisms of all industrial agreements. The task was simply not possible for a relatively small agency such as the ICC. It appeared preferable, therefore to start with the simpler task of gathering information and to work progressively toward becoming an embryonic register during 1934. In this case, the privacy of the ICC made it preferable to the LoN, which would have found it easier to attract the collaboration of managers.[25] Changes to national laws made it too difficult to suggest a common policy. In two countries, Germany and Hungary, new cartel registration legislation and national preventive supervision of agreements were settled during 1932, attracting the LoN's curiosity (Tschierschky 1932). The ICC debate was quickly enlarged to include both private cartels and the new national versions of state intervention in the economy.[26]

The main problem with establishing a private register for cartels was the rapid change in the nature of cartels during the 1930s. Cartels were no longer mere 'private agreements'; in many cases, political intervention was evoked as a necessity for international economic governance. This emerged during the economic conference of London in 1933. Although the conference did not devote the same attention to cartels as the conference of 1927, it focused mainly on monetary issues, it recognised the necessity to formulate international plans to reduce global industrial output, and the need for firms and government to cooperate to achieve this goal (Société des Nations 1933: 75–80). The main novelty was that, for the first time, the cartel problem was not presented as a solution to be adopted only by private producers. Instead it was argued that, along with the desirability to create a Bureau des Cartels, the ICC had to consider the existence of two types of agreements, one of which involved governments. While the usual industrial cartels were presented as the outcome of private actions, raw materials agreements required the intervention of governments, given these materials underpinned national economies. From this point, until the 1940s, the division of the cartel problem into two became mainstream in the debate (Mason 1946; Lovasy 1947).[27]

The artificial divide between industrial cartels or raw materials agreements

The theoretical debate was supported, as it was during 1926–1927, by specific examples. During this same period some cartels were being reshaped either directly by governments or through public bodies contributing to their administration. The direct involvement of public administrators helped create compromises. The perfect example was the International Steel Cartel (ISC), which replaced the former Entente Internationale de l'Acier. Both the British and the German governments played key roles in reshaping the agreement following the use of 'home-markets' reservation and export quotas (Wurm 1988; Berger 2000). Similarly a proposal to substitute general quotas with 'home-market' reservations and export quotas was discussed in the board of the aluminium cartel around the same time (Bertilorenzi 2014). In another two cases, the difficulty of particularising general plans made by private actors pushed the public authorities to intervene. In the case of tin and rubber, new types of agreements emerged, which were written under the control of political authorities to reduce outputs and stockpile excess (Hillman 2010; Coates 1987). These two cartels were not only innovative because governments played a new role, they also acted as buffer stock schemes, meaning that instead of only reducing production, the governments administered the stocks and their buffering on the market. This kept some of the unsold stocks outside the market, allowing price manipulation and minimising output.

The main problem for programmes of output restriction was that the general economic crisis of the 1930s made accepting sacrifice difficult. Governments' new role also emerged as a problem within the study group and created issues concerning the ICC's role in the arbitrage of international cartels. The earlier definition of cartels as voluntary and private did not suit the new environment. Louis Marlio argued the CEII should promote only private cartels, while Lammers argued that the role of government in the economic regulation was not negligible because it made these organisations more cohesive and effective. Benni summarised that the crisis was changing the range of cartels. In his opinion, while during the 1920s cartels served to provide international governance in the international markets, the crisis of the 1930s meant involving new regulations at a national level. This necessitated the involvement of governments in the general discussions on international cartelisation.[28] The division between private cartels and public interventions had been progressively reshaped by the artificial distinction between 'industrial cartels' and 'raw material agreements.' This divide continued and another category of agreements was created: 'International Commodity Agreements'. From our present standpoint they could be considered cartels as well, but their key feature was the involvement of governments in their formation and administration (Davis 1946; Mason 1946). At the end of 1934, Stoppani called on the CEII to broaden its work to include these forms of agreements, seeking the creation of a specific study group on raw materials. The LoN again asked for the collaboration of the ICC, the expertise of which was considered a critical factor in achieving impartial but penetrative studies.[29]

The work of the CEII was reshaped by these double components. During 1935, various reports claimed advances in gathering information about existing cartels, and associated with this, the LoN's study group on raw materials continued. It seems that the ICC and the LoN had a division of tasks; the ICC became the centre for private cartels assessments, while the LoN made inspection of commodity agreements. This does not mean the two spheres were completely separated. For example, the work of the LoN included private cartels, such as aluminium (Oualid 1938). Similarly, the 1937 congress of the ICC, which was largely devoted to Lammers's group on cartels, discussed various forms of cartelisation using three case studies. The aluminium industry, described by Louis Marlio, was presented as the *idealtypus* of the private cartel. The tin and rubber industries, by contrast, were described by Sir John Campbell, who according to Hilman (2010) was their leading crafter, as examples of agreements under strict governmental control. Between these two categories, Meyer described the steel industry as a combination in which public powers endorsed and helped the establishment of the cartel (International Chamber of Commerce 1937).

The ICC adopted this conceptual framework in its 1937 congress, during which Lammers proclaimed the need to continue his original idea of a private register for cartels. However, the idea of providing expertise was never invoked again. Rather the ICC was expected to gather information about cartels and to share this in confidence, with the CEII. Thus, the original idea to form a private *organon* was adapted to the existing possibilities and limited to those businessmen who believed in the necessity to harmonise the works of cartels.[30] On the other hand, the LoN continued its activities on commodity agreements, periodically producing reports. These were distributed to governments to keep them informed about the principal agreements, both private and intergovernmental that were evolving. The intention was not survey cartel activity. Rather, because these agreements were viewed as tools of public interest, they constituted important data for the formulation of the international economic policy of each government. The documents suggest that the LoN wanted to harmonise national political actions with the international agreements.[31]

Besides gathering confidential information about cartels, the specific role of the CEII was to perform a public relationship exercise to enhance cartels' reputation and public awareness of them. In this context, the 'Bureau d'information privé des Ententes Industrielles Internationales' (BEII) was formed as a financially autonomous section of the ICC. The BEII was the final outcome of the on-going debates held within the CEII. Its tasks were to collect available documentation and to publish a special review (*Ententes internationales: Revue du Bureau des Ententes industrielles internationales*) in English, French and German. Two issues appeared before the war and their content reflected the central paradigm of presenting private cartels and ICAs as two faces of the same economic and political governance problem in the industrial world. The publication of this review was an evolution in the cartel study group's strategy; while confidential information was not disseminated, the review tried to spread the debates on cartels, their achievements and their transformations outside the CEII. It was not possible to determine the real significance of the information on cartels gathered by the BEII. When war stopped the activities of the ICC, however, Lammers declared that

> Le BEII est la seule organisation qui soit habilitée internationalement pour grouper des renseignements sur tous les cartels existants et suivre l'évolution des législations en cette matière. ... Les cartels ont un rôle à jouer à l'égard non seulement de la production, mais aussi de la consommation. Ils peuvent éviter des perturbations sociales, assurer un certain équilibre, et faciliter la reconstruction économique internationale.[32]

It is unclear whether this work continued during the war, and in particular what role was played by either the ICC or the LoN. During the final phase of war, a proposal to create an International Trade Organisation emerged, with the task, among others, of surveying international cartels and commodity agreements (Wells 2002; Freyer 2006). Many features of the debate about the cartel problem, as settled during the final part of the 1930s, were to be revitalised to cope with the same issues after the end of hostilities. Even if their recognition and desirability was dramatically reshaped during the war, the long lasting debated of the 1920s and the 1930s was a legacy for future policies. Many economists during the 1940s thought that the good side of the cartel experience, (the intergovernmental agreements), could have helped public welfare and growth and stabilisation policies after the war (Mason 1946; Hexner 1946; Bennett 1949). Schumpeter (1942) himself was not immune to this debate. This evolution was underlined in 1947 by one of the few official reports of the United Nations on international cartels, which eventually had access to the cartel documentation gathered by the CEII during the 1930s. The chief economist of the UN, Gertrud Lovasy, explored the old-fashioned distinction between private industrial cartels and public raw material agreements. She claimed that the first were essentially schemes to reduce production in response to market conditions, while the latter aimed to use stocks as anti-cyclical tools to keep price and employment stable. In other words, the desirability of economic tools to cope with business cycle was saved, while private interests had been replaced by governments in the settlement of public policies (Lovasy 1947: 24).

Conclusions

The CEII produced the first international chronicle of cartels, even though it was created neither to survey the cartel activity nor to regulate it. Its ability to obtain the direct involvement of businessmen from cartelised industries was critical in helping it gather information about cartels, but it also affected the political vision of the desirability of cartels that emerged from this review. In fact, the private review was designed to promote cartels and their impact on the international economy. This suggests that the reputational credit that cartels received during interwar period was not only the outcome of the lack of an anti-trust policy (or ideology). It was also the direct consequence of a discourse, imposed by both businessmen and civil servants who shared the same positive opinion about of cartels and their success in overcoming discordant voices. Its main creators, who served the CEII as experts, would not have critiqued the cartel movement.

The discourse about cartels during the interwar period aimed to transform private and secret organisations into instruments of public utility. In this process of recognition, a key role was played by the acquisition of power and authority by a network of people, initially elected as neutral expert representatives. The permanence of figures such as Marlio, Meyer, Lammers, Benni, De Rousiers, Duchemin, Oualid, McGowan, Stoppani and Tschierschky in this network of experts influenced the way in which the cartel problem was approached by the LoN and the ICC and necessarily the way it was disseminated outside. These organisations were the creators of a positive discourse about international cartelisation, which legitimised cartels both economically and politically. The need for cartels was a paradigm self-legitimised by the expert authors who were also key supporters of international cartels of the time. The outcome of the cartel committee can be described as a process of induction, which went from the practice to the theory, and through which cartels were legitimised.

This study has focused on the evolution of the debates of the CEII. It has basically ignored the factual corroborations of what exactly cartels did; this could be done through a comparative analysis of some case studies. The aim of this study is not to assess whether the CEII was correct in proposing cartels as an optimal tool of economic or political governance. Rather, the main argument is that, whatever the real nature of cartels (aside from any moral dimensions), the CEII existed as an official channel for the flow of information and ideas. This channel was able to propose a bloc of coherent arguments, which were globally used and adopted in almost all subsequent discussions on cartels. In other words, the way in which 'the cartel problem' was settled passed through official spheres to become a consistent ideological paradigm. Business practitioners, policy makers, scholars, and civil servants compromised to make cartels neither a standard political tool, nor an enemy of public interests, but a practical and tolerable fact. The construction of this rhetoric was shocked only by the Second World War and by the settlement of another discourse, born in the United States, that presented cartels as an evil *per se* (Maddox 2001; Taylor 1981).

It would be naïve to imagine, however, that the paradigm of competition replaced the cartelised view in a few years. The marriage of public utility with private cartels was progressively questioned during the 1930s, when the main attributes of the cartel movement of the 1920s were placed under criticism. It has been shown that the 1920s view, which presented cartels as a 'private and voluntary' tool of economic management, was progressively eroded during the 1930s. Cartels were not replaced with competition policies, but with a change in the role of public powers as administrations of international trade reduced the private and voluntary aspects of cartels. In other words, it was not the tool but the administrator of this tool that changed. The new economic dimension of the state in international trade reshaped the nature of cartels and made them less desirable than before. The invention of a new category of cartels (i.e. the International

Commodity Agreements) denotes this institutional and cultural transformation, which is the starting point of a new paradigm. Even if the 1920s view of the members of the cartels committee, had left cartels free to act without any political control, this idea would have changed during the 1930s. At that point, states would have no more allowed international trade free to be self-regulated, than they would have allowed cartels to remain uncontrolled.

Acknowledgements

This research could be possible thanks to the access to the archives of the League of Nations, at UN in Geneva, and of the International Chamber of Commerce, in Paris. I acknowledge these institutions for the liberal approach to my enquiries and for providing access to their documents. In particular, I would like to express my aknowledgement to Sylvie Picard-Renaut (ICC). Many thanks also to Dominique Barjot, Valerio Cerretano, Margrit Müller, Harm Schröter, Luciano Segreto, and Ray Stokes for their comments and suggestions. A special thanks is for Susanna Fellman and Martin Shanahan, not only for having invited me to contribute to this collection, but also and above all for their valuable readings to the previous drafts. As usual, I remain alone responsible for mistakes and inaccuracies.

Notes

1 Procès-Verbal du 21 Conseil, 25 June 1926, Archives ICC, n.c.
2 L'Ouevre économique de la SDN. Rapport et projet de résolutions présentés par la Deuxième commision à l'assemblée, Genève 1931, document A.75: 4, Archives LoN, R.2830, file 31254.
3 Procès-Verbal, 27 Conseil, 29 June 1929, Archives ICC, n.c.
4 Cartels. Memorandum du Sécretariat préparé sur les indications du Comité consultatif économique, 1929, Archives LoN, R.2828, file 6890. Société des Nations, Tableau provisoire des ententes ind. et com. Internationales. E.713, 20 June 1931, Archives Historiques du Ministrère des Affaires étrangères, B39, Dossier 1, Folder 1931.
5 Pietro Stoppani (LoN) to Sydney Chapman (Board of Trade), 1 June 1929, The National Archives, BT/64/388.
6 Procès-Verbal 29 Conseil, 29 March 1929, Archives ICC, n.c.
7 Procès-Verbal, 8 May 1929, Comité Consultatif Economique, Sous-Comité I, Industrial Questions, Archives LoN.
8 Consultation d'Experts en matière d'ententes industrielles. Service d'un expert Français, 29 December 1929, Archives LoN, R.2857, file 16770.
9 Ententes Industrielles, Collaboration de MM Lammers et Benni, 1929, Archives LoN, R.2829, file 13731.
10 Cartels. Memorandum du secretariat preparé sur les indications du Comité Consultatif économique, 1929, Archives LoN, R.2828, file 9989.
11 Ententes Industrielles. Pubblications de Monographies, 1930, Archives LoN, R.2830, file 20773.
12 Cartels. Memorandum par les trois experts juristes, 1930, Archives LoN, R.2829, file 9989.
13 Procès-Verbal du 32 Conséil, 4 March 1930, Archives ICC, n.c.

Legitimising Cartels 47

14 Libbey-Owens.
15 Procès-Verbal, Comité des Ententes Industrielles Internationales, 15 July 1931, LoN Archives, R.2857, file 21575.
16 Joseph Avenol (LoN) to Louis Marlio, 27 January 1930, Archives LoN, R.2857, file 16770.
17 'Cartels are associations in which independent firms, either of the same industrial branch or of similar branches aim to ameliorate production or sales conditions'.
18 'Avoid the ruinous consequences of cutthroat competition amongst large producing units that, during periods of economic depression or during periodical over-production crises, can no longer work at economics of scale.'
19 Note on list of International industrial agreements, 12 January 1929, The National Archives, BT/64/388.
20 Note explicative du Secretariat général sur la preparation de la 36ème session du Conséil, 23 October 1931, Archives ICC, n.c.
21 'The ICC expresses the idea that international industrial cartels, when well settled and when they are respectful to the interest of consumers from all countries, are able to provide highly satisfying outcomes and their further diffusion can contribute to ameliorate the actual situation of the productive system. ... The Council of the ICC, considering it helpful to extend the adoption of cartel to all industries not yet touched by this form of organisation, charges the General Secretariat to put forward the study of cartels and, in case of need, to offer to be at disposal of private industries, if they would like to meet in a neutral field, to examine the means to achieve new international cooperation.' Procès-Verbal du 36 Conseil, 23 October 1931, Archives ICC, n.c.
22 Note explicative, 23 October 1931, Archives ICC, n.c.
23 Procès-Verbal du 46 council, 30 July 1931. Archives ICC, n.c.
24 Comité Executif. Doc. 4580, enclosed to the Procès-Verbal du 46 council, 30 July 1931, Archives ICC, n.c.
25 Procès-Verbal du 46 council, 29 June 1934, Archives ICC, n.c.
26 Procès-Verbal du 34 council, 30 October 1932, Archives ICC, n.c.
27 Procès-Verbal du 34 Comité Executif, 20 July 1933, Archives ICC, n.c.
28 Procès-Verbal de la Commission des Ententes Industrielles Internationales, 27 and 28 Jun. 1934, Archives LoN, serie 11803, file 13855.
29 Stoppani (LoN) to Vasseur (ICC), 2 October 1934, Archives LoN, Section 10A, file 13855.
30 Procès-Verbal du 36 Comité Executif, 30 May 1938, Archives ICC, n.c. In this meeting the settlement of the charter of a 'Bureau des Ententes Industrielles Internationales' was discussed.
31 Note, La Situation actuelle des cartels internationaux, 20 November 1939, Archives LoN, section 10A, file 13855. International Economic Collaborations, regional agreements, producers agreements. A note by the LoN secretariat, 1 July 1938, The National Archives, BT/64/388.
32 'The BEII is the only organisation internationally qualified to gather information about all existing cartels and to follow the evolution of the legislation about them. ... Cartels have a big role to play not only in concerning production but also in regards to markets. They can help us avoid social diseases, to ensure certain economic equilibrium, and to promote the recasting of the international economy'. Procès-Verbal du 61 conséil, 30 October 1939, Archives ICC, n.c.

4 Competition policy in the European Economic Community, 1957–1992

The curse of compulsory registration?

Laurent Warlouzet

Introduction

The European Union (EU)'s competition policy is unique in the world as it is fully federal. Until the recent reforms introduced in the twenty-first century, it was implemented by the European Commission alone, with only a consultative voice from member-states. Its decisions can be overturned only by European Federal Courts. It is also unique in its range, as its remit includes cartels, mergers, abuse of dominant positions, state aid and deregulation (Cini and McGowan 2009).

Its history has not, however, been smooth and linear. Between its establishment in 1957 at the birth of the European Economic Community (EEC), with the Treaty of Rome, and its replacement by the European Union (EU) in 1992 it has been the subject of widespread debates. Based on extensive primary sources from national and European institutions and a growing body of literature in history, political science and law, this chapter underlines the conflicts between various actors involved in the development of the EEC competition policy.[1] It focuses in particular on the regulatory regime for cartels, which was the first to be defined, in 1962.[2] Its enforcement mobilised most of the energy of the European commission during its first decades. It was based on a procedure of compulsory notification for companies concluding agreements until its replacement by a new European law in 2003. Critical to many was the question: Was the registration process a curse or a necessity for the EEC competition policy? Differing views on this issue were at the core of many of the debates between opposing various actors, including the European Commission, France and Germany. It also divided officials within the Commission and within national governments.

Four chronological steps will be underlined here: the origins of this unexpected regime; the decision to opt for a compulsory registration; the difficulty in setting up an effective anti-cartel regime; and in the 1980s and 1990s, the decisive reinforcement of the competition policy combined with the end of the registration procedure.

The European rules at the crossroads of influence

Why were provisions dealing with competition policy inserted in the Treaty of Rome? The questions seems trivial today but it was not so in the period between the end of the World War II and the signing of the Treaty in 1957, at the time when competition policy was almost unheard of in Europe.

In those days, if we exclude the German decartelisation law imposed by the Allies, and the pro-cartel legislation of the interwar period, only two countries from the EEC had a competition law; France and the Netherlands. In both cases it was embryonic. The Dutch system was based on registration and a broad tolerance on cartels (see Chapter 5 of this volume). France had the oldest national law in the original EEC, dating back to 1953. The expression 'competition policy', however, was largely unknown in those days. Provisions against cartels were embedded in price policy the aim of which was to fight against 'restrictive practices' that resulted in inflation. A severe stance was maintained against some types of distribution agreements as they were supposed to hamper the modernisation of the distribution sector. Severe sanctions were ordered by the Courts against so-called 'restrictive practices'. In contrast, cartels as such were not particularly discouraged. The 1953 law had established a consultative committee linked to the Ministry of Economics which examined a couple of cases of cartels each year. There was no registration. The cartels were generally cleared, sometimes after a few adaptations, and 'no drastic sanctions' were taken (Riesenfeld 1962: 469). Competition policy had existed in the UK since 1948 (for monopolies and mergers) and since 1956 (for restrictive practices) but the UK was not part of the ECSC, nor of the EEC before 1973.

This situation explains, in part, why the first discussion about competition policy in Europe was heavily influenced by the American example. US antitrust policy dates back to the Sherman Act of 1890. In that legislation there was no registration and it was implemented by multiple actors, including the courts, the Department of Justice and the Federal Trade Commission. Moreover, the US was at the peak of its influence over Western Europe between 1945 and 1953, when the Western European countries not only depended on American funds to finance their reconstruction, but also relied on the US nuclear umbrella as a shield against the aggressive Stalin-led Soviet Union. American influence spread in particular through the diffusion of free-market values, and antitrust was part of this package. Numerous trips to study US antitrust policy were organised for European experts. The US also promoted these values through European organisations, the first being the Organisation for European Economic Cooperation (OEEC) of 1948, whose purpose was to progressively restore free-trade in Europe. There were, however, no antitrust provisions in the OEEC treaty, a situation that was identical globally with the 1947 General Agreement on Tariffs and Trade (GATT). In both cases, there were political problems; whereas it was possible to find an agreement on custom duties, ceding sovereignty in terms of public regulation of companies seemed unachievable.

It was against this background that the first treaty creating a semi-federal international institution, the European Coal and Steel Community (ECSC), was negotiated among the six countries which later formed the EEC: West Germany,

France, Italy, Belgium, the Netherlands and Luxembourg. The aim of the ECSC was to create a common market for coal and steel. A common approach to the regulation of restrictive agreements was seen as technically logical. In order to promote the integration of markets, it was important to avoid the substitution of public obstacles to trade, like custom duties, by private obstacles like cartels; especially in cartel-prone sectors like coal and steel. More precisely, three motivations lay behind the development. First, French officials wanted to control the de-concentration of the German coal and steel industries in order to avoid the rebuilding of the great *Konzerne* of the interwar period (Poidevin-Spierenburg 1992: 223). Second, French companies sought access to German coal at the same price as their German counterparts. Last, the transatlantic networks that linked the Americans, Jean Monnet and German ordoliberals (despite differences in economic doctrine) wanted to use competition policy as a tool to establish a modernised Europe, that was more economically and politically efficient than in the pre-war period (Leucht 2010).[3]

As a result, the Treaty of Paris creating the European Coal and Steel Community (ECSC) included antitrust provisions that had no real precedents in Europe. These provisions were linked to two important principles. First, decision-making power was granted to a supra-national institution – the High Authority – that was formally independent from the member state governments. Second, the High Authority was given the jurisdiction to regulate a wide range of commercial practices. Its mandate went beyond cartels as such (restrictive and unjustified agreements between independent companies) and covered mergers (or 'concentrations' between companies) and other forms of potentially distortive commercial conduct (in particular, the ability to deal with price discrimination). With regard to cartels, no registration requirement was explicitly set up (Treaty of Paris, article 65), whereas there was a system of preliminary notifications of all mergers (Treaty of Paris, article 66). There was a stark contrast, however, between these strong legal provisions and the weak policy that was actually put into practice by the ECSC High Authority. The competition policy, as implemented, was in fact timid and dominated both by interstate bargaining (in particular by Paris and Bonn) and by the efforts of companies to influence their governments, and hence the High Authority (Witschke 2009: 338–341). Eventually, the High Authority authorised the vast majority of the cartels and mergers (ECSC 1963).

As a result, when the negotiations over a treaty to create a 'Common Market' opened up in 1955–1956, there was no strong pressure to construct a comprehensive competition policy (Warlouzet 2011: 21–34, 273–275). The failure of the ECSC's competition policy, the very limited development of any national provisions, and the diminishing influence of the US did not bode well for the development of an ambitious European policy. However, the technical argument, to promote the integration of markets, remained. Furthermore the situation changed in West Germany. Germany had no national cartel law when the Treaty of Rome was negotiated, except the allied imposed law of 'decartelisation'. It was, however, in the last stages of a longstanding policy debate which ended in July 1957 with the adoption of the law against the restriction of competition in July 1957. Some of its features were already visible in 1956, when the Treaty of Rome was negotiated. Two of these contrasted vigorously with the French example. First in Germany competition policy was considered crucial to the building of a new democratic and liberal nation, which would break with the past, as the National-Socialist era was associated with cartelisation (Gerber 1998: 232–65). A new school of thought, ordo-liberalism influenced many German officials, including the powerful economics minister Ludwig Erhard (1949–1953). For these officials, economic liberalism was strongly linked to political liberalism and competition policy played a central role in this process. It was part of an 'economic constitution' designed to ensure that individual freedom was guaranteed. Second, the principle of prohibition had already been largely accepted in 1956. It meant that all cartels were banned, except if they were explicitly authorised by an authority. The prohibition principle in German law contrasted with the abuse principle adopted in France (where all cartels were authorised unless explicitly banned). There was no merger control. Economics Minister Ehrard, despite his ordoliberal connections, did not want to weaken industry by stringent provisions against concentration (Berghahn 1986: 159). The German law of 1957 created a system of registration managed by an independent institution, the *Bundeskartellamt* (BKA; see Chapter 11, this volume). All cartels (with some clear exceptions such as export cartels) had to be registered with the BKA, which then decided to accept or to ban them. The BKA decided alone, although the Minister of Economics had the right to authorise a cartel previously banned. The influence of an ordoliberal approach meant that competition policy had a more central place in German state economic policy than in France or the UK. Price control and industrial policy were far less important in Germany. It does not mean, however, that it translated into a very strict and severe competition policy, as Chapter 11 of this volume shows.

The Treaty of Rome negotiations were largely dominated by a debate between French and Germans over competition policy. US experts were far less influential than during the ECSC negotiations. By the late 1950s the death of Stalin, the end of the Korean War, and the restoration of the financial situation of most Western European countries reduced dependence on the US. In terms of competition policy, the passing of the French law in 1953 and the longstanding debate on the German law meant that there was indigenous expertise in this domain. During the Treaty of Rome negotiations, the French proposed a competition policy based on the abuse principle, and on the same treatment of all restrictions on competition, cartels, concentration and individual practices (Warlouzet 2011: 274–275, 294–296). They feared the competition of the larger German companies. The Germans had a contrary position. They emphasised the fight against cartels, and were more lenient toward concentrations. Above all, Alfred Müller-Armack, the German negotiator and a close collaborator with Ludwig Erhard, insisted on securing the prohibition principle. He explained that it was compulsory for domestic reasons; if the prohibition principle was not upheld at the EEC level, it would be threatened at the national level.[4]

The two sides agreed on one point. They did not want to give increased power to the European authorities. For the French, competition policy was only a minor field, especially considering the failure of the ECSC policy in merger control. For the Germans, the most important issue was to preserve their future national law the longstanding negotiations of which, were not yet completed. Thus both countries accepted the compromise presented by Hans von der Groeben, the president of the group negotiating the articles on competition policy.[5] It left the main questions largely unanswered. Article 85 EEC (article 81 EU/article 101 TFEU)[6] contained the prohibition principle in the first paragraph, but also exception in the third paragraph. Cartels could be banned according to article 85-1, but also authorised if they fulfilled the criteria of article 85-3 (contribution to technical progress, etc.). Article 87 EEC left the implementation of the first two articles to a further regulation. This additional regulation is a European law which is proposed by the supranational institution, the European Commission, and which has to be accepted by the Council of Ministers, itself comprising representatives from the six member-states. It was clearly stated in the Treaty that this future regulation should take into account national laws (article 87-2e), and 'the need, on the one hand, of ensuring effective supervision and, on the other hand, of simplifying administrative control to the greatest possible extent' (article 87-2b). In other words, no clear institutional framework was defined by the Treaty.

In terms of substantive provisions, article 85 EEC could be interpreted either as an outright ban on cartels (the German interpretation) with exemptions, or it could be seen as establishing the principle of 'abuse' (the French interpretation – which relied on the fact that the wording of article 85 of the EEC was close to that of article 59 *bis* of the 1953 French Law).[7] Some German officials would have preferred a clearer ban on cartels.[8]

As a result, the Treaty of Rome left unresolved important institutional and substantive features of EEC competition policy, and in particular the question of whether or not a system of cartel registration needed to be created. This conundrum was solved in 1962 with the decision to create a cartel register.

The choice of the cartel register

The establishment of an effective European competition policy, one that could have an impact on the regulation of markets, was a difficult task. The EEC officials chose to target cartels first with an ambitious law, the 'Regulation 17/62' of 1962. It interpreted article 85 as a ban on cartels. As a result, an institution was required to grant the exemptions mentioned in article 85-3 EEC. The Commission fulfilled this role. It had a monopoly on information, via the notification procedure; all cartels which had an effect on intra-EEC trade (thus excluding those with a purely national dimension) had to be declared to the Commission. As a result, the sub-unit of the Commission in charge of competition, the so-called 'Directorate General IV' (DG IV) created a cartel register. It was not public as only the Commission had an access to it. This was the result of the information monopoly the Commission acquired with Regulation 17/62. It also had a monopoly on decision making. The decision-making process had four steps. First, the Commissioner for Competition, assisted by his/her administration, the Directorate General IV, had to evaluate the admissibility of each cartel with regard to the Rome Treaty and Regulation 17/62. Second, the Commissioner presented his/her proposed decision to the college of commissioners, which voted on it. Third a committee of member-state experts was consulted. Its opinion was not binding and could be ignored. This in effect confirmed the monopoly possessed by the Commission. Fourth the decision could be contested at the Court of Justice of the European Communities.

Regulation 17/62 was the result of a compromise between the Germans and the French, but the German model was the closest to the regulation 17/62 system.[9] In both cases an institution managed a ban on cartel through notification and a de-facto monopoly of decision (bar an appeal to the Courts). It was not, however, a pure adaptation since the Commission was a political institution, and not an independent administrative authority like the BKA. Moreover, the German government had not always been willing to grant large powers to the Commission. When the first draft of the regulation was proposed in 1960, the German's Ministry of Economics did not want to develop a supranational EEC competition policy steered by an influential European Commission.[10] Its priority was to preserve the proficiencies of the newly-founded BKA. The Ministry appeared quite doubtful of the ability of the EEC institutions to implement a genuine and efficient cartel ban.

Many alternatives to Regulation 17/62 (monopoly of information and of decision on the Commission) were envisaged. The most radical came from the French negotiators. From the start, they had defended an interpretation of the Rome Treaty based on two different premises: the abuse principle (and not the principle to ban cartels), and a decision-making process implemented through an association of the Commission and of the member states, and not by the Commission alone (Warlouzet 2015a). In this framework, a cartel register would have been pointless, except for voluntary registration. The French based their interpretation on the fact that the wording of article 85 was somewhat close to article 59 of the 1953 French law, which was interpreted as an abuse law. At the beginning of the negotiations, many member-states defended the principle of abuse. France stuck to its interpretation until the very end of the negotiations, submitting a counter-proposal along the same lines in early December 1961, a fortnight before the final compromise.[11]

To thwart this danger, Bonn actively supported the Commission's proposal in 1961. In the end, a twofold compromise was struck between Paris and Bonn. At a general level, Germany secured a competition policy based on the interdiction principle (hence its own national law was not threatened), while France got agreement on the Common agricultural policy; finalised on 14 January 1962 (Moravcsik 1998: 218; Pitzer 2009: 407). This bargain does not appear clearly in the archives although the link between both issues was mentioned on both sides of the Rhine.[12] The second compromise dealt with cartels. France accepted a regulation in tune with German's priorities, but she secured an agreement for a future tougher regime for exclusive dealing agreements (Warlouzet 2016a).[13] The French policy against these type of cartels was more severe than the Germans', as the German law targeted horizontal rather than vertical restraint (Riesenfeld 1962: 473; Gerber 1998: 295). The severity of the French policy against distribution agreements lay in her willingness to fight business practices that were accused of stoking inflation; such as the refusal to sell. As a result, article 22 of Regulation 17/62 stipulated that, within a year of the regulation's entry into force, the Council (on a proposal from the Commission) was to examine the possibility of making the notification procedure mandatory for certain types of agreements. This clearly meant distribution agreements.[14]

As a result, the EEC law on cartels was not a blueprint of the German model, but rather a reinterpretation of it by the European commissioner von der Groeben. The Commissioner for Competition was a German Christian-Democrat but he had not always been on the same path as the German representatives, especially the responsible officials in Bonn, Minister Erhard and his deputy Müller-Armack who represented Germany in the negotiations on cartel regulation. During the Treaty of Rome negotiations, both had appeared as relatively timid towards European integration, whereas von der Groeben had been much more enthusiastic. In those days, he had already proposed to establish a strong European institutional framework to ensure the implementation of competition rules (Löffler 2002: 548–552). On the whole, Commissioner von der Groeben appears to have been the most successful actor in these negotiations, even though he also made concessions. He agreed to alter his initial proposal of 1960, by taking specific requests from the European Parliament and French government. The main challenge was to implement this ambitious piece of legislature, by creating an efficient cartel register.

A Pyrrhic victory: the 'backlog'

The setting up of the registration system for six countries proved to be a daunting task; both in practice and intellectually. The European Commission was still a very young institution; it had only begun in 1958. In 1964, the DG IV had only 78 officials (McGowan 2010: 128–129). It was a multilingual institution composed of civil servants, each with their own working habits and backgrounds compared to national ministry which could be united by an 'esprit de corps'. The problem was compounded by the very different economic policies of the six member states. Half did not have any competition policy, and the rest had very contrasting experiences. It was not only a problem of information, as national cartel registers were either inexistent or incomplete and anyway they were not available to the European Commission, but also a problem of criteria. The national competition authorities and judicial bodies had to decide what to do with the agreements in their registers, in particular which agreements should be banned, which should be authorised, and which should be authorised after modifications.

Thus, it is not surprising that in 1962, the interpretation of Regulation 17/62 was unclear for both the officials and business organisations, particularly with regard to distribution agreements.[15] Companies were not sure if they had to send notification of their agreement or not.[16] To settle this problem, the Commission encouraged notification. It adopted Regulation 153/62, which introduced a simplified notification procedure for certain exclusive agreements, and it published a communication on the subject of notification (EEC Commission, 1962). In a letter to UNICE (Union des industries de la Communauté européenne) – the main EEC-wide business organisation – von der Groeben expressly asked companies to submit notification of their distribution agreements, including those for which the need to notify was unsure.[17] He said that the Commission would be 'moderate' and 'understanding' for the companies that 'trusted' it. Von der Groeben probably sought to encourage further notifications because the Commission received only a handful during the first months of implementation of the regulation.[18] Only 800 notifications were gathered in November 1962.[19] A few months later, more than 36,000 notifications were being sent to the Commission in a single year, most of them distribution agreements.[20] This triggered another impossible situation for the DG IV. It was too small to deal with thousands of cases, especially in the absence of any proper doctrine. The DG IV was unable to issue a single decision before September 1964, when it decided the famous Grundig–Consten case (EEC Commission, 1964). This case concerned a distribution agreement between a German producer (Grundig) and a French distributor (Consten). After this landmark case, the Commission took only a handful of formal decisions. Indeed, only four decisions were formally taken between Grundig–Consten and the completion of the Treaty of Rome's 'transitional period' in July 1968.[21] Most of the notified cases were never dealt with directly, or only after a considerable delay. This was the so-called 'backlog problem'. The fact that the Commission's first formal decision and the first block exemption (see below) both concerned distribution agreements shows the Commission's policy making and enforcement activities were significantly limited because of the early emphasis on vertical agreements – and in particular on distribution agreements.

As early as July 1962, Von der Groeben had been aware of the risk posed by excessive numbers of notifications that the Commission would be unable to study.[22] As a consequence, he proposed the issuing of 'block exemptions' whereby the Commission would be able to exempt certain types of agreements, *en bloc*, from the prohibition against restrictive agreements. A category of agreements would be eligible for a blanket exemption if the Commission considered that, even if the particular agreements did restrict competition, any harm would be offset by their expected economic benefits. The Commission's proposal was submitted officially in November 1962.[23] The aim was twofold: to avoid receiving notifications of agreements unlikely to be pernicious, and to lift the burden of declaring *ex post* that most of the agreements that had already been notified were harmless. From the Commission's perspective this tool would have been a logical addition to Regulation 17/62: on the one hand, Regulation 17/62 had the effect of centralising information and putting it under the Commission's control; on the other, block exemptions would have allowed the Commission to prioritise the flow of information.

The member states, however, rejected the proposal. They underlined the fact that Regulation 17/62 gave to the Commission an obligation to implement Article 85 in a comprehensive way, without any possibility to exempt categories of agreements by itself. The Council insisted on reserving its legislative prerogatives to such a significant reform.[24] It was also argued that the Commission needed a sound jurisprudential foundation before deciding on exemptions.[25] After protracted negotiations (five of the six member states were still opposed to the Commission's proposal in September 1964),[26] agreement was reached only in February 1965 with the Regulation 19/65.[27] This Regulation gave the Commission power to propose block exemptions to the Council. The first Regulation concerning block exemptions was designed specifically to deal with distribution agreements, but it was not adopted until March 1967 (Regulation 67/67), almost five years after von der Groeben proposal in mid-1962. The Commission continued to propose several block exemptions (which defined the conditions to exempt a specific type of cartel, for example R&D agreements) over the following years but each had to be accepted by the Council, which led to protracted negotiations. The Commission managed to progressively solve the backlog problem in the 1980s thanks to block exemptions, but the process was slow. There were still more than 4000 pending cases in 1979 (Temple-Lang 1980: 20). In the meantime, making decisions about previously notified cartels remained difficult.

The difficult implementation of the European cartel register

The Commission faced many difficulties to effectively monitor anticompetitive practices based on a cartel register. From the 1960s to the mid-1980s the environment was not favourable for the Commission. Most national competition policies were either embryonic, non-existent (the first Italian law dates back to 1990 for example) or if apparently extensive, subordinated to other economic policies. In the UK, for example, despite important laws in 1948, 1956 and 1973, competition policy remained largely secondary to price and industrial policy. It was the same in many countries, particularly France, despite the pro-competition credentials of the Prime Minister Raymond Barre (1976–1981). His government passed a statute in 1977 reinforcing French competition law, while at the same time liberating prices. It seemed apparent that the regulation of prices had shifted from state control to market dynamics. But the approach did not work out as planned because of both persistent high inflation, and because of cartels. For example, as soon as the price of bread was liberated, bakers engaged in informal price-fixing agreements to prevent any shop selling baguettes, a staple of French food, below a floor price. This was the infamous affair of the '1 franc baguette', which triggered a large-scale investigation by the Ministry of Economics in 1981 (Warlouzet 2016b). As a result, it was difficult to implement a similar public policy at the European level. More precisely, specific obstacles impeded the Commission at critical moments. In the early 1960s, the youth of its administration limited its efficiency. In 1965, the 'Empty Chair' crisis subdued the supranational Executive for two decades. Triggered in 1965 by the French leader Charles de Gaulle, who was opposed to the federalist plan of the President of the Commission Walter Hallstein, the crisis resulted in the French government removing its representatives from the EEC institutions, hence the name 'Empty Chair'. It ended in 1966 with a reassertion of the prerogatives of the member-states, through the Council of Ministers, against the Commission. With notable exceptions, most European commissioners became more cautious, until the Delors Commission (1985–1995) restarted the engines of integration.

The second impediment came from within the Commission itself. It came under the guise of commissioners and civil servants who were opposed to the free-market ideology that underpins the development of an extensive competition policy. Most of them were not hostile to a strong cartel policy, but they considered that it had to be subject to other policies, like planning or industrial policy. Early in the 1960s, the French commissioner Robert Marjolin developed a comprehensive European planning project that led, in 1963, to the creation of a committee for mid-term policy, just one year after Regulation 17/62 (Warlouzet 2011: 339–396). Marjolin was a socialist and a former deputy head of the French planning agency. His project involved the coordination of all national and European policies at a European level, with competition policy being only one sub-field among others. Marjolin and von der Groeben frequently clashed within the Commission, either directly or indirectly through their deputies, when either planning or competition policy was discussed (ibid.: 370–380). Another important project which impaired the development of an autonomous and bold cartel policy was industrial policy. The creation of a European policy designed to foster the growth of industry, especially in high-technology, was advocated by several Italian commissioners; first by Colonna di Paliano (1967–1970), and then by Altiero Spinelli (1970–1976) (Warlouzet 2014). Industrial policy was envisaged not only for the high-technology sectors, but also for managing the decline of old sectors, such as coal mining, steel, textile, and shipbuilding which all suffered massive crises at the same time around Europe in the late 1970s. Between 1977 and 1984, the Belgian commissioner for industrial affairs Etienne Davignon managed to implement a successful European industrial policy in the steel sector (Leboutte 2008: 486–492). As a result, competition policy was embedded in a larger framework, under the direction of the commissioner for industrial policy. There was no cartel policy, as the Commission managed a de facto cartel. The only task of the DG IV was to monitor state aid. Davignon tried to extend this approach to other sectors, such as textile and shipbuilding but with mixed results. Nevertheless, the industrial policy remained very influential both at the national and at the European level.

Finally, the Commission had to confront reluctant member states. Opposition came not only from countries which did not have any competition policy, or which promoted another model, like France, but also from Germany. This was despite the fact that the German experience was the most important inspiration of Regulation 17/62. Although many officials at the European commission in the 1960s were German Christian-Democrats (especially the first commissioner for competition, Hans von der Groeben, and his close collaborator Ernst Albrecht), they were not puppets of the German government. Indeed, the Gruding–Consten case even led to a conflict between Bonn and Brussels. The decision proposed by the Commission – to ban the Gruding–Consten agreement in 1964 – was against the German government representative's position, for whom exclusive dealing agreements were a useful tool to penetrate foreign markets (and thus increased competition within the Common market).[28] The fact that Grundig was a German company certainly also played a role. The German government later decided to support Grundig's appeal of the decision at the Court of Justice of the European Community. The German officials in the Ministry of Economics took this decision after consulting with the advocate-general of the Court of Justice of the European Community, Karl Roemer.[29] In the end, however, the Court only annulled part of the decision and broadly supported the Commission.[30] On the whole, the Court of Justice supported the Commission for political reasons – to bolster the European integration process, but it frequently criticised its decisions on judicial and economic grounds (Warlouzet and Witschke 2012). This case clearly demonstrates that the cartel register provided by Regulation 17/62 gave very strong powers to the Commission to decide alone, without consulting member-states. The only possibility for member-states to contest the Commission's decision on cartels was an appeal to the Court of Justice. As demonstrated in the Grundig–Consten case, however, the Court was often broadly supportive of the Commission. Despite these important institutions powers the Commission did not have the material, intellectual and political means to implement effectively the cartel register.

The last hurdle to overcome was the economic crisis of the 1970s. The two oil shocks of 1973 and 1979 triggered a dramatic rise in unemployment and inflation. The industries of the First Industrial Revolution, such as coal, steel, textile and shipbuilding, entered a steep and relentless decline, while more modern sectors, such as cars and chemicals underwent sharp contractions. In this situation, cartel busting was not a priority for governments. Within the EEC, most countries not only subsidised ailing companies, but they tolerated or even encouraged the formation of cartels to limit the decline in revenues, or to level out losses. Crisis cartels were used to foster rationalisation, or sometimes to prevent it by ensuring that all competitors could get a share of the market. The operation of the Directorate General for Competition was made even more difficult by internal divisions within the Commission; the Commissioner for Industrial affairs Etienne Davignon being much more influential than the Commissioner for Competition Raymond Vouel in the late 1970s.

The man-made fibres sector offers a fascinating example of how difficult it was for the commission to implement a smooth cartel policy based on registration. This sector is at the crossroad between textiles and chemicals. In 1977, the industry in Europe was beset by falling prices, flat demand, increasing competition from abroad, and increasing output capacity triggered by massive national subventions. As a result, in the summer of 1977, the Commissioner for Competition, Vouel asked the member-states to stop their subsidies.[31] The Commission was too weak, however, to enforce state-aids rules, especially against Italy which considered the expansion of its man-made fibres industry a strategic imperative. To solve the problem, Davignon brokered the creation of a crisis cartel among all the main European companies, with an association of US subsidiaries.[32] Production had to be stabilised to maintain prices. According to the archives of the German Ministry of Economics, which was averse to these official crisis cartels (the Minister of Economics being the free-marketer Otto von Lambsdorff), the Commissioner for Competition Vouel expressed concerns on the compatibility of these cartels with

EEC law, but he was not motivated enough to intervene.[33] In the spring of 1978, the most senior official of the Commission's unit for competition, Director General Willy Schlieder, proposed a system to reconcile the need to implement competition rules, with the serious sectorial crisis. He suggested a new regulation complementing article 87 but which did not rely on registration. Instead, he proposed a two-step process that involved first, the Council of Ministers (which had to declare the 'state of crisis' in a certain sector for a given period of time) and then the Commission (which would manage the request for authorisation of crisis cartel in this sector).[34] This system would clear the problem of the man-made fibre crisis cartel; the DG IV had suggested in April 1978 after a preliminary review that it would probably not be exempted under the current system of Regulation 17/62.[35] Schlieder's proposal was partly inspired by German legislation, which contained an exception for crisis cartels. As the scheme was not based on a registration system, it is likely that the process of notification was considered to be unsuitable; such specific agreements often had a strong political element. The German Ministry of Economics and the Bundeskartellamt were not hostile to crisis cartels in principle, but they could only accept them if there was a stringent commitment to reduce capacity.[36] Moreover, Bonn did not like the public supervision of cartels favoured by Davignon. Bonn feared that the regulation of crisis cartels would ultimately play into the hands of Davignon, and not of Vouel, as the former was much more influential than the latter. On 27 March 1978, *Business Week* called Davignon 'Europe's architect of cartels'.[37] In the end, the proposal was abandoned.

In the meantime, on 20 June 1978, the agreement (the expression 'cartel' was avoided) between the man-made fibres companies was officially signed, and subsequently notified to the Commission.[38] The agreement mostly contained provisions to reduce output, and not to fix prices. It mentioned the necessity to rely on the Commission and the member states to ensure the implementation of the agreement by particular member states, Italy being especially targeted. On 8 November of the same year Vouel announced to the Commission that the man-made fibres agreement notified in July could not be authorised.[39] He asked the Commission for the authorisation to launch proceedings against the cartel but there was no majority within the college of commissioners to support him. The face-saving solution was to declare that the agreement was not actually implemented; an outcome that clearly demonstrated the futility of cartel busting in the midst of the 1970s crisis.[40] In fact, in addition to the problem of backlogs, the cartel register solution suffered from the European Commission's lack of authority to enforce regulations in sensitive cases. The situation changed in the 1980s.

The cartel register defeated by Americanisation?

The implementation of Regulation 17/62 was not a complete failure for the Commission. Over several decades it had progressively built a jurisprudential and legislative framework which allowed for the gradual development of a European competition policy. To overcome the backlog the Commission used three tools: decisions from relevant cases that could set a legal precedent that were useful both to solve already notified cases and to avoid further notifications; the use of 'soft-law', via non-binding communications designed to orient business practices; and third, it used block exemptions (Temple-Lang 1980: 20–26). Block exemptions, however, were difficult to get as the Council had to agree. Moreover, most were only granted for a precise time period so they had to be renewed. One example illustrates the difficulties of the Commission; the 1985 block exemption for exclusive dealing agreement in the car sector studied by Sigfrido Ramirez (Ramirez 2008). The issue began in 1981. The Commission wanted to impose strict conditions on agreements that limited the price of cars sold in different EEC countries, but it had to yield to the pressure of automobile lobbies. In the end only a diluted set of conditions was adopted. The Commission considered it as a success, however, as it solved all the remaining cases in the car sector involving exclusive dealing agreements in one go.

On the whole, the cartel issue was progressively solved in the 1980s even if the problem remained acute, leaning heavily on DG IV resources. There were still more than 3500 cases pending on the 31 December 1986 (European Commission 1987: 55). When he became Director-General for Competition in 1990, Claus-Dieter Ehlermann still considered his main task regarding cartels was to alleviate the burden of the remaining 3000 cases waiting decision.[41] It ultimately took several decades for the Commission to overcome this burden. However, this chronology was not exceptional if one considers the national level. It was over this same period that French competition policy was decisively upgraded with important legislation in 1986; that Thatcher launched large-scale reforms to increase competition in Great-Britain; and that countries previously without competition policies adopted their first laws in this field (Italy in 1990, Belgium in 1991). In the meantime, cartel busting became less central to European competition policy as the Commission extended its remit from cartels to the deregulation of sectors previously sheltered from competition. From 1987–1988 onwards, the Commission extended its reach, beginning with air transport and telecommunications; merger control (1989) and monitoring state aid (in the 1980s). European competition policy was benefiting from a more favourable climate, with the development of national competition policies mirroring the rise of neoliberal ideas and economic recovery. Neoliberal ideas were not always in favour of creating strong competition policy but they certainly worked against industrial and prices policies. Thus another tool to monitor markets had to be created.

Multinational companies also put pressure on national governments to adopt European-wide rules instead of national ones (Büthe and Swank 2007). At the EEC level, the dynamic of the Single Market (1986–1992), the Court of Justice and pressure from some segments of European business favoured European level regulation ahead of 12 different national competition policies.[42] Together these factors supported the efforts of dynamic commissioners for competition policy (Frans Andriessen, 1981–1985; Peter Sutherland, 1985–1989; Leon Brittan, 1989–1993) (Cini and McGowan 2009: 31; Warlouzet 2016a). Within the expanding jurisdiction of European competition policy, the role of cartel busting tended to decrease.

The relative decline in efforts to confront cartels was compounded by the many criticisms of the registration system and its implementation. The loudest critics came from scholars influenced by the second Chicago School (i.e. Robert Bork and Richard Posner). It posits that government intervention – including competition policy – should be reduced to a minimum, as markets tend toward a natural equilibrium (Kovacic and Shapiro 2000: 53–55). Predatory conduct is difficult to sustain in the long run. A 'more economic approach' based on an increasing use of economic tools, rather than on the legal assessment of cartels, would allow the competition authorities to take more realistic decisions, in tune with the goal of maximising 'consumer welfare'. The European competition was considered too formalistic. Its legal approach led it to condemn some agreements because they paid regard only to legal form, rather than to economic effect. This criticism was particularly focused at the Commission's policy against vertical agreements, which had been its priority since the first implementation of Regulation 17/62. The criticism was also supported by scholars outside the 'second' Chicago School, who thought the Commission should have a more economic approach, and as a result, should concentrate more on horizontal rather than vertical cartels. One of the first scholars who led the charge against EEC cartel policy was Valentine Korah, an English professor of competition law. Her criticisms were evident at early as 1978, when she highlighted that through article 86, the Commission seemed more interested in protecting competitors than competition and consumers.[43] She advised the Commission to follow the US example in this area (Korah 1982: 225). She has been a fierce critic of both the UK and the EEC competition authorities for being too legalistic, too cumbersome and not paying enough attention to economic realities (ibid.: 284–285). She particularly criticised the DG IV 'dogmatic' severity against vertical agreements, whereas some of the contracts could have been useful to avoid 'free-riders' (companies who benefit from an expensive service provided by another company, such as after-sale service, without paying for it through an exclusive dealing agreement). Like many economists of the second Chicago School, she found that the concerns about barriers of entry were excessive. She denounced a European policy guided by political motivations –namely the desire to protect small and medium enterprises (SMEs) – rather than by a genuine quest for economic efficiency (Korah 1986: 145–146). In the 1990s, she was one of the first to call for a transformation of the EEC competition policy by adopting the goal of efficiency, as in the US (Gerber 2007: 1248). Another early critic of EEC cartel policy was Barry Hawk, who in 1980 criticised the economic reasoning of the Commission (Hawk 1980: 49). He published an influential article in 1995 which criticised the 'form-based' treatment of vertical restraints, while he promoted a US-style 'effect-based' analysis (Hawk 1995). A year earlier, Korah published a book that included a section entitled 'The paucity of economic analysis in the Commission's public decision' (Korah 1994: 266).

In the 1990s, there were also internal pressures for change within the Commission (Wilks 2005: 235–237). The prospect of a massive enlargement in membership through the entry of eastern European countries had daunting implications for the flow of notifications. Moreover, there was a willingness to shift from a reactive approach to a proactive one. In a system of registration, the action of the competition authority was largely guided by the notifications it received. Decisions had to be made in response to give companies legal certainty. It meant that resources were concentrated on notifications, rather than in looking for hidden cartels through extensive economic analysis. Despite resistance within its ranks in the late 1990s the Commission decided to shed the registration process (Gerber 2007: 1241). It proposed to the Council a new regulation to replace Regulation 17/62. It was adopted in 2003 as Regulation 1/2003.

The new system abolished the registration procedure. The national authorities became primarily responsible for implementing competition policy but they are now encompassed in a European Competition Network (ECN) dominated in two respects by the Commission. First it is the Commission which examines the most important cartels. It is also the same institution which can decide in certain case to allocate a cartel decision to a national authority or not. Second, the doctrine is defined by the European Commission because European law has primacy over national law, and because new methodologies emphasising economic analysis have been developed and circulated throughout the ECN. Since there is no longer a registration process at either a national or European level, competition authorities have to identify problematic cartels on their own; either through analysing market behaviour, or after denunciation (mostly by competitors). To increase the efficiency of this process, a 'leniency' procedure was adopted in 1996. Inspired by the US example, it provides advantages to the first company which denounces a cartel. This system was further strengthened in 2002. Full immunity can be guaranteed to the first whistle-blower, while the fine can be reduced for those which voluntary collaborate. For David Gerber these evolutions convey a dynamic of 'Americanisation' as the European system has become closer to the US both in terms of substance and institutions (Gerber 2007: 1259–1260). According to Stephen Wilks it is a striking success for the Commission; rather than 'decentralising' European competition policy it has 'Europeanised' the national competition regimes (Wilks 2005: 433).

The abandonment of the register system does not mean it was a complete failure. From the Commission's perspective, the system of the cartel register helped it to get information on cartels and to progressively nurture its own doctrine, at a time when there were hardly any comprehensive competition policies in Europe. Only in the 1990s were those policies fully established at the national level. With the widespread diffusion of a competition culture, and the development of new tools like economic analysis and leniency, the time was ripe to adopt a new system. The emphasis too changed, with more focus put on prosecuting horizontal restraints rather than vertical agreements.

Conclusion

European competition policy towards cartels was especially difficult to establish. Not only had the European Commission to understand contrasting national markets and legislations, but it had also to overcome the reluctance of member-states and private companies to give information and to devolve powers to this new

Competition policy in the EEC 63

supranational institution. The choice to establish a cartel register in 1962 must be understood against this difficult background.

The cartel register was both a curse and a necessity for the Commission. On the one hand, the flow of notifications created a backlog problem that lasted for decades. It discredited the Commission and rendered its policy more reactive than proactive, as the priority lay in managing the thousands of notifications. On the other hand, the register was an irreplaceable source of information, especially as several European countries did not have any competition authorities until the 1990s.

Tensions around the development of competition policy abounded. At one level, the classical opponents were France against Germany. The former being the classical example of the 'dirigist' country which favoured price and industrial policies, while the latter liked to present itself as a pro-market country relying on competition policy. This contrast was certainly true in the debate between European industrial policy and European competition policy. When one looks into the case-study more closely, however, the picture becomes blurred. French officials were keen to fight vertical agreements. As a result, they supported the Commission's action in this area, whereas West Germany was much more doubtful; hence its opposition on Grundig–Consten. The difficult debates surrounding the man-made fibre cartel of 1978 showed that many supporters of competition policy were also ready to accept cartel agreements in specific circumstances.

In the end, the system of the cartel registration was lifted in 2003 for many reasons, but mostly because it was no longer useful. It was seen as indispensable in the beginning, when the Commission was a young institution with very little information about the extent of cartelisation within the EEC. After more than forty years of experience, the Commission has developed a large body of case-law that established criteria for the admissibility of cartels. Moreover, it has also learnt how to locate information about cartels, especially since it has developed the new tool of leniency. It has adopted a more proactive stance. Today, the most important action for companies is not to register properly, but to be the first to betray the cartel agreement.

Notes

1 EEC/EU archives have been consulted from the 1950s to the mid-1980s; national archives have been scrutinised in France, Germany and in the UK; interviews of former EEC Commission's officials working in the Competition Policy Department have been conducted.
2 For a history of EEC competition policy following an historical institutionalist angle, and linking the cartels and the mergers issues, see Warlouzet 2016a.
3 Ordoliberals refers to a view situated between social liberalism and neoliberalism that sees the State's role as assisting the free market reach its theoretical potential.
4 Note of the secretariat, 'groupe du Marché commun', debates of 7 September 1956; note of 5 November 1956 of Meyer-Cording, EU archives, CM3/236; note of 8 November 1956, published in Schulze and Hoeren (2000: 194–195, 204–205).
5 Document of 20 November 1956 ('groupe du Marché Commun'), EU archives, CM3.
6 The EEC refers to the European Economic Community set up by in 1957. The articles

were renumbered in the Treaty of Amsterdam of 1997 on the European Union (EU), and again in the Treaty on the Functioning of the European Union (TFEU) of 2007.

7   Note DG Prix, 1 March 1961, French archives (Foreign Affairs), DECE 1258.
8   Vermek betreffend die Konferenz über den Gemeinsamen Markt vom 05.11-07.11.1956, Bonn, November 1956, (Bundesarchiv, Koblenz, Bestand B 141) in Schulze and Hoeren (2000: 204–205); Müller-Armack statements during the meeting of the 13 November 1956, document of 20 November 1956, EU archives/CM3.
9   The historical literature on the Regulation 17/62 is quite large now (Hamblocht, Leucht, Pitzer, Ramirez, Seidel) but it is not focused on the influence of the French negotiators and on the division of the German actors as this article does: see more details in Warlouzet 2016a.
10 Note BMWi, 3 October 1960; note on the meeting of representative of governments on 6 October 1960; note on the discussion with von der Groeben on 15 October 1960, German archives, B 102/134644.
11 Note BMWi, Obernolte, 6 December 1961, German archives, B 102/259229.
12 Note BMWi, 13 novembre 1961 German archives, B 102/259228; Note Debré for De Gaulle, 6 December 1961, French archives (FNSP), 2DE30.
13 Note BMWi, Epphardt, 16 décembre 1961, German archives, B 102/259229.
14 Letter from Verloren van Themaat to Fontanet, 28 October 1960, French archives, 1979.0791/264.
15 Note on a meeting of the International Chamber of Commerce (ICC)/'Commission des pratiques restrictive affectant la concurrence', 6 February 1962, Archives of the French Business Organization (Conseil national du patronat français or CNPF, 72 AS 1504.
16 Note on the meeting of the CIFE, 'comité de l'intégration', 3–4 January 1963 CNPF Archives, 72 AS 812; Letter from de Koster (UNICE) to von der Groeben, 5 January 1963, EU archives, BAC 89/1983/9/145.
17 Letter from von der Groeben to de Koster (UNICE), 23 January 1963, EU archives, BAC 89/1983/9/213.
18 Note 'MC', 15 January 1963, French archives (Foreign Affairs), DECE 1259.
19 Proceedings of the 12th conference of experts in Competition Policy, EEC, 22–23 November 1962, French archives, 1979.0791/262.
20 Proceedings of the meeting of experts on Competition Policy, 18 September 1963, French archives, 1979.0791/262.
21 *DRU-Blondel* (no. 65/366/CEE, 8 July 1965); *Hummel-Isbecque* (no. 65/426/CEE, 17 September 1965); *Maison Jallate-Hans Voss* (no. 66/5/CEE, 17 December 1965); *Transocean Marine Paint Association* (no. 67/454/CEE, 27 June 1967).
22 Note on a meeting between UNICE's representatives and von der Groeben, 15 July 1962, CNPF Archives, 72 AS 1544.
23 Telex from the permanent representative, 12 November 1962, French archives (Foreign Affairs), RPUE 609.
24 Proceedings of the 12th conference of experts in Competition Policy, EEC, 22–23 November 1962, French archives, 1979.0791/262; Telex REP, 12 November 1962; RPUE 615, telex REP, 27 February 1964, French archives (Foreign Affairs), RPUE 609.
25 Note of Ph. Cuvillier, 11 February 1964, French archives (Foreign Affairs), RPUE 615.
26 Telex from Jean-Marc Boegner, 21 September 1964, French archives (Foreign Affairs), RPUE 615.
27 Note of the Council EEC, 2 February 1965, French archives, 1988.0516/6.
28 Note BMWi, 1 June 1965, German archives, B 102/259100.

29 Note BMWi, Everling, 14 July 1965, German archives, B 102/259100; 'Conclusions de l'avocat général M. Karl Roemer, présentées le 27 avril 1966', *Recueil de jurisprudence*: 507–556.
30 Note BMWi, 14 July 1965 and 7 October 1965, German archives, B 102/259100.
31 Letter Vouel, 19 July 1977 German archives, B 102/278124.
32 Note 1 February 1978, German archives, B 102/278120.
33 Note 10 February 1978; note BMWi for Schlecht, 21 February 1978, German archives, B 102/278120.
34 Note 1 March 1978 German archives, B 102/278120.
35 Note BMWi, 25 April 1978, German archives, B 102/278120.
36 Note 17 July 1978; B 102/278124, Kartte to Schlieder, 2 August 1978, German archives, B 102/278124.
37 'Europe's architect of cartels', *Business Week*, 27 March 1978.
38 Note BMWi, 26 September 1978, German archives, B 102/278126.
39 'Special' minutes of the Commission meeting, 8 November 1978, EU archives.
40 Note BMWi, 12 April 1979, German archives, B 102/278126.
41 Interview of the author with Claus-Dieter Ehlermann, Brussels, 31 July 2013.
42 There were six member-states in the EEC in 1957, nine in 1973, ten in 1981, twelve in 1986 and fifteen from 1995 onwards.
43 An article of Valentine Korah dating from 1978 was referred to in Temple-Lang, 1980: 35.

5 How the tortoise became a hare

On the initial sclerosis and ultimate modernisation of Dutch competition policy

Lilian T. D. Petit, Jarig van Sinderen and Peter A. G. van Bergeijk

Introduction

Dutch economic policy making traditionally aims at consensus and cooperation between employers, trade unions and the government to find a balance between sustainable growth, a low level of unemployment and acceptable wage increases. In this so-called Polder Model, the different parties attempt to strike a balance between the freedom to negotiate legally on wages and working conditions, and the impact of these negotiations on economic and social goals. The Polder Model was also clearly evident in the Dutch policy towards cartelisation through much of the twentieth century. Cooperation and consensus was desired between both the participants in the markets and between the government and the market (see also Bouwens and Dankers 2012). From 1935 until 1998, competition legislation allowed the formation of domestic cartels. Particular statutes in 1935, 1941 and 1958 arose from the changing circumstances at that time. The relatively tolerant Competition Law of 1958 remained in effect for about 40 years. This finally changed in 1998 when the Netherlands passed a new Competition Law that met international standards and also established an independent competition authority.

This chapter investigates the social, legal and economic transformation processes of Dutch competition policy from the 1930s until 1998. We identify four periods that reflect the shift from the Netherlands being regarded as a 'cartel paradise' to a situation, which began in 1998, where competition in the product and service markets was explicitly viewed as a core element of Dutch economic policy. In broad terms the periods can be categorised as:[1]

- 1930–1950, when the foundations of the 'cartel paradise' were established;
- 1951–1958, a period of modification, starting with the introduction of the Economic Competition Act (1958);
- 1959–1986, when the Netherlands was considered to be a cartel paradise – a period of policy inertia; and finally
- 1987–1998, when Dutch policy adapted and harmonised with EU policy, resulting in the introduction in 1998 of the revised Dutch Competition Law.

For each phase we identify (1) international determinants and developments (2) the social, political and economic changes that occurred and (3) changes in Dutch regulation and policies.

Our analysis reveals that the change in competition policy from one that enabled a cartel paradise towards a competition law shaped policy according to EU legislation, was primarily driven by economic circumstances and EU pressure. Our analysis also clarifies, however, that institutions designed in response to a concrete policy environment may prevent necessary change later on. This is where the 'tortoise' makes its entrance. The self-centred policy of the 1970s and 1980s provided limited room for discussion. Dutch corporate culture meant that the few discussions that occurred on changing the system were not easily settled. Further, the economic research needed to motivate change as an outcome of an academic debate simply did not exist. Eventually, it became exceedingly obvious that the relatively stagnant Dutch economy of the 1980s was a result of failing competition and that a change in attitude towards competition policy was necessary. This transformation gradually occurred in the 1990s. An outdated straggling policy demanded rapid reforms. The tortoise, so to say, had to be made ready to be transformed into a 'hare'. European integration required reform and Dutch academic research on the impact of competition policy took off. Proposed policy transformations that prohibited anti-competitive behaviour accelerated and finally succeeded in 1998.

Cartels and cooperation (1930–1950)

The key to understanding economic policy developments between 1930 and 1950 is to recognise that the Dutch economy was confronted with two major crises: the Great Depression and the Second World War. Prior to the crisis in the 1930s, both government and Dutch academic economists were inspired by the Austrian School

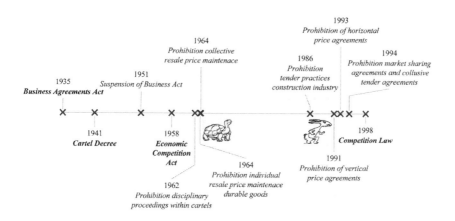

Figure 5.1 Timeline of the different competition acts in the Netherlands.

that favoured free markets and a small government (Dullaart 1984: 5). This policy orientation changed dramatically after the Great Depression which reduced trust that market clearing would also produce socially acceptable results. Indeed, markets were now distrusted and a majority of economists and policy makers were convinced that cooperation between companies, government and trade unions was essential for recovery. Government had to guide the recovery process. One should place the development of a pro-cartel policy in the 1930s against this background.

International developments

The Dutch view on competition policy in this era did not deviate from that of almost all other European countries. Generally speaking, cartels were considered to provide a solution to the economic crisis and to protect local producers from international competitiveness. Cartels 'were particularly pronounced as an essential, accepted and even government-orchestrated feature of business activity in German-speaking Europe throughout the first half of the twentieth century' (McGowan 2010: 14). Other countries that also had a positive attitude towards cartels in the inter-war period were: Austria, Belgium, Czechoslovakia, Finland, France, Germany, Norway, Sweden and Switzerland. Conversely, countries which officially prohibited cartels at that time were: Argentina, Australia, New Zealand, US and Yugoslavia (Schröter 1996; Chapter 7, this volume).

Starting in 1929 after the Wall Street Crash, the League of Nations constructed a database of various international cartel agreements (Chapter 3, this volume). The League of Nations saw merit in providing transparent and publicly available information on, for example, essential facts of production, price developments and world supplies, as this would 'assure the consumer of accurate knowledge so that he might not be misled through any misrepresentations by international industrial groups' (Klein 1928: 456). The presence of the Netherlands was notable in the cartelisation data recorded by the League of Nations. In the 1930s the Netherlands participated in 17 of the 47 identified international cartels. Other European countries, such as Germany, France, the UK and Belgium took part in respectively 23, 14, 13 and seven cartels (United Nations 1947; Chapter 13, this volume).

National developments

The developments in Dutch competition policy were a reaction to the economic circumstances that supported central organisation, cooperation and consensus. The Great Depression led to protection of national markets and the widespread notion that firms should cooperate rather than compete in order to survive and to guarantee their international competitiveness. Leading Dutch economists in this period, such as Jan Tinbergen, argued in favour of government involvement and considered free competition to be unsustainable. Tinbergen constructed the first macro-econometric models and showed that the economic crisis was caused by a lack of effective demand. He was convinced that policymakers should employ an active demand management policy to control the business cycle. Other leading Dutch economists such as François de Vries (the first chairman of the Dutch Social Economic Council formed in 1950) and Johannes Veraart (leading the Dutch employers' organisation) were in favour of self-regulation within sectors to control competition and curb the crisis. De Vries and Veraart, however, opposed the increased government intervention suggested by Tinbergen, and instead advocated a corporatist model. Veraart proposed the 'organisation of industry' and introduced the concepts of 'reasonable prices' and 'reasonable wages' (Dullaart 1984).

The idea of self-regulation was put into practice after the Second World War. In 1950 the Industrial Organisation Act (*Wet op de bedrijfsorganisatie*) was introduced providing a legal foundation for the cooperation of employers and employees at industry level. The core of this policy legalised a centralised regime of wage and price restraint. This policy improved international competitiveness and kept unemployment at about two percent of the labour force in the late 1940s (Statistics Netherlands 2014). In this period average economic growth was about four percent annually (Statistics Netherlands 2014). The Social Economic Council (Sociaal Economische Raad; SER) played a prominent role in this cooperative model of recovery. In this council, the cooperative model for negotiation between employers, employees, government and independent specialists was formalised. This typical Dutch model of economic decision making later became known as 'the Polder Model'.

Institutional and regulatory change

Business Agreements Act

In 1935 the Dutch government introduced the Business Agreements Act (*Ondernemers-overeenkomstenwet*). This law was intended to enhance and support cooperation among entrepreneurs and organisations: 'Its main aim was to curtail the deleterious effects of excessive (domestic) competition on prices and employment' (Asbeek Brusse and Griffiths 1998: 16). The idea was that in following this law, Dutch businesses and thus employment would remain secure. The act contained two instruments to regulate and support agreements.[2] The most important was the government's right to declare agreements binding within a specific sector. The purpose was to force entrepreneurs or organisations in a particular sector, to take part in, and act in accordance with, an agreement, even if they had initially declined to participate.

The Business Agreements Act was limited to the extent that enforcement required a formal request from stakeholders, rather than being initiated by the government. The law was seen as an instrument promoting socially desirable market outcomes, as long as participating firms did not abuse the market power they derived from the agreement. As Dullaart (1984) argues, they were expected to serve the public interest. The government also could declare agreements non-binding. The minister of Economic Affairs decided on a case-by-case basis whether an agreement should be declared binding or non-binding (Bervoets 2000). From January 1935 until December 1939, 45 requests for binding agreements were filed.

Only a few proved successful after assessment by the government. Of the 45 requests, fifteen were declared binding, sixteen were not granted, four were withdrawn while the remainder were still under discussion in 1940, when Nazi Germany occupied the Netherlands. Of fifteen successful requests to declare an agreement binding, seven were new, and the rest concerned eight requests for extension of an already binding agreement. Requests to declare agreements non-binding were rarely submitted; this occurred a mere three times and those that were submitted, all failed within a few months.

Cartel decree

In 1941, under the Nazi regime, the Business Agreements Act was replaced by the Cartel Decree (*Kartelbesluit*). Under this law the government had virtually unlimited powers to regulate the market (Tweede Kamer 1953). The principles of binding and non-binding agreements remained the same. The most important amendment to the 1935 law was that the Cartel Decree also allowed the government to enforce government-initiated cartels and to intervene ex officio: on the ministries' own initiative, similar to the German legislation from 1933 (Chapter 11, this volume). In 1943 another new element was introduced that allowed the government to act against dominant economic positions in specific markets (Verbond van Nederlandse Werkgevers 1958).

Parties that were engaged in a cartel agreement were obliged to report their agreements to the Ministry of Economic Affairs. During the German occupation no actual decisions were taken and only the requirement to report business practices to the ministry was enforced (ibid.). Agreements were archived in a confidential cartel register (*kartelregister*). Again, the German practise was followed. Germany had a register from 1936 which was also confidential (Chapter 11, this volume). The cartel register was a piece of war legislation consistent with the idea of full control of the economy; it was parallel to the German cartel legislation at that time (Chapter 11, this volume). Reasons for the requirement of confidentiality of the Dutch register are unclear (Tweede Kamer 1980). It was assumed that cartelisation details only concerned the government and the practising firms (ibid.). The register introduced in 1941 would stay in effect until 1998.

Social Economic Council (1950)

A major institution of the polder model, which is still in place today, is the Social Economic Council (*Sociaal Economische Raad*). At present it 'represents the interests of trade unions and industry, advising the government (upon request or at its own initiative) on all major social and economic issues' (Sociaal Economische Raad n.d.). In 1950 the SER's impact on the Dutch economy was much stronger than today because the law then demanded that the Council be asked for advice in all important economic decisions. The SER's influence diminished over time, but it always continued to play an important role in advising the government, also while representing industry, and changing competition legislation.

Modification (1951-1958)

The increased importance of public interest as part of cartel evaluation began in 1951 with the introduction of the Suspension of Business Regulation Act (*Wet Schorsing Bedrijfsregelingen*). It was followed in 1958 by the Economic Competition Act (*Wet Economische Mededinging, WEM*). The increase in economic prosperity after the Second World War made the government reconsider the efficacy of cartels. This saw a decisive shift away from the legislation framed in times of crisis towards regulation based on the idea that only those cartels that benefitted the public (a concept which later appeared an inconvenient criterion), should be permitted.

International developments

In the 1950s the Netherlands was a leading proponent of European integration. Along with France, Germany, Italy, Belgium and Luxembourg it was one of the founding countries of the European Coal and Steel Community (ECSC), established by the Treaty of Paris in 1951. The ECSC promoted mutual economic interests between the former foes Germany and France (Chapter 4, this volume). It also reflected the recognition by policy makers, that the success of the USA emerged from competition (Motta 2004). In 1957 the Treaty of Rome established the European Economic Community (EEC) or 'Common Market'. Article 85 of the Treaty prohibits cartelisation affecting trade *between* member states and specifies particular practices that are incompatible with the common market.[3] The article provided the direction towards stricter competition policy that was eventually taken by all member states (Chapter 4, this volume).

Before the formation of the EEC, various European economies had already started to prohibit cartels. In 1945 France prohibited restrictive business agreements of all kinds if their purpose or effect was to impair competition 'by preventing a decrease in costs or selling prices or by facilitating an artificial increase in prices' (Souam 1998: 206). Their first competition statutes (Le Décret du 9 Août 1953) came into effect in 1953 (ibid.). A *rule of reason* policy was applied; only those cartels that would result in increased prices were prohibited. In 1956 the UK introduced the Restrictive Trade Practices Act; it did not prohibit all kinds of restrictive business practices. Its main principle, however, was that 'restrictive agreements are in general adverse to the public interest unless shown otherwise' (Symenoidis 1998: 56). From 1958 the German GWB (*Gesetz gegen Wettbewerbsbeschränkungen*, the act against restraint of competition) prohibited cartels in general. Yet, a considerable number of cartels could opt for exemption under the GWB, such as cartels on conditions; rebate cartels; those formed because of crisis; rationalisation cartels; specialisation cartels; cooperation cartels; cartels involved with imports and exports and ministerially decreed emergency cartels (Chapter 11, this volume; Haucap, Heimeshoff and Schultz 2010). A Federal Cartel Office (*Bundeskartellamt; BKA*) was established to enforce the GWB. Cartels had to be registered at the BKA, who determined whether they would be accepted (Chapter 4, this volume).

Overall there was a major re-orientation of policy on competition issues in France, the UK and Germany. This is relevant because of the central role of Germany and France in the European integration process and also because all three countries were important trading partners of the Netherlands. As with the Dutch legislation, there was still room for some types of cartels in all three countries. Up to this point all these countries had a similar perspective on competition.

National developments

During the 1950s the Netherlands enjoyed the fruits of economic cooperation and consensus between economic agents as the reconstruction and recovery from the Second World War progressed. Between 1951 and 1958 real average GDP grew at more than four percent per annum, unemployment averaged less than two percent and inflation was around three percent (Statistics Netherlands 2014). Employment increased and the welfare state gradually expanded. Keynesian ideas of government intervention were generally accepted and cooperation and consensus continued to develop.

The government no longer needed to promote cartelisation and curb excessive competition to overcome an economic crisis or assist recovery from war. In fact, by the end of the 1940s the Ministry of Economic Affairs had begun receiving various requests to act against specific cartel agreements (Verbond van Nederlandse Werkgevers 1958). As a prelude to the regulatory changes yet to come, between 1945 and 1955, the ministry intervened when it considered business behaviour adverse to the public interest. Its priorities were in cases where there was:

- exclusion of firms in horizontal and vertical relationships;
- conditional inclusion of firms in such relationships;
- a risk or threat of exclusion of firms in such relationships;
- prescription of distribution channels;
- limitation of production;
- prescription of minimum prices and
- tender agreements.

The good condition of the economy meant that cartels were not needed; in fact minimum price cartels could even jeopardise economic objectives such as controlling inflation. The perception of cartels shifted from a presumption that they provided an economic advantage for the country, to a conditional acceptance that cartels may use their advantage only in specific situations.

Institutional and regulatory change

Suspension of the Business Regulation Act

The 1941 Dutch Cartel Decree was complemented in 1951 by the Suspension Act. This served as a temporary solution until the Economic Competition Act was ready to be introduced in 1958. By 1951, the Economic Competition Act was at the drafting stage (Verbond van Nederlandse Werkgevers 1958). Both laws were enacted during a period when the Labour Party (Partij van de Arbeid) and the Christian democratic parties (KVP, CHU and ARP) formed the Cabinet. Under the old legislation it was time-consuming to declare agreements non-binding once they were found to be contrary to public interests. The successive governments of the 1950s however, all recognised the urgency to dissolve such agreements as the economy started to grow (Verbond van Nederlandse Werkgevers 1958). The 1951 Act complemented the Cartel Decree and provided for immediate suspension of agreements that conflicted with public interests. Both the Suspension of the Business Regulation Act and the Cartel Decree remained in effect until 1958.

Economic Competition Act

The Economic Competition Act (WEM) was passed in July 1956 and came into force in November 1958. It remained in operation for four decades. This act permitted cartels as long as they did not run counter to the public interest. The term 'public interest' was, however, undefined in the initial legislation and remained so until the WEM was terminated in 1998. Despite noteworthy attempts by De Roos (1969) and Kuin, Becker and Admiraal (1982) to define public interest, it was problematic to develop uniform criteria that could be applied in specific cases ('T Gilde and Haank 1985: 5). Aspects such as productivity increases, price stability, economic development, employment and balanced public finances were all mentioned as belonging in the public interest domain (ibid.). The WEM specified the roles of different players in the assessment of agreements. The Ministry of Economic Affairs carried the prime responsibility of enforcement of the Act.

An important role in securing objectivity was played by the Committee for Economic Competition (Commissie Economische Mededinging, CEM). The CEM was appointed by the minister and was able to provide advice. The minister was obliged to ask the CEM for (non-binding) advice under specified circumstances (see Appendix 1a). In the final analysis it was the minister who decided whether an agreement conflicted with the public interest or not.[4]

The WEM provided the minister with four instruments to intervene in *agreements*:

(i) On request of the firms involved, the minister of Economic Affairs could declare an agreement binding on all the firms within an industry. This was the case if the turnover of the firms involved in the cartel exceeded the turnover of the 'outsiders'. (WEM 1956, s 6);
(ii) The minister of Economic Affairs could declare an agreement (partly) non-binding and generally non-binding in the event that it interfered with public interests; for a maximum of five years, (with possibilities for extension. (WEM 1956, ss 10, 19(1)(b));
(iii) The minister of Economic affairs could (partly) suspend a specific agreement. Suspension is a temporary but immediate measure to declare an agreement

non-binding until the decision of the Committee for Economic Competition (WEM 1956, s 23);
(iv) The ministry could publicise (parts of) the agreement in cases where it interfered with public interests (WEM 1956, s 19(1)(a)).

In addition to intervening in agreements, the WEM provided five instruments to tackle *market power* which could harm the public's interest (see Appendix 1a).

The agreements were archived in the cartel register, an inheritance from the former Cartel Decree. The registration pertained to those agreements that regulated economic competition between owners of firms. Agreements that regulated non-economic competition in the Netherlands were exempted from registration (WEM 1956, s 4(1)). The definition of non-economic competition was not clearly defined in WEM. The goal of registration was to gather comprehensive insights into the economic competition agreements affecting the Dutch economy. The key prerequisite for a complete cartel register was considered to be confidentiality. Transparency towards the public was not considered appropriate. For example, it was argued that community members would not be able to judge the information objectively.[5] Therefore, the government fulfilled the role as 'guardian' of public interests. Since the system was based on anti-abuse, and cartels were by definition, considered neither harmful nor beneficial for the economy, the ministry required information about the agreement. Once registered, the ministry could assess the agreements on their merits; particularly on whether they were conflicting with the public interest. In cases where certain aspects appeared dubious for the ministry, its employees and the concerned firms tried (informally) to reshape the agreement so that it would become acceptable. Thus the cartel register functioned as an instrument for the government to safeguard excessive behaviour. Each year, an overview was published about the number of cartel agreements by industry and by type of agreement (price agreements, market sharing, conditions, etc.; see Chapter 13, this volume).

The WEM provided for the publication of information on the existence of certain agreements. First, agreements that would conflict with the public interest could be published in detail (WEM 1956, s 19(1)(a)). Second, decisions on agreements that were declared binding (WEM 1956, s 6(3)), exemptions from binding agreements (WEM 1956, s 8(4)), exemptions from general prohibitions (WEM 1956, s 12(7)), and agreements declared non-binding or which were published in detail (WEM 1956, s 19(2)) should be announced in the government gazette. Third, agreements that were subject to advice from the CEM should be announced in the government gazette as too, agreements that were suspended (WEM 1956, s 23(2)).

In summary, the WEM was designed as a neutral law, but one that was equipped with the tools to act against harmful cartels. What was considered harmful was to be decided by the government. In that sense the public had to rely on the Ministry's judgment. Only in a few circumstances, mainly when action had already been taken, were particular cartels made public.

Institutional inertia (1959–1986)

From 1959 to 1986 the Dutch regulatory cartel framework put in place in 1958 remained unchallenged and comparatively static, although other major European countries reoriented their competition policy. The process by which the Dutch institutional regime became obsolete was gradual and went by largely unnoticed. Even the economic crisis of the 1980s did not, at first, have much impact on Dutch competition policy. Stagflation (double digit inflation combined with high unemployment) however, meant that the traditional macro-policies of demand management appeared to be unsuccessful for economic performance in the long run. Restructuring the supply side became the main focus of policy. At this point there was little discussion on the adverse results of competition policy on the goods and services markets.

International developments

With the establishment of the EEC, cartel practices that were likely to harm interstate competition between countries became regulated and were subject to prosecution if proven illegal.

While the Netherlands was clearly part of the EEC, the country preserved its own attitude to cartels. The first example of a cartel fined by the EEC was the 1969 quinine cartel, organised between Dutch, French and German firms. It involved many types of illegal conduct such as agreements on export quotas, conditions on the sale of quinine, price calculations, etc.[6] From 1970 until 1990, around 40 percent of the EEC's decisions on serious competition infringements concerned Dutch firms (De Jong 1990; Asbeek Brusse and Griffiths 1998). Bouwens and Dankers (2012) identify 21 serious infringements from Dutch firms between 1970 and 1989. Among these decisions one particular intervention illustrates the divergence between the Dutch government's view on cartels and that of the EEC at the time. In 1982 the European Commission fined a Dutch cigarette industry. The Netherlands had been dominated in the 1970s by a cartel that limited competition between cigarette companies at the retail level.[7] The firms were fined a total of 1.47 million ECU (European Currency Unit). This cartel stood out because it also involved the Dutch government which was also influencing retail prices by setting excise duties.

By 1986, several European countries had each established a competition regulator. As mentioned, Germany established its regulator (*Bundeskartellamt*) and its prohibition-oriented law in 1957. The UK established its regulator (Office of Fair Trading) together with the Fair Trading Act in 1973 and the Restrictive Trade Practices Act in 1976 (Symenoidis 1998). The UK law also relied on abuse principles. France introduced its first regulator (*Le Conseil de la Concurrence*) together with new competition rules (*Ordinance relative a la liberté des prix et de la concurrence*) in 1986. This ordinance 'established the free market economy as the model to be used in France' (Souam 1988: 209). By contrast, the Netherlands did not establish its competition regulator until 1998.

National developments

The early 1980s saw a deterioration in the Dutch economy. The Netherlands were in a recession from 1980 to 1982; economic growth was negative and the budget deficit increased above six percent in 1982. Unemployment rose to approximately ten percent in 1983 (Statistics Netherlands 2014). With the public interest as its priority, the WEM equipped the ministry with tools to react to changing economic circumstances. Yet, the interventions were very limited during the crisis itself.

The first reason was that the crisis was primarily considered a problem of public finance and wage restraint which together caused a deterioration of the competitiveness of the Netherlands and a worsening of the labour market. Second the WEM's legislation implied that government intervention only took place when there were complaints or signals from third parties. The crisis had a lagged impact on the change in competition policy. After the change from a policy of Keynesian driven demand management towards an economic policy which was based on neo-classical principles, the lack of flexibility in the product market became more and more evident (van Sinderen 2000). The momentum for change was also stimulated by international developments.

Limited proactive powers

The idea of cooperation and consensus are deeply rooted in the Dutch mind-set and in the regulatory system. Market outcomes were affected by, among other things, the WEM, the Wage Law (*Wet op de loonvorming*), the Price Law (*Prijzenwet*), and the social partners (employers' organisations and trade unions). One problem with this institutionalised polder model was that it allowed significant influence to be exerted by lobby groups and sectorial interests. For example if the minister of Economic Affairs wished to rule that an agreement was in conflict with the public interest (meaning that prohibition was appropriate), he was obliged to involve other relevant ministers in the decision thus ensuring specific interests were always represented in the debate (Chapter 6, this volume). Asbeek Brusse and Griffiths (1998) and the Sociaal Economische Raad (1994) argue that the implementation of the WEM was driven by complaints which were resolved by internal discussions between civil servants and firms. Peeperkorn (1987: 67) even claims that competition policy was controlled by the government and the cartelised firms and that the Ministry of Economic Affairs was biased in favour of trade interests and industry at the expense of 'third parties' (consumers and/or competitors) who were neither involved nor informed about the cartel agreements.[8]

Under the WEM little recourse existed for consumers or parties not directly involved in the cartel practises but who were nevertheless dissatisfied with particular cartel's conduct. In essence, the policy was kept in-house. After 1969, some efforts were made to change this situation; all were unsuccessful.

Political inconsistency

Two attempts at change illustrate the political climate surrounding competition policy. First, a recurring issue was the secrecy of the cartel register. A debate between the government and Parliament occurred in 1969, and the SER was asked to advise on proposed policy changes. In 1971, the SER was asked not only to advise on whether the previously secret register should be made public, but also on specific revisions to the WEM, including a general prohibition of horizontal price agreements. The SER advised in favour of public disclosure of the register in 1973. A new bill authorising public disclosure of the register's contents was submitted to the SER for advice in 1977 and in January 1981 a bill was sent to the House of Representatives (*Tweede Kamer*). It was eventually passed, only to be rejected in June 1986, by the Senate (*Eerste Kamer*).[9] The most important parties which were opposed to the bill were the liberal party (*Volkspartij voor Vrijheid en Democratie*) and the Christian Democrats (*Christen-Democratisch Appèl*). Eventually, in 1987, the state secretary for Economic Affairs, Evenhuis saw a chance to use the Freedom of Information Act (*Wet openbaarheid van bestuur*) to allow parts of the cartel register to be disclosed on demand (Peeperkorn 1988). Evenhuis acted in advance of this development and published a list of certain existing agreements. Employers' representatives reacted furiously (ibid.). The State Council (*Raad van State*) then decided that the Freedom of Information Act was overruled by the original pledge of secrecy adopted in the WEM. From that moment, the debate about publicity of the cartel register was closed and would not be resumed; the register would remain confidential.

Second, in addition to advising in favour of public disclosure in 1973, the SER gave an opinion on horizontal price agreements. The SER argued against a general prohibition on horizontal agreements and proposed that specific legal criteria should be used to identify 'condemnable' price cartels; those which would undeniably conflict with the public interest. Eventually in 1977, a bill dealing with prohibition principles for price agreements was filed by the minister of Economic Affairs, but rejected by Parliament. Obviously, the firms themselves were content with the current policy ('T Gilde and Haank 1986).[10] In their advice to the SER, industry representatives stated that firms saw no justification for changing the law (Sociaal Economische Raad 1973). The SER also argued that regulation of collective labour agreements was in line with the rigidity of the markets for goods and services. Thus any amendment to the regulation of goods and services markets would also require a change in the regulation of labour markets. The latter would have been politically difficult for the government since changing labour market policy was a challenge that would bring them into conflict with the labour unions. These fruitless torturous journeys illustrate the political inconsistency associated with developing Dutch competition policy.

Ministry inertia

The passive attitude of the ministry is illustrated by its formal decisions and the continued existence of the cartel register. From 1960 until 1983 only one decision was taken about a binding agreement; four general prohibitions were declared; one decision was taken on a non-binding agreement; and there were no publications of agreement details (Barendregt 1991). The role of the cartel register during the period of inertia remained; to assess new agreements on their merits. The political call to make the register public, and so inform society about cartel agreements, remained fruitless. Simultaneous with seeking advice from the SER in 1973, an enquiry was launched to update the content of the cartel register. This led to a downward adjustment in the number of registered, operational, agreements. Of the 654 agreements then recorded, 111 appeared to have already been terminated.[11] Interestingly, the enquiry concluded that neither the rules and regulations of the WEM, nor firms' obligations to notify an agreement to the ministry, were generally known (Tweede Kamer 1973). After this enquiry the urgency to keep the content of the register up-to-date lost priority so that by 1984 the ministry concluded that another 74 agreements had expired (Tweede Kamer 1985). Overall, the register continued to exist but was updated infrequently

This might have been due to the confidential character of the register, no detailed information was to be published so there was no incentive to maintain it accurately. Note, however, that in Finland the register was public, and it too suffered from lack or updating (Chapter 6, this volume). Another reason may have been that with few modifications to the legislation there was no urgency to reassess existing cartel agreements.

Academic inertia

While policy makers created no catalyst for change, neither did academics. There was virtually no research in the Netherlands on the lack of competition at either a micro or macro level, and no assessment of the impact of cartels on competition. Industrial organisation was part of the curriculum of all Dutch economics faculties but was held in low esteem and typically was descriptive in nature (van Gent 1997). Economic policy was mostly macro-oriented. Van Bergeijk and van Sinderen (2000) identify three reasons why academic research was absent at the micro level: the barriers to obtaining (confidential) government information; the limited size of the Dutch economy; and/or the poor short-term rewards of developing specific models on this topic, which all resulted in limited funds for researchers.

Institutional and regulatory change

Economic Competition Act

The Economic Competition Act of 1958 remained basically unchanged, except for minor changes from 1959 until 1986. The three modifications that were made to the WEM occurred in the 1960s: a prohibition against disciplinary proceedings within cartels (1962); a prohibition against collective resale price maintenance (1964); and a prohibition against individual resale price maintenance for various durable consumer goods (1964).[12]

Resale price maintenance was, at that time, considered highly anti-competitive. It was argued that resale price maintenance curbed the competition at retail level, and hence there was less incentive to increase efficiency in distribution. Moreover, resale price maintenance provided no opportunities to decrease prices and increase sales, diminishing the incentive to decrease costs for inefficient distributors (Sociaal Economische Raad 1971). In the 1970s and 1980s the only serious challenge to the regulations surround cartels had been the SER advice on the transparency of the cartel register and horizontal price agreements.

Transformation (1987–1998)

After such a long period of inertia change became almost inevitable. Poor economic performance showed that the reigning policy required reorientation to improve economic outcomes. Researchers, aware of the impact of regulatory changes in other countries began to study product and services markets in the Netherlands more closely. Dutch policy makers realised the need for legislation prohibiting cartel behaviour and the divergence of their country's policies from the rest of Europe; something that had to be altered if the Netherlands were to continue to be aligned with EEC policy (Bouwens and Dankers 2012).

International developments

The signing of the Maastricht Treaty in 1992, which came into effect in 1993, was a milestone in EU convergence. Nonetheless Dutch cartel regulation was not yet aligned with EU requirements. For example, at the beginning of the 1990s the European Commission (EC) scrutinised the Dutch construction sector, in particular the 'Association for co-operative and price arranging organisations in the construction industry' (*Vereniging van Samenwerkende en Prijsregelende Organisaties in de Bouwnijverheid, SPO*). According to the EC, their agreements harmed trade in other member states. The EC decided that the SPO's practises did not comply with European legislation and in 1992 imposed a 22.5 million ECU fine.[13] The EC also initiated proceedings against the Dutch government.[14] In 1995 the EC concluded that the rules for public procurement in the Netherlands did not comply with the Treaty on the Functioning of the European Union (TFEU). Dutch competition policy was also becoming problematic for other individual EU countries.[15] Geelhoed, Secretary-General of the Ministry of Economic Affairs at the time, and an important promoter of the new Competition Law, used these examples to argue that the Dutch competition regime had become outdated and the regime raised eyebrows internationally (Den Hoed, Buevink and Keizer 2007).[16]

In the meantime, several other countries had adopted policy and competition principles that prohibited cartel behaviour. For example, Italy and Belgium introduced their first laws in 1990 and 1993 (Haffner and van Bergeijk 1996: 26–28). The pressure to change Dutch competition policy and cartel regulation was becoming irresistible. This was also the case in Sweden and Finland in 1992 in conjunction with their EU membership applications (Chapter 6, this volume).

National developments

The end of the 1980s marked the first changes in attitude towards competition issues. In July 1987, the minister of Economic Affairs explicitly stated that a well-functioning market mechanism was crucial for Dutch welfare (Tweede Kamer 1987). It was argued that competition yields an incentive to produce efficiently, keep prices low and adjust services and goods to the buyers' preferences. There was, however, no call to abandon the WEM. Instead, the state budget outlined a strategy to increase the effectiveness of competition policy within the context of the WEM (ibid.). This scheme included: (i) a critical assessment of new competition agreements; (ii) a reconsideration of previously applied agreements; (iii) a prompt reaction to complaints and other signals; (iv) computerising the cartel register; (v) provision of more information about competition policy, and (vi) enhanced control on decisions and actions to be taken under WEM (ibid.).

The cartel register was reviewed in 1987 and 1988. Cartel members recorded in the register were contacted by mail and asked about their agreement's current existence. Approximately sixteen percent of the firm's responses revealed the register included outdated agreements that were already terminated (Tweede Kamer 1988). Consequently, the Dutch government launched a campaign in June 1988 called 'the new vision on free competition' (Tweede Kamer 1988, 1989). This campaign defined the policy's principles, the need for registration of existing cartels and the opportunities to file complaints. Especially, in the period of transformation the ministry required data about new and existing cartels. The activated policy also manifested itself in an increase in the number of decisions. From 1984 until 1990 six (partly) non-binding decisions were taken (compared to two between 1958 and 1983) and one decision on a binding agreement took place in the bakery industry (compared to one in the sugar industry between 1959 and 1983) (Barendregt 1991).[17]

The economic crisis of the early 1980s caused politicians to look for solutions outside the long used, but increasingly ineffectual standard policies. Wages and prices were spiralling upward and serious questions were raised about the limits of the welfare state. The Netherlands, like many other members of the OECD, opted for structural reforms, including tax reform and more flexible labour markets (van Sinderen 1990). One of the most important influences of this restructuring in the beginning of the 1990s was the scheduled completion of the European internal market ('Europe 1992'); something that clearly required a level playing field across a number of areas including competition policy. Bouwens and Dankers (2012), studying the role of trade associations, cartels and mergers, show that in late 1980s mergers become increasingly popular. The more stringent anti-cartel policy may have provided firms with the incentive to merge instead of continuing to cooperate via cartels (ibid.).

Most Dutch economists, however, remained more interested in studying the labour market and international phenomena than examining the effect of more competitive goods and services markets. It became increasingly apparent that the lack of research into the economic impact of uncompetitive Dutch markets was making it difficult to convince politicians that the WEM was almost obsolete and that the economy urgently required increased competition. Even the Netherlands Bureau for Economic Policy Analysis (*Centraal Planbureau; CPB*) found it difficult to supply any analysis. The CPB is the independent agency responsible for advising the government on economic policy. Although it became interested in the economic impact of structural reforms to competition policy, it was slow to engage in economic modelling. This was because, the agency argued, there were few modelling tools available to quantify the effects of institutional change (van Bergeijk and Haffner 1994). The economic proof needed to allow the CPB to forecast accurately the consequences of reform remained elusive (van Bergeijk 2005).

Policy makers thus encountered a critical problem. They could not provide estimates of the costs and benefits of any contemplated changes in the competition policy regime. By the beginning of the 1990s, however, empirical research had increased sharply. The first empirical academic research on the functioning of Dutch markets was published in 1987, followed by two more in 1991 (De Wolf 1987; van Schaik 1991; Kuipers 1991). The research then gathered pace, with an average 6.5 studies per year over the next decade (van Bergeijk 2002). In an effort to provide the necessary empirical evidence, economists at the Ministries of Economic Affairs and Finance published a number of articles estimating the costs of rigidities in product markets, although none drew on the cartel register for data.

A plethora of studies revealed the extent of anti-competitive elements in the economy; market rigidities and distortions by Dutch institutions and the government (including certain legislation such as the Establishment of Businesses Act (*Vestigingswet*) and Shopping Hours Act (*Winkelsluitingswet*); business agreements under WEM; market inertia; and other Dutch regulations (Kremers 1991; van Bergeijk, Haffner and Waasdorp 1993; van Sinderen *et al.* 1994) Others demonstrated the economic gains to be made through reform (Gradus 1996; van Bergeijk and van Dijk 1997). Collectively this substantial increase in research helped to substantiate the claim that the Netherland's lagging competition framework created substantial macroeconomic costs. There was much to gain from liberalisation and reregulation of labour and product markets (van Bergeijk and Haffner 1996).

Under pressure from the looming 'Europe 1992', the minister of Economic Affairs argued in 1991 that the Netherlands competition policy should be made more congruent with European practices (Tweede Kamer 1991). The WEM and its institutional regime was not compatible with the introduction of free capital and goods markets. It was initially decided to simply modify the WEM, but by 1992 the design of a new competition law was announced (Tweede Kamer 1992). In 1994 the government also launched an initiative to deregulate the economy and improve the functioning of markets. The aim was 'to increase the dynamics and competitiveness of the Dutch economy by comparing, critically examining and adapting Dutch legislation to modern requirements' (Ministerie van Economische Zaken 1996: 9). Revision of the competition policy, the WEM and its institutions, was part of this project. Geelhoed pleaded for more competition in both Dutch product and labour markets to stimulate economic growth (Geelhoed 1996). This position was partly based on the research carried out within his ministry.

Economists and policymakers were now keen to stimulate change in the national competition regime.

Institutional and regulatory change

Economic Competition Act

In the last operating decade of the 1958 Dutch Economic Competition Act there was slight movement towards the prohibition of cartels. For example, in 1986 a ban against certain tender practices in the building industry was introduced. Five years later a general prohibition against vertical price agreements was enacted. By 1993 the prohibition of horizontal price agreements was introduced, followed the next year by the prohibition of market sharing and collusive tender agreements.

In 1995 aspects of the WEM were amended as an interim solution before the proposed Competition Law came into effect (Ministerie van Economische Zaken 1996). The government's changed view about the effectiveness of the WEM is summarised in the 1996 annual report.

> The WEM regime, which is based on control of abuse combined with a number of general invalidations – i.e. prohibitions – of certain severe forms of cartel, is not enough ... for this. Firstly, supervision of abuse is intrinsically ineffective, because action must be provided for the assessment of a conflict with the general interest. Secondly, the system of general invalidations of agreements and decisions combined with enforcement under penal law is a cumbersome one. Thirdly, the system of separate general prohibitions for different types of competition agreements inevitably entails problems of definition.
> (Ministerie van Economische Zaken 1996: 3)

Again, the question of how to assess the public interest was identified as a shortcoming of the prevailing policy. Even though general prohibitions were introduced in 1993 and 1994, definitional problems arose in the practical application of the policy. The prohibitions were based on the legal form of the agreement, rather than capturing the effect of the agreement (i.e. an object approach). Conversely, the WEM initially concentrated on the outcomes for the public. Overall, however, it is clear that the Dutch government had by now recognised the lack of effectiveness of the WEM and adopted a positive attitude towards modernisation and a prohibition system. By 1996 the minister of Economic Affairs, appears to have accepted that the lack of competition between 1984 and 1990 had led to considerable macro-economic costs for the Dutch economy (Tweede Kamer 1996).

The new Competition Law

In May 1996, the new Competition Act was submitted to Parliament. It was referred to as a 'radical break with the regime of the present Act' (Ministerie van

Economische Zaken 1996: 1). Cartelisation was simply prohibited; assessing cartels on their merits was not an option. The cartel register maintained under the abuse system became obsolete and was no longer used after 1997. The new Competition Law (*Mededingingswet*) was based on the prohibition principle and a separate body, the Netherlands Competition Authority (*Nederlandse Mededingingsautoriteit; NMa*), was established. In 2005 it became an (independent) non-departmental public body.

By the beginning of 1998 Dutch competition policy was at last aligning with European practices. Section 6 of the Competition Law, based on Article 101 of the TFEU, prohibits cartels: 'Agreements between undertakings, decisions by associations of undertakings and concerted practices of undertakings, which have the intention to or will result in hindrance, impediment or distortion of competition on the Dutch market or on a part thereof, are prohibited' (Competition Law 1998, Section 6, paragraph 1). Abuse of dominant positions is similar to Article 102 of the TFEU and addressed in Section 24 of the Competition Law: 'Undertakings are prohibited from abusing a dominant position' (Competition Law 1998, Section 24, paragraph 1). Although it had taken decades to achieve, cartels were finally prohibited.

The new competition policy

While cartels were prohibited *per se* from 1998, it took until 2004 for the NMa to deal with a series of exemption requests. Firms could apply for exemption as a transition from the old WEM to the new prohibition system. In total only 39 of 315 requests for exemption of Section 6(1) of the Competition Law were granted; and most only for a transition period (Chapter 13, this volume). Early in its administration, one of the biggest cartels prosecuted by the NMa was in construction.[18] This prosecution was made possible by a whistle-blower providing inside information (van Bergeijk 2008). Other cartels that received attention were in shrimp fisheries, bicycle manufacture and in the flour industry.[19] While the concept of free competition was embedded in the NMa's policy approach, the organisation soon started to face new challenges.

Nationally, third parties began to question free competition as a goal, rather than looking at the final market outcomes of competition enforcement. Debate about the value of free competition was revived with the introduction of competition in the healthcare sector in 2006. Over time the debate influenced the NMa's merger policy in the healthcare industry and its successor the Authority for Consumers and Markets (*ACM, Autoriteit Consument en Markt*). Competition policy came under more attack after the banking crisis of 2008 turned into both a national and international economic crisis. In such a climate, some politicians found it expedient to plead for a relaxation of the stringent competition rules. The NMa also received requests from, for example, the inland navigation industry, which requested exemptions from the Competition Law to help accommodate cut-backs in their industry. Until now, the NMa has resisted the pleas for exemptions submitted by self-interested industries (Don *et al.* 2013). Politicians too sought to make the ACM more 'accountable' to the community. To quantify the merits of its interventions, the ACM publishes an annual estimate of the monetary value of its activities on consumer welfare in the Netherlands (van Sinderen and Kemp 2008).

Institutionally the ACM's policy gradually shifted to an effect (impact) approach, rather than the formal object (motivation) approach. The ACM has the consumer as its main focus. Consumer surplus, therefore, is the most important variable to consider, but there is also scope in its policy decisions to include other elements of the public interest, that includes granting exemptions on the prohibition of cartels. The new authority has a broad array of instruments, from fines to other interventions to enforce Competition Law (Ottow 2014). The Netherlands, once a jurisdiction with little interest in combating cartels, now possess a policy regime well equipped to ensure firms operate in a competitive market place.

The Netherlands was one of the first countries in Europe to consolidate its regulatory powers. With the establishment of the ACM in April 2014 (a result of a merger between the NMa, the Independent Post and Telecom Authority and the Consumer Authority) the organisation regulates the whole domain; from competition and regulation to consumer protection. This has occurred ahead of the international trend to consolidate regulators (e.g. Spain, UK).

Concluding remarks

Competition policy and social and economic developments are interconnected. The transformation of Dutch competition policy in the second half of the twentieth century has both shaped, and been shaped by important social and economic changes to the Netherlands over the same period. Competition policy is not an isolated field of decision making.

Changes in competition policy are much more effective if combined with reform in other areas – such as labour markets. Initially, the consensus policy framework and their enabling laws in effect after the Second World War were an endogenous barrier to change in the Netherlands. Combined with the introverted competition policy of the WEM the result was a significant institutional and cultural barrier to change. The introverted policy was also expressed in the confidential cartel register. Firms had to notify their cartel agreements at the ministry, which had the exclusive right to assess these agreements. Due to the confidentiality of the cartel register, there was limited room to provide the society information about the scope of cartel agreements. Attempts in the 1980s to make the register open to the public, so that society could also (re)act against cartels, were fruitless.

In this context, external economic and international developments became critical to making policy change in the Netherlands. From the start of the EEC, competition was vital to ensure market integration. The economic breakdown of the 1980s and the failure of alternative economic policies to combat these problems increased pressure to change. 'Europe 1992' provided still further impetus for integration. Cross-border competition was essential to the pursuit of the goals of European integration. In order to achieve a level playing field convergence of national policies was essential. In sum, these changes meant that the Netherlands' policy tortoise of the 1950s to 1980s transformed into a policy hare in the late 1990s – a position from which it now leads other nations adapting to new challenges.

Archival and printed sources

Ministerie van Economische Zaken 1996, *Annual Rapport Competition Policy*, Ministerie van Economische Zaken, The Hague.

Sociaal Economishe Raad n.d., *About the SER*. Available from: www.ser.nl/en/about_the_ser.aspx (accessed 21 May 2014).

Sociaal Economische Raad 1973, Advies inzake herziening van de Wet Economische Mededinging en versterking van het mededingingsbeleid uitgebracht aan de minister van Economische Zaken, no. 6, 15 June, 1973, The Hague.

Sociaal Economische Raad 1994, Advies nieuwe mededingingwet, Advies inzake de nieuwe mededingingswet uitgebracht aan de minister van Economische Zaken, no. 13, 21 October 1994, The Hague.

Statistics Netherlands 2014, *Nationale rekeningen; historie 1900–2012 (Binnenlands product – Bruto, marktprijzen)*. Available from: http://statline.cbs.nl/StatWeb/selection/?DM=SLNLandPA=7343NRandVW=T (accessed 2 June 2014).

Statistics Netherlands 2014, *Consumentenprijzen; prijsindex 1900 = 100 (Inflatie)*. Available from: http://statline.cbs.nl/StatWeb/selection/?DM=SLNLandPA=71905NEDandVW=T (accessed 2 June 2014).

Statistics Netherlands 2014, *Beroepsbevolking; vanaf 1800 (Werkloosheidspercentage)*. Available from: http://statline.cbs.nl/StatWeb/selection/default.aspx?DM=SLNLandPA=71882NEDandVW=T (accessed 2 June 2014).

Statistics Netherlands 2014, *Nationale rekeningen; historie 1900 – 2012 (Overheidstekort (-)/overschot (+))*.Available from: http://statline.cbs.nl/StatWeb/selection/?DM=SLNLandPA=7343NRandVW=T (accessed 2 June 2014).

Tweede Kamer 1953, Memorie van toelichting: Regelen omtrent de economische mededinging, no. 3295-3, The Hague.

Tweede Kamer 1955, Memorie van antwoord: Regelen omtrent de economische mededinging, no. 3275-7, The Hague.

Tweede Kamer 1973, Verslag over de toepassing van de Wet economische mededinging, no. 12 413, The Hague.

Tweede Kamer 1985; 1988; 1989, Rijksbegroting voor het jaar 1986; 1989; 1990 – Memorie van Toelichting – Appendix no. 11;10;11, Kamerstuk no. 19 200; 20 800; 21 300, chapter 13, no. 3, The Hague.

Tweede Kamer 1987, Brief van de Staatsecretaris van Economische Zaken, 19 700, chapter 13, no. 118.

Tweede Kamer 1991, Brief van de staatssecretaris van Economische Zaken: Mededingingsbeleid, 22 093 no. 1, The Hague.

Tweede Kamer 1992, Nieuwe regels omtrent de economische mededinging (Mededingingswet) – Memorie van Toelichting –24 707, no. 7, The Hague.

Tweede Kamer 1996, Nieuwe regels omtrent de economische mededinging (Mededingingswet) – Memorie van Toelichting –24 707, no. 3, The Hague.

Appendix: extracts from the Economic Competition Act 1958, Wet Economische Mededinging (WEM)

Appendix 1a

The minister was obliged to ask the CEM for (a non-binding) advice *before*:

(i) Declaring an agreement binding (WEM 1956, s 7(1));
(ii) Declaring an agreement generally non-binding (WEM 1956, s 11(1));
(iii) Declaring an agreement non-binding (WEM 1956, s 20(1));
(iv) Publicising (parts of) the agreement (WEM 1956, s 20(1));
(v) Granting exemption for general prohibitions (WEM 1956, s 13(1));
(vi) Acting against dominant positions (WEM 1956, s 25(1));
(vii) Invalidating an agreement due to non-notification (WEM 1956, s 5(2)).

In addition, the minister was required to seek advice of CEM *at the moment* he took a decision on a:

(i) Suspension of an agreement (WEM 1956, s 23(3));
(ii) Temporary solution for dominant positions (WEM 1956, s 27(3)).

Source: WEM (Wet Economische Mededinging, 1958).

Appendix 1b

The WEM provided five instruments to tackle market power which could harm the public's interest. The minister could:

(i) Publish information about the market power in question (WEM 1956, s 24(1)(a));
(ii) Force involved firms to desist from engaging in certain practices (WEM 1956, s 24(1)(b)(1));
(iii) Oblige supply of certain goods or services (WEM 1956, s 24(1)(b)(2));
(iv) Prescribe prices of certain goods and services (WEM 1956, s 24(1)(b)(3));
(v) Prescribe conditions governing delivery of specific goods and services (WEM 1956, s 24(1)(b)(4)).

Notes

1. The categorisation aligns with Asbeek Brusse and Griffiths (1998). They distinguish 1935–1956 (pro-cartel phase); 1956–1987 (indifference); 1987–1997 (anti-cartel drive).
2. In 1937 a similar act was introduced for collective labour agreements. At the request of stakeholders, the government could declare an agreement on wages binding, or non-binding. Whereas the Business Agreement Act dealt with regulation among firms, collective labour agreements were concerned with terms of employment and were arranged between employers and employees. Together, both laws regulated labour and product markets.
3. There were, however, some issues of interpretation. The prohibition legislation could also be interpreted as abuse legislation (see Chapter 4, this volume).
4. The minister of Economic Affairs was also obliged to involve the ministry concerned with the particular sector in his decision.

5   In for example Finland, Norway and Sweden public transparency was considered an instrument to regulate cartels. Public opinion would discipline the degree of cartelisation (see Chapters 6, 8 and 12 of this volume).
6   European Commission, 69/240/EEG, Celex number: 31969D0240, Quinine.
7   European Commission, 82/506/EEG, Celex number: 31982D0506, SSI; Tweede kamer, vergaderjaar 1986 – 1987, 19 700 chapter XIII, no. 3: 92.
8   This also appears partly true in Finland and Sweden (see Chapters 6 and 12 of this volume).
9   There were at least four reasons given for this rejection. First, the parties argued that the position of small and medium-sized enterprises was still too weak for publicity. Second, as only horizontal agreements were to be subject to publicity, this would result in inequity. Third, publicity would not conform with the Freedom of Information Act. Finally, it was argued that the parties acknowledged resistance from businesses themselves (Eerste Kamer 1986).
10 As in Germany businesses tried to push the system towards abuse instead of prohibition (see Chapter 11 of this volume).
11 The obligation to announce the termination of the agreement was often ignored. This was also true in Sweden and Finland.
12 These goods were, radio and television sets, record players, tape recorders, electric refrigerators, toasters, mixers, vacuum cleaners, washing machines, centrifuges, plat irons, dry-shavers, hair dryers, passenger automobiles, cameras, photo or film projectors, and phonograph records (Staatsblad nos. 110, 352 and 35).
13 European Commission, 92/204/EEG, Celex no. 31992D0204, Building and construction industry in the Netherlands.
14 European Commission, C-359/93, Celex no. 61993CJ0359, Commission of the European Communities v Kingdom of the Netherlands.
15 Other countries also had problems. Portugal was reluctant to promote competition for several years. Barros and Mata (1998: 273) claim that 'the presumption was that most firms in Portugal are too small to be competitive by international standards'. The Belgian government regulated prices until the 1990s. Sleuwaegen and van Cayseele (1998) argue that price regulation is usually employed to correct undesirable market outcomes, however in Belgium it was used as a policy instrument to secure fair prices and an equitable distribution of benefits. Belgium enacted a modern competition law in 1993.
16 See also van Bergeijk (2008) on the construction sector cartel.
17 The backing agreement was abandoned in 1988 and the sugar agreement in 1989.
18 Netherlands Competition Authority, Case 4155/GWW-activiteiten.
19 (Shrimp) Netherlands Competition Authority, Case 2269/Garnalen, (Bicylces) Netherlands Competition Authority, Case 1615/Fietsfabrikanten and (Flour) Netherlands Competition Authority, Case 6306/Meel.

6 Creating the 1957 cartel law

The role of pressure groups on Finland's competition policy and cartel registration

Susanna Fellman

Introduction

Finland belonged to that group of countries which maintained a cartel register in the post-war period. The Finnish register was established when the first 'cartel law' was passed in 1957. It ended in 1992, when a new law was passed in conjunction with Finland's signing of the European Economic Area (EEA) Agreement and the country's application for European Union membership. In one stroke, the new legislation replaced a relatively tolerant legislative framework with one which was strongly hostile. Until the legislative reform of 1992, cartels could work fairly openly; the focus of competition legislation was aimed only at preventing the most 'abusive' behaviour. Finland has been classified by researchers as one of the most cartelised economies in Europe (Schröter 1996; Chapter 12, this volume).

Although the statutes were revised and renewed several times during the postwar decades as the control of restrictive practices became stricter and some types of agreements were banned, overall the legislation was very tolerant towards restrictive practices right up until 1992. In this chapter, Finnish competition legislation and the cartel register will be the focus of investigation. In particular, the role of pressure groups in influencing, or attempting to influence, the country's legislation and registration system, will be discussed. I will also briefly deal with subsequent legislative discussions as the Act was revised several times prior to 1992, but the main focus here is on the law of 1957 and the processes leading up to its enactment.

The Finnish legislation and system of registration showed close similarities with several other countries, not the least Sweden. International influences and trends clearly reached Finland and the Finnish competition authorities followed especially closely the developments in other Nordic countries. Tony Freyer has stressed that anti-trust legislation and competition policies cannot be studied in isolation, but that they have to be put into the broader institutional context (Freyer 2006: 2–5, 394). One notable feature in the development of Finland's regulatory system is that the legal and institutional framework regulating cartels and other forms of agreements between firms to restrain competition was often connected to other economic-political targets and was occasionally part of a broader legislative package, especially concerning price regulation and price surveillance. In this, it was similar to many other countries including, for example the Netherlands (Chapter 5, this volume). The country also followed its own path, however.

Interest groups and the early competition legislation

Interest groups had a significant influence on Finland's competition policy and legislation. The initial legislation and the processes that lead to its introduction provide a good example. It has been claimed that few other committees had as many members from different interest groups with vested interests in competition policy as did the 'cartel committee' (Virkkunen 2003).[1] Correct or not, the fact is that apart from the chair person, all the members were representatives of some interest group (see Table 6.1).[2] As no prior legislation existed, the committee had quite far-reaching opportunities to influence the outcome and to lay out the basic principles of the new law. The interest groups also had considerable influence in the actual implementation of the legislation, as they had representatives in the competition authorities' various bodies until the 1990s. The role of interest groups in policy implementation has been dealt with in detail elsewhere (Fellman and Sandberg 2015). In this chapter I will reveal the opinion of the various pressure and interest groups (trade unions, agrarian groups, consumer cooperatives and the different associations and federations of trade and industry) to the competition legislation and, in particular, towards a system of registration.

My focus will be on the first statute, the 'cartel law' of 1957 (an Act on the Control of Practices Restricting Economic Competition – *Laki talouselämässä esiintyvien kilpailurajoitusten valvonnasta*), which came into force in 1958.[3] It was

Table 6.1 Composition of the 1948 Cartel Committee.

Chair	Representative, profession
Kyösti Sipilä (until 1950)	Professor of labour law
Paavo Ant-Wuorinen (from 1950)	Director, Finnish Patent and Registry Office
Members	
Yrjö Fellman	Deputy director, Suomen Teollisuusliitto (Finnish Federation of Industries), Lic. of Law
Paavo Korpisaari (until 1950)	MP for Conservatives, Secretary for Suomen Liikemiesyhdistys (Association of Finnish Businessmen)
Lauri Kirves (from 1950)	Director, Suomen Tukkukauppiaden Liitto (Finnish Wholesalers' Association)
Onni Koskikallio	Director, Maataloustuottajien Keskusliitto MTK (The Central Union of Agricultural Producers and Forest Owners), Dr. of Agricultural and Forestry Sciences,
Frans Jalmari Laakso	Director, Kulutusosuuskuntien Keskusliitto KK (Central Association for the Consumer Cooperatives)
Secretary	
Tauno Niklander	Government Secretary

Source: Kartellikomitean mietintö KM A 1952:48: 1.

this law that laid out the basic principles and framework for the legislation and the registration procedure, which, despite some changes, remained consistent with its basic rationale until 1992. The events leading up to and including the passage of the first statute were what Jacob Hacker (2002: 307) has called a fateful, or critical, juncture in policy reform (i.e. a reform during a short period of time which moulds future development for the longer term).

In the post-war decades, Finland can be characterised as a highly coordinated market economy (Fellman 2008). Finland also developed strongly neo-corporatist features with the aim of promoting compromise and consensus (Pekkarinen *et al.* 1992; Christiansen *et al.* 2009). Although the neo-corporatist consensus evolved during and immediately after the Second World War, its roots can be traced to earlier periods. In general, the system of neo-corporatism signifies a structure where interest groups have influence over, and play an important role in, the organisation of economic activity and policy-making. In essence, the state delegated some policy issues to the negotiation table of the employers and employees (or other groups). These features were most noticeable in the labour market and in social policies, where the target was to avoid confrontations and strikes which had detrimental effects on the economy. Contestation inevitably demanded that the various interest organisation had to restrain their members. According to Hugh Compston governments were willing to trade away some of their political power for the commitment of powerful interest groups and so extend their own role in managing the economy (Compston 2003). Interest groups also influenced other policy fields, including competition and price policies. Similar corporatist models were found in many other countries in the post-war period, although the models varied. For one example, the Dutch 'polder model' (see Chapter 5, this volume).

The influence of interest groups was highly visible in a system where state committees played a role prior to important policy reforms (Rainio-Niemi 2010). The role of committees especially increased in the 1960s and 1970s, when an "administrative ideology', which presupposed closer contact between the bureaucracy and its clients' was in vogue (Helander 1979: 226.) It was not only in state committees, however, that interest groups played a role; they could also be influential in those state authorities charged with implementing legislation. In neo-corporatist systems it was common for both intermediation and a certain degree of concerted action between the state and the various groups also in administration (Molina and Rhodes 1992; Compston 2003; Schmitter 1982). The relation between the state and interest groups within the administrative authorities and even in the judicial bodies (such as the Competition Council and market court) seems to have been especially significant in the field of competition policy (Fellman and Sandberg 2015).

Background to the legislation

Prior to 1957 cartels were permitted to work openly in Finland. During the liberal inter-war period – liberal in the sense that the state interfered as little as possible in the market mechanism – the prevailing doctrine was that firms should be able to organise their activities as they thought best. Non-interference in business and freedom of contracting were considered basic principles of commercial life. Cartels were also seen by many as a legitimate way to organise. For example, big export cartels were often viewed as advantageous for a young nation which had only achieved independence in 1917. As with many other European countries, it was commonly argued that cooperation between firms could promote rationalisation and technological advancement, and smooth out cyclical swings within specific branches of the economy (Rissanen 1978: 46). Cartels and cooperation, instead of cut-throat competition, was viewed by many as a 'more civilised' approach to capitalism.

Some associations and individuals were worried about the power of cartels and monopolies, however, and called attention to the need for some kind of legislation against them. One reason was an increasing concern about the prevalence, power and negative effects of big international cartels and trusts. Although, one has to be cautious with drawing any far reaching conclusions due to lack of systematic research, it appears that the Finnish economy experienced increasing cartelisation during the first decades of the twentieth century (Alfthan 1921; Salonen 1955: 60–63). For example, the left-wing consumer cooperative, *Kulutusosuuskuntien Keskusliitto* (KK), in their representatives' meeting of 1928 issued a proclamation in which they urged the state to implement some kind of control over trusts, cartels and monopolies in Finland. The KK was an ideological 'umbrella' for the so-called progressive (i.e. left-wing) cooperative movement, later usually called the E-movement (*E-liike*).[4] The KK's proclamation was based on a pamphlet published in 1927 by the director of the insurance company Kansa, Sulo Suortti; the company also being a part of the 'progressive' movement.

One reason for their interest in this issue was the discussions in Sweden and Norway. They carefully followed the debates occurring in their Nordic sister organisations *Kooperativa Förbundet* and *Norges Kooperative Landsförening*. Moreover, Norway had enacted their Trustlov legislation in 1926, which, naturally, they also noted (Chapters 2 and 8, this volume). Suortti even proposed a register similar to the Norwegian instrument (Suortti 1927: 129).

A more immediate reason for the interest in the increasing power of monopolies and big trusts, was that *Osuustukkukauppa OTK* – the wholesale cooperative within the E-liike – had made a deal to buy matches from the powerful Swedish match trust (the Kreuger imperium). People close to the KK debated if it was ethically correct that a progressive cooperative, aiming to promote the interest of the workers and 'ordinary people' was engaged in business transactions with an international trust (Aaltonen 1953: 472–473; Suortti 1927: 76–77).

The KK's initiatives and discussions did not lead to any concrete measures at the time, however. The prevailing ideology was freedom of contract and there was overall, a great reluctance to interfere in business life; impeding commerce was not on the agenda. No other groups showed any real interest in the issue. Moreover, the political influence of the KK was weak. Although the cooperative movement in the early twentieth-century in the Nordic countries grew into a powerful movement, the Finnish cooperative movement had been troubled by drawn-out internal conflicts since the early 1910s (Hilson 2010). Originally the farmers and the workers had organised a joint consumer cooperative *Suomen Osuuskauppojen Keskuskunta* (SOK), but growing political tension in the 1910s ended up dividing the cooperative into two fractions; the left-wing, progressive KK and the neutral (i.e. non-socialist) consumers' cooperative SOK. The political left was also fragmented and weakened after the Civil War in 1918 and this too affected the left-wing KK. As a result of these divisions and focus on internal politics, the policies on cartels and trusts remained inactive and highly tolerant until after the Second World War.

The need to implement some form of control on cartels and monopolies was taken up again by the KK in 1948. In 1942, the director of the KK, Jalmari Laakso had stated that concentration of the wholesale and retail trade sectors and the evolution of trade chains were particular problems in the Finnish economy (Laakso 1942: 38–42). Economic regulation during the war had promoted cartelisation and cooperation within many industries and in some branches practically forced cartelisation. Thus, after the war, the extent of monopolisation and cartelisation in Finnish business became a real concern. One of the leading persons in the KK, a social scientist by the name Antero Rinne, took up Suortti's ideas in new a publication (Rinne 1948). This resulted in a new proclamation at the association's representative meeting in 1948.[5] Cartels and monopolies were to be put under government control.

Balancing conflicting interests: the 'progressive' cooperative movement

The KK did not demand a total ban on cartels and restrictive practices, however, and in spite of a left-wing agenda, the association did not call for the overall socialisation of monopolies, either. In fact, even Suortti had admitted that monopolies and rings were not always harmful (Suortti 1927: 24, 84–86, 113). In line with much of the rhetoric of the interwar period, he argued they could even have some beneficial effects by, for example, providing secure employment opportunities and controlling prices. The same argument was repeated by Rinne, although cartels and monopolies had occasionally 'matured to such an extent that it was feasible to consider society taking them over' (Rinne 1948: 90). The KK representatives emphasised, however, that cartels and monopolies raised prices for consumers; something they considered problematic. Of special concern for them were the devastating effects of 'monopolistic rings and combinations' on small independent producers, as the powerful rings often forced their members to boycott small outside producers. Therefore, they argued, that the big rings and trusts and their activities should be put under state control; boycotts and unfair trading should be banned (ibid.: 116, 128). No suggestion for a total ban on restrictive practices was put forward, however. The best alternative was to put cartels and trusts under state control according to the 'Swedish system' (i.e. with anti-abuse legislation and a system of registration and publication).[6]

Why did the KK not promulgate non-tolerant legislation or even a total ban on restrictive practices; or perhaps even demand the socialisation of monopolies? On reason for their conciliatory views might have been simple; their director, Jalmari Laakso, was a member of the cartel committee (Table 6.1), which gave him influence over the preparatory work, but at the same time also tied his (and the KK's) hands.

Another, perhaps more important reason, was that the KK – and the cooperative movement in general – simultaneously represented several partly conflicting interests. The association represented urban wage-earners and their interests as consumers, but many of its members were also small-scale entrepreneurs and producer cooperatives. The introduction of far-reaching bans would also have affected the KK's own members. Their focus in the debate was primarily directed to measures against monopolies and big trusts. This also explains why the KK wanted the government to take measures against 'unfair competition' and delivery boycotts; issues which especially threatened small independent entrepreneurs and cooperatives.

Judging from their statement, it appears that the KK's main concern was the protection of the small independent cooperatives, rather than the consumers. The KK emphasised, however, that consumers and small cooperatives had common interests and the best protection for the consumers was to support small cooperatives (Rinne 1948: 105; Rinne 1942: 60–61). A law that would control the cartels and monopolies would therefore be beneficial also for workers and the consumers. Small cooperatives were – at least at the rhetorical level – the solution to big business capitalism. Nevertheless, during the legislative process the KK advocated a somewhat stricter legislation than many other organisations (see below).

One committee, one report ...

A few months after the proclamation by the KK, the government (then a left-wing agrarian coalition) appointed a cartel committee to consider the need for a law controlling cartels and, if they decided it was needed, to draw up its basic framework. The time was now right for progress. The political situation had changed. State regulation became more accepted. Moreover, there was growing support for left-wing parties, and especially some leading social democrats, like Väinö Tanner (one of the leading social democrats and a minister on several occasions) and Veikko Helle (long-time MP and several time minister of labour in the 1970s and early 1980s), were active in the progressive consumer movement. Tanner had in fact been director for the OTK early in his career and he followed international cartel debates. He was sentenced to prison after the end of the Second World War on Soviet insistence and during this imprisonment he translated the work of Wendell Bergen *Cartels, Challenge to a Free World* into Finnish. Thus, the KK had the ear of influential social democratic politicians.

The issue also received attention in other circles during these decades. Cartel legislation emerged in many countries, an issue which did not go unnoticed in Finland. The Swedish law of 1946 was particularly mentioned in debates. Finland often looked for policy models from Sweden. That country was considered more advanced in many respects, and, more importantly, the institutional framework was quite similar, meaning that Swedish reforms were usually considered suitable for the Finnish situation.

The work of the cartel committee turned out to be difficult and slow, however, and the report was not submitted until 1952. One reason was that the committee started from scratch and it thoroughly investigated legislation from other countries. But the committee also suffered from severe internal conflicts. There were in 1949 rumours, for example, that the chair wanted to dissolve the committee. The KK complained several times that the group was a form of 'obstruction committee'.[7] Jamari Laakso, KK's representative on the committee, became increasingly frustrated with its slow progress and in January 1950 he sent a letter to the chair in which he threatened to resign.[8] In the end, it was the chair of the committee who left.[9]

The change of the chair apparently solved the worst crises and after this the work resumed at a better pace. Finally in May 1952, the committee submitted its report, including the draft of a new law. The model was basically taken from the Swedish legislation (i.e. the committee suggested legislation based on controlling and monitoring restrictive agreements). The committee explicitly abstained, however, from proposing bans on any type of competition restrictions. Before any bans could be introduced, it was necessary to get more information about which types of competition restrictions there were in the market. The committee also considered that it was not their task to resolve which types of agreements (if any) were to be banned. They concluded, however, that the authorities were to be granted the right to remove agreements and clauses, which had 'harmful' effects.[10]

The committee proposed a system of registration. Restrictive agreements were to be brought to the attention of the authorities, so that they would know the types of agreements, their frequency and their content, and which entrepreneurs and associations were involved. Moreover, a register would also provide information which could be used as the basis of further legislative reforms. The register was to be public so that both consumers and competitors would receive information about restrictive agreements. Making the agreements public was designed to have a deterrent effect on the entrepreneurs and prevent abuse of the cartels' and monopolies' market power.[11] The publicity of the register was in fact one of the key issues in the debate during the legislative process, and one which the business lobby groups gave special attention (see further below).

... and many voices

The committee's report did not lead to any immediate legislation. One reason for the – again – slow progress was the extensive process of referral and consultations (*remiss*) which started after the report had been submitted; a process which was tied tightly to the committee system. The Ministry for Trade and Industry asked for comments and statements from several groups. From these statements the variation in attitudes towards the legislation became visible.

The KK proposed especially that resale price maintenance should be banned and emphasised this in their statements. Moreover, the association wanted the legislation to include a broader range of 'restrictive agreements'; for example control of dominant market position, mandatory notification on the entrepreneurs' and cartel organisations' own initiative, and that big monopolies and the banking and insurance industries should be included in the register.[12]

An on-going dilemma: the agrarian producers and the competition legislation

The agrarian producers' and forest owners' voices in social and economic issues were heard primarily through two associations, the Central Association of Agrarian Producers, the MTK (*Maataloustuottajien Keskusliitto*), which also had a representative in the committee (Table 6.1), and the Pellervo Society (*Pellervo Seura*) an organisation basically representing agrarian non-socialist cooperatives. The agrarian lobby was, like the consumer cooperatives, hostile in principle towards big business, monopolies and in particular, international trusts. In fact, the agrarian lobby organisations were to support stricter legislation in the post war period. At the time of the committee's report, however, the MTK strongly objected to its proposals. The MTK's representative Onni Koskikallio presented the only dissenting opinion to the 1952 committee.[13] His main objection was that the agrarian producers and even farming itself were viewed as entrepreneurial activities to be covered by the law. This was something Koskikallio could not accept. The MTK also strongly opposed the system of registration, arguing that no registration should be introduced before the market had been thoroughly studied.

The Pellervo Society was slightly more conciliatory. According to the Society, the proposed law was not a problem, as such agreements did not exist within the agrarian sector, because of 'its specific nature'. Individual farmers could not control and restrict output and/or prices, as 'they are at the mercy of nature and the weather' (Salonen 1955: 159). A similar argument had previously been presented by Suortti (1927: 139) and was now repeated by Koskikallio in his dissenting opinion.

Like the KK, the Pellervo Society represented several, partly conflicting, interests. In spite of their ideological schisms, the Pellervo (non-socialist) and the left-wing KK could often unite in efforts to protect small-scale cooperatives. On the other hand, many agrarian cooperatives were large; like the dairy cooperative Valio, which had an almost dominant position in the Finnish market. Thus Pellervo occasionally also represented big business interests. Unlike the KK, the conflicting interests in Pellervo were not so much between consumers and businesses, but between small and big cooperatives. Within the cooperative movement the mode of ownership was frequently used as an argument for them being less damaging than other monopolies and big businesses. As Suortti argued, cooperatives were owned by the consumers and a result they had common interests with the owners (Suortti 1927: 138).

No unified business interests

Within the business sector there was, not surprisingly, fairly strong opposition, or at least significant reluctance, towards any kind of legislation interfering with their activities. Freedom of contract was seen as overriding any consumer interest and the strong export cartels were considered to be working in the interests of the nation. Moreover, many representatives of the business lobby stated that it was odd that 'free competition' was to be promoted by state regulation, an argument later put forward in the parliamentary debate both by liberal and conservative MPs (Fellman 2010). Another common statement among business representatives was that no such law was needed as no such agreements existed in the Finnish market (Salonen 1955: 154).

The business interest groups were not completely unified in their views, however. The corporate sector was at the time divided into several different branch and trade associations and many groups did not belong to any of the big confederations. A consolidation of the various associations and generally increasing cooperation occurred during the war, but the private sector was represented by many voices. This is evident from the many associations that were asked by the cartel committee to give their opinions and from the many statements it received (Salonen 1955: 150–153).

The circumstances and experiences of different industry sectors and between small entrepreneurs and big business also varied. Associations representing small businesses within manufacturing and handicraft organisations were, in general, more positive towards some form of legislation. These businesses occasionally felt they had problems competing with big business and influential cartels; delivery and sales boycotts against those not belonging to a 'ring' were not an uncommon problem. In many ways, their situation was similar to those of the members of the KK. As the committee's proposal did not contain bans on any competition restrictions, small businesses viewed the report favourably and gave it their support.

On the other hand, the representatives of big business, especially the associations of the strong and influential export industries, strongly opposed any legislative measures. For instance, the Central Association of the Finnish Wood Processing Industry (*Suomen Puunjalostusteollisuuden Keskusliitto*), which represented a highly cartelised sector, argued that the effects of competition restrictions were nothing compared to the devastating effects of the state companies and state regulation. According to the Association, there were actually no 'real' cartels or monopolies in Finland, or at least many fewer than in the foreign market (Salonen 1955: 156). This was an interesting (and clearly self-serving) statement coming from this sector. Representing the main export industry, the Association was satisfied with one recommendation, however; the proposed legislation would not involve the export industry.

The Central Chamber of Commerce was also harsh in its statements against the proposal and provided a long list of its weaknesses. They admitted that cartels and monopolies occasionally could have serious adverse effects on society and in such cases the authorities should be able to prevent such activities. According to them, however, there were much more severe problems to be solved first. Like the

Association of Wood Processing Industry, the Chamber of Commerce argued that the strict post-war economic regulations, state companies and the high and devastating level of taxation were the real problems of the Finnish economy, not cartels and private monopolies. Until these other issues had been satisfactorily solved, there was no need to regulate private businesses and their agreements. Actually, they argued that the dreadful economic environment faced by the private companies was probably *the* single most important reason for co-operation between entrepreneurs and increasing cartelisation; it was the only way to survive in the 'appalling' Finnish economy. According to the Chamber, apart from the state monopolies – the real villains – there were only a few private monopolies, which were mostly 'natural' monopolies (Salonen 1955: 154–155).

The Federation of Industries joined the chorus, and although they admitted there were some cartels and agreements restraining competition in Finland, the Federation emphasised they were few and of little significance compared to the situation in large countries (Salonen 1955: 157).[14] The Federation also maintained that cartels and other forms of voluntary cooperation to restrict competition between firms were often beneficial for the consumers in the long run as they led to 'rationalisation and more ingenious solutions in production and distribution.'[15] Similar statements can be found in the committee report, perhaps put forward by the Federation of Industries' representative, Yrjö Fellman.[16]

The Federation was a little more appeasing than the Chamber of Commerce, however, and agreed that such legislation might be needed to do away with some restrictive practices. The Federation's position was more delicate, as their deputy director Yrjö Fellman had been a member of the committee and stood behind the proposal. They argued such a law was only needed in case 'free competition' was restored, probably meaning that all other kind of government regulations were abolished. The Federation was also pragmatic. They could probably see that a law was coming at some stage. In spite of their fundamental objections, the Federation stressed that, *in case* such a law was to be enacted, it should be of 'European' form (i.e. based on control and monitoring, and including a system of registration). Similarly, the Wholesalers' Association concluded that if there was a need for some kind of regulation, then a system based on notifications and registrations was the best alternative. It would, they argued, be best to tread carefully, however, and no bans should be introduced.

A question of secondary importance: the trade unions and the cartel law

Within the Finnish neo-corporatist environment during the post-war period, the unions gradually achieved a prominent position. Despite this, neither the Finnish Confederation of Trade Unions SAK (*Suomen Ammatiliittojen Keskusjärjestö–Finlands Fackföreningars Centralorganisation*), nor the Confederation of Intellectual Workers (*Henkisen Työn Keskusliitto – Unionen för Intellektuellt Arbete*) had any representatives on the cartel committee. It was seen an issue more for producers and consumers. The SAK's attitude to cartels and to the cartel law also appears to have been fairly cautious – even indifferent. On one occasion in

1949, the SAK had argued that the role of the state in controlling 'capitalist big business' which had achieved a dominant or monopoly position should be strengthened.[17] The same year, the SAK's meeting of delegates also declared that the state should break-up price fixing and promote competition between companies and entrepreneurs to lower consumer prices.[18] Despite this, no strong statements about the devastating effects of 'rings and trusts' and the need for a specific law to control them, similar to those presented by the KK, can be found. Nor did the SAK give any statements relating to the committee report. The only employee organisation giving a statement was the Confederation of Intellectual Workers, in which they stated that they supported the framework for such a law (Salonen 1955: 152).

Why this weak interest from the SAK? John Lapidus has argued that the Swedish social democratic party was quite permissive in its attitude towards cartels in the inter-war period as cartels were seen by some left-wing organisations as making socialisation easier (Lapidus 2013). Sulo Suortti had in fact depicted similar attitudes in Finland; cartels were considered by some socialists as a higher form of organisation 'which could easily be converted to serve the socialist system' (Suortti 1927: 86). This attitude might have influenced the SAK. According to Suortti big business and monopolies also often paid higher wages than smaller, independent firms (Suortti 1927: 105). It is likely that the SAK's members would be affected differently by any bans on cartels. The strong unions within the paper and metal industries were employed within highly cartelised sectors and these unions were probably more interested in preserving their members' (fairly well-paid) jobs, than putting limitations on these export cartels.

Perhaps the most important reason, however, was that it was not yet clear if labour market organisations were to be covered by the law. For example, the business lobby argued emphatically in their statements that trade unions were a form of cartel and should be covered by the law. The MTK argued that if agrarian producers' activities, not to mention farmers' and forest owners', were to be regulated by the law, so should the activities of unions. When it was later clear that the unions were exempted from the legislation, the SAK generally argued for stricter legislation.

A legislative proposal in 1954

This commentary round took some time, and in 1954 the KK again felt the need to press the government for concrete measures. The same year, a legislative proposal was submitted to parliament. The proposal basically followed the committee's outline, but included both a ban on bid rigging and on resale price maintenance. Resale price maintenance was banned during this period, or at least included for consideration to be banned, in several other countries (Chapter 7, this volume). The Finnish consumer associations' representatives had also considered it a particularly harmful form of restrictive practice (Annala 1953).

The proposed bans were not to the taste of the business interest associations, however. Although the Federation of Industry had been quite conciliatory before, the proposal met with fierce protests. The ban on vertical agreements especially made the Federation see red. The leading people argued that there was little knowledge of the frequency and harmfulness of these types of agreements. Thus, the market situation should be investigated first. This is an interesting claim, as according to a contemporary analyst, Viljo Annala, one of the few things that had been investigated previously was the occurrence of resale price maintenance (Annala 1953).

Not only was there little knowledge about the frequency of resale price maintenance but, according to the Federation:

> The fixing of sales prices for the next step in the chain was in most cases to the advantage of the consumers, as that put consumers in different parts of the country in similar and equal position. Otherwise prices would fluctuate depending on the transport conditions.[19]

The Federation also actively lobbied MPs and was, for example, in contact with the Minister for Trade and Industry. They reminded him that the committee had not wanted to ban any restrictions, especially not in resale price maintenance.[20]

The parliamentary process also took a long time. Extensive referral processes and consultations with specific interest groups and associations were carried out at every step. The legislative proposal remained an especially long time in the parliament's commerce committee (*talousvaliokunta, ekonomiutskottet*). In this part of the process, the ban on resale price maintenance was watered-down from the original. The lobbying of the Federation of Industry (and others) had perhaps born fruit.

The interest groups and the system of registration

One issues for debate during the parliamentary process was the system of registration. The committee had, as mentioned, looked towards Sweden and Norway for models and suggested a system of registration. The committee report, however, was quite vague on how the system would work in practice. The MTK strongly opposed a register, but that was consistent with their objection to a law altogether. Although objecting to a law of any form, most business interest associations claimed that if there was going to be a law, then a system of registration was the best alternative. For example, the Central Chamber of Commerce believed that the registration and publication of competition restrictions could actually be a quite effective tool. The corporate sector feared a system of collecting information about their agreements and then making them public, as this would reveal crucial trade secrets and other confidential information.

Thus, the Chamber of Commerce's representatives strongly urged the authorities not to collect more than the absolute minimum information and then only the clauses of the agreements rather than documents should be published. Detailed information was only to be for the authorities' use (Salonen 1955: 154–155).[21] The Federation of Industries put forward similar arguments; only the actual agreements and the compiled report were to be made public. Moreover, they suggested that the parties to an agreement should have the right to inspect and accept the reports compiled by the authorities, before they were made public.[22] The Wholesalers' Associations suggested that the information should not be made public, at least not until the authorities had gained more experience from the system of registration. The association did not demand full secrecy, but suggested that reports should only be on display in the cartel authorities' offices, and accessible only on demand.[23]

On these issues, the demands of the business lobby appear to have been heeded. When the legislation was presented to parliament, the business lobby's worst fears had disappeared. In 1957, the Federation of Industries could reassure their members that their business secrets would not be handed over to the authorities, nor were issues other than restrictive clauses and a summary of the agreement to be made public.[24]

The other issue raised by the business lobby was the plan for compulsory notification. The question was whether every entrepreneur must report their agreements or if some smaller ones would be excluded, and whether notification had to be carried out on their own initiative or only on request from the authorities. The committee had proposed that all agreements should be notified on the instigation of the entrepreneurs, cartels and trade associations themselves. This also received support from, for example, the KK. The business lobby opposed this, but primarily for pragmatic reasons. It would, they argued, be impossible to get their members informed about the process and to respond to such a regulation with such short notice. This proposal also collapsed because of its own impracticality – it was generally recognised that the authorities would have been flooded with notifications. A similar 'backlog' problem would occur as in the EEC registration system (Chapter 4, this volume).

Finally a law in 1957

Finally, in 1957, the 'cartel law' was passed. This law was based on the abuse and publicity principles as the committee had suggested. Only one form of restrictive practice, bid rigging, was declared illegal. During the parliamentary process the ban on resale price maintenance had been removed, although the law declared that resale price maintenance agreements could be compulsorily removed, in cases where they were considered to have harmful effects.

In principal the law covered all businesses, both manufacturing and trade and services. In 1964 the banking and financial institutes were excluded from the competition legislation as they had their own legislative framework. Agreements concerning the labour market were made exempt from the law. The legislation covered only agreements in the domestic market. Thus the strong exports cartels were not required to report their agreements, unless they had effect on the domestic market as well. The 1957 law did not exempt agrarian producers either. The majority of the parliament supported the view that agrarian production was to be considered an entrepreneurial activity (Finnish: *elinkeinoharjoittaja*; Swedish: *näringsidkare*). This did not please the agrarian lobby of course, and was an issue they raised when the legislation was later renewed. In fact the position of the agrarian producer cooperatives was on the agenda every time amendments to the legislation were considered.

A system of registration was introduced. The entrepreneurs and cartel associations on request from the government office were to notify the authorities of their agreements. The authority was to investigate the agreements and if it considered them to be restrictive as defined by the law, include them in the register. The main contents of the agreements were to be made public. A public register would increase transparency; consumers and competitors would know what kinds of agreements had been signed, but it was also believed that this would have a deterrent effect and encourage firms to abstain from exploiting a dominant market position. The openness of the register was also linked to the principle of public access to official records – a principle strongly associated with Nordic public bureaucracy (Chapter 8, this volume). The Finnish law on openness of government records had been initiated in 1951, but the Swedish legal tradition was strong (Mäenpää 2008: 2).

Apart from minor details, the Finnish law was a copy of the 1946 Swedish Act on Probation on Restrictive Business Practices (Chapter 12, this volume). The Swedish law, however, had already been revised in 1953. The government proposal was also quite similar to the 1953 Swedish law, but in the end the Finnish Parliament opted for the more 'cautious' version exemplified by the 1946 law (Rissanen 1978: 35–45). One reason was that there was unanimous agreement that the authorities needed more information about existing cartel agreements and their effects before a stricter, more prohibitive legislation could be implemented. Another reason appears to have been the strong lobbying of the business organisations during the parliamentary process.

The fairly lenient legislation was also a deliberate decision not to alarm the corporate sector. The deputy director of the Finnish competition authorities Martti Virtanen emphasised there was an explicit fear among the authorities that the cartels would otherwise go underground; something which was often argued when outright prohibition was discussed.[25]

With the law, a new authority, the Cartel Bureau (*Kartellivirasto – Kartellbyrån*), was established within the National Board of Patents and Registration. The Cartel Bureau was to administer the notifications and registrations and to carry out branch investigations. This bureau was small – at the outset only five employees – and suffered from high employee turnover. An Advisory Board for Cartel Issues (*Kartelliasiain neuvottelukunta*) was also formed with members from various interest groups, which was to give advice on matters of principle concerning restrictions of competition in Finnish society.

To make the content of the agreements public, a periodical *Kartellirekisteri – Kartellregistret* similar to the publication in Sweden was established (Chapter 12, this volume). The first entry into the register was made in 1959. The number of agreements reported – and registered – remained low, however (see Table 6.2). In the first year, a total of 97 agreements were registered and by the beginning of 1964, fewer than 400 cases had been entered into the register. The Cartel Bureau had only a handful of employees and at regular intervals they complained that they did not have enough resources to carry out their tasks. The real reason for the low number of registered agreements was that entrepreneurs and cartel associations were slow in reporting. The authorities did send out numerous inquiries and reminders. For instance, by 1962, more than 9700 inquiries had been sent out, which resulted in around only 240 registrations. A further 115 branch investigations had also been under-taken (Table 6.2).[26] According to the authorities there were two reasons for the slowness in reporting. First, there were no sanctions for non-compliance. Second, many within the corporate sector did not understand the legislation. The law was vague in formulation and occasionally difficult to interpret even for the authorities, not to mention the public. Also the deterrent effect of making anti-competitive agreements public appeared to have been negligible (Fellman 2010).

The largest problem with the legislation was, however, that the authorities had no instrument with which to intervene in cases where an agreement was suspected of having harmful effects.[27] In fact, during the first years of the legislation, no case suspected of being harmful to the public was brought forward; the authorities could only register, carry out branch investigations and give statements. Thus, the legislation was soon considered inefficient both from the perspective of preventing possible harmful effects and from the perspective of controlling and monitoring the market situation. Voices calling for more strict legislation began to be raised.

A new law in 1964

In 1962 measures to revise the legislation were started. This time the process was fast; by 1964 a new statute, the 'Law to Promote Economic Competition', had replaced the existing law. One reason for this speed was that the task was given to

Table 6.2 Registrations, inquiries and investigations by the Cartel Bureau/Bureau for Freedom of Commerce, 1958–1966.

	Information and investigations*			*Requests for additional information*	*Registrations*		
Year	Investigations	Inquiries	Reminders		New	Changed	Abolished
1958	13	876	–	200	–	–	–
1959	34	1985	194	217	97	–	–
1960	45	2085	399	250	56	–	1
1961	76	2597	590	291	80	1	2
1962	67	1996	141	206	77	–	5
1963	103	2190	505	105	56	2	7
1964	74	1805	22	189	52	–	6
1965	74	2052	161	233	38	60	36
1966	79	1957	267	242	44	80	53

Note: * Includes also previously started, not yet concluded investigations.
Source: 'Yhteenveto Elinkeinovapausvirastossa suoritetuista tutkimuksista 1967' (Archive of the National Board of Trade and Consumer Interests).

a committee already working on other issues. The task was also clearer; to come to grips with the worst problems. There was an almost unanimous view that there were problems with the registration process and a lack of instruments to intervene against agreements considered harmful.

The KK was, not surprisingly, urging for a stricter law and the association especially, continued to push for a ban on boycotts. They also wanted the system of registration to be reformed. The KK emphasised that the registration system had brought restrictive agreements to the public's attention and shown that cartel organisations were much more common than previously had been known. The law had also revealed that many of these restrictions had taken forms that had dubious effects on consumers. The system of registration had not been successful in bringing any but a small number of agreements to the public's attention, however. Therefore notification had to become mandatory. Moreover, the KK also suggested agreements not in the register should be declared null and void.[28]

The agrarian lobby, with the MTK in the lead, again raised the issue that agrarian producers should be exempted from the legislation, especially as the labour unions were not covered by the law. The Pellervo Society, in turn, continued to emphasise that small cooperatives could not be seen as business activities in the same way as big business and that small cooperatives were in fact, a real balancing factor against the big monopolies (Isopuro 1962). The idea that cooperatives could not form cartels overall was also repeated (H. R. 1968). To strengthen their point, the leaders in the Society invited a Swedish 'expert on Finnish affairs', Torsten Odhe, to write an article in their journal, in which arguments why the agricultural cooperatives should be exempted from the law were presented (Ohde 1961). The strong demands from the agrarian producers has to be seen against the sensitive balancing between the wage-worker's and the agrarian populations' interests during the decades after the war. The agrarian lobby felt that it was unfair that agrarian cooperatives were covered by the law, while the trade unions and other labour market organisations were not.

This new committee took a different stance to the old cartel committee on what should be covered by the legislation. It stated that it was inclined to exclude farming, fishing and reindeer herding from the legislation, but that agrarian cooperatives were indeed an entrepreneurial activity and that the largest cooperatives even fulfilled all the characteristics of big business.[29] In the end, primary production (i.e. farming and fishing) was left outside the legislation, but the processing, sales and marketing of agrarian products, irrespective of ownership form, was covered by the law. This continued to be the case until 1988, despite agrarian producer cooperatives' continual complaints.

This time the business lobby paid less attention to the law, as long as no far-reaching new bans were to be introduced. For example, the Federation of Industries repeated the standard line that further bans on cooperation and cartel agreements should be avoided.[30] The trade unions, on the other hand, paid more attention to the legislation and the SAK provided both an official statement and mentioned the issues in other venues and fora. At the SAK's assembly of representatives in 1961, a declaration in support of the renewal of cartel legislation was made.[31] In their formal response to the legislative proposal, the SAK supported both reforming the law and pursuing more active measures, as otherwise the new law would continue 'to remain a form of "pilot" legislation'. The planned ban on resale price maintenance was also welcomed by the SAK. Like the KK, the confederation urged that notification of agreements become mandatory.[32]

In spite of this growing interest in the competition law, the system of price control and price monitoring was an issue of greater priority for the SAK.[33] During these decades, a significant division in the Finnish bargaining system was between wage-workers' interests and agrarian interests. This division influenced many social-political and economic policies and was a source of occasional political tension. Wage bargaining was, to a large extent, a balancing act between the unions' demands for higher wages and the agrarian interest groups' demands for higher food prices.[34] On the question of price control, the SAK and the Confederation of Employers (STK) were occasionally even allies in their pleadings to the government.[35] The fact that the SAK and the STK could find common ground on price controls might also explain why the SAK was cautious about competition policy during this period. Later the SAK developed a stronger view on competition legislation. For example, when a new law was planned in the early 1980s, the SAK sought a total ban on both horisontal price and quota agreements.[36]

A new statute was enacted in 1964, with the name, Act on the Promotion of Economic Competition (*Laki taloudellisen kilpailun edistämisestä L 1964/1*). Now resale price maintenance (vertical price-fixing) became conditionally banned (i.e. such agreements were illegal, provided it was not explicitly stated by the firms that their recommended price could be undercut (Rissanen 1978: 39). Under the new law it became mandatory for formal trade associations or cartels to notify their agreements on their own initiative. Firms and entrepreneurs who had independently signed restrictive agreements still had to report their agreements only on request. Non-compliance with the notification requirement could result in fines. The KK was, however, disappointed that again, no ban on boycotts was introduced.

In conjunction with the revised law, the Cartel Bureau became the Bureau for Freedom of Commerce (*Elinkeinovapausvirasto – Näringsfrihetsverket*), with a larger number of employees. As can be seen from Table 6.2, the number of registrations gradually increased after 1964, but no dramatic shift occurred. Although it had become mandatory for associations to report their agreements on their own initiative, most of the notifications were still done only on the request of the authorities. For example in 1968, 48 new agreements were added to the register, and none on them were done on the cartels' or associations' own initiative. The previous year, five notifications had been instigated by association members.[37]

Perhaps the most important reform was that a negotiation procedure was introduced. In cases where an agreement was suspected to have harmful effects, the cartel members or signatories of an agreement could be called into negotiations with the authorities with the intent to remove clauses or the whole agreement. A Council for Freedom of Commerce (*Elinkeinovapausneuvosto – Näringsfrihetsrådet*) was also established, which consisted of seven members from various interest organisations and was, like its predecessor the Advisory Board, to provide statements on issues which were considered of 'public interest' and/or matters of principle. The Council's main task, however, was to initiate and conduct negotiations, although it had no jurisdictional power. If negotiations were unsuccessful, the Council could only transfer the issue to the Government, which could make the agreement invalid or remove a specific clause for a period of one year (later altogether). During the Council's first two years, no cases were brought to full negotiations.[38]

The legislative development in 1970s and 1980s

In 1973 the legislation was again renewed, when among other things, resale price maintenance became totally prohibited and horizontal price agreements between individual entrepreneurs were to be compulsorily reported on the participants' own initiative. Sanctions for non-compliance with notification requirements became harsher. The most important reform, however, was the change in the organisation of the competition authorities; namely the establishment of a National Board of Trade and Consumer Interests (*Elinkeinohallitus – Näringsstyrelsen*). The goal was to better synchronise competition policy with price regulation, in order to, among other things, fight inflationary pressures.[39] In conjunction with this reform, a Competition Ombudsman (*Kilpailuasiamies – Konkurrensombudsman*), similar to the Swedish Ombudsman of Freedom of Commerce was established, while a new Competition Council (*Kilpailuneuvosto – Konkurrensråd*) replaced the Council for Freedom of Commerce.

In the early 1980s the competition legislation came up for renewal again, but this time the preparatory work only led to some minor amendments of the existing law. The final legislative reforms occurred in 1988, shortly before Finland adopted legislation non-tolerant of cartels in 1992. The legislation then became stricter in every respect. Controls over firms with dominant market position were introduced and the competition authorities were also granted the right to require information concerning mergers and acquisition whenever the company had, or could achieve, a dominant market position. Stemming from the legislative reform of 1988 a new administrative body was instigated, the Finnish Competition Authority (FCA) (Purasjoki and Jokinen 2001). The Competition Council's jurisdiction was also enlarged. The legislation was, however, still based on the same principles as before (preventing abuse, control, publicity and negotiation). The registration procedures were continued, but after 1988 the number of new registrations started to decline (Hyytinen and Toivanen 2010). The interest groups' influence in the committees declined to some extent, but they were still well represented in all the committees and administrative bodies dealing with competition policy. The authorities, and especially the Competition Ombudsman, however, strongly argued for more active promotion of competition and still stricter legislation.

The register as a tool for policy implementation

The Finnish register was first and foremost a tool for the authorities to obtain information on the types of agreements in the market. This information could then be used when considering stronger measures to combat anti-competitive behaviour. The information in the register was also to provide the public (consumers and competitors) insight into various agreements. It was believed that by making agreements public, firms and cartels would engage in self-restraint and avoid abusing their market power. After the negotiation procedure was introduced, material in the register was also used when agreements were being considered to be called in for the negotiations. Moreover, information in the cartel register, together with material from price surveillance, was intended as primary material for the authorities in economic policy making.[40] The low number of cases in the register diminished the role of the register as a policy tool.

The system of registration followed quite a complex procedure. First, the authorities made initial investigations concerning individual firms, specific branches or trade associations. If they suspected that there was an agreement which should be included in the register, they sent out an inquiry and a standard form. As in Sweden, this appears to have been done in a fairly random manner. The authorities primarily followed economic journals and newspapers to learn about existing agreements, or it came to the authorities' knowledge by anecdotal evidence that agreements to restrict competition existed within one sector. As a result, requests were usually sent out simultaneously to several firms and/or associations within the same sector. This resulted in agreements within certain industries being registered in clusters and several agreements from within the same industry are often found in the register with consecutive numbers (Fellman and Sandberg 2015).

On receipt of an inquiry, the businesses or cartel organisation were to notify (report) their agreements to the authorities by filling in the form and submitting the requested documents. When the authorities had received the documents, they began an investigation into whether the agreement fulfilled the criteria of a restrictive agreement (or 'restraint of competition' which was the direct wording of the law) and if it was to be registered or not. If it was considered a restrictive agreement covered by the legislation, the authorities wrote an account (*selostus – redogörelse*) about the content of the agreement. The signatories of the agreement then had the right to inspect this account and when they had approved the content and the wording, the agreement was given a case number and included in the register. After that, the account and the main clauses of the agreement were published.

As already described the authorities experienced extensive problems with non-compliance. The committee report from 1962 emphasised that new legislation was needed to get more cases into the register. This was important for acquiring deeper insight into restrictive agreements.[41] This was an issue of on-going concern during the whole period, however. The issue was again on the agenda prior to the 1973 legislation, when the competition authorities strongly urged that notification be made mandatory for all entrepreneurs and that the sanctions for non-compliance should be more severe. It was also considered unfair that different agreements and businesses were treated in differently.[42] The authorities were well aware, even until the 1980s, that non-compliance with the notification requirement was considerable. A committee giving its report in 1982 stated that it was evident that 'only a minority of the competition restrictions existing in the market were to be found in the register'.[43] The authorities recognised that non-compliance was not always the result of deliberate violation of the law, but may be because the 'law was not well-known among the entrepreneurs'.[44] From the start, the authorities could see that if they themselves had problems in interpreting the goals of the legislation, individual business owners were unlikely to understand what was meant by 'competition restrictions' and what was to be notified and what was not.[45] In support of this interpretation, businesses were nearly as slow to report changes in their agreements and the demise of an agreement as new agreements. The Dutch encountered similar issues (Chapter 13, this volume).

As a result of the low number of cases in the register, the goal of getting more information, for the authorities and to the public, was not fulfilled. Nor did the publicity principle work as a deterrent. The circulation of the cartel periodical was miniscule and ordinary newspapers revealed little interest in reporting the new registrations the authorities published.[46] In the 1970s the periodical was changed into a journal, with the name *Hinnat ja Kilpailu* ('Price and Competition'), which also published articles of more general interest. This enlarged its circulation, but even in 1982 few individuals took an interest in the information on the register.[47]

An additional problem with the registration system was that, according to the authorities, the business sector had started to frame their agreements in such a way as to avoid notification requirements.[48] The fear of agreements 'going underground' had apparently been partially realised.

Concluding remarks

It is safe to say that one reason behind the tolerant legislation and the system of registration was the influence of strong business interest groups. The corporate sector and business lobbies were well represented in the first committees, which created the basic model. They were also active in the public debate, making statements and exercising influence on the parliamentary process. Many of these interest groups had direct contact with specific parties. In the evolving neo-corporate model such influence was not only enabled, but often promoted. One of the aims of the neo-corporate model was to increase various parties' trust in the system, and thus improve its operation (Rothstein 1992). This was one aim of allowing interest groups to influence competition policy implementation. Another goal was transparency. An open and transparent system would make the super-vision of the agreements and cartel behaviour easier, especially as authorities feared that the cartels would otherwise go underground.

The register, in spite of its weaknesses, was initially based on good intentions. The idea to investigate and study businesses in order to receive more information about their agreements, and to be able to monitor and control restrictive agreements and cartel behaviour was in principle a good idea. The information that was gathered, especially combined with information from the price monitoring authorities, was also thought to become useful for policy makers in the coordination of economic policy; the authorities needed statistical data about prices, quotas, production etc. from different sectors to assist in their policy decisions. In practice the system was less successful, however. On the other hand, as in Australia the system and the legislation brought the public's attention to these issues, and showed that restrictive practices were by no means unproblematic (Chapter 9, this volume). Although non-compliance was a severe problem as long as the register existed, it enabled information for the authorities to make branch investigations. Some important information was thus received. As a tool for pushing forward decartelisation, however, it was not useful.

Compared to other countries, the Finnish system of registration seems to have been one of the least successful in curbing restrictive practices. Non-compliance was common, and the authorities' potential - and perhaps also their willingness - to interfere was scarce (Fellman and Sandberg 2015). One common explanation has been that collaboration and collusion was a 'habit of the country'. Many other countries, however, also considered themselves 'cartel paradises' (Chapter 5, this volume). Another reason might have been the significant influence of interest groups in implementing the legislation; there was always somebody obstructing more active measures and the result was a weak compromise. On the other hand, some of the problem seems to have stemmed from the 'architecture' of the registration process itself, although the authorities did the best they could.

Notes

1. See also Kilpailukomitean mietintö (KM) 1991:15, Helsinki, 1991.
2. Only the chair and the secretary were civil servants and experts. Ad hoc committees at the time usually had interest representatives, and increasingly so in the 1960s and 1970s. Despite this according to one investigation interest groups representatives exceeded 50 per cent of the members in less than 4 per cent of the *ad hoc* committees in the mid-1960s making the cartel committee an extreme case (Helander 1979).
3. The English name of the law comes from the one used by OECD (OECD 1975, vol. III: Finland).
4. The letter 'E' came from the word *edistyksellinen*, which means 'progressive' in Finnish.
5. KK 1948, 'Monopolistiset yhtymät kuluttajien vaarana'. *Vuosikirja 1948*, Kuluttajaosuuskuntien Keskusliitto, Helsinki: 470–473.
6. Ibid.: 459, 466, 470–473.
7. 'Kulutusosuuskuntien Keskusliitto (KK) Pöytäkirja 8.2.1950.' Kulutusosuuskuntien Keskusliitto archive, The People's Archive.
8. 'Kirje Jalmari Laakso-Arvo Sipilä.31.1.1950. Liite. KK Pöytäkirja 8.2.1950', Kulutusosuuskuntien Keskusliitto archive, The People's Archive.
9. 'Kirje Sipilä/kartellikomitean jäsenille 3.2.1950. Liite 3. KK Pöytäkirja 8.2.1950', Kulutusosuuskuntien Keskusliitto archive, The People's Archive.
10. Kartellikomitean mietintö B 1952:33 (KM B 1952:33) Helsinki: 34.
11. KM B 1952:33: 19.
12. KK 1954, 'Määrähinnat kuluttajan rasituksena'. *Vuosikirja,* Kulutusosuuskuntien Keskusliitto, Helsinki: 312.
13. 'Liite 1. Eriävä mielipide', KM B 1952:33,
14. Suomen Teollisuusliitto 1952, 'Kartellilainsäädäntö', *Teollisuusliiton Tiedonantoja*, no. 2: 17; Suomen Teollisuusliitto, 'Lausunto 12.11.1957', Finnish Federation of Industries archive, ELKA Central Archive for Finnish Business Records.

Creating the 1957 cartel law 109

15 'Muita taloudellisia ja teollisuuskysymyksiä', *Suomen Teollisuusliiton vuosikertomus 1952*: 4; also 'Lausunto 15.10 1952', Suomen Teollisuusliitto, Finnish Federation of Industries archive, ELKA Central Archive for Finnish Business Records.
16 KM B 1952:33: 18.
17 SAK 1949, *Mitä SAK nyt tahtoo? SAK viidennen edustajakokouksen julkilausuma sodanjälkeisestä kehityksestä ja päätöslauselma lähiaikojen toimintaohjelmista*, Kustannusosakeyhtiö Yhteistyö, Helsinki: 8.
18 SAK 1949 (1951), 'Pöytäkirja Suomen Ammattiyhdistysten Keskusliitto SAK r.y.n Valtuuston ylimääräisestä kokouksesta 19. joulukuuta 1949. Liite n:o 3', *SAK Vuosikirja 1949*, SAK, Helsinki: 98.
19 Suomen Teollisuusliitto 1952, 'Kartellilainsäädäntö', *Teollisuusliiton Tiedonantoja*, no. 2: 18.
20 'Yrjö Fellman kirje jäsenille 30.8.1954', Finnish Federation of Industries archive, ELKA Central Archive for Finnish Business Records.
21 See also KM B 1952:33: 28.
22 'Lausunto 12.11.1957', Suomen Teollisuusliitto, Finnish Federation of Industries archive, ELKA Central Archive for Finnish Business Records.
23 'Kartellikomitean mietintö. Suomen Tukkukauppiaiden Liiton lausunto', *Kauppalehti* 21, October 1952.
24 Suomen Teollisuusliitto 1957, *Tiedonantoja* no.7: 18.
25 M. Virtanen, personal communication, 8 April 2010.
26 See also *Ehdotus laiksi taloudellisen kilpailun rajoitusten valvonnasta perusteluineen* 1962:4 (KM 1962:4): 20.
27 KM 1962:4: 21.
28 'Johtokunnan pöytäkirja 8.2.1961'; 'Johtokunnan pöytäkirja 4.4.1962'. KKn pöytäkirjat. Kulutusosuuskuntien Keskusliitto archive, The People's archive.
29 KM 1962:4: 9.
30 Somen Teollisuusliitto 1964, 'Lagen om främjande av konkurrens.' *Teollisuusliitto Tiedottaa*, no. 1: 16.
31 SAK 1962, *SAK Vuosikirja*, Helsinki: 25.
32 SAK 1962, 'Lausunto Kauppa- ja teollisuusministeriön kauppaosastolle. Asia: Hallituksen ehdotus laiksi taloudellisten kilpailunrajoitusten valvonnasta', *SAK Lausuntoja*, SAK archive, The People's archive.
33 For example, SAK 1964 (1963), *SAK Vuosikirja 1963*, Helsinki: 51.
34 SAK 1971, 'Pöytäkirjaa SAK edustajainkokous 29.6–2.7.1971', *SAK Pöytäkirjat*, SAK archive, The Peoples' archive.
35 SAK 1962 (1963), 'Hintapolitiikka', *SAK Vuosikirja 1962*, Helsinki: 24.
36 'SAK Lausunto kilpailutoimikunnan mietinnöstä 3.2.1983'; 'SAK Lausunto hallituksen esityksestä Eduskunnalle laiksi taloudellisen kilpailun edistämisestä annetun lain muuttamisesta. 4.10.1984', *SAK Lausunnot*, SAK archive, The People's archive.
37 'Kertomus Elinkeinovapausviraston ja -neuvoston toiminnasta v. 1968', *Kilpailunvapauslehti*, 1969, no.1: 12–13.
38 'Elinkeinovapausviraston toimintakertomus vuodelta 1966': 4. Elinkeinohallitus, Archive of the National Board for Trade and Consumer Interest.
39 Hinta- ja kilpailukomitean mietintö B 1972: 52 (KM B 1972:52), Helsinki: 53.
40 'Hinta ja kilpailuvalvonnan tavoitteet. Elinkeinohallitus 25.5.1984', Elinkeinohallitus, Archive of the National Board for Trade and Consumer Interest.
41 KM 1962:4: 21.
42 KM B 1972:52: 82; 'Elinkeinovapausviraston vuosikertomus 1964 Kauppa- ja

teollisuusministeriölle', Elinkeinohallitus, Archive of the National Board for Trade and Consumer Interest.
43 Kilpailutoimikunnan mietintö 1982:49 (KM 1982:49), Helsinki: 64.
44 Ibid.: 65.
45 'Kartelliviraston lausunto Kauppa- ja teollisuusministeriölle12.2.1965', Elinkeinohallitus, Archive of the National Board for Trade and Consumer Interest.
46 KM 1962:4: 21.
47 KM 1982:49: 65.
48 'Patentti-ja rekisterihallituksen kartelliosaston (Kartelliviraston) toimintakertomus vuodelta 1963', Elinkeinohallitus, Archive of the National Board for Trade and Consumer Interest.

Part II
Registers in different countries

7 Cartel registers around the world

Martin Shanahan and Susanna Fellman

Introduction

This chapter provides a comparative overview of some of the most well-known cartel registers that existed in the twentieth century.[1] These registers had a common purpose; to record information about firms' involved with restrictive trade agreements and the main elements of these arrangements. Outside of this, however, they varied significantly in their coverage, operation, methodology, timing, transparency and intended use across the countries that adopted this form of competition regulation.

While it appears that the first use of a register occurred in Norway in 1920, it was really in the 1950s and 1960s that this form of regulation was most widely used across the world. By the 1980s and 1990s, and in some cases much earlier than this, registration as a form of information gathering and identification had fallen from favour. These forms of regulation were usually replaced by legislation that prohibited outright most of the forms of restrictive trade practices that had previously simply been monitored.

The registers recorded agreements that firms had organised between themselves, in order to restrict competition and control market forces. The many ways in which this was done make an exhaustive list impossible, but the most important forms of restrictive agreements included: cartel arrangements; resale price maintenance, vertical and horizontal agreements that restricted prices, quantities or markets, bid rigging (of tenders), collusion of many forms, full line forcing (which requires retailers to stock an entire line of goods, not just a selection); exclusive dealing or selling, refusal to deal with some firms/competitors; boycotting of competitors, among other things.[2] Some registers recorded institutional structures, as well as behaviour (i.e. where mergers or acquisitions had reduced competition; where one firm dominated the market; where trade associations were involved; and occasionally when foreign ownership was involved). Evidence of restrictive practices was also critical, so in some countries, while agreements in writing had to be registered, non-written agreements were automatically illegal (Germany, Austria); in others, such as the UK, written or oral agreements, legally enforceable or not, were subject to registration (Borrie 1994: 358).

Where registers were designed to capture only those agreements involving 'abuse' of consumers or competitors, the range of registrants was obviously different from registers designed to record 'prohibited' agreements and the firms involved. As will become clear from the examples that follow, there is also significant variation in the registers as a result of the variety of exemptions, interpretations and the administrative vigour with which they were constructed. For researchers this can be particularly frustrating, as even within a single country, what was legislated against, and what was actually recorded, may vary depending on the administrators involved.

For example, administrators were often given important powers of interpretation and discretion. In most countries, agreements were evaluated by competition authorities before they were recorded (Finland, Sweden and Australia). The definition of what constituted 'restrictive business practices' was often vague and could be interpreted either narrowly or broadly by the administrative authorities. In the UK a court interpretation was required (Edwards 1967: 54; Symeonidis 2002). In many situations the determinations turned on whether the agreements had 'harmful effects' or were 'against the public interest'; phrases both important and vague. The legislation seldom clearly defined what could be considered 'abuse' and what 'public interest' meant.[3] As the authorities themselves occasionally struggled with this, it was often difficult for firms to know what they had to do, or whether their agreements were 'restrictive' under the Act. This could lead to both confusion and the opportunity for non-registration.

The actual recorded content of the registers varied too. Some jurisdictions required the full text of the written agreements, and full terms of unwritten agreements be recorded, (and in some cases even how the agreements came into existence, who was not in the agreements, penalties for non-cooperation etc.). Such elements were required in Denmark, Finland, Norway and Sweden, and Austria, for example.[4] Other countries required little information. Some registers were open to the public (and even published in gazettes) while in other countries their contents and the firms involved were kept secret.[5]

This chapter presents a summary of what we know about the countries and their use of registers as a regulatory device in the twentieth century. It reveals many of the contexts in which the registers were created, the goals and targets of these registers, how they were maintained, the main principles identifying what was to be registered, and how they were used by the authorities. We also examine the longevity of the registers and the circumstances of their demise.

Origins and timing of the registers

The first register of non-competitive market behaviour appears to have been in Norway, which in 1920 introduced temporary legislation, which required registration of restrictive business practices (Chapters 2 and 8, this volume). The Norwegian Act on the Control of Restraints of Competition and Price Abuse of 1926, (Trust Act), is commonly characterised as Europe's first 'real' competition law (Gerber 1998: 156). Although the Trust Act came after the 1923 German Decree against the Abuse of Economic Power Position, the 1920 Norwegian legislation marks a clear change in approach, and when combined with the 1926 developments initiated the first 'modern' European competition legislation and the use of a restrictive business practices register (Espeli 2002).[6]

In 1931 the Inter-Parliamentary Union (IPU), an international organisation of parliaments established to promote democracy and dialogue, met in London. The delegates discussed the problem of cartels, ultimately recommending that individual countries should introduce a system of registration and thus control cartels through publicity (Boje and Kallestrup 2004: 102; McGowan 2010: 64). This was noted in a number of countries. For example, Denmark took heed, and in 1937 introduced a notification system which allowed the control authorities to investigate individual markets. According to Boje and Kallestrup (2004: 125–128), however, it was not until 1955 that the system began to control firm behaviour effectively. The Danish registration statues were directly inspired by their Norwegian neighbours.

Bulgaria, Czechoslovakia, Hungary, Latvia, Poland and Yugoslavia also introduced registers before the Second World War. All these countries established registration procedures, and a cartel court or commission. With the abolition of the market economy in these countries after the Second World War, the register and governing systems disappeared (Timberg 1953; Edwards 1967). To our knowledge only the Danish and Norwegian systems survived the war.[7] Information about regulations in the Eastern European countries is sketchy. The Hungarian legislation, for example, implemented in 1931, was heavily influenced by the 1930 German legislation and the Norwegian register. According to Article 2 of the law, as long as one party to an agreement was of Hungarian domicile both national and international agreements had to be registered (Tschierschky 1932). The Czechoslovakian register was reputed to be voluminous (Teichova 1974).

The prevailing opinion in the interwar period considered restrictive practices could have positive effects. With the benefit of hindsight, cartel registers were a first step towards an ultimately more restrictive view on anti-competitive behaviour, even in countries where such restrictive business practices had not previously been seen as detrimental to economic efficiency or consumers.

In the post-war decades when the economic environment had changed and legislation to curb restrictive business practices and cartels were introduced, registers emerged in an array of counties. Although the war had weakened international cartels, a new attitude had also evolved; government regulation in the public interest was preferred to self-regulation. The American view on anti-trust also started to penetrate the European tradition (McGowan 2010: 84ff.; Maclachan and Shaw 1967: 117–119). Increasingly governments began to consider that the restrictive practices of cartels and trusts had seriously negative effects on consumers and the economy. Such activities were seen to inhibit the free flow of trade and economic integration as they could block market entry and hamper growth. The inter-war examples of the German cartels and Japanese *Zaibatsu* were also considered especially devastating (Hoermann and Mavroidis 2003).

Gradually supranational arrangements, like the European Coal and Steel Community (ECSC), the European Economic Community (EEC) and the OECD began to require countries pay attention to local firms' anti-competitive behaviour.

For example, the EEC policies aimed to control and restrict those cartels and restrictive practices that directly affected the free flow of goods and services within the Community (Chapter 4, this volume). The OECD collected information about existing competition legislation in member countries and gave occasional recommendations.

In Germany and Japan the occupation forces broke up powerful cartels and implemented legislation intolerant of restrictive practices in these countries. The success of the American pressure on the regulatory and legislative outcomes in these countries has, however, been debated (Dumez and Jeunemaître 1996; Freyer 2006: 160ff.). In both countries the legislation was quickly relaxed when the bans on restrictive agreements were perceived as detrimental to reconstruction (Chapters 10 and 11, this volume). The final outcomes were regulations that tolerated some restrictive agreements, but which also required fairly tight controls, via notification and registration. In the UK, post-war reconstruction saw the register emerge as the authorities sought to combat anti-competitive behaviour (Symeonidis 2002: 24–26). In the case of Israel, which introduced a register in 1960, the original purpose of the law was to enhance competition to promote economic efficiency and growth in a small economy with sheltered markets. The growth criterion, however, negatively affected the implementation of the law as competition restrictions and monopolies were often justified as promoting efficiency (Kestenbaum 1973).

Table 7.1 compiles basic information about many of the countries that had registers. The table includes comments on the prevailing attitudes to anti-competitive practices at the time the registers were introduced and whether they were open or closed to the public. Apart from those variations which can be observed from Table 7.1 closer inspection of the individual registers reveals a number of additional variations. These can be broadly categorised as differences that depended on (i) the aims of the register and the regulatory authorities, (ii) the way in which the authorities used the registers, and (iii) their ultimate effectiveness in tackling restrictive trade practices in their jurisdiction. These issues will be looked at in turn.

Examining the dates many of the registers began (and ultimately ceased), reveals that the 1950s and 1960s were the decades when these instruments were most used by regulatory authorities. It is also true, however that in several countries such as Norway, Sweden, Denmark, Austria and Japan, the register was a remarkably persistent remaining in place for several decades. Other nations such as New Zealand, barely created the process before it was abandoned. The cessation of many of the registers in the 1980s and 1990s also reveals the impact of changes to international attitudes toward restrictive practices.[8]

Aims of the registers

Registers were created for a variety of reasons and in a variety of contexts. In countries with legislation primarily motivated to prevent abuses, the primary aim was to control and monitor restrictive business practices and to gather information for use by the authorities and policy makers.[9] A common element was that the authorities had little or no prior information about the extent of non-competitive agreements in their domestic markets. To be able to promote competition and deal

Table 7.1 Countries with cartel registers in the twentieth century.

Country	Start date	Type of register	Original legislation	Initial extent of tolerance to restrictive practices
Norway	1920	Public	Price Regulation Act	Tolerant
Denmark	1937	Public	Law on Price Agreements; replaced by Monopolies Supervision Act 1955	Highly tolerant
Italy	1942	n.a.	Civil code of 1942 articles 2612–15	n.a.
Sweden	1946	Public	Act on Probation on Restrictive Business Practices	Highly tolerant
Japan	1947	Public	Act on Prohibition of Private Monopolization and Maintenance of Fair Trade	Highly intolerant
United Kingdom	1956	Public	Monopolies and Restrictive Practices (Inquiry and Control) Act	Intolerant
Germany	1957	Public	Act against Restraints of Competition	Intolerant
Finland	1957	Public	Act on the Control of Practices Restricting Economic Competition	Highly tolerant
Netherlands	1958	Secret	Economic Competition Act	Highly tolerant
New Zealand	1958	Public	Trade Practices Act	Intolerant
Austria	1951	Public	Cartels Act	Tolerant
Israel	1960	Public	Restrictive Trade practices Act	Intolerant
Spain	1963	Public	Act to Afford Protection against Activities that Reduce Competition	Intolerant
Australia	1967	Secret	Trade Practices Act	Highly tolerant
India	1969	Public	Monopolies and Restrictive Trade Practices Act	Intolerant
Pakistan	1970	Public	Monopolies and Restrictive Trade Practices Ordinance	Intolerant
South Korea	1980	Public	Monopoly Regulation and Fair Trade Act	Intolerant

Note: Degrees of tolerance are: Highly tolerant (ban no restrictive practices; only control them); tolerant (bans some specific restrictive practices, but no generalised bans); intolerant (in principle bans, but allow many exemptions) and highly intolerant (bans most restrictive practices and only minor exceptions). This table includes is not exhaustive. We exclude, for example, Hungary, Poland Bulgaria, Czechoslovakia and Yugoslavia as records on these are scarce. Other registers may also have been created, but we have no systematic information about them.

Sources: compiled from Edwards (1967); OECD (1964, 1967–1975, 1971, 1978); Borell (1998); Hunter (1963); Thorelli (1959); Yang (1985); Jaffe (1967); Linder and Sarkar (1971); Rampilla (1989).

with firms' abusive behaviour the authorities first had to find them. The registers were, thus, often a first step to gather required information. The evidence gathered by the register could also form the basis for making the legislation stricter. Beyond just gathering data, the authorities sometimes intervened in agreements that violated good trade practices or which were considered harmful for the general public or economic efficiency.

In countries where restrictive trade practices were based on a prohibition principle (i.e. prohibiting anti-competitive practices rather than focusing only on those firms that caused detriment) and the attitude towards firm cooperation was intolerant, the register was a tool for controlling 'exempt' or 'approved' agreements. This was the case for example, with the registers in Germany, UK, Japan, Israel, Spain and South Korea (Edwards 1967: 49). In the case of the UK it was also a way to inform affected third parties of the existence of restrictive agreements (Frazer and Waterson 1994: 89–93).

It is clear registers assisted some governments in regulating anti-competitive practices. Governments, however, have a range of policy targets, and thus the registers were not always created in an environment totally focused on promoting more vigorous markets. In some circumstances competition may have been a secondary consideration. For example, in Japan industrial policy 'overruled' anti-monopoly concerns, and in many cases promoting competition was seen as incongruent with growth targets (Freyer 2006: 162; Wise 1999). In Finland and Sweden, economic efficiency and firm rationalisation aimed at enhancing economic growth were highly prioritised and the promotion of competition *per se* was secondary. The collective wage bargaining systems, which existed in many European countries like Denmark, Sweden and Finland, allowed for indexed wage increases and required price control legislation. The public register could potentially help governments in their efforts to tackle inflationary pressures through a register that identified firms engaging in price agreements. By contrast, Australia also had wage indexation, but it introduced a secret register in 1967 to gather information rather than shame firms and control prices. Nonetheless, pressure for the register had emerged from state level enquires in the 1950s into the link between price rises and restrictive practices (Round and Shanahan 2011).

Cartel registers were frequently designed to be pragmatic element of economic strategy. The Israeli law was primarily designed as a practical instrument of economic policy (Jaffe 1967). In Finland the register was at least thought to provide information for the state-led, top-down, economic policy making of the post-war period (Chapter 6, this volume). In the Netherlands the register was to be used to invigorate an economy believed to have grown moribund because of anti-competitive behaviour (Chapter 5, this volume). The Spanish register established in 1963 was part of a general stabilisation plan designed to re-establish the market economy; as such it was just one part of a much broader policy change.

In the Asian countries mentioned here, the main objective of competition legislation appears to have been concern with the concentration of economic power. The target of the Indian law from 1968 was especially to counter the strength of monopolies, although many other forms of anti-competitive agreements were also recorded (Rampilla 1989; Rao and Sastry 1989). In Pakistan, the motivation behind their first law was to modernise the economy. It was also observed that the overall concentration in business had led to an increase in wealth inequality. As a result the Pakistani law also targeted, apart from unreasonably restrictive practices, undue concentration of power and unreasonable monopolisation (Linder and Sakar 1971).

In South Korea, the original 1970s legislation was motivated by concerns about the effect big monopolies and *chaebols* had on the price-level (Choi 2014). As a result, the first form of anti-competitive behaviour mentioned in the Monopoly Regulation and Fair Trade Act was abuse of market-dominating position. Cartel agreements were to be controlled by law and included in the register (Yang 1985, 2009). The South Korean legislation fell between those types of regulation based on principles of non-tolerance and those aimed at preventing abuse. It did not ban outright restrictive practices, but collaborative agreements had to be registered in order to be permitted. Unregistered agreements were illegal and declared null and void. In case a registered agreement was considered against the public interest and lead to 'substantial restriction of competition in the particular field of trade', the authorities could reject registration or ask for revisions prior to registration (Yang 1985).

The cartel registers were thus established for a range of reasons – but with a common suspicion that firms cooperating together needed to be watched, sometimes controlled, and occasionally banned.

Secret or public registers

Registers could be public or secret (closed). Most of the registers were public. In the case of the closed registers, as in the Netherlands and Australia, the aim was ostensibly to provide information to public authorities, but not more broadly. In the Australian case, it was hoped that by guaranteeing anonymity, cases of abuse would be easier to identify and dismantle, as the firms involved could both volunteer information about their arrangements and negotiate privately with the authorities (Round and Shanahan 2015).

Where the registers were public, the rationale was that competitors or consumers should normally be informed of agreements existing in the market. Such publicity, it was hoped would restrain conspiring firms and cartels and thus have a deterrent effect. The publicity principle was an important feature in the Austrian, Swedish, Danish, Norwegian and Finnish registers; so important that Finland and Sweden adopted the principal from the start. This did not mean everything on the record was open; usually only some of the information was made public. In Finland, Sweden and Austria summaries of the agreements were published, while in the Finnish case, examples of specific agreements could be supplied, fully disclosing their total content. In Austria the authorities outlined the general types of agreements, but the information provided was very brief. In countries like the UK and Spain, where only agreements exempt from prohibition were recorded, the register was, for obvious reasons, usually open. The Israeli register was so open that all submitted documents were in the public domain, unless specifically granted secrecy (Jaffe 1967).

The content of the registers

The exact contents of the registers varied. One must be wary of assuming that the contents of a register in one country match the contents recorded in another. First, the registers usually do not include all the sectors or industries of a country. As a general statement, the labour market, parts of the agricultural sector and most major exporters were not usually required to register. In the UK, the system of registration initially covered only manufactured goods, while in Sweden, Finland and the Netherlands service agreements were included. After 1979 service industry agreements were also included in the UK. In most countries export agreements were usually excluded, although Japan was an exception. In Norway and Japan agreements including foreign companies and foreign ownership were to be registered, while in others the interests of the foreign company had to cross a set threshold before it was compulsory to register. In Australia only agreements involving trade across state boundaries had to be recorded.

Even where registers existed, and particular forms of arrangements were proscribed, not everyone who had such agreements was necessarily required to register them. The regulations varied extensively between countries. For example, in Finland, initially cartel associations had to report their agreements on their own initiative, while individual firms and entrepreneurs reported agreements only on request. After 1973 all horizontal agreements had to be notified on the parties' own initiative. In Sweden it was mandatory to report all agreements, but also only on request. In both cases the underlying reason was a fear that the authorities would be overwhelmed by notifications. In Sweden and Finland small entrepreneurs and businesses could be asked to report their agreements, while in some other jurisdictions the register mostly captured large companies. In the Netherlands only legally binding agreements had to be reported, while in Denmark informal agreements were registered in case they had major effects.

Second, in those countries which had non-tolerant legislation the register included only those agreements which had received exemptions from the ban. In Germany, for example, official policy required horizontal agreements as well as resale price maintenance to be banned and they were not included. The many agreements which received special exemption (like rationalisation and depression cartels) were of course included (Chapter 11, this volume). In Spain 'crises' and 'rationalisation' agreements as well as export cartels could be approved. The Israeli register contained a large variation; approved agreements, agreements which had been cancelled as well as possible hearings called by the Board (Jaffe 1967: 938). Exemptions were usually given to cartels which tended to 'protect the continued existence of an entire branch, which is of advantage to the Israeli economy, or the enhanced efficiency of production or marketing or to increase production or to reduce prices or to check a rise of prices' (ibid.). In broad terms, the model that Israel followed was the British Restrictive Trade Practice Act of 1955.

In countries where the legislation was more tolerant of restrictive practices, and where the primary aim was to control and monitor these, the type and number of recorded agreements was usually quite large. Here too there was considerable difference between countries. While some only required the notification of vertical

Table 7.2 Selected contents of agreement registers, 1961–1970.

What was reported	Australia	Austria	Denmark	Finland	Germany	India	Israel	Japan[a]	Netherland[b]	Norway	Pakistan	Spain	Sweden	UK
All restrictive agreements	Yes	Yes	Yes	Yes		Yes	Yes		Yes	Yes	Yes		Yes	Yes
Agreements subject to approval or exemption[c]					Yes							Yes		Yes
International agreements								Yes						
Dominant firm		Yes	Yes	Yes		Yes				Yes	Yes		Yes	
Merger & acquisition					Yes[d]	Yes		Yes			Yes	Yes[d]		
Foreign ownership								Yes		Yes[e]				

Notes: Tables 7.2 and 7.3 represent on the major content categories and are not exhaustive.

(a) Japan's register also included information about Interlocking directorships; Stock held by large non-financial Companies; where >10% of stock was held by financial institutions; >10% stock was in competing companies, and trade associations.

(b) The Netherlands also required foreign firms to register restrictive agreements

(c) The regulations of countries recorded in this row included a range of exemptions that were subject to separate approval processes.

(d) Only if after the acquisition the firm would have 20% of the market or more in Germany; 30% or more in Spain. India also aimed to include a wide range of other types of restrictive agreements, among others, collective bidding, collective discrimination and boycotts from trade associations

(e) If foreign firms exceeded minimum share ownership, or market share criteria

Sources: based on Edwards (1967: 48), with additional information from OECD (1964); Jaffe (1967); Linder and Sarkar (1971); Rao and Sastro (1989); Fatima (2012)

or horizontal cartel agreements, others required the notification of firms with dominant market positions, mergers and acquisitions, monopolies, or other types of price agreements. Regulations about the necessary detail included in the register also changed over time, making both an overview and an interpretation of the registers even more difficult.

To complicate issues further, some types of restrictive agreements were under surveillance in some countries, without even being included in the register; in other countries, restrictive agreements were recorded, but outside the cartel register (OECD 1978). The net effect is a lack of consistency in what appears on the surface to be quite similar regulatory instruments. In some countries, mergers and acquisitions appeared in the register, in others they do not. In Sweden for example, after 1968 mergers and acquisitions were controlled and registered, but not in the cartel register.

Tables 7.2 and 7.3 extend the first major post-war effort to summarise the regulations on restrictive trade practices which was authored by Corwin Edwards (Edwards 1967).[10] Building on this work we summarise the contents found in the registers of fifteen countries in the 1960s and 1970s. Our table adds several more countries, while also depicting the type of register being used. Given regulatory legislation evolved over time, what is recorded should be considered cross-sectional snapshot relevant for the time periods under consideration. Taken together the tables reveal the range of agreements and their use in a variety of countries.

As can be observed from the tables, a wide range of restrictive practices were recorded, although we have only included the most commonly used categorisations. As the content varied considerably over time we report the results from the two key decades when the use of registers was at their most wide-spread.

As the twentieth century progressed, in every jurisdiction, competition legislation gradually became increasingly hostile to anti-competitive agreements and other activities that reduced the operation of free markets. This meant that in some countries, mergers and acquisitions, and firms with dominant market positon were included in the register. This increased the number of mandated activities to be recorded. Running counter to this, the increased hostility also meant that certain types of agreements were totally banned, with the result that they disappeared from the registers. For instance, vertical agreements, i.e. resale price maintenance, and collusive tendering (bid rigging) were banned in many countries in the 1950s and 1960s.[11] Thus by the 1970s these agreements had mostly vanished from the registers (see Table 7.3).

Individual countries emphasised different types of restrictive agreements. For example, it has been said that European countries especially aimed to control cartels; and in particular the so called 'hard core' horizontal price-fixing cartels. Resale price maintenance was also of particular interest to the European legislators (for example, Norway banned this in 1953), while they were less concerned by monopolies (Thorelli 1959). Thus, the main types of restrictions to be included in the registers in these countries were horizontal and vertical price agreements. On the other hand, over time mergers and acquisitions and dominant market position also became the target of the authorities in many countries. The variation in Europe

Table 7.3 Selected contents of agreement registers, 1971–1980.

What was reported	Austria	Denmark	Finland	Germany*	India	Israel	Japan*	The Netherlands	Norway	Pakistan	South Korea	Spain*	Sweden	UK*
Horizontal agreements registered	Yes	Yes	Yes		Yes	Yes		Yes	Yes	Yes	Yes		Yes	
Horizontal agreements banned (exemptions allowed)				†Yes	†Yes	†Yes	†Yes			†Yes	†Yes	†Yes		†Yes
Resale price maintenance banned (exemptions allowed)	Yes	†Yes	†Yes	†Yes	†Yes	†Yes	†	†Yes	†Yes	†Yes	Yes	†	†Yes	†
Dominant firm	Yes	Yes	Yes	o	Yes	o	o	o	Yes	Yes	Yes	o	Yes	o
Merger & acquisition	Yes		o	Yes	Yes		o			Yes	Yes	Yes	o	o
Exclusive dealing/ selective selling	Yes	†	Yes	o	Yes	Yes	†		Yes	Yes	Yes	o	Yes	
Refusal to sell/ boycott					Yes	Yes				Yes	Yes			†
Foreign ownership							Yes		Yes					

Notes: * Countries where restrictive business practices were illegal, and only those agreements having received explicit exemption were to be included in the register.
† Banned outright. o Controlled but not in register.

This table only includes those types of restrictive practices most commonly referred to as being subject to registration. Many other forms of restrictive practices were either only important in particular countries, or fell outside the registration process For example, the table excludes collusive tendering, joint ventures, boycotts, and agreements relating to industrial and commercial property. For more examples see OECD (1978). Japan's register also included information about international agreements, interlocking directorships, stock held by large non-financial companies, where >10% of stock was held by financial institutions, >10% stock was in competing companies, and trade associations. In South Korea also international cartels and trade associations had to register. India also aimed to include a wide range of other types of restrictive agreements, among others, collective bidding, collective discrimination and boycotts from trade associations.

Source: Based on OECD (1978); Rao and Sastro (1989); Yang (1985); Fatima (2012); Wilson (2006).

was also large. For instance, in the Netherlands, a very wide range of agreements were included in the records, including 'other' agreements; something that even encompassed the terms and condition of sales and conditions of transport and packaging (Chapter 5, this volume). In India too, the regulations could catch a wide range of institutions and activities; for example, monopolies, dominant firms and cartels could all be included in the records and the legislation covered twelve forms of restrictive practices.

As Chapter 10 of this volume shows, Japan is quite different from the other countries included in these tables. There the register also included anti-competitive practices that involved international agreements, consideration of the extent of significant shareholdings and interlocking directorates.

Registers' contents varied not only because of differences in legislation and definition, but because in many countries, public servants were entrusted with significant powers of interpretation to decide what was to be registered and what was not (Fellman and Sandberg 2015). This was particularly important where the legislation allowed a great deal of discretion. This open-endedness was especially common in jurisdictions where the aim was not to prohibit behaviour, but rather, to gather information (Edwards 1967: 53). The relatively free hand to interpret the legislation possessed by many competition authorities had a negative impact. They often considered the notification and registration procedures to be problematic. For example, defining exactly which types of agreements the law included, what kind of information was to be reported, and what was to be included were subject to interpretation; something that could be narrow or broad depending on the authorities vigour and concern. Clearly this could affect the final recorded content.

Non-compliance with the obligations to notify agreements was occasionally a problem. In the UK, the Department of Trade and Industry suspected that deliberate evasion existed.[12] In Finland, the competition authorities were frustrated that not all agreements that should be advised to the register had been notified. In the 1970s and 1980s the threat of fines made the Finnish legislation more effective, but still non-compliance seems to have been fairly common (Chapter 6, this volume). In Sweden fines, and later imprisonment, was the punishment for not reporting, but as nobody had to notify on their own initiative, non-compliance was less of a problem.

While the authorities were often aware of the difficulties in getting compliance, in many countries it was assumed that only a few firms did not report. The threat of considerable fines, or as in the Australian case, making registration *prima facie* evidence that the agreement was legal, provided an incentive to register. In some countries, such as the Netherlands, Austria and Norway, criminal prosecution could be instigated for non-registration. In Denmark an unreported agreement was legally invalid and unenforceable, while in Austria, an unregistered agreement was both invalid and unlawful.[13] In Austria and also in Israel, the completion of registration at the same time signified approval of an agreement (Edwards 1967: 50). This induced entrepreneurs to notify their agreements.

A bigger problem than non-compliance was when firms framed their agreements so that they looked innocuous (ibid.: 60–61). As legalisms increased, so more frequently the form of the agreement became more important than the substance- ironically making it occasionally easier to avoid registration.

The use of the registers and their effectiveness in combatting restrictive trade practices

For some decades registers constituted a key instrument for monitoring and controlling national markets and cartel behaviour. As discussed, the registers served as a general source of information for the competition authorities and governments about the types of agreements in existence. It was often stressed, both in hostile and lenient competition environments, that it was important first to know about the agreements in the market prior to taking action. The registers were also an important source of information on which to base action against harmful agreements and in evaluating behaviour detrimental to the public. They formed the basis both for further legislative measures and in the actual implementation of policies.

In spite of differences in attitudes and in the degree of tolerance of non-competitive behaviour, the actual administrative and judicial procedures were fairly similar in many jurisdictions. In the more tolerant policy milieus, there was an emphasis on investigation, and in some cases negotiation. Only after these steps were completed, might there be court proceedings. The negotiations were usually instigated by the administrative authorities and/or by an independent authority like a competition ombudsman. Occasionally the public or potential competitors could request authorities to investigate.

The most informal processes were in countries where administrative authorities negotiated with a firm to remove harmful clauses or even complete agreements. This was typical for the three Nordic countries, Denmark, Finland and Sweden, and also Australia (Edwards 1967: 37). If the negotiations failed, the case could be transferred to the government or some judicial authority to suspend the agreements. In the Netherlands, where the register was secret, investigations could be instigated by the Minister of Economic Affairs and the other relevant Ministers. They had a wide range of possible response options. In Norway the decision and actions were to be taken by the administrative authorities, and not the courts. The Cartel Court or Trust Council was independent of ordinary courts and political bodies, making the system very independent (Espeli 2002).

In those policy environments that were less tolerant of anti-competitive agreements, recourse to court procedures was more common. For example, in the UK, where the register was established in 1956, a 'case-by-case' approach was initially adopted. No explicit prohibition was implemented, but a judicial procedure was adopted to assess every case and their impact on the public interest. The Director General of the Office of Fair Trading was obliged to investigate every registrable agreement. Until a decision was made it was allowed to continue. Non-compliance with the Court's decision was however, punishable. The majority of agreements in the UK were gradually abolished (Symeonidis 2002: 21). In 1976 the legislation was renewed and the new law became still more hostile towards restrictive agreements, although a total ban was still not implemented.[14]

In the German case, the authorities had two ways of proceeding. One process saw the cartel authorities investigate specific agreements and on completion publish their decision. The other approach was an administrative procedure where the authorities could impose a fine and/or prosecute (OECD 1978: 177–196; Chapter 11, this volume). In Spain, to instigate an exemption, the parties had to ask for an investigation and apply for provisional registration. In case of suspicions or illegal practices, the administrative authorities, the Service for the Protection of Competition, first investigated those practices and this was followed by proceedings in the Court for the Protection of Competition. The implementation of the Spanish legislation was, however, extremely inefficient and few cases were reviewed or registered before the 1980s (OECD 1978: 177–196). According to Israel's 1960 Restrictive Trade Practices Act, every cartel was prohibited until permission had been given by the Control Board. The Chairman of this Board could decide to issue a temporary permit. Unless the cartels had sought approval or received such a temporary permit, its operation was an offence, punishable with up to eight months in prison (Jaffe 1967: 938). In Japan which cartels were exempted and which were authorised in the register depended on the outcome of deliberations between the anti-monopoly authorities and particular ministers who often had other goals, in particular to promote industrialisation and economic development (Chapter 10, this volume).

In India, the registered agreements were investigated by the MRTP Commission which assessed them against the test of 'public interest'. The authorities had to balance rationalisation and possible cost savings, against the public interest and if permitted, the agreements were said to have passed through a 'gateway' that allowed them to proceed. The gateways were many and frequent. As a result, it has been judged that although fairly intolerant in theory, in practice the law was tolerant. Moreover, while the actual register included several thousand agreements, very few cases were ever dealt with in the Commission (Rampilla 1989; Battarchajeya 2012; Rao and Sastry 1989). The procedure in Pakistan was that the authorities should only make inquiries based on records included in the register; so from the start, it was less ambitious than the Indian legislation (Linder and Sarkar 1973). In the end the authorities could only make recommendation to the government (Fatima 2012).

The proceedings and the decisions could be either secret or public. In those countries with a legislation based on prohibition, the procedures seem to have been more open, with public court cases. In reality however, in those countries the actual hearings were usually not open, especially not at the negotiation stage, although the decisions were generally made public eventually. In the Netherlands the secrecy appears to have been at its highest; both the registers and the procedures in case of abuse, were kept totally secret. The final decisions were, however, published. Similarly, in Australia which also had a secret register, if firms revealed illegal levels of cooperation (i.e. against the public interest) confidential negotiations were conducted to dissuade them. Only when firms refused to amend their behaviour after such negotiations, were public court cases conducted and prosecutions undertaken. In Australia this amounted to a total of three public court cases from over 14,000 registered agreements over a decade (Chapter 9, this volume).[15]

According to some experts, the 1963 Spanish legislation remained unimplemented until 1978, when it was reformed, but even then it was only partially enforced (Cases 1996; Borrell 1998). Similarly, although the UK authorities were intolerant in principle, they were not very active, especially during the 1950s and 1960s (Wise 2003). The Act, renewed in 1976, was considered to be quite effective by the 1980s as it controlled formal agreements on horizontal price fixing and market-sharing agreements. Simultaneously, however, the firms and entrepreneurs become more skilled in drafting agreements that did not have to be registered (Frazer and Waterson 1994: 89–94). Administrative procedures tended to be more focused on whether an agreement was to be registered (its form), rather than whether it had detrimental effects (Borrie 1994). Similarly in several countries, it was not uncommon for firms to redraft their agreements to avoid the legal forms that brought them to the attention of authorities. By contrast the Israeli law seems to have been difficult to avoid. Of the 257 cases registered by 1967, only 33 had been approved (Jaffe 1967). However, by the early 1970s it was claimed that the law had been less effective than originally intended. As one expert argued, this was not the fault of the legislation, but a consequence of the authorities' ambivalence towards enhancing competition and their concern with other economic and regulation issues (Kestenbaum 1973).

Around the world, as the legislation gradually became more hostile towards restrictive agreements, processes became more legalistic. This is usually considered to have meant more effective implementation of the legislation. The initially more lenient countries also made small modifications over time which gradually improved their processes, while others adopted sweeping changes that 'jumped' their competition policies to a new level.

A formalistic approach also meant that many agreements without anti-competitive consequences were registered while firms could also draft them in such a way as to evade registration. For example, according to the DTI (in the UK), the 'catch-all' characteristic of the Act was considered unnecessarily burdensome on business and one of the prominent weaknesses of the legislation. Thus even in the UK, with its case-by-case approach, one of the key problems was that competition law was form-based and not effect-based (Borrie 1994; Wilks 1996).

How effective the registration system was in preventing restrictive practices or abuse in each country can be debated. It is difficult to evaluate. Contemporary criticisms were that the systems had difficulty in judging what was against the public interest and that overall, the systems were generally slow and ineffective, with few cases actually being resolved. These perceived weaknesses may well have accelerated the demise of the registration system. The neo-corporatist countries were particularly criticised on these grounds, but, on closer inspection the evidence suggests that informal discussions and the threat of negotiations did tend to result in a change or abolition of harmful agreements (Fellman and Sandberg 2015; OECD 1978: 192).

The demise of registers

The fate of the register and the particular notification process can be traced out in each country. Table 7.4 reveals the dates when the cartel registers in each country ceased, either because they were abolished or because they became redundant; mostly because the agreements previously registered were now totally prohibited. As the table shows, most registers ceased to be operational in the late 1980s or early 1990s although some (as in Australia and New Zealand) were phased out as early as the mid-1970s. In New Zealand, the register in fact only existed for around three years, as it was never fully accepted as necessary and it was removed under pressure from business lobbies (Collinge 1969). In contrast, the register in Israel is still in force, although a fundamental renewal of the competition legislation has been under debate for years (Dabbah 2011).

While the policy approaches seemed to converge, the process of shifting to a stricter regime varied in each country - just as had the goals and scope of the original registers. Competition legislation and anti-cartel policy is deeply embedded in the local legal, institutional and historical settings. A good example of the twists and turns of policy is the UK. By the late 1950s its approach to the register marks it as having a high intolerance of cartels and restrictive agreements. Relative to other EEC countries it was also an early mover towards market liberalisation. Nonetheless its shift to adopting competition legislation congruent with the EU competition policy and implementation of real penalties for unlawful restrictive practices was fairly slow. At least one reason was its internal politics of the 1980s, which were directed towards the privatisation of state companies. Competition legislation was transformed only later (Wise 2003).

In Finland, there were already strong voices for much stricter competition legislation in the early 1980s but it was only in 1992, with the application for membership to the EU, that the legislation changed. The reform was implemented rapidly, to assist the successful acceptance of membership, but discussions around the new legislation suggest a readiness for a new 'cartel-hostile' environment (Fellman 2010). Similarly in Australia, the legislation replacing the register (in 1975) was seen as long overdue. Although not compelled by application for membership of an international body, the Australian debate focussed on the need to modernise the economy by advancing competition and outlawing anti-competitive practices (Round and Shanahan 2015).

In Japan the register's phasing out was partly a result of the authorities' reluctance to authorise cartels which were growing stronger as the policy milieu grew more hostile. The continuous trade tensions with the US also pushed forward the implementation of stricter policies towards restrictive practices as the golden age of economic growth persisted (Chapter 10, this volume).

In South Korea the register was abolished in 1986 by legislation that was not tolerant of restrictive practices. The original 1980 statute had not been able to deal with the problems it was supposed to target. After the new legislation, the number of cease-and-desist cases grew every year (Choi 2014). In India, there were internal and external pressures for reform in the 1990s, but the process was slow. In conjunction with general liberalisation of the economy a new non-tolerant statute was passed in 2002; it was not implemented until 2009 (Battarchajeya 2012).

Table 7.4 The year selected registers closed.

Country	Year of closure	Replacement legislation	Context
Italy	1947	No replacing legislation at the time	Reform after fall of Fascist government
New Zealand	1961	Trade Practices Amendment Act	Abandoned due to lobby groups
Australia	1975	Trade Practices Act 1974	Shift to stronger pro-competition legislation
Germany	1985	Law on unnecessary economic regulation	Shift to stronger pro-competition legislation
South Korea	1986	Monopoly Regulation and Fair Trade Act – Amended 1986	Shift to stronger pro-competition legislation
Israel	1988	Restrictive Trade Practices Law	Shift to stronger pro-competition legislation
United Kingdom	1989	Competition Act	Harmonisation with EU rules
Denmark	1989	Competition Act	Harmonisation with EU rules
Spain	1989	Competition Act	Harmonisation with EU rules
Finland	1992	Competition Act	EEA Agreement, EU membership application
Norway	1993	Competition Act	EEA Agreement
Sweden	1993	Competition Act	EEA Agreement, EU membership application
Netherlands	1993	Competition Act	Harmonisation with EU rules
Japan	1999	Anti-Monopoly Act – Amendment	Gradual phasing out in 1990s
India	2002	Competition Act	International pressure; stronger pro-competition legislation
Austria	2006	Cartel Act and Competition Act	Harmonisation with EU rules
Pakistan	2010	Competition Ordinance – Renewed	International influence. stronger pro-competition legislation

Sources: OECD (1991, 1995, 1997, 2007); Wise (1999, 2000, 2003, 2005); Borell (1998); Collinge (1969); Battarchajeya (2012); Sturm (1996); Fatima (2012).

The impetus for phasing out registers was often because the processes of negotiation and registration were perceived to be too slow. Too often the processes appeared to deal first with restrictive agreements of lesser importance, focusing excessively on what was to be registered, rather than the negative consequences of more influential restrictive agreements (Wilks 1996: 169). As Warlouzet emphasises in his chapter, the system of registration was reactive rather than proactive.

The system was also frustrating, because the authorities in general gathered too little information. On the other hand, if they had received all the information that was available, it would have over-whelmed even the best resourced government authority. As Warlouzet notes, one of the problems with the EEC register was the large number of notifications that had to be examined. As a result there was a long delay in dealing with specific cases. The first MRTP law in India was considered to be inefficient. One reason was that the MRTP Commission was understaffed and underfunded, which led to a massive backlog, both of registrations and in determining the agreements themselves. Moreover, as anyone (a consumer, competitor or trade association) could complain to the Commission, it was drowned in allegations of 'unfair' behaviour and all kinds of consumer complaints, many of which were unrelated to competition (Battarchajeya 2012; Rao and Sastry 1989). Similarly, as Fellman relates in Chapter 6 of this volume, the Finnish authorities decided that it was impossible to require all cartels, trade associations and entrepreneurs to notify their agreements on their own initiative, as the authorities would have been swamped by these notifications.

Conclusion

The many and varied paths to the creation of registers of restrictive practices, and the numerous differences between them, run counter to the prevailing view that after the Second World War, the Americanisation of business regulations, and changes to antitrust legislation, was both swift and uniform. Rather, countries developed registers in different ways, responding to particular local issues, with objectives, that while seeking to enhance competition, often had different strategies. For a period during the middle of the twentieth century the registers were a popular mechanism by which to detect, and sometimes deter anti-competitive behaviour. They were also a good example of how regulatory ideas were transmitted across national boundaries; the legal framework in one country can, and sometimes did, influence the regulatory frameworks of their neighbours.

The registers mostly exempted export-orientated firms, labour unions, service sectors such as banking and health; and they often (although not always) omitted firms involved with the agriculture, transport and insurance sectors, and those parts of the economy with sufficient political influence to ensure the legislation did not cover their fields of operation.

Despite the many compromises and efforts to find a middle path, the registers themselves were not particularly successful in preventing firms from entering into agreements to engage in uncompetitive behaviour, nor in breaking up existing restrictive practices. Given the many exemptions and exclusions, neither were they particularly successful in detecting many of the anti-competitive practices in existence over the periods they were enforced. Ironically, in those jurisdictions where some enforcement was successful, the quantity of work involved in administering the system (often the result of the compromised processes that resulted in multiple checks and assessments before registration) frequently made the system impractical. In the end the general public in most countries showed a distinct lack of interest in the names appearing on the lists.

Nonetheless, and even accepting there were failings with this regulatory approach, several authors assert that the processes around registration were successful in changing business attitudes to anti-competitive behaviour. Simply raising the issue that many restrictive practices were an abuse of consumers and fellow companies seems to have had an effect on business attitudes. The reality of submitting documentation outlining those practices and the risk, no matter how small, of having those practices revealed publically, also seems to have been salutary, not only for individual firms, but for business interests generally.

Ultimately, in most countries it was international pressure that put an end to the registers. This was not because of direct efforts to remove the registers, but because they simply became irrelevant. By the early 1970s international organisations such as the EU, and increased international trade made local (national) cartels and other anticompetitive practices either illegal or mostly redundant. International trading partners would not accept prices and conditions that did not deliver goods and services as cheaply and efficiently as possible. Competition from external sources made internal restrictive arrangements almost impossible to maintain. The result; in only a few years, cartel registers became a relic of business regulation as competitors and policy makers either undermined the restrictive practices in the market, or declared the practices illegal.

Notes

1. As no definitive list of registers has ever been created, we have checked multiple sources. Nonetheless we cannot be absolutely certain we have identified all the registers that existed. We would be grateful to receive information about other registers.
2. The OECD put significant effort into defining 'restrictive trade agreement' when a special expert committee under the European Productivity Agency aimed to harmonise legislation and practices (OECD 1971: 1–6).
3. The problem was less in countries which specified what offences were illegal. For example, the Australian legislation only prohibited collusive tendering and collusive bidding – but exactly what constituted these still had to be determined by the court.
4. One reason for extensive reporting was the variation in what constituted cooperative behaviour (Fear 2006, 2008).
5. In Australia this is still the case: individual firms and agreements cannot be identified more than 40 years after the register ceased operation.
6. The competition authority was comparatively independent from both political authorities and civil courts; a characteristic of modern European legislation.
7. In Poland, registration existed between 1933 and 1939. A form of it reappeared in 1990 when new legislation required firms with dominant market position, and those intending to merge, be recorded (Blachucki 2013).
8. Early in the twenty-first century a number of countries again introduced the process of registration, but in this case their objective was to signal their willingness to transition toward EU competition policy standards. The countries that appear to have used registers for this purpose include Bulgaria, Estonia, Lithuania, Montenegro, Poland and Serbia (UNCTAD 2009). One African country that has adopted a register of

restrictive trade practices in recent years is the United Republic of Tanzania (ibid.: 877–986).

9   The use of a register does not exhaust all the possible non-prohibitive regulatory approaches to restrictive trade practices. Different in form, but not in substance, South African legislation in 1949 involved a tribunal examining reported activities. If these were shown to restrict trade to the detriment of the public, the Minister could request its discontinuance. If this request was not obeyed, details of the practice and people involved could be published (Cowen 1950). The process was changed by legislation in 1955 (South African Government, 1977). There are other examples of similar procedures, for instance in Chile (Furnish 1971).

10 Corwin Edwards was chief economist of the American Federal Trade Commission in the 1930s to 1950s. A specialist in anti-trust economics, he was an advisor to the US delegation to the United Nations for many years, as well as leader of the US mission investigating Japanese combines in 1947. He received the Veblen-Commons award for his work in institutional economics in 1978. He died in 1979.

11 Norway was again forerunner in this area (Espeli 2002). In the UK, resale price maintenance was identified in the legislation in 1964 and the Restrictive Practice Commission was more hostile towards resale price maintenance than towards horizontal price fixing agreements (Symeonidis 2002: 22, 32).

12 In the UK, it was not an offence not to report an agreement, but if unreported it was unlawful to give effect to the restrictions (DTI review of RTP policy, quoted in Frazer and Watershed 1994: 91).

13 In the Austrian register, cartels with very small effects (*Bagatellkartelle*), which commanded less than five percent of the market, did not have to register (OECD 1974: 202).

14 According to Eyre and Lodge (2000) the UK competition policy was characterised by a pragmatic and administrative investigative style, with a focus on the "public interest" and the economic consequences rather than legal considerations.

15 Three other cases, all challenging the constitutional legality of the register also emerged from this process (Round and Shanahan 2011).

8 Transparency of cartels and cartel registers

A regulatory innovation from Norway?

Harald Espeli

Introduction

The Norwegian Act on the Control of Restraints of Competition and Price Abuse of 1926, normally called the Trust Act, has been characterised as Europe's first 'real' competition law (Gerber 1998: 156). Norway was the first European country to implement specific legislation enabling competition control including intervention against abuse of restraints on competition. Norway was also the first European country to introduce compulsory notification and registration of restrictive business arrangements and market dominant enterprises as well as including subsidiaries of foreign multinational companies through the provisional Price Regulation Act of 1920. That Act marked the beginning of the official cartel register, which existed to 1993. Short summaries of the main elements recorded in the notified information were printed in the *Norsk Pristidende* – the official gazette – of the Price Directorate (1920–1926) and in *Trustkontrollen* – the publication of its successor, the Trust Control Office (1926–1940) a number of times per decade. Both the public and businessmen normally gained a cursory but roughly correct impression of the relevant restrictive business arrangement notified through the gazette. The complete information of the cartel register was also accessible to the public, including the press, at the office of the Price Directorate until the enactment of the Trust Act in 1926.

Cartel registers were introduced by a few countries in the inter-war years; notably Denmark, Bulgaria, Poland and Czechoslovakia, copying Norway in various ways (Brems 1954; Andersen 1937: 109–124; Boserup and Schlichtkrull 1962: 68–70). In the post-war period West Germany, Britain, Finland, Sweden, Austria, the Netherlands and Spain were among the countries adopting different forms of compulsory notification schemes (OECD 1978a: 165–175; Chapter 7, this volume).

The purpose of this chapter is to investigate the roots of the principle of notification and the register of cartels, monopolies and dominant market actors in Norway in the 1920s. I will analyse the legislative history, including the preparatory works of the provisional Price Regulation Act of 1920 and its amendments, as well the Trust Act of 1926. One important question is where the idea of notification and registration of cartels originated. There was no obvious domestic or foreign model or pattern which could be copied. Another important question regarding the cartel register was its degree of transparency towards the public and other business actors. The most radical version of transparency was that all notified information should be accessible to anyone willing to pay a moderate fee for a copy. This was the original proposal in Norway. The opposite extreme was that notified information should be withheld from the public and only be accessible to the administrative body controlling cartels. In Norway no-one advocated for this alterative, which seems to have been implemented in the Netherlands after the Second World War (Goldstein 1963: viii).

The concept of controlling cartels, monopolies and dominant market actors, which included compulsory notification of their existence, and intervention against abuse of economic power, was among the most controversial political issues of the 1920s in Norway. The Norwegian business community and its core organisations, notably the Norwegian Federation of Industries (NFI; *Norges Industriforbund*) and the Norwegian Federation of Commerce (NFC; *Norges Handelsstands forbund*) were very critical of the proposals by the Trust Commission on permanent legislation controlling cartels, market dominant companies or monopolies. The business organisations were, however, unable to form a united front on basic issues. This had important implications for the final outcome because it increased the scope of action among non-socialist politicians.

An important regulatory aspect of the Trust Act and its notification procedures was that any cartel agreement or other arrangements restricting competition, which had a stipulated duration of more than one year and a term of notice of more than three months, demanded an explicit acceptance by the Trust Control Council (Trustkontrollrådet). Any formal decision by the Trust Control Council, after considering such agreements, would be printed quickly in the gazette of the Trust Control Office, together with the recommendation of the Trust Control Office, which would normally give more than core information about the agreement. Public transparency of such long term restraints on competition was thus usually more wide ranging than the publicly known parts of the cartel registers. I will discuss the regulatory control resulting from these decisions which offered the trust controlling authorities the possibility to set precise conditions and demand specific changes if these long term agreements to restrict competition were to be accepted.

The historiography of the Trust Act

The struggle over the shaping and implementation of the Trust Act, as well as its legal predecessors, has attracted significant interest from many researchers. These have included scholars in jurisprudence in the interwar years (Knoph 1926; Andersen 1937) and later historians (Haaland 1994; Kili 1993; Hodne 1989; Espeli 2002) and an economist (Munthe 1954). With only one exception (Epland 2012), none of the works have concentrated on the establishment of the principle of notification and the cartel register. Researchers usually ascribe a prominent role to the industrious and vigilant Wilhelm Thagaard (1890–1970), who was the Director General of the governmental administrative body, the Price Directorate (1920–

1926, 1940–1942 and 1945–1960) and Trust Control Office (1926–1940). Thagaard, a trained lawyer and economist, was no bureaucrat or civil servant in the Weberian mould, but combined administrative and political activities between which the borderlines were often fluid. The comparative uniqueness of Thagaard, who more or less personified the Norwegian price and competition policy regime and the autonomy of its bodies for 40 years, is beyond dispute (Espeli 2002: 629ff). In this chapter, however, there are reasons to play down Thagaard's importance. Although he belonged to the radical and state interventionist wing of the Liberal Party, the predominant governing party in Norway between 1884 and 1935, other prominent members of the Liberal Party as well as politicians from other parties were also important in shaping legislative principles until 1926.

Historians have underestimated the political importance of the unstable parliamentary power relations that existed after the Liberals lost their parliamentary majority in the general election in autumn 1918. Between 1918 and the enactment of the Trust Act of 1926, Norway was governed by seven minority governments, three led by the Liberals and four by the Conservatives. For example, historians seem to have overlooked completely the trust law proposal by the Conservative government in 1924, which excluded notification procedures and a cartel register. During the years 1918 to 1926 all parliamentary decisions demanded support from at least two of the four major parliamentary parties, which also included the Farmer's Party and the comparatively radical Labour Party. During the 1920s, the three non-socialist parties often endeavoured to avoid giving Labour or smaller socialist parties any significant parliamentary influence. With one important exception that was also the case regarding the core questions dealt with here, but in 1926 important proposals on the Trust Act by the Farmer's Party gained a parliamentary majority.

Although Labour sided with the Liberals in the legislative process in 1926 they were much less ardent supporters of the act than the Liberals. As the Social Democrats in Sweden, Labour considered cartels and trusts as progressive economic developments in the sense that the age of cartels and trusts were viewed as both more efficient and closer to socialism than markets characterised by free competition and numerous actors (Lapidus 2013). Labour's lack of enthusiasm for a Trust Act reflected the fact that the possibility to intervene against abuse of markets power could protect and vitalise capitalism.[1]

Another important element in the research of Trust Act, and the provisional legislation on price regulation preceding it, is that researchers have virtually ignored that all forms of cooperation and collusion by Norwegian business related to exports and foreign markets, including membership of international cartels, were excluded from legal regulation. This oversight is less critical however, as most export cartels among Norwegian manufacturing industries also tried to regulate the domestic market, and were thus indirectly encompassed by the regulations. That was not the case for the large and internationally based Norwegian shipping industry (cf. *Trustkontrollen* 1926: 58–62). This was important because the normally very influential Norwegian Shipowners' Association never found it necessary to engage in the political struggle considered here. Across business as a whole, researchers have also underestimated the importance of the previously mentioned political divisions between the NFI and the NFC.

The origins of the regulatory innovations

In 1916 the Liberal (*Venstre*) government led by Prime Minister Gunnar Knudsen, appointed a trust commission to study the problems of abuse of market power in Norwegian business and to propose measures to counteract such activities. The Trust Commission made little progress until Johan Castberg was appointed as its new chairman on 24 September 1918. Castberg had been minister of Justice as well as Trade in Knudsen's governments and been one the main architects of the controversial concessions laws enacted from 1906. The concession laws made it possible to regulate the influence of direct foreign ownership, as well as limited companies owned by Norwegians, in Norwegian business. Castberg was chairman of the radical Labour Democrats (*Arbeiderdemokratene*) which functioned as the radical wing of the parliamentary group of the Liberals on many issues. Castberg, an educated lawyer and a Supreme Court Judge from 1924 to1926, was one of the most influential politicians and members of the Norwegian parliament (*Stortinget*) at the beginning of the twentieth century. He was chairman of its standing committee on justice from 1915 to1921 and again in 1925–1926 which formulated recommendations on the principles and wording of the Trust Act. Castberg's importance has been underestimated, especially as compared to Thagaard in the most thorough studies of the period 1918 to 1926 (Epland 2012: 39ff.; Haaland 1994: 88ff., 146ff.).

The Trust Commission presented two preliminary principal proposals to the Ministry of Justice on 9 January 1919. This was seven weeks prior to Thagaard being appointed as a member of the Trust Commission and one year prior to his becoming director of the Price Directorate. Most researchers, however, have tended to focus on the one proposal which was enacted by parliament – the act of 14 April 1919 which obliged all businesses to supply the Trust Commission with any information it found necessary for its work. Although the act included relatively severe penalties for not supplying the information, the proposed law was rushed unanimously through parliament.[2] There seems to have been no protests from business organisations against this wide ranging enabling law.

The Trust Commission's other, mostly overlooked proposal to the Ministry of Justice, was more far-reaching and of particular interest here. It proposed a permanent law demanding notification from all business associations, as well as individual companies whose activities might influence production, prices or markets in the country as a whole or in any part. Only employer organisations and trade unions were, as in the later Trust Act, excluded. The associations were to supply all relevant information, such as lists of all their individual members, their bylaws, criteria for membership and exclusion, as well as all collective decisions that could influence markets. Cartel members owned by foreign firms should be specified. In addition to the cartels, individual firms which might influence markets nationally or in part of the country were required to supply additional information.

That should include any memberships in business associations intending to influence markets, and ownership in other companies, as well as if major owners were represented in the leadership of the company through board members. Notification of interlocking directorates was also required.

The Trust Commission argued that such a law be enacted immediately, regardless of what measures the commission would eventually suggest to 'fight' abuses by trusts and cartels. In addition to the far reaching notification demands, it was proposed that the information given by business to the notification authority (to be the Price Directorate established in 1917) should be published regularly. Probably the most controversial part of the proposal was that all notified information in the register should be accessible to the public who were required to pay only a moderate fee. This approach was based on the principle of freedom of information (*offentlighetsprinsippet*). This principle was then well established in Sweden with regard to state administration in general (Hirschfeldt 2008). By contrast, the freedom of information principle in public administration was not enacted in Norway until fifty years later, in 1970. Although some aspects of the licences given to companies controlling waterfalls, mines and industrial real-estate through the concession acts were public and transparent via the parliamentary record, there was no freedom of information principle relating to concession applications in Norway.

The Trust Commission's report did not, however, refer to Sweden's freedom of information principle in its proposal for a transparent cartel register. This raises the question: where did the idea of a far-reaching notification system and a publicly accessible register came from? The Trust Commission referred to two foreign examples: The US, and in particular the 1914 Federal Trade Commission Act, and an Austrian cartel law proposal from 1898, which was never enacted. No details were given in either case. The most important argument for obliging cartels, trusts and large businesses to notify administrators of their agreements, and that this information should be accessible to the public, was that this was probably the best method to regulate their activities. Even experts who were convinced about the economic and societal advantages of trusts and cartels had not expressed any serious objections against notification and transparency about their existence and their way of functioning. It was felt that public awareness and criticism would increase and this would make business actors think twice before they exploited their market power in a 'ruthless' manner (Castberg 1919: 36–37). Castberg published the two law proposals to put pressure on the government. The Ministry of Justice, as well as the rest of the Liberal government, however, was sceptical about his second proposal, and it was never presented to parliament.[3]

In 1919 the Trust Commission's secretary published a survey of trust and cartel legislation in numerous countries as part of a comparative study of the commission's work. The survey showed that the US Trade Commission Act of 1914 only made public information that the commission considered useful, and not as general principle. The act did not establish a federal register on competition restraints. The Trust Commission's final report shows that an Austrian cartel law proposal from 1898, and to a lesser extent a Hungarian proposal from 1904, were the obvious role models behind the Commission's proposal for transparency (*Trustkommisjonen* 1921: 30). The Austrian proposal said the cartel register should be public, meaning that anyone could ask for a copy of any notified information but they had to pay the copying costs. The publicity principle underpinning the Austrian government's proposal was widely accepted. The chaotic parliamentary conditions in Austria from 1897, however, created a legislative deadlock lasting about ten years. The influence of the Austrian ideas on German cartel legislation in the 1920s is well known (Gerber 1998: 43–67). It now seems equally clear that the Austrian influence was also essential for the Norwegian Trust Commission and its cartel register proposals.

In contrast to both the proposal by the Trust Commission and later cartel regulations in Norway, the proposed Austrian law specified explicitly that cartels which did not adhere to notification procedures, were illegal. Later Norwegian legislation only stated that members of cartels not providing the necessary information were free to act in contradiction to decisions by the cartel. Compared to the Austrian case, the Trust Commission offered two major extensions. The Austrian suggestions only encompassed cartels regulating the most important consumer goods on which the government imposed excise taxes. The aim was to intervene against cartels' abuse of power against consumers, which also undermined government finances. In contrast, the Trust Commission not only included cartels from any economic activity but also included monopolies and market dominant companies. This second extension was inspired by the US anti-trust regulations as well as the Norwegian concession laws. Only employer associations and trade unions were excluded following the principles of freedom of association (Øvergaard 1919: 77–78, 119–122, 129–131).

The provisional trust control 1920–1926

Prior to the Trust Commission's final recommendations, submitted in 1921, the Parliament enacted a provisional law on price regulation in August 1920. This was just prior to a general domestic price fall caused by international developments. Most other European countries having imposed price regulations during the First World War had lifted or eased these regulations in summer 1920. The act should be considered as one of a number of political decisions taken to appease the comparative radical Norwegian labour movement (Danielsen 1984: 18–35; Maurseth 1987: 27–218; Olstad 2010: 230–284). The provisional act gave the Price Directorate increased powers to intervene against price increases, to set maximum prices and the right to demand access to all relevant business information. The provisional act only covered the price of physical goods, not services. The Act's first section also established a wide ranging system of notification of competition restraints by any monopoly or large enterprise as well as 'all arrangements and agreements among businesses, which have *the aim* of reducing free competition'. This element of the act – which was the beginning of the cartel register – had neither been included in the Liberal government's proposal nor in the parliamentary committee's recommendations. Despite this, the motion from the floor by a Labour

MP, being an unclear enabling clause, met very little parliamentary resistance. The Conservative minister of Provisions, Rye-Holmboe, responsible for the administration of the Act, and the parliamentary chairman of the Conservatives and later prime minister, Ivar Lykke, explicitly supported the motion. Thagaard subsequently argued that this support was crucial for the outcome, which he found surprising. Historians seem to agree with Thagaard's surprise (Epland 2012: 49–52; Haaland 1994: 177–179).

The outcome was less surprising than it seems. In autumn 1919, the committee of four of the most important national business organisations, including the NFI and NFC, had negotiated with the Price Directorate on new ways of controlling prices. They had proposed a wide ranging notification obligation for monopoly-like companies as well as all agreements defined as 'obstructing free competition'. The intention behind the proposal was that public price regulations should be delegated to the price cartels and monopoly-like companies. The role of the Price Directorate was to control the prices set by these actors but the Directorate should have no competence to overrule them. The business organisations would also accept an extensive principle of notification on restraints of competition and a register of this information at the Price Directorate, but not that there should be any public transparency on these restraints.[4] As a consequence, business organisations did not initially protest against this part of the provisional Price Regulation Act in 1920 as they did with other parts of the act (*Handelsstandens Maanedsskrift* 1920: 232–233).

Lykke, a leading member of the NFC, supported the motion because he considered that a cartel register with some sort of public transparency would demystify the number, importance and influence of cartels. The most important explanation as to the almost unanimous support of a cartel register in 1920, however, was that it would only be provisional. It did not include Thagaard's and the Price Directorate's proposal. The Price Directorate had proposed a permanent statue on price regulation which not only included a cartel register but also general power to ban specific restraints on competition which the Price Directorate found improper. The Price Directorate also meant it should have powers to intervene more generally against cartels, monopolies and large companies which could be 'considered damaging to the general public'.[5]

The controversies related to notification and the cartel register started after the Ministry of Provisions (*Provianteringsdepartementet*) issued its administrative regulations of the provisional Price Regulation Act in November 1920. Notifications included oral agreements and understandings to restrict competition. The regulations also stated that the cartel register would be public and anyone could order a copy of registered information for a fee of two Norwegian kroner (NOK) per page. The cartel register would include the 'main features' of the fairly comprehensive and extensive information to be notified. Business secrets related to technical devices and production methods would not be registered however.[6] The NFC was extremely critical of a publicly transparent cartel register and considered that agreements to 'regulate', but not 'restrict' competition should not be notified. The NFC's linguistic differentiation between regulation and restrictions and their advice to members were equivalent to open civil disobedience by a major business organisation. NFC's advice proved to be influential. Thus on the initiative of the Price Directorate, and supported by the Liberal government, the parliament in the autumn of 1921 amended the provisional Price Regulation Act, against the votes of the Conservatives. The amendments made it clear that in deciding which actions that restrained competition that were to be notified, a broad definition, which included 'regulate' as well as 'restrain', should be used. The NFC gave in. The principle of public transparency of the cartel register, however, was not an issue in the parliamentary debates.[7]

Additional amendments to the provisional act in 1922 extended its scope to include handicrafts and the liberal professions. The amendments did not, however, include banking and insurance where cartels flourished. The 1922 amendments also gave the Price Directorate explicit legal powers, although the provisions were not very transparent, to control and regulate prices set by cartels and large companies. Although the Price Directorate had initiated such controls and regulations in 1921 prior to the amendment, the legal basis for this was at best unclear. It should be emphasised that this critically important amendment met little opposition, even from the Conservative party (Haaland 1994: 186–191; *Prisdirektoratets beretning VIII*/the Price Directorate's annual report for 1921: 2). Consequently the years 1920–1926 have been called period of 'provisional trust control' (Knoph 1926: 12).

The many business critics of the Price Directorate's regulatory activities concentrated their efforts on the Trust Commission's proposals and the content of a permanent Trust Act. It should, however, be mentioned that cartels and large companies generally accepted their obligations to extensive notification from 1921–1922. From 1922 to 1926 the number of cartel-like agreements and monopolies and large scale companies (notifying units) varied between 630 and 700 of which about 90 were companies and the rest various forms of cartels (Epland 2012: 68). The Price Directorate publicised core elements of the notified information in its gazette emphasising that the whole cartel register was public and accessible to anyone for two hours every day at its office (*Norsk Pristidende*: 3619ff., 3847ff., 3945ff., 4005ff., 4059ff., 4153ff.). Very few if any important controversies were related to these procedures until the Trust Act was put into effect in July 1926.[8]

The proposals of the Trust Commission and the debate on the Trust Act

Some of the Trust Commission's members had dissenting views on several important issues. Unfortunately, there is no space to go into these here. The recommendations regarding the scope of notification and transparency of the notified information, however, were unanimously supported. The proposals on the scope of notification were a follow-up to previous suggestions. The Trust Commission argued, as previously, for a wide-ranging application of the principle of freedom of information. In annexes to its recommendation, the Trust Commission printed extensive summaries of the information it had received via the 1919 enabling act as well more detailed information about the actual workings of the cartels. This is still the most detailed and comprehensive public survey of cartels and other competition restraints of the Norwegian economy prior to the Second World War (*Trustkommisjonen* 1921: 30–31, bilag 3–5).

The main business organisations were very critical of the Trust Commission's proposals but were split on how to react and what to recommend to political lawmakers. The NFI pleaded to the government to dismiss the legal proposal altogether and send the report to the archives. The Norwegian Federation of Handicrafts concurred. The NFI argued that the obligations on cartels and large companies to supply large amounts of information would be too expensive both for the notifying units and taxpayers. More critical was the fact that the cartel register should be publicly transparent. That would be particularly beneficial to foreign business interests. The NFI did not believe that the trust controlling authorities would be able to control foreign trusts and monopolies efficiently. Thus trust control would unilaterally damage Norwegian companies and cartels and companies and as a consequence Norwegian society (*Norges Industri* 1922: 440–447; Hodne 1989: 164). It should be noted that the NFI's opposition to any such legislation was not motivated by its humiliating experience with trying to establish a competitor to the very powerful fire insurance cartel in the years 1922 to 1926 (Espeli 1995: 18–23).

The NFC largely agreed with the NFI's critique of notifications and on the disadvantages of a public cartel register. The NFC did consider, however, that a legal option to intervene against unreasonable remuneration and restraints to competition which were damaging to society (*samfunnsskadelig*), would be useful. In the beginning of 1924 the NFC proposed a law in line with such aims but without any notifying measures or a cartel register (*Handelsstandens maanedsskrift* 1924: 6–23).

Later in 1924 a Conservative government proposed a law under the same headings as the NFC had proposed, based on similar evaluations and principles. A state control board could intervene against 'unreasonable prices' and 'improper restraints on competition' in all kinds of private business activity; employee-related affairs excluded. Thus, banking and insurance was included despite warnings and opposition from the business organisations representing them.[9] The later Trust Act encompassed all private and municipal business activity. Commercial boycotts of cooperatives, including refusals to sell, would normally be illegal, while other boycotts might be acceptable (Knoph 1926: 122–127; Espeli 1990: 176ff.).

In 1925 a new Liberal government proposed yet another Trust Law based on the recommendations of the Trust Commission but excluding its most controversial issues such as the ban on 'control companies' (i.e. where a parent company of operating companies functioned as a trust).[10] This proposal, which also allowed the government to grant dispensations to otherwise banned companies, was the basis for complicated parliamentary decision making, but which ultimately resulted in the Trust Act. The extensive parliamentary debates of 1926 have not yet been properly analysed by historians. Despite a heated debate on the precise wording of the scope of notifications, there was little parliamentary disagreement on the principle of notification on restraints of competition which could influence national or regional markets. The Conservative MPs were deeply split on the issue. This was surprising considering that the Conservative government had, in principle, opposed notification in 1924.

The cartel register and its transparency

The main disagreement regarding notification and transparency of the cartel register during the 1926 parliamentary debates concerned large companies' membership of national cartels, being subsidiaries of foreign multinationals, or influencing national or regional markets because of their size. These large companies, defined as companies with a taxable wealth or share capital of one million NOK or more, were required to supply their annual accounts. This was enacted with the smallest possible parliamentary majority. The minority, who opposed notifications altogether, gained the majority, again with the smallest possible margin, on the other controversial issue. This was that companies report their cash dividends and payments made to the CEO and board members, and that this information be made public through the Trust Control Council. The Liberals and the labour parties supported the supply of such information, but lost the vote. The purpose of this proposed transparency was obviously to inform the public directly on possible excessive remuneration and cash dividends from large companies benefitting from high market shares.[11]

The issue of the public transparency of the cartel register was raised in the parliamentary debate in 1926, even after the Liberal government proposed ending the freedom of information principle for the register that had existed since 1921. The only argument given for this policy change was to 'prevent a misuse of the register', which to that date, had not been documented. Future public access to the register was to be made dependant on a decision by the Trust Control Council.[12] The motivation for the policy change proposed by the Minister of Justice, Paal Berg, normally the senior judge of the Supreme Court, might have been to appease business interests.[13] More important, however, was the fact that Norwegian lawyers were generally opposed to the freedom of information principle. The fact that the principal policy change did not create any political or public controversy is a clear indication that newspapers had not utilised the opportunities of the transparent cartel register.

The precise content of the notified information that should be published by the Trust Control Office was not regulated in the Trust Act. This was to be decided by the independent Trust Control Council which formulated the administrative regulations (*Trustkontrollen* 1928: 174–176). These regulations followed the Price Directorate's publishing practises concerning notified competition restraints, themselves based on the provisional Price Regulation Act. The published summaries gave the public concise fact-based information on the formal organisation and functioning of existing cartels, often organised as nationwide or regionally based business interest organisations of various branches. Based on the information published from the cartel register, it was often impossible for an outsider to understand whether the cartel agreements represented the core or a much less important element of the activities of a business interest organisation. It should be emphasised that the published information concerning large companies was shorter and usually much less informative than the information on the cartel agreements (e.g. *Trustkontrollen* 1928: 257–259). According to the Trust Act, the content of the cartel register, except those abstracts being published, were not accessible to anyone. This was in stark contrast to the Trust Commission's original proposals that were founded on the principle of freedom of information. The very restricted transparency of the information contained in the cartel register was probably aimed to reassure business leaders who were generally sceptical about the notification demands.

As mentioned, the Trust Control Council could make specific parts of the cartel register accessible by an individual decision if this was 'desirable' for the work of the control office or if 'general considerations demanded it' (§7). This exemption clause was used only once, in June 1933. That was soon after the Trust Act had been changed in the wake of the international depression, making it possible for the Trust Control Council to intervene and set minimum prices to stop what was considered to be destructive or dangerous cut-throat price competition. The exceptional case is interesting from various perspectives. It was the culmination of the trust controlling authorities' attempts from 1929 to regulate the car insurance market. This market was dominated by the car insurance cartel trying to stop new entrants from outside the cartel surviving and becoming competitive. The decision in 1933 by the Trust Control Council to give the public free and complete access to all new notifications from the car insurance cartel, and two recent former members of the cartel, were likely be part of the Council's same agenda. It would appear that the explicit aim of allowing public access was to ensure that an earlier Trust Control Council decision setting minimum prices was accepted and followed by members of the car insurance cartel (Espeli 1995: 26–31; *Trustkontrollen* 1932: 106–108).

One may ask why Thagaard, as the director of the Trust Control Office, did not ask the Trust Control Council for greater transparency for parts of the cartel register. Although the office had not more than about ten employees in all, and was neither staffed nor organised to cope with numerous inquiries of this sort, the cartel register had been public prior to the Trust Act. One explanation was that such transparency could undermine the normal working methods of Thagaard and his staff. These were based on confidentiality. There were also the problems caused by conflicting parties, when the Control Council could be required to give a decision favouring one or other party. Increased public transparency of parts of the cartel register might also increase consumer criticism towards Thagaard's and the Trust Control Council's increasingly positive attitude to cartels and their willingness to set minimum prices. This was a kind of enforced cartelisation, which occurred in a number of industry sectors after 1932.

Reduction in the scope of notifications but increased control of long term cartels

The Trust Act reduced the scope of notifications to include only the competition restraints of cartels, agreements and large companies which could influence national or regional markets. Thus the number of individually registered entries decreased from about 600 in 1926 to less than 300 up to 1933. Between1933 and 1939 the number of entries of the cartel register increased to 431. The number of listed large companies was stable at around 40 from 1926 while the number of cartels increased rapidly from the beginning of 1930s, reflecting increased cartelisation in Norwegian business generally (Epland 2012: 96).

The cartel register was the basis for the control of competition restraints and it facilitated the possibility of intervening against specific forms of restraints, which could be considered an abuse. The most obvious example was that any cartel agreement restricting competition which had a stipulated duration of more than one year, and a term of notice of more than three months, required an explicit acceptance by the Trust Control Council (§16). Researchers have not studied the control of these agreements as such (Andersen 1937: 256–257). Such long term agreements usually implied a greater degree of public transparency by the *Trustkontrollen* than the normal short notices or excerpts printed in the cartel register. The procedure opened the possibility for the Trust Control Office to set conditions if Thagaard recommended that the Council should accept such long-term agreements. In direct contradiction to the printed sources, researchers have argued that such control was not possible (Munthe 1954: 20). The greater public transparency of such agreements, and the increased possibility for active control from the regulatory authorities, meant that most cartels, if possible, avoided long term agreements. Mergers and acquisitions, an obvious alternative to long term cartel agreements, was not controlled through the Trust Act during the inter-war years, although some new companies that resulted from mergers or acquisitions could be defined as 'large' companies and were subject to notification.

The first long-term cartel agreement considered by the Trust Control Council was the set of arrangements between Norsk Hydro and IG Farben in 1927 which included cross shareholding and it spanned 15 to 25 years. The agreements were also part of an international market sharing agreement regarding nitrogen fertilisers. Thagaard scrutinised the parts of agreements directly related to the Norwegian market and recommended the agreement on the condition that Norsk Hydro was free to set its prices in Norway. The Council agreed to this (*Trustkontrollen* 1927: 145–147; Andersen 2005: 275–284).

The Trust Control Council accepted a number of such long term agreements in individual sectors without Thagaard proposing specific conditions. This included a wide ranging market sharing agreement among domestic cement factories. In most of these instances the public transparency of the agreement documented was short and not very informative. On a number of occasions Thagaard recommended and the Trust Control Council endorsed a flat refusal of such agreements while only providing summarily information for their decision (e.g. *Trustkontrollen* 1927: 457–458, 473–474; 1929: 473–74; 1930: 675–676).

From the late 1920s, the fact that long-term cartel agreements had to be accepted by the trust control authorities was particularly important in creating new and comprehensive cartels in two major markets and industries. The most controversial of these, politically and in the parliament, was the cartelisation of the margarine industry. Thagaard and the Trust Control Council played a central role, both in informing the public about the cartel agreements in 1930 and in bringing about the downfall of the Liberal government in 1931. The core of the political conflict was how accommodating Norwegian authorities should be to demands by Unilever. The outcome of the conflict was that the government mostly had to give in to Unilever's demands. Neither Thagaard nor the Trust Control Council's independent role was undermined by the conflict, however (*Trustkontrollen* 1930: 765–848; Sandvik and Storli 2013; Sandvik 2010).

Thagaard and the Trust Control Council played a much less central role in the extensive cartelisation of the milk market and the dairy industry in the 1930s. Their acceptance of long-term regional cartel agreements in 1931 was, however, essential in creating a secure organisational basis for the regional cartels dominated by producer dairy cooperatives. This was also one of the relatively few examples of Thagaard being overruled by the Trust Control Council. It accepted agreements with a duration of three years while Thagaard had recommended only a two year agreement (*Trustkontrollen* 1931: 974–980,1042–1046; Espeli et al. 2006: 40–59).

Another controversial issue in the 1920s was the so-called tobacco war between Batco (British American Tobacco), popularly labelled the tobacco trust, and the association of Norwegian tobacco-producers. This included a well-organised boycott campaign against Batco, which Thagaard and the Trust Control Council supported. The outcome of the tobacco war was that the biggest domestic tobacco producer, Johan H. Andresen, made a separate long term agreement with Batco. Ultimately, this made Andresen and his personally owned company, J. L. Tiedemanns Tobaksfabrik, the real victor of the prolonged struggle, while excluding the other domestic tobacco producers. They felt betrayed and demanded that the Trust Control Council should set conditions, which would improve their interests, in return for accepting the agreement. Thagaard and the Council flatly refused this. After the Council's decision had been made, Thagaard emphasised his satisfaction with the outcome of the struggle which showed that 'Norwegian companies in competition on the domestic market could prevail against a powerful international trust, when only the will to self-assertion was there.' It should also be emphasised that the core elements of Andresen's agreement with Batco were kept secret from the public as well as the other domestic producers (*Trustkontrollen* 1930: 855–860; Sogner 2012: 314–317; Nordvik 1994).

The trust controlling authorities were deeply involved in setting or influencing specific conditions in the long-term agreements, including conditions on extensive market sharing. This formed the basis for one of the most stable and powerful cartels created in the 1930s; the beer or brewery cartel. The comprehensive and nationwide cartel replaced and supplemented previous, much less ambitious price and markets sharing cartels between the breweries. In 1931 Thagaard and the Trust Control Council refused to accept a 100–year agreement between the breweries in Oslo, largely due to its duration. When, in 1932, the proposed duration of the agreement was reduced to ten years, with an automatic continuation of an additional 15 years and some other minor adjustments, Thagaard and the Council accepted it. This accepted long-term cartel agreement was followed by 30 other similar or identical long term agreements between breweries in the years 1933 to 1938. The beer cartel was also extended to local breweries who were obliged to buy and sell mineral water from the only soft drinks company owned by the three Oslo breweries forming the core of the beer cartel (*Trustkontrollen* 1931: 1049–1053; 1932: 1245–1249; 1938: 59–60; Hovland 1995).

The last major industry notifying long-term cartel agreements differed extensively from the others in being mainly an export industry. The paper industry was one of Norway's core export industries and was well organised in the interwar years. Its cartels participated in a number of international paper cartels among exporters, which was outside the legal scope of the Trust Act. A central element of the agreements between the export cartels of Norway, Sweden and Finland was, however, that domestic paper producers and their cartels should have a monopoly in their home country (Fasting 1967; Clemensson 1948). In such instances long-term cartel agreements with domestic paper wholesalers was a useful tool to avoid domestic competition. That could obviously undermine the Nordic export cartels although this was not clearly stated in the published sources. The detailed implementation of the domestic paper cartels led to numerous conflicts between the trust control authorities and the agreements between the associations of the producers and wholesalers.

These conflicts were mainly related to the conditions for acceptance as wholesalers, and the specific conditions for differentiating wholesaler discounts from prices fixed by the producers. Thagaard and the Council never seemed to have investigated whether the Norwegian paper cartels implemented price discrimination, demanding higher domestic prices compared to export markets, and thus respecting the core functions of the cartels. Thagaard and the Council repeatedly refused to accept long-term cartel agreements during the 1930s, however, because they considered the detailed conditions for wholesalers were unclear and lacking transparency and objectivity. Not until December 1939 was a long-term agreement accepted by Thagaard and the council (*Trustkontrollen* 1935: 239–246; 1938: 95–131; 1940: 173–192).

The Trust Act also allowed for intervention and a ban against the use of fines or other enforcement measures used by cartels against disloyal members, if the use of these measures was considered 'unreasonable' or in conflict with 'common considerations' (*almene hensyn*) in section 19 of the Act. Most of the relatively few interventions and bans based on these clauses were decided prior to the 1930s depression which affected the Norwegian economy from 1931. Most of the bans (21 in all between 1926 and 1940) were probably also directly or indirectly based on individual complaints to the Trust Control Office. There are reasons to believe, however, that a number of these bans were based solely on the notified cartel agreements (e.g. *Trustkontrollen* 1927: 125–129, 185–193; 1930: 757–764).

The Trust Act and cartel agreements on tenders and other secret cartels

The most far reaching enabling clause of the Trust Act (§20) permitted the general dissolution of cartels or large companies if they exercised a damaging influence on domestic markets or if their actions were considered 'improper' (*utilbørlig*). This enabling clause was never applied literally. The clause was in fact interpreted in a very restricted sense, encompassing bans on specific elements of a cartel agreement and not the agreement as a whole. In a few instances it seems that the council intervened and banned specific elements of a cartel agreement based only on the notification documents. These bans were often linked to minimum prices on tenders and others forms of collective agreements on tenders (*Trustkontrollen* 1927: 68–74, 116–117; 1929; 1930: 757–761; 1931: 1002–1004; 1934: 58–63).

The Trust Act demanded that prolonged or permanent cartel tenders should be notified like other cartel agreements. Few such cartel tenders were notified and all seem to have been banned by the Trust Control Office. Cooperation between tenderers in relation to a specific tender was not covered by the obligation to notify the Trust Control Office, however. Instead any formal or tacit agreements with other bidders in a tender had to be declared when delivering the offer (Knoph 1926: 108–109; *Trustkontrollen* 1929: 417–418). It is highly unlikely that participants in prolonged or *ad hoc* cartel tenders informed the tender issuer after 1926. With the exceptions of the few notified prolonged cartels, the Trust Act and the cartel register did not improve the transparency of such cartels; rather, it was the other way around. Such tender cartels were kept secret and not notified to the relevant actors in accord with the law (Espeli 1993: 34ff.).

After the enactment of the Trust Act in 1926 there are, with the important exceptions of permanent or *ad hoc* tender cartels, very few documented examples of important cartels clearly violating the obligation to notify their existence to the cartel register. In 1933, two Norwegian companies producing telephone equipment, made an extensive geographical market-sharing agreement which effectively wiped out direct competition between the two for decades. The two companies, Elektrisk Bureau and Standard Telefon og Kabelfabrikk, dominated the Norwegian market for such products. Both were controlled by multinationals of the telephone equipment industry; L. M. Ericson and ITT respectively, which had a greater international market sharing agreement. This Norwegian cartel was effective until the 1980s when the state telecom monopoly chose to break up the duopoly, which it had tacitly accepted since the 1930s, through an international tender of telephone switches (Espeli 2005: 202–205; Thue 2006: 144ff.).

Interventions and bans by the Trust Control Council

In most of the numerous individual cases considered by the trust controlling authorities between 1926 and 1940 the archiving of ordinary notified information in the cartel register was not particularly important. The majority of the cartel control cases were based on complaints about the actual behaviour of the cartels and large companies. When considering such complaints the Trust Control Office either demanded or was given freely more information about the conflicts than the notification procedures of the cartel register required. In these conflicts the core question was whether the activities could be considered as either, an illegal boycott, an illegal exclusive agreement or an illegal unfounded price difference. The question was answered by following the relatively flexible legal provisions of the Trust Act and the pragmatic interpretations and evaluations of the Trust Control Office and Trust Control Council. In 1932 the Trust Act was amended so that the Council could also intervene against prices being too low, and not as previously only against prices being set too high. The power to set minimum prices was aimed to stop dumping through imports, as the tariff schedule had no provisions to counter such activities, and to prevent the destructive effects of domestic cut-throat price competitions. The enabling power to set minimum prices, a kind of enforced cartelisation, was only used seven times and in no case against dumping (Munthe 1954: 42ff.; Espeli 1995: 30–31). In these cases the cartel register was irrelevant.

The Norwegian cartel register – a regulatory innovation inspired from Austria

The establishment of the cartel register was meant to create public transparency of cartels, large companies and other restraints on competition. The Trust Commission originally proposed a radical freedom of information principle in 1919 for the cartel register, arguing that publicity would make cartels and large companies think twice before they exploited their market powers in unacceptable ways. The idea that the wide ranging transparency of cartels and other competition restraints would function as a deterrent against unacceptable market behaviour was never really tested in Norway although anyone could come to the office of the Price Directorate until July 1926 and copy information about the registered cartels. The Trust Act of 1926, however, departed from the principle of freedom of information and replaced it with a minimum form of public transparency for the cartel register, based on the printed excerpts in the official gazette the Trust Control Office.

The ideas underpinning the original cartel register were clearly inspired by an Austrian cartel law proposal from 1898 and to lesser extent from a Hungarian cartel law proposal from 1904, neither of which were ever enacted. The discussions and regulations in the US, particularly those related to the Clayton Act, were much less important. It should be noted that the proposed Austrian cartel register was limited to consumer goods, while the Norwegian Trust Act encompassed almost all forms of economic activity and incorporated all forms of services including banks and insurance. Although export cartels were excluded, their activities in regulating domestic markets were not. The influences of domestic concession laws on the development of the cartel register is difficult to document. The public transparency on applications of concessions varied significantly and in an incidental manner. No one seems to have advocated for a national register of concessionaires. The inclusion of large companies in the Trust Act and the cartel register was, however, obviously influenced by the possibility to regulate the conditions of ownership of limited companies in the concession laws. The register of business enterprises from 1890 was public but the information to be notified was very limited (Beichmann 1890).

The establishment of a *permanent* cartel register with some kind of public transparency was extremely controversial among the national business organisations within commerce, handicrafts and manufacturing industries between 1921 and the enactment of the Trust Act in 1926. Animosity to a permanent register was mainly based on opposition to a permanent and independent government control body of cartels and large companies with wide ranging but unclear powers to intervene against what it considered an abuse of market powers. The proposed legislation also meant an infringement on the freedom of contract which was the basic principle of commercial law in Norway (and Denmark) at the time. The clearest indication of a tactically based resistance against the notification requirements of the register is that after 1922 there are no indications of organised collective actions trying to sabotage the provisional notification demands administered by the Price Directorate. Nor after 1926 did the national business organisations make any critique of the cartel register and the notification obligations in the Trust Act. In the 1930s the numerous and often fierce political controversies related to Thagaard and the Trust Act were usually related to Thagaard's suggestions to extend significantly the enabling powers of the trust controlling authorities.

Norway was the first country to introduce a cartel register, which began functioning in 1920. The German cartel legislation from 1923 did not include a cartel register but knowledge of the Norwegian legislation became known through the leading European periodical on cartels and competition, the *Kartell-Rundschau* (Gerber 1998: 158–159). In 1930, competition legislation was a major topic during the Interparliamentary Union Conference in London, considered to be a relatively influential international body at the time. The unanimous resolution of the Conference stated that cartels and trusts were a natural part of the economy but they might have a 'harmful effect both as regards public interests and those of the State [and] it is necessary that they should be controlled'. The states should thus 'seek to establish supervision over possible abuses and to prevent those abuses'. In this work regulations creating publicity and disclosure on cartels would be useful. This was close to the purpose behind the Norwegian cartel register (Gerber 1998: 161–162).

The most obvious European county influenced by Norwegian cartel legislation is Denmark. Its act on price agreements in 1937 included a notification procedure for cartels as well as a publicity principle similar to the Norwegian Trust Act (Boje and Kallestrup 2004: 102–128, esp. 127). Poland (1933), Czechoslovakia (1933), Yugoslavia (1934) and Bulgaria (1931) also established various forms of notification procedures and cartel registers in the 1930s and as such followed the Norwegian example although the direct influence is less clear.

In Norway the political controversies regarding the cartel register disappeared after 1926 while its regulatory importance for long-term cartel agreements which needed the explicit acceptance of Trust Control Council increased. After the outbreak of the Second World War, however, the situation changed radically. Soon most of the registered cartels and business associations with powers to regulate prices were integrated into a comprehensive public regime of price control and price regulation swiftly established by Thagaard. Its aim was to reduce the inflation created by the war, mainly through imports. Numerous national, regional and local price commissions were established to control any price increase in their spheres of competence. The national price commissions were normally organised at a branch level with the national cartel or business organisation functioning as secretariat but with representatives from consumer and retailer interests if the commission were to regulate production prices. These corporatist bodies could decide to increase price quotations but actual price increases were, in principle, dependant on the consent of the Trust Control Office. At the beginning of the war the price commissions usually agreed to increase prices without requiring consent because the Trust Control Office did not have the administrative capacity to review all the recommended price increases from the price commissions. Thus the price commissions, with the cartels at their core, were in reality being delegated state authority to regulate prices according to the guidelines formulated by Thagaard and his staff. They, however, had the power to intervene against any decision by the price commissions they considered contradicted price regulation provisions (Espeli 1990: 533–535; *Trustkontrollen* 1939: 352ff., esp. 407ff.).

Thagaard's involvement of the cartels in the state's detailed price regulations increased their legitimacy within organised business significantly. That was one essential element in the relatively successful implementation of detailed price regulations from September 1939 to May 1945. Such a swift administrative delegation of price regulation authority would have been impossible without a cartel register. The tight involvement of the cartels in implementation of the detailed price regulations from 1939 however, also made it difficult to recreate price competition after 1954 when state price regulations were abolished. The Price Act of 1953, replacing the Trust Act, continued the cartel register more or less unaltered. Significant efforts were made to update the register, which had decayed during the period of comprehensive price regulation since 1940. The cartel register was updated and summaries of the notifications were published from 1956. The register did not, however, play any important part in the decision making processes leading to the prohibition of resale maintenance in 1958 and the prohibition of horizontal price agreements in 1960. These prohibitions, although liable to dispensation, meant that two of the most important forms of cartels were banned (Espeli 1993, 2013; Rathke 2013). This reduced the importance of the cartel register although it continued to be maintained with small administrative resources.

The cartel register was finally closed with the Competition Act of 1993. The basic argument for discontinuing notification to a cartel register was that extensive notification had not proved effective in improving competition since 1980. None of the interventions against competitive restraints had been based on notified information. Since the prohibitions of 1957 and 1960 the control of these bans were not based on notified information. Notification of competition restraints, and bans on such restraints, were normally alternative policy approaches. If notification were to be continued it would require comprehensive and large administrative resources to maintain and control such a system. Ultimately it was agreed that these administrative resources should be diverted to other and more effective methods of competition control (Ryssdal *et al.* 1991: 166–168).

Notes

1 OT (Odelstingstidende): esp. 172, 176–178. Norwegian Parliamentary Records (PR) 1926. See also Myrvang (1996).
2 PR 1919, Ot.prp.nr.19, Indst.O.nr.20, OT: 32–37; LT (Lagtingstidende): 10–11.
3 Ministry of Justice to Ministry of Trade 27. January 1919, draft with comments, PR 1920 OT: 470–471 National Archives, Riksarkivet (RA), S-3212, Dd 144; see also Ot.prp.nr.50: 60–66.
4 PR 1920, Dokument nr.22: 1–14.
5 PR 1920, Ot.prp.nr.50: 49–50.
6 PR 1921, Innst.O.XV: 3–7, *Norsk Pristidende* 1920: 3092–3100.
7 PR 1921, Ot.prp.nr.4, Dokument nr.22, Innst.O.XV, OT: 1514–36. 1864; LT: 429–35, 454.
8 One of the exceptions to the rule, see *Handelsstandens Maanedskrift* 1922: 81–84.
9 PR 1924, Ot.prp.nr.48.
10 PR 1925, Ot.prp.nr.43.
11 PR 1926, Innst.O. II, Dokument nr.4, OT 1926 OT: 127–355, esp. 238–288, 383–385; LT: 61–114.
12 PR 1926, OT.prp.nr.43: 6.
13 Hem (2012: 296–297) does not mention this issue.

9 The secret register and its impact in advancing competition in Australia, 1900–2010

Martin Shanahan

Introduction

> [J]ust about every restrictive trade practice known to man is used in Australia.
> (Karmel and Brunt 1963: 94)

Australia has a long history of anti-competitive practices in its markets. From the time of the first fleet, individuals and groups sought to control markets and profit from manipulating prices (Round and Shanahan 2015: 1–10). Despite the Federal Government passing legislation inspired by the Sherman Act before the First World War, it paid no real attention to ensuring competitive markets for almost half a century. Under the shelter of tariff walls, centrally planned wages, and small markets, many firms coordinated collectively, either formally or informally, to control markets. It was only after the Second World War, and the urgency to modernise, industrialise and grow the economy, that serious attention was paid to ensuring competitive internal markets existed. This chapter describes the pre-war attitudes that had developed, and how the introduction of the Trade Practices Act in 1965, which included a secret register, helped transform business attitudes to competition. Extending the perspective to the present day, it is clear that the 1965 Act and the changes that it triggered played a major role in shaping Australia's current competition policy.

Government efforts to tackle anticompetitive practices have waxed and waned over the past 120 years. After Federation in 1901, the new country, concerned to advance, but anxious about the outside world, passed legislation to protect workers and their wages (via conciliation and arbitration laws), the local European descended community (through a restrictive immigration policy) and industry (with tariffs). To protect against trusts and combines, in 1906 the Federal Government passed the Australian Industries Preservation Act 1906 (AIPA), based on the United States Sherman Act, with Prime Minister Alfred Deakin promising to defend Australia's producers, workers and consumers against monopolies (*Melbourne Age*, 22 December 1905).

Despite passing the AIPA, during the first half of the century Australian attitudes to cartels and restrictive trade practices fell somewhere between the hard-lined US attitude and the more benign European view that some good could come from cartels in some circumstances. Australians were aware of the costs of anti-competitive behaviour by firms, but they were especially wary of foreign competitors' efforts to control markets. They were also pragmatists. Australia's internal markets were small and disparate; wealth was drawn largely from the primary sector. The climate was harsh while distances were great, and entrepreneurial capital limited. Many of the larger enterprises, financial institutions and even the primary sector were controlled by outsiders, principally from Britain (Ville and Fleming 2000). In such circumstances, small businesses found it hard to survive alone.

The small enterprises that did develop primarily serviced the agricultural, pastoral, dairying and mining industries; all highly variable in production. Public ownership of essential services was accepted because of the general perception these could not be provided by private operators. Nor did the government abuse its dominant position. It sought neither monopoly profits nor did it provide excessive subsidies (Butlin et al. 1982: 24–25).

For local producers, foreign imports were not the only competition. Tariff free interstate trade meant competition from producers in other states; a problem for small businesses outside the two largest states of New South Wales and Victoria. In an economy with relatively small markets, high wages and large transport and logistics costs, success was difficult. There was price collusion among competitors, particularly in staple homogeneous goods with few substitutes, as were agreements on quality control and output (Ville 1998). Services, too, such as banks and insurance companies, formed mutually beneficial pricing arrangements (Merrett and Ville 2000).

AIPA aimed to prevent the dumping of cheap goods by foreign companies and to prohibit monopolisation by both Australian and overseas companies. The Attorney General Isaacs, while acknowledging the act could be used against Australian firms, conceded that its real aim was to preserve Australian industry from foreign (read large) businesses (CPD, House, 4 July 1906, 1016–1017).[1] AIPA was aimed to protect local industry from the 'unfair' foreign competition that had already been experienced in the agricultural machinery, tobacco, meatpacking, oil, beef and steel industries. Supporters of the Bill argued that predatory pricing, while it enhanced the profits of a few, increased costs for the many.

The Act (s. 4) made it an offence for anyone to enter into a contract or combine 'with intent to restrain trade or commerce to the detriment of the public'. It also included a similar prohibition on 'any foreign corporation or trading or financial corporation formed within the Commonwealth' (s. 5). In the Parliament much of the debate centred on how to word the legislation to stop only those industries whose anti-competitive aims were driven by greed (that is, American firms), rather than as the outcome of enterprise (Australian firms).

In 1908 parliament was presented with a detailed list of combines and trusts that involved intrastate and interstate collusion in both consumer and producer goods. The list included artificial fertilisers, bicycle parts, bricks, confectionery, flour milling, jam, meat, oil, photographic equipment, railroad trucks, shoe machinery, barbed wire and nails, biscuits, cement, condensed milk and tobacco

(CPD, House, 29 July 1909: 1796). In most instances the Crown Solicitor recommended against prosecuting, either because of lack of evidence, or the collusion was confined within one State and fell outside the federal jurisdiction, or it was deemed that the combine did not cause detriment to the public. In 1909, when considering prosecuting confectionery manufacturers for anti-competitive practices, the Crown Solicitor found the price rises were to maintain the industry rather than cause detriment to the public. He did not proceed with the case (CPD, House, 29 July 1909: 1796).

The first real test of AIPA was The King and the Attorney-General of the Commonwealth v. The Associated Northern Collieries and Others (1911); the Coal Vend case (Shanahan and Round 2009). Five coal mining companies in northern New South Wales formed the Associated Northern Collieries. They established a common labour policy, jointly raised the price of coal, followed the same rules when dealing with foreign customers, abided by established quotas, assigned output, and restricted the opening new mines if that meant a member would produce more than their quota.

The Vend joined with four major shipping companies that had colliery interests: Adelaide Steamship Co. Ltd, Howard Smith Co. Ltd, Huddart Parker and Co. Pty Ltd and McIlwraith McEachern and Co. Pty Ltd. The companies united in the Steamship Owners' Association and along with two others formed a Joint Purse agreement in July 1902 that established a management committee to charter members' ships. The companies in the agreement reportedly owned nearly all the wharves in Australia and had some control over the remainder (*Adelaide Register*, 12 November 1909).

The colliers agreed to sell all the coal required for the interstate trade only to the four shipowners, and the shipowners agreed to only deal with Vend sourced coal. The Vend collieries effectively ceased competition with each other, as did the shipowners. The agreement between the collieries was horizontal, while the agreement with the shipowners was vertical. Under the terms of their agreement, the coal companies were the dominant parties.

The government issued a writ alleging that the coal and shipping companies were an unlawful combination and that their agreement was in restraint of trade to the detriment of the public. The companies were charged with attempting to monopolise the trade and forcing consumers to pay higher prices for coal than if there had been no combination.

Despite the strong evidence of collusive activity, proving it was difficult. While prices were set for the shipping companies, the scale varied depending on the location and coal type. In special situations, higher prices could be charged, and the parties could agree to different prices for large contracts. Final prices were adjusted for changing insurance and freight charges. Changes in demand, accidents, strikes or war were specifically cited as factors that might trigger a reconsideration of the price regime. This flexibility reflected practical realities but also made it difficult to detect patterns of collusion so the Court considered them 'as a whole'. Together with the restrictions on transportation, it found the supply of coal was completely controlled by the Vend.

The fact that Vend members remained in the scheme and would pay significant penalties for transgressions reveals its profitability. After extensive and careful economic assessment, the judge held that consumers overpaid between six pence and one shilling a ton for their coal, a significant profit for the proprietors. The court held that the cartel's actions had been detrimental to the public.

The defendants, however, successfully appealed to the Full Bench of the High Court which found the Vend had no intention to cause detriment to the public, a group which included not only consumers, but producers and workers. They held that Vend members intended to restore the Newcastle coal trade to a level where they could sell at a satisfactory profit and pay adequate wages to their workers; actions which did not intend to cause detriment to the public. They applied a nineteenth-century interpretation of restraint of trade:

> Cut-throat competition is not now regarded by a large portion of mankind as necessarily beneficial to the public ... The mere fact that the effect of such combinations may be to raise the price of commodities to the consumer is not regarded. It is recognised that consumers of a commodity are a part, not the whole, of the public, and that in considering the question whether a contract in restraint of trade is detrimental to the public regard must be had to the public at large. It may be that the detriment, if it be one, of enhancement of price to the consumer is compensated for by other advantages to other members of the community, which may, indeed, include the establishment or continuance of an industry which otherwise could not be established or would come to an end.
>
> (*Commonwealth* v. *Associated Northern Collieries*: 76–77)[2]

The Commonwealth Government unsuccessfully appealed to the Privy Council in England, at the time Australia's highest appeals court.[3] The Privy Council held that the colliery proprietors and shipowners had not entered into contracts to restrain trade or commerce, or agreed to combine, with any intent to restrain trade or to monopolise to the detriment of the public. As with the Full Court, the Privy Council considered that the term, the public, was not merely the coal consumers and gave greater weight to the mine proprietors and workers.

The case represented the high water mark of the federal government's actions against anti-competitive behaviour for almost half a century. Launched at a time of multiple investigations into cartels and monopolies, efforts to combat market exploitation and encourage competition were virtually abandoned for the next 50 years. Between 1908 and 1965 the AIPA, despite being amended and remaining in the statute books, was used in only three minor prosecutions. It would not be until after the Second World War, and the realisation that the Australian economy desperately needed invigoration, that federal politicians seriously returned to the issue of stimulating competition in markets around the country.

Despite the lack of effective government action to promote competition, between 1901 and 1939 there were, at the Federal level, at least twelve royal commissions and enquiries into monopolies, cartels and other combinations, and twenty two at State government level (Round and Shanahan 2015: 49–51). Of the dozen Federal enquiries, nine occurred before the First World War. While the majority found the existence of a combine or cartel, and all but three clearly found detriment to the public, none resulted in changes to legislation or institutions that enhanced competition in the industry under examination. While public exposure may have caused firms in the spotlight to modify their behaviour, none of the enquiries appears to have actually advanced competition through triggering long-term change to firm behaviour or structural changes to markets.

Before the Second World War there were also several State inquiries into apparently anti-competitive behaviour. The investigations included areas such as food, drink, and construction (i.e. bricks, roofing tiles), the cost of living, and retail stores, revealing public disquiet with firm behaviour, particularly as it affected individuals and families. The enquiries, which peaked in the years of rising prices in the First World War and again towards the end of the 1930s Depression, reveal State governments' relatively ineffective response to popular pressure. In all but three of the 22 cases the inquiry found there was detriment to the public. Only one, however, resulted in any subsequent legislation (Stalley 1956; Gentle 1979; Borchardt 1958, 1970; Round and Shanahan 2015: ch. 2).

Thus in most of the enquiries, evidence of collusion, price fixing, or market sharing that was detrimental to the public interest, was found. The sheer number of enquiries and the diversity of industries involved, suggest a persistent use of anti-competitive practices in some industries.

Part of the explanation for politicians' lack of action against these types of activities lay in the range of anticompetitive organisations involved in the economy. There was a mixture of government monopolies (perceived as beneficial); a small number of potential foreign (US) combines (mostly viewed as predatory); locally based firms with foreign origins (which if British were seen as benign, but otherwise suspect) and local businesses (usually perceived as struggling). Politicians needed to respond to all these constituents. When the Australian Industries Preservation Bill was debated several Labor members actually spoke in favour of certain monopolies and trusts because they were good for the workers (CPD, House, 19 September 1911: 625). When on the opposite side of the parliament, the same politicians opposed the trusts and charged their political opponents with supporting such groups. While Australian politics and institutions were focused on the importance of workers receiving a living wage, much less attention was paid to the price of goods they purchased, or how these prices were set.

The Australian Constitution also hampered the Federal Government. Section 51(i) of the Constitution, which empowers the Commonwealth to regulate trade and commerce between the States was interpreted to mean the Commonwealth could only control *inter*state trade. Monopolists that operated nationally could incorporate *within* each State and be immune from prosecution. To amend the Constitution required a referendum supported by a majority of electors in a majority of States. Only eight out of 44 referendums have passed in Australia over 115 years, and all efforts to change the constitution to tackle monopolies or to control prices failed.

The writers of the Constitution, aware of the difficulties in resolving commercial disputes, designed an Inter-State Commission (ss. 101–104). It was intended to have the power to legislate on trade and commerce and monitor prices. The Commission's first investigations began in 1913, and in total it produced 70 reports in just less than five years.[4] While its primary focus was tariffs (i.e. external trade), it also revealed cartel behaviour within industries. The Commission found positive evidence of price fixing and other cartel behaviour to the detriment of the public in just under a third of the industries it investigated (Round and Shanahan 2015: 50–51). As its role was broader than the control of monopolies, however, it lacked the necessary authority to penalise monopolists (Brown 1914: 179–182).

The war years from 1914 to 1918 were critical in shaping Australian attitudes to anti-competitive behaviour. Under the War Precautions Act 1916, a Prices Adjustment Board was established, together with marketing boards to ensure the supply of commodities such as wool and wheat (Scott 1936). In the challenging years of the late 1920s and 1930s, marketing and price control boards were adopted for many agricultural products. These became a ubiquitous feature of Australian agriculture until at least the 1970s (Dyster and Meredith 1990). Such mechanisms, particularly when comprised of both public and private sector interests, desensitised consumers to price setting and orderly marketing and blurred the distinction between private and public sector interference in markets.

In total, over 65 separate industries were alleged to be run by combines between 1901 and 1939. These included both inter- and intrastate combinations and covered industries as diverse as agricultural machinery to fresh fish; insurance to roofing tiles. Table 9.1 identifies many of the pre-Second World War industries where prices were artificially set, distribution channels controlled or other forms of market manipulation conducted. The wide range of industries, and their direct impact on consumers, reveals the penetration of such structures and anti-competitive behaviour in the Australian economy at this time.

In the areas of banks, breweries, dental supplies, groceries, hotels, insurance, kerosene, matches, petroleum, photographic materials, press and cable services, retail trade, salt, timber, tobacco, wheat milling the agreements covered all the states in Australian. Another fifteen covered only either New South Wales or Victoria, which were the two dominant States in Australia. While the starting dates and length of the combination varied between industries, the blanketing of States suggests a coordinated approach to creating anti-competitive structures.

Almost all industries involved in these cartels dealt in essential goods and services, where rival sellers' products were largely undifferentiated, demand was inelastic and for which there were few close substitutes. Manufacturing, distribution and retail industries all feature heavily. About one-third of the industries were involved in manufacturing producer goods. Few of the industries experienced only short periods of cartel activity – most lasted for a decade or more, and several for over two decades.

At the federal level, for four decades from 1913, protection, nation building and economic development took precedence over tackling concentrated market structures and anti-competitive behaviour. Not until the mid- to late 1950s, with war economy problems being a thing of the past, did the interests of consumers emerge as a subject of concern for governments. It was only with the hardening of international views against cartels that Australians begin to reassess the detrimental effect of firms cooperating to lessen competition.

Post-Second World War

The First World War had highlighted Australia's vulnerability because of the nation's distance from the UK and relatively small population and economy. The Second World War underlined the problem of defending a small population of only seven million spread over a vast land area. As a counter, the government set out on a programme of population growth through assisted immigration and industrialisation (Schedvin 2008).

By the late 1950s and early 1960s, modernising the Australian economy was important to all politicians. Overseas, governments had introduced legislation controlling restrictive practice. Such legislation had been introduced in the UK, while the US was the home of free enterprise. The success of the British legislation in examining individual circumstances contrasted to the American approach of banning monopolies; something considered difficult in the Australian context (Kenwood 1995: 90–90). Decisions of the High Court too had broadened the interpretation of the Constitution to provide the Federal government with more opportunity to intervene in the economy (Zines 1992).

There were two main motivations for the move to introduce trade practices legislation in the early 1960s. The first was nation building and modernising, especially increasing the industrialisation of the economy. According to Attorney-General Barwick, antitrust legislation in America was introduced at almost the same stage of its economic development (NAA, A432, 1966/2098, Minutes, 11 August 1961: 10). Even the Chief Justice of the United States, suggested that for Australia to 'grow up' it needed anti-trust legislation (NAA, A432, 1966/2098, Minutes, 15 September 1961: 84).

The second concern was rising prices, often the result of bottlenecks in production. Assisted migration raised family formation and demand for housing and automobiles (Whitwell 1989: 61). Virtually full employment and a rise in consumer spending increased demand. Growing affluence increased the pressure to remove anti-competitive arrangements even as a centralised wage system eased pressure on businesses to compete on price (Whitwell 1989: 15–18; Dyster and Meredith 1990: 182–225). Reliant on a cushioned market, the majority of manufacturers and retailers believed that, for all to share in the abundance, they needed to suppress competition. 'Orderly marketing' (i.e. sharing the market rather than competing) was the rule. The government began to realise that the introduction of a truly competitive market would force businesses to change, and result in lower prices to consumers.

Table 9.1 combines the industries identified pre-the Second World War as cartels or combinations with 102 industries identified by academics as cartels or engaging in restrictive trade practices in the 1960s. The results identify 38 cartels and a wide range of industries with restrictive practices from 1901 to 1961. While some industries had documented evidence of cartels in only one of the two periods, 29.5 per cent operated as cartels over an extended – although not necessarily continuous – period. The cartels encompass goods and services, distribution and manufacturing, and consumer and producer goods, and largely comprise products that were either essential inputs for the economy to operate or were necessary daily consumables for which there were no ready substitutes. Among the more important goods the markets for which were manipulated, were agricultural machinery, banks, bread, breweries, brickmaking, butter, cement, flour millers, glass, hotels, insurance and assurance, iron and steel, lime, paper products, petroleum products, pharmacies, rolling stock, roofing tiles, rubber products, timber and tobacco. Many of these goods served as inputs into other parts of the economy, as for example, cement, brickmaking, insurance, iron and steel, petroleum, rolling stock.

These records suggest that the cost of cartels and other anti-competitive behaviour to the Australian economy persisted over decades. The impact of this for the trajectory of Australia's economic growth was profound. The costs of doing business in Australia were clearly higher because of cosy arrangements and orderly marketing.

In 1960 Barwick travelled to the USA, Canada and the UK to examine their anti-trust legislation (Merrett, Corones and Round 2007). He wanted to introduce a simple law with substantial impact. The 1961 Liberal Party platform promised protection from all forms of anti-competitive behaviour by firms that acted the public interest (Liberal Party Platform November 1960).

One proposal to address restrictive trade practices was the establishment of a register – a mechanism that could help transition businesses away from their anti-competitive practices and towards more competitive attitudes. As Attorney-General Barwick knew, the biggest hurdle would be to overcome the opposition of vested business interests unused to revealing their anti-competitive practices to anyone, let alone a public body.

He did not want to follow either the UK legislation, which included a public register but had no penalties, or the US legislation, which focused on criminal sanction. He argued that a secret register would lead to frank and full disclosure of restrictive practices and more information, while an open register would drive agreements 'underground'. Nonetheless, the States urged that the register be public. Ultimately, it was suggested that a secret register would give businessmen the opportunity to adjust (NAA, A432, 1966/2098, Minutes, 27 July 1961: 30). As a compromise between openness and secrecy, it was proposed that people with an 'appropriate' interest would be allowed to look at the register. In the end, the register remained secret.

While some of Barwick's proposals were new, others borrowed from overseas, such as promoting public welfare rather than focusing on competition *per se* (Barton 1963: 130–131). Unlike the UK, the Act was to cover not only bilateral and multilateral restrictive arrangements but also unilateral actions by individual companies. This was to ensure that not only associations with many members, or cartels with a few members would be included, but also that monopolies, which had the power to operate in isolation, would not be immune (CPD, House, 6 December 1962).

Table 9.1 Cartels and industries involved in restrictive practices, 1901–1939 and to the 1960s.

Industry	1901–1939	1961	Industry	1901–1939	1961
Agricultural machinery *	X	X	Ham and bacon trade	X	
Aircraft manufacture and maintenance		X	Handkerchiefs		X
Artificial flowers		X	Hardware trade*	X	X
Artificial manure	X		Heavy machinery		X
Asbestos cement sheets		X	Hotels*	X	X
Automotive parts		X	Ice	X	
Banks*	X	X	Ice cream		X
Barbed wire and nails	X		Industrial chemicals		X
Barristers	X		Insurance and assurance*	X	X
Batteries		X	Internal combustion engines		X
Bicycle parts*	X	X	Iron and steel*	X	X
Biscuits*	X	X	Jams and preserves*	X	X
Boot making equipment	X		Jewellers	X	
Boots and shoes – retail	X		Kerosene	X	
Bread*	X	X	Lime*	X	X
Breweries*	X	X	Margarine		X
Brickmaking*	X	X	Masonite		X
Butter*	X	X	Matches*	X	X
Canvas goods		X	Meat	X	
Carpets		X	Milk – distributors*	X	X
Cement*	X	X	Milk – producers	X	
Chains		X	Motor vehicles		X
Cheese	X		Newsagents*	X	X
Coal	X		Newspapers and periodicals*	X	X
Coke works		X	Non-ferrous metals		X
Condensed milk	X		Paints		X
Confectionery*	X	X	Paper products*	X	X
Copper refining		X	Petroleum products*	X	X
Cotton/spinning/weaving	X	X	Pharmaceutical industry		X
Cutlery and flatware		X	Pharmacies*	X	X
Dental supplies*	X	X	Photographic materials*	X	X
Driving schools		X	Plastic materials		X
Dry cleaning		X	Plumbers' goods		X
Electric cables		X	Plywood		X
Electric lamps		X	Poultry		X
Electrical contracting		X	Printing trade	X	
Electrical equipment		X	Quarried materials		X
Engine reconditioning		X	Rabbit exporters	X	
Explosives*	X	X	Racehorse training		X
Fencing and netting		X	Radio receivers		X
Fibrous plaster*	X	X	Radio valves		X
Firewood	X		Railway rolling stock*	X	X
Fish – canning		X	Refrigerators		X
Fish – fresh	X		Retail trade	X	
Flax mills		X	Rice	X	

Table 9.1 Continued.

Industry	1901–1939	1961	Industry	1901–1939	1961
Floor and wall tiles		X	Roofing tiles*	X	X
Floor coverings		X	Rope and cordage*	X	X
Flour millers*	X	X	Rubber products (inc. tyres)*	X	X
Fluorescent tubes		X	Salt	X	
Footwear – repairs		X	Shipbuilding		X
Footwear – sales*	X	X	Shipping	X	
Fruit – dried	X		Soap and candles		X
Fruit – fresh*	X	X	Soft drinks		X
Furniture manufacture		X	Sugar	X	
Glass*	X	X	Tanneries*	X	X
Grocery trade (manufacture wholesale/retail)	X		Timber*	X	X
Hairdressing		X	Tobacco*	X	X

Note: * signifies industry is comprised of cartels.
Source: Round and Shanahan (2015), combined with data from Cook (1961), Hunter (1961), Karmel and Brunt (1963), Sheridan (1974).

While the contents of the Register of Trade Agreements under the Trade Practices Act 1965 were to be kept secret, its administrator, the Commissioner of Trade Practices, was free to examine any agreement and bring to an end those deemed against the public interest. Following section 35, if the Commissioner (Mr Ron Bannerman) or his office 'determined' an 'examinable' agreement, it was effectively dissolved or modified to a form that was judged not to be harmful to competition. The process was one of consultation and negotiation.[5] Together with the register, this was to prove a key factor in ultimately altering business attitudes. Over the register's seven-year life, just over 3250 of the 14,480 registered agreements were determined; all *in camera* (i.e. in secret).

Businessmen had a major incentive to register their agreements. Not only would their arrangements be kept secret, but notification exempted the businessmen from immediate liability. Only if their arrangements were deemed examinable, and after secret negotiations with the Commissioner they refused to have the agreement determined, was it possible that they would be taken to court. As a consequence of this initial indemnity, every type of conduct listed in section 35 is found in the registered agreements. Horizontal agreements alone covered 52 of the 56 divisions in the Standard International Trade Classification. Over half of the registered agreements (just over 5900) consisted of vertical distribution agreements between a manufacturer or a wholesaler with its outlets, often covering several hundred distributors. The manufacturer or wholesaler often competed with its own retail outlets such that the agreement effectively was between competitors. These agreements were typically about resale price maintenance, which was rampant throughout Australia, or involved forms of exclusive dealing. Distribution agreements commonly reinforced horizontal agreements, whereby rival producers would agree on prices or other terms of sale, and the distribution agreement would force the distributors to abide by their supplier's specified price (Commissioner of Trade Practices 1970).

After three years of operation, the annual report in June 1970 provided some details on the industries which had ceased anti-competitive agreements. Businessmen were slowly recognising that their old habits of engaging in comfortable agreements, especially those relating to prices, were under serious threat. Price-fixing agreements in gypsum and plasterboard, tyres and tubes, builders' hardware, welding electrodes, rubber footwear, sporting ammunition, nails, paint, engineers' cutting tools, greeting cards, metal control valves, and ham and bacon, all ceased in that year. In the case of producer goods, themselves inputs into downstream activities, these changes meant the benefits from increased competition were likely to start flowing through the production chain.

The majority of the determined agreements involved the manipulation of distribution, while many others related to pricing agreements, both horizontal and vertical. In the activities of motor vehicle distribution and financing, for example, one hundred percent of the registered agreements were against the public interest; the highest proportion of all the industries considered by the Commissioner. In the fields of welding equipment, phosphate and household chemicals, iron and steel products and hardware, at least nine out of ten registered agreements were against the public interest. In all, around 4000 firms were parties to agreements that were eventually determined. This was out of a total of just over 12,700 firms that were parties to registered agreements; many were also subsidiaries of foreign companies. Sixteen individual companies were parties to over one per cent of all registered agreements involving consumer durables, financial services, wholesaling and distribution of timber products, chemicals, welding equipment, engines, and agricultural services. One company selling and financing consumer durables (broadly defined) accounted for 4.4 per cent of all registered agreements, but 19.4 per cent of the determined agreements; 98.7 per cent of its registered agreements were determined. Another single company involved in the provision of financial services was responsible for the fifth highest percentage (2.47 per cent) of all registered agreements and the second highest percentage (6.4 per cent) of all determined agreements; these determined agreements representing 58 per cent of all of its registered agreements. As few as nine companies (0.2 per cent of all the companies that were parties to agreements that were determined) were each responsible for two per cent or more of all determined agreements. While this may seem small, overall these companies accounted for almost half of all determinations, and the 18 companies which were involved in one per cent or more of the determinations were associated with 61 per cent of them.

The files reveal, therefore, not only the extent of anti-competitive agreements across the Australian economy, they also reveal that for some companies, and in some fields, agreements that were against the public interest came as second nature, and was their standard method of doing business.

Publicly, the Commissioner was much more circumspect in what he revealed about the agreements. Nevertheless, the first annual report the Commissioner recorded almost 3000 horizontal agreements, of which around 1400 were trade association agreements, from 968 trade associations (Commissioner of Trade Practices 1968). Of these, 375 were in manufacturing and 367 in wholesaling associations, almost 130 were associated with retailing, and the other 285 were between trade associations and others (often other trade associations). In the other 1555 horizontal agreements, over 680 were in manufacturing industries; over 250 in wholesaling and around 40 in retailing. Almost 500 were in livestock and wool trading where the agreements were mainly between agents at different selling locations and coordinating commissions or restrictions on bidding at auctions. Finally, just fewer than 100 occurred in service industries.

For the next six years Bannerman updated these statistics in each annual report. Occasionally there was no doubt which companies were involved, even though he never named individual firms. In his second report for example, he noted that pricing agreements in the concrete pipes, ceramic tiles, tyres and tubes, and arc welding electrodes industries had ceased, commenting that in each case the manufacturers accounted for all, or almost all, of the total Australian production of these goods (Commissioner of Trade Practices 1969: 4).

The annual reports provided details about a subset of cases where the anticompetitive behaviour ceased, or was modified after intervention by the Commissioner. He mentions a total of 285 determined agreements, of which 58 per cent involved horizontal restrictions, 35 per cent were vertical agreements and seven per cent covered both. This was a marked deviation from the overall structure of the Register discussed above. For example, the public record suggests 48 per cent of the determined agreements were among manufacturers, while in reality it was around 10 per cent. Similarly the annual report suggests associations were involved in 28 per cent of the targeted agreements, rather more than the 11 per cent were actually in the overall Register.

The 285 more public determinations, some of which covered multiple activities, included 181 agreements with price fixing (63 per cent), 91 with discount fixing (32 per cent), 119 with resale price maintenance (42 per cent), 18 with bid rigging (six per cent), 53 with exclusive dealing (19 per cent), 17 with market sharing (six per cent), 14 with output restrictions (five per cent), and three with refusals to deal (one per cent). It appears the Commissioner and his office sought to highlight price fixing and other price agreements. He also targeted the fixing of discounts. While the number of determinations as a result of direct action was not large, the percentages of determinations attributable to intervention by the Commissioner were also relatively high for output restrictions, bid rigging and refusals to deal.

Once the problem was determined with the parties, satisfactory outcomes were usually achieved without the need for the use of more formal consultations (s. 48). Only 15 cases went this far. Three related to a variety of fibreboard containers and two to electric lamps, and other major industries included concrete pipes, asbestos cement products, ceramic wall tiles, electric cables, tyres and tubes, gypsum plaster, and plasterboard. The Commissioner was successful in all three cases that ultimately went to a Tribunal (frozen vegetables, fibreboard containers, and books). Other businesses, as in cement, avoided the Tribunal by merging and restructuring. In 1971, after a new Trade Practices Act was passed, the Commissioner initiated several more cases alleging resale price maintenance, successfully obtaining injunctions against prominent companies in industries as diverse as cosmetics and toiletries, cattle tickicide, evaporative air conditioners, electrical appliances, television sets, petrol and blankets.

The Commissioner also regularly complained of slow progress, but by year four he was optimistic for the future (Commissioner of Trade Practices 1971: 13; *Australian*, 21 August 1971). In the next year a constitutional challenge to his office, subsequently rejected by the High Court, and Parliamentary debates, attracted wide publicity. In May 1972 the Attorney-General introduced proposals to strengthen the legislation and widen its scope (CPD, Senate, 24 May 1972: 1956–1969). The government lost office before it could proceed.

The Commissioner used his sixth annual report to show the need for stronger trade practices legislation. He revealed that some companies were using the twilight period before the introduction of new laws to continue their price agreements. Many businessmen still needed the threat of enforcement to behave competitively (Commissioner of Trade Practices 1974: 2). Nonetheless he felt the legislation had successfully demonstrated the extent of the problem of anticompetitive practices in Australia, and the need for additional legislation (ibid.: 1).

In his final report he wrote that businesses were abandoning price agreements because 'the climate has changed and ... the attitudes of businessmen generally are different from what they used to be' (ibid.: 1–4).

After the secret register

It is impossible to determine quantitatively the impact of the secret register on firm behaviour and anticompetitive arrangements. Too many things have changed in the 50 years since the Act was passed that created the register. Nonetheless, it is possible to follow the change in regulatory standards that has occurred since; the change in attitudes held by the government and business, and to reflect on the range of anticompetitive behaviour that has been successfully detected since the mid-1970s.

A new, more interventionist Labor government was elected in 1972, determined to press further against anti-competitive behaviour. ALP Senator Lionel Murphy condemned the Restrictive Trade Practices Act 1971, and the 1965 Act, as completely ineffective (CPD, Senate, 30 July 1974: 540). This was really just rhetoric. The modern Trade Practices Act 1974 that he introduced and its ultimate acceptance by business would have been much harder to achieve without the register and the work done to enforce it.

The Trade Practices Act 1974 prohibited outright, contracts, arrangements and understandings in restraint of trade or commerce, monopolisation, exclusive dealing, resale price maintenance, price discrimination and anti-competitive mergers. As a consequence, registration of agreements was discontinued and secrecy was confined to confidential information. Secrecy around the contents of the old Register was, however, retained. The Act accelerated the process of eliminating unfair agreements and practices, and allowed those affected to bring private proceedings in the courts. Penalties were increased. In consumer law, mandatory consumer standards replaced the principle of caveat emptor as the default approach (CPD, Senate, 30 July 1974: 540–547).

The 1974 Act brought Australia into line with then contemporary overseas legislation promoting competition. As well as aiming to stop anti-competitive mergers and the misuse of market power, the Act specifically banned horizontal and vertical price and non-price agreements and retained the prohibition of resale price maintenance.

For Australian executives, their cosy collusive days were over. Nor could they hide behind a secret register and avoid exposure of their anti-competitive actions. For the first time, cartel behaviour could be made public through the record of Trade Practices Commission (TPC) investigations and court decisions. Even though such information was the tip of the iceberg of corporate collusion – all that is known is the action taken by the agency – it still signalled a significant shift in the attitudes of government, administration and the private sector.

While Australia was making progress in convincing local firms to compete rather than collude, internationally, regulations covering anticompetitive behaviour, and cartels were advancing. While the Trade Practices Act 1974 was Australia's first modern trade practices law, it was introduced at the tail end of the global shift towards harsher antitrust laws; a movement consistent with increased international trade. The many trade agreements implemented in the 1970s and 1980s triggered a strengthening of regulations against cartels and anti-competitive behaviour (Freyer 2006; Joelson 2006; Wells 2002). For Australia to participate in international commerce meant Australian businesses had to learn higher standards of behaviour (Spier and Grimwade 1997). The EU, for example, introduced new standards of competition that transcended national boundaries, and required participant countries both inside and outside the EU to modify their internal trade practice regulations (McGowan 2010). The TPC, later, the Australian Competition and Consumer Commission (ACCC) worked to help Australia catch up to international policy standards (Grabosky and Braithwaite 1986). Internationally pressure mounted to make serious cartel conduct (including price fixing) a criminal offence. Although it took many years to be introduced in Australia, the Labor government finally made serious cartel conduct a criminal offence in 2009.

Although the competition agency has an enviable win/loss record over the last three decades, especially against firms that fix prices, the evidence suggests that collusion remains a problem in Australia. Examining the successful TPC/ACCC court cases between 1974 to 2004 provides a restricted insight into the extent of continuing anticompetitive behaviour late in twentieth century Australia. Forty four firms were found guilty of fixing prices over the thirty years to 2004. They include many familiar industries including those in beer production, building and construction materials, bricks, concrete, petroleum products, pharmaceuticals, retailing, and sugar, as well as newer industries in animal vitamins, automobile parts and windshields, internet access services, barbeque equipment, foam products and retail department stores (Round and Shanahan 2015: 215).

It is also possible to examine which industries exhibit persistent tendencies to engage in anticompetitive behaviour. Table 9.2 identifies 15 industries that, in one form or another, have been identified for over a century as engaging in cartel practices in Australia. About half are directly involved in final retail sales to consumers, and involve essential commodities, such as banking services, bread, beer, groceries, sugar and petroleum. Others are key inputs into important production processes, such as bricks, cement and concrete, iron and steel, and rubber products. Collusion is present at all major functional levels of the chain of production and distribution – manufacturing, wholesaling and retailing.

While a single cartel agreement can be viewed as a 'one-off' event, created in response to changes in market conditions, the external regulatory environment, or changes in firm identity or its management team, it is clear that for some industries it is also a preferred way of doing business. Product type, industry background, environment and culture predispose some Australian industries to the easy life promised by anti-competitive practices. Such cartels are also resilient to social, political and judicial concerns about the damage they do to social welfare.

Conclusion

It took Australia more than half a century to move beyond the ineffective Australian Industries Preservation Act 1906 and introduce national legislation to inhibit

Table 9.2 Cartels present throughout the twentieth century.

Present pre-war and 1961	Present 1969–2009
Banks	Banking – mortgages
Bread	Bread retail
Breweries, hotels	Breweries, also wholesalers of beer, wine and spirits
Brickmaking	Bricks/clay bricks
Cement, lime	Concrete (also pre-mixed), aggregate
Ice*	Ice
Iron and steel	Steel pipes
Groceries – manufacture, wholesale, retail	Retail – supermarkets, wholesale frozen foods
Petroleum products	Petrol and petroleum products, petrol retail
Pharmacies – retail	Pharmaceuticals – wholesalers
Retail trade	Retail (department stores)
Roofing tiles	Roof tiling
Rubber tyres and related products	Rubber tyres and related products
Sugar*	Sugar
Wheat and flour milling, wheat trade	Wheat and flour milling (wholesale)

Note* Signifies cartel present in pre-war period but not in 1961. Appeared again from 1974 onwards.

Sources: Cook (1961); Hunter (1961); Karmel and Brunt (1963); Sheridan (1974); Round (2000); Round and Hanna (2005); Round and Shanahan (2015); Round and Siegfried (1994); Round, Siegfried and Baillie (1996); and updates from ACCC (2004–2009) and www.law.unimelb.edu.au/cartel.

anti-competitive behaviour. The Trade Practices Act 1965 was brought in amongst howls of outrage from many business leaders (*Melbourne Age*, 25 August 1970; *Australian Financial Review*, 20 October 1970; *Sydney Morning Herald*, 10 November 1970; *Canberra Times*, 9 February 1971).

In 2010, the Competition and Consumer Act replaced the Trade Practices Act 1974. Cartels were prohibited and virtually all forms of anti-competitive behaviour now require an assessment of their substantial purpose. In 2012–2013 the ACCC examined over 800 complaints and enquiries, reviewed almost 300 mergers and was involved in 15 proceedings before the Federal Court of Australia on competition matters. There were 11 civil actions for cartel. Where the secret register meant the rationale for the authorities pursuing particular agreements had to be inferred, the ACCC now publically lists the reasons behind its pursuit of particular firms (Coops and Hendrick 2014).

In recent years the ACCC listed its competition priorities as: cartel conduct; anti-competitive agreements; and misuse of market power. Unconstrained by the earlier constitutional interpretations, and in an era of globalisation, the Competition and Consumer Act 2010 crosses multiple borders – something almost impossible for the first trade practice legislators to achieve. The Act applies to conduct, even if engaged in outside Australia, if the party engaging in the conduct is incorporated in Australia, registered as a foreign company in Australia, carries on a business in Australia (including nominees or agents) or is ordinarily a resident of Australia.

Penalties too have increased. While leniency, cooperation and discussion are still options, penalties for breaching civil and criminal competition prohibitions are now clear. Australians no longer accept that firms can collude to fix prices, or divide up the market. It is unacceptable for business to rig tenders or force their goods on unwilling retailers. Cartels are no longer tolerated. Much has changed since Ron Bannerman, reflecting on the 1967 Trade Practices Act wrote:

> There was sometimes a club-like attitude. The rules were known to the members, but they did not want to talk about them to other people … price agreements between competitors were common, although the customers were not told … often … not only was price fixed, but also who could trade, and how … competitors could be excluded and new entrants deterred.
> (Bannerman 1985: 84)

The secret register was an important institution that helped change Australian's attitudes to anti-competitive practices. It paved the way for more modern Trade Practices legislation and the promotion of competitive attitudes and markets. The true value of its impact in advancing Australian business practices is yet to be fully calculated.

Acknowledgements

This chapter builds on the work of several colleagues in the Centre for Regulation and Market Research at the University of South Australia, in particular K. Round,

Z. Brunkova and D. K. Round. I thank them for their assistance and generosity in allowing me to use our work here. All errors remain my responsibility.

Archival and printed sources

Australian Competition and Consumer Commission and the Australian Energy Regulator, Annual Report 2012–2013, www.accc.gov.au/system/files/ACCC%20Annual%20Report%202012-13.pdf (accessed 8 July 2014).

Commissioner of Trade Practices, Annual Reports (1968–1974) Government Printer, Canberra.

Commonwealth Parliamentary Debates [CPD], House of Representatives [House], various years, Government Printer, Canberra.

Cases:

Attorney-General of the Commonwealth of Australia v. *The Associated Northern Collieries and Others* (1911) 14 CLR 387

Attorney-General (Commonwealth) v. *Adelaide Steamship Co Ltd* (1913) 18 CLR 30.

Notes

1. Commonwealth Parliamentary Debates (CPD), House of Representatives (House).
2. *Attorney-General of the Commonwealth* v. *The Associated Northern Collieries and Others* (1911) 14 C.L.R. 387.
3. Appeals to the Privy Council were abolished in 1986.
4. It also examined the cost of living (1917); cost of clothing (1918); cost of rent (1918) and the sugar industry (1919). They found cartels were ubiquitous but generally not injurious to the public. When the appointments of the initial members expired no new members were appointed.
5. Section 35 defined an examinable agreement as one between two or more persons whose businesses competed with each other in the supply of goods or services, and which accepted any of the following restrictions: (i) terms or conditions on prices or any other matter,(ii) concessions or benefits, including allowances, discounts, rebates or credit, in connexion with, or by reason of the dealings; (iii) quantities, qualities, kinds or extent of goods or services produced, acquired, held or supplied, or the resources or methods used, or the resources acquired or maintained for use; (iv) places in, to or from which goods or services may be supplied; or (v) the persons or classes of persons who may be dealt with, or the circumstances or the conditions under which, persons were dealt with.

10 Policy transfer and its limits

Authorised cartels in twentieth-century Japan

Takahiro Ohata and Takafumi Kurosawa

Introduction

The history of cartel registration in Japan deserves special attention for several reasons. First, the country had the world's most institutionalised and encompassing cartel registration system during the second half of the twentieth century. A systematic international comparison conducted by Corwin Edwards, a renowned trust-buster in US and founder of Japan's post-war antimonopoly law, showed that the scope of reporting requirements was the widest in Japan among the 11 nations compared (Wells 2002; Edwards 1967: 48).

Second, Japan's system clearly exhibits the dual nature of the cartel register; namely, authorisation of cartels on the one hand, and containment of them on the other. The balance between these two factors changed over time, reflecting the industrial structure, the role of state intervention, and the international environment. Additionally, Japan is representative of how the practice of cartel registration flourished in the spheres between the general prohibition of cartel and economic liberalism, where *laissez-faire* meant the liberty of contract and relative freedom for cartels.

Third, Japan's cartel registration system exhibits the uniqueness as well as the universality of the nation's experience. Its uniqueness lies in the dramatic volte-face in the competition policy following American occupation and policy transfer immediately after the Second World War. The huge leap from the promotion of cartels and a war economy to the other extreme of an idealistic and draconian post-war antitrust law was ordered and supervised by the General Headquarters of the Supreme Commander for the Allied Powers (GHQ/SCAP). It was part of the 'greatest experiments in trust-busting' in the world, which was intended to transform the economic, social, and political structure of Japan (Hadley 1970: 6). This unprecedented policy shift was the reason why Japan developed its highly systematic cartel registration system after the end of the occupation. This case also demonstrates how the gap between the imported policy framework and the conditions of the local society was addressed. The post-war cartel registration in Japan can be interpreted as an outcome of 'Americanisation' and its subsequent 'Japanisation'. It is also true, however, that the longer trends in the rise and fall of cartel registration in twentieth-century Japan are remarkably similar to those of most other nations.

The extant literature on cartel and competition policy in Japan in English and Japanese is quite extensive (Dore 1986; Tilton 1996; Haley 2001; Beeman 2002). The rise of the Japanese economy by the end of the 1980s and trade frictions with its major trade partners motivated a plethora of studies on cartels, cartel policy, and the business-state relationship in Japan (Johnson 1982; Gao 1997; Schaede 2000). Non-competitive trade practices and cooperation between economic entities were the focus of most English-language studies on the Japanese economy. Interestingly, however, the concept of cartel register was rarely used by researchers and contemporaries in Japan, despite its wide use in practice. Given the post-war anti-cartel legislation in Japan, and the system of a general ban with exemptions, the register nominated all kinds of legitimate cartels. Thus, the register was taken for granted and barely received research attention. In this chapter, we address the gap between the extant literature on cartels and the recent studies on cartel registration from a comparative and long-term perspective.

This chapter is organised into five sections. In the first, we describe the long-term transition and shift in Japan's competition policy, using a conceptual diagram. The second section deals with the developments before the Second World War and the third discusses the impact of the US occupation in Japan. The position of the cartel register as well as the process and organisation of the policy shift will be illustrated. In the fourth section, the framework of the post-war cartel register is analysed using a typology, while the fifth section traces the overall rise and decline of the system.

Swings, continuity and discontinuity of policy: an overview

The development of competition policy in Japan was far from linear. It was marked by swings, especially when one focuses on the formal policy settings. We present a bold simplification via a conceptual diagram (Figure 10.1) to illustrate the long-term fluctuations.

In this figure the vertical axis shows the chronological developments of policy. Major events and background context are presented in the left column. In the central part of the horizontal axis, the direction of the cartel policy is depicted by movements in the line that is drawn following a highly simplified dichotomy of anti-cartel (left) and pro-cartel (right). At the far right, the domain of 'war mobilisation and controlled economy' is a separate section because it went beyond the 'pro-cartel' policy in the market economy.

The bold curved line, partially dotted, shows the transition of the cartel policy in the twentieth century. The line starts from the upper centre, meaning that the policy was neither anti-cartel nor pro-cartel at the end of the nineteenth century. Subsequently, the trajectory shows several swings. Both the rupture in 1945 and the backlash after the recovery of political independence are impressive.

The ellipses along the curve and their titles show the different phases of cartel registration. The following classification of the periods is given in the diagram (with some overlaps):

A   'Authorised cartels by local trade associations' (1884–1920s)

Policy transfer and its limits 171

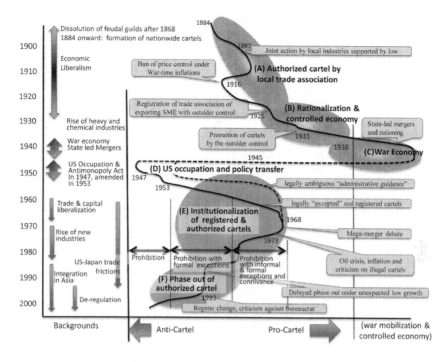

Figure 10.1 Swing, continuity and discontinuity in Japan's cartel policy, 1884–2000.
Note: See text for explanation of labelling used in the diagram.

B   Rationalisation and controlled economy (late 1920s–1937)
C   War economy (1937–1945)
D   US occupation and policy transfer (1945–1952)
E   Institutionalisation of registered and authorised cartels (1953–1970s)
F   Phase out of authorised cartels (1980s–mid-1990s)

The bases of the classification of the periods and the features in each period are explained in the following sections.

There are three points to note about the conceptual diagram. First, a fundamental change in the position of cartels in the mid-twentieth century set a limit on the effectiveness of the criteria based on the pro- and anti-cartel dichotomy. Before the Second World War, there was no general prohibition on cartels. The liberty of contract, including the freedom to make cartel agreements, used to be the principle. Thus, the dichotomy is not applicable during this period. The cartel registration-related policy before the Second World War was introduced to provide local or industry-level trade associations with the legal authority to exercise outsider control, in addition to existing private sanctions. All businesses out of the scope of such special legislations had no duty to report their cartel to the authority. In short, cartel registration was 'optional' for business circles, not a general obligation. In contrast, after the Second World War, cartels and any other restrictive trade practices were generally prohibited. Hence, all such activities required special legislations or authorisation by the government, which were always bundled with reporting obligation. The cartel registration was no longer an option, but a duty.

Second, the curve in the diagram portrays only the basic settings and orientation of the competition and cartel registration policy. It does not necessarily show the intensity or effectiveness of cartels or any other restrained trade practices. It has been argued that the network among companies, and that between business and the state, were formed and intensified under the war economy and succeeded in post-war Japanese economy (Kikkawa 1994). It is not possible, therefore, to say that the pro-cartel policy during the 1930s was more effective than the one in the post-war era. Similarly, the nation's industrial structure experienced several changes independently from this swing in policy; through mergers under the war economy; the division of *Zaibatsu* (mostly family-owned large corporate groups) under occupation, and because of a dynamic wave of new entries during the high growth period after the war.

Third, the ranges shown by the double arrows in the lower part of the diagram, namely, 'prohibition', 'prohibition with formal exception', and 'prohibition with informal exception and connivance' do not apply to the first half of the twentieth century.

Cartels and cartel registration before the Second World War

Authorised cartels by local trade associations (1884–1920s)

The early history of cartel and related competition policy in Japan bears a significant resemblance to that of other industrial nations, although certain delays and early maturings can also be observed. As early as in the mid-1880s, nationwide trade associations had sprung up in some transplanted large-scale sectors of industries (e.g. paper and cotton spinning). They often worked as a body of cartel agreements (Minobe 1931). Some of these cartels, such as those in cotton spinning, were powerful and others were vulnerable to challenges by outsiders and were short-lived. Given the dominance of economic liberalism, the government had neither the intention nor the tools to be involved in cartels or to control them.

In this context, the first policy on the registration of collective actions appeared not as a policy about cartels, but as part of the legislation on local trade associations. In 1872, soon after the Meiji Restoration, the new government abolished *Nakama* (guild-like organisations). They were classified as feudal and anti-modern, and they were regarded as incompatible with the idea of free trade. A decade later in 1884, however, the Ministry of Agriculture and Commerce announced the Rule on Trade Associations (*Junsoku-Kumiai*), which gave prefectures the administrative power to approve local trade associations. By 1886, there were 1579 authorised associations based on this decree (Shirato 1981: 71). Although the authority of prefectures was indirectly denied for a while by the promulgation of the Constitution (1889), which ensured freedom of residence, it was restored soon after by another decree in 1891. At the end of the nineteenth century, laws on association for important (exporting) local industries had been enacted (1897/1900). In 1921, there were 1020 associations based on these laws (Shirato 1981: 80).

These associations often set the price, quality, and wage rate in their industry, and the information on such activities was reported to the government. This system, therefore, can be deemed a proto-type of cartel registration. These trade associations had the legal power to control outsiders because membership was compulsory if they organised more than 75 per cent (1884) or 60 per cent (1990) of the business entities in the industry in a given region (Ministry of International Trade and Industry 1964: 17–20).

The main objective of these decrees, however, was not the regulation of cartels but the promotion of collective action for the improvement, standardisation, and inspection of local products. The improvement of reputation in the export markets was particularly important (Hashino and Kurosawa 2012).They were also only applied to small and medium-sized enterprises (SMEs) in the regional clusters.

It is well known that the state played a decisive role in the transplantation of Western culture and the establishment of modern industries in Japan. Following the privatisation of the major state-owned enterprises in 1880, however, economic liberalism was the norm in Japan through the late 1920s. Even the First World War did not change the situation. When the sudden drop of imports led to inflation, the reaction was neither systematic rationing nor adoption of a controlled economy (Yoshino 1962: 99–100). Instead, a decree was passed that suspended the trade associations' powers to set prices for several years.

Rationalisation, controlled economy, and promotion of cartels (late 1920s–1930s)

The idea of cartel registration per se first appeared in the late 1920s in Japan. A reversal of the dominant economic views occurred following a spate of economic crises during the 1920s, with the rise of new and capital-intensive industries after the First World War. The argument to emphasise the superiority of public and national interests over private ones was intensified. It was believed that control of the joint action of private companies, not free competition, would improve public and national interests. The global debate on 'organised capitalism' and rising nationalism were also decisive factors.

The Important Industries Control Law (1931) heralded a new era in Japan (Ministry of International Trade and Industry 1961: 158–169; 1964: 47–76). It was the first cartel registration law targeting large and modern industries. The nationwide geographical scope was also new. The law and related policy had several significant features.

First, all cartels and agreements related to 'control' in 'the important industries' had to be reported to the supervisory ministry if they involved more than half of the business entities in the industry. Thus, registration was not an 'option' for the dominant cartel organisation, but an obligation. If the organisation involved more than two-thirds of the companies in the industry nationwide, the Ministry could order non-members to comply with the rules set by the dominant cartel. Sanctions against outsiders could be implemented by the state law, overcoming the limits of private contract. A variety of restrictive practices was included in the 'control' agreements: production and sales amounts; segmentation of products; price controls; sales channels; and joint selling. Subsequently, the establishment of new firms and the expansion of capacity were added to the issues that required reporting and authorisation, as deemed necessary by the government. This authority was utilised in the latter half of the 1930s, together with the new legislation, to promote specific strategic industries.

Second, the power to select an 'important industry' rested with the Ministry. A similar method was in use through the 1925 law (The Important Export Products Trade Association Law; Ministry of International Trade and Industry 1964: 21–25). In the 1925 statute, the Ministry specified special segments and regions, and facilitated cartels and joint projects by dominant trade associations. Dominance was understood as the participation of more than two-thirds of the businesses in the region; this condition allowed control of outsiders. By adopting similar methods and relaxing the requirement to half of the companies (not regionally but nationally), the 1931 law focused on large businesses. It covered exporting industries (e.g. cotton spinning) as well as a wide variety of 'basic' industries (e.g. coal mining and pig iron). Starting with five industries, the law was eventually applied to 24 industries.

Third, reflecting the *Zeitgeist*, the law had a clear bias toward the promotion of cartels. One reason for the origin of the policy concerned with exporting SMEs. For policy-makers, this sector was ridden with structural problems; firms were too small, the entry barrier was too low, and massive entries and exits brought about excessive supply, low quality, and low profit. The results were disorder, low productivity, and economic crisis, which triggered price dumping and led to criticism from abroad. The 1925 law allowed regional organisations to tackle this problem. From the mid-1920s, the word 'rationalisation' became popular and was seen as a solution to these problems. Simultaneously, the expansion of the pro-cartel policy to include big industries was suggested. In 1930, the Temporary Industrial Rationalisation Bureau was established under the Ministry of Commerce and Industry (Ministry of International Trade and Industry 1961: 12–110). Slightly later, 'controlled economy' became the buzzword. The policies to promote cartels and mergers in the 1930s were justified and advertised using such keywords. While the 'controlled economy' became unpopular and obsolete in post-war Japan, the notions of 'excessive' competition and rationalisation survived and served as an important logic to justify authorised cartels.

Fourth, the other side of the cartel register, namely, the containment of harmful cartels, was explicitly discussed. At a session of the Diet, Shinji Yoshino, the designer of the law, faced criticism from advocates of conventional economic liberalism and standard anti-monopoly theory. Yoshino defended the bill, emphasising that the register of cartels and possible disclosure would deter their abuse (Yoshino 1962: 204–207). The government would have the power to check the contents of restrictive agreements, and if deemed necessary, it could order change or reject granting the authorisation.

The extent to which the law had an impact on the reshaping of industrial organisations, however, remains debatable. With only one exception (cement), all the cartels authorised by the law had influential cartel activities well before the legislation. Private businesses utilised this policy to intensify their cartel and mergers and acquisitions (M&A) activities; however, the drive towards organised capitalism already had its own strong momentum. On the other hand, those sectors where private businesses had strong self-regulation or capability to conduct business on their own, resented the state intervention and distanced themselves from it. Thus, the effect of the law was limited to strengthening the control of outsiders on the existing cartel organisations.

Finally, there were strong international influences. The shift in paradigm in economic and social thought and the transformation of economic organisations in Western countries had a profound impact on Japan. It is well-known that Germany was taken as Japan's model, however, its policy makers' attention was not limited to Germany. Together with the potash cartel in Germany, they studied the coal mining cartel in the UK and various cartel-related legislations in small nations, along with a series of reports by the League of Nations. Interestingly, the Norwegian cartel registration system in existence in 1925 was explicitly mentioned in the debate on the deterrence effect of publicity (Yoshino 1962: 204–208; 1935: 324–338). Both a simultaneity in action (the cartel register in Norway and the SME cartel register in Japan in 1925) and self-motivated international policy transfer from Europe to Japan can be observed.

The war economy (1937–1945)

The war economy transformed the nature of cartels and their registration. The second Sino-Japanese War (July 1937), the earliest phase of the Second World War, was the turning point for the expansion and intensification of the state's control over the economy (Ministry of International Trade and Industry 1964: parts 3–5). At this stage, the control of economic crisis and rationalisation was replaced with a militaristic goal as the reason for state intervention. The National Mobilisation Law of 1937 gave the government significant discretion in allocating natural resources, foreign currency, the labour force, goods, and money. From 1940, the 'New Economic Order' based on the principle of planned economy fundamentally re-organised industrial organisation. First, the 'industrial adjustment' forced small or inefficient companies to merge or exit the market. Second, new intermediate entities were institutionalised to control each industry. Former cartel associations were used as important foundations for such large-scale national organisations.

The associations, however, were no longer self-determining organisations. They served the state as a rationing channel. Therefore, the label of 'cartel' was no longer used. Instead, 'control association' became the norm. The war economy was the end of private cartels, although the principle of private ownership was not abandoned officially until the end of the war.

US occupation and policy transfer (1945–1952)

Policy transfer and cartel register in the international context

The American occupation of Japan after the Second World War fundamentally changed Japan's anti-cartel policy. For the international comparison of cartel register, three elements are important.

First, the direct transfer of the radical American anti-cartel policy made the registration of cartels pervasive. In principle, all cartels were prohibited by legislation as per the Antimonopoly Law of April 1947. This principle is maintained even today. There was, however, a massive contradiction between the new principle and local policy. Hence, as soon as the control of the occupational army waned and eventually ended, the government introduced a range of legal exceptions, while the principle of general prohibition was officially maintained. The government controlled these exceptions through legal and administrative measures. These were essentially 'registered' cartels. The terms such as 'cartel registration,' 'registered cartel' and 'to register a cartel' were hardly used because these were just part of the conditions for authorisation. Instead, these 'exceptions' were called 'exempted cartels' because they were exempt from the basic rule of the Antimonopoly Law.

Second, the anti-cartel and antimonopoly legislation under occupation was the world's most draconian and idealistic at that time. It was even stricter than its model, the American anti-trust policy, which was at its peak exactly in the mid-1940s. The famous (infamous in American business circles) 'trust-busters' were dispatched to Japan in an attempt to build an ideal country with economic democracy (Edwards 1946; Hadley and Kuwayama 2002; Wells 2002). In this context, the 'backlashes' (i.e. series of relaxations after the end of the US occupation) did not mean that Japan became a country with an overly cartel-friendly policy in global comparison.

Third, Japan's situation was different even from that of post-war Germany. The GHQ/SCAP, the US occupation authority in Japan, passed policies related to this subject in their own capacity, with little communication with their government back home and without coordination with their Allied counterparts. Japan's anti-cartel legislation of 1947 came ten years earlier than that in West Germany. This made Japan's anti-cartel policy framework in the first phase of the post-war era far more rigid than that in Germany. The dramatic 'Japanisation' during the 1950s – the swing between sphere (D) and the early phase of (E) in Figure 10.1 – should be interpreted in this context.[1]

Process of policy shift and the Antimonopoly Law of 1947

The process of law making and the formation of policy organisation show how reluctantly the Japanese government accepted the unfamiliar policy. The preparation of the Antimonopoly Law started with an order from the GHQ/SCAP dated 11 November 1945. Officials in Japan had limited knowledge and experience with the American anti-cartel policy. Both the government and businesses had no motivation for a radical change and disregarded it as being harmful and useless. The bills prepared by the Japanese government were rejected every time. Eventually, the government succumbed to the repeated orders from the occupation army and prepared a bill based on instructions from the Anti-Trust and Cartels Division (AC, renamed Fair Trade Practices Division in 1949) of the Economic and Scientific Section (ESS/AC) of the GHQ/SCAP (Office of the History of Finance, Ministry of Finance 1982: 385–455; Nishimura and Sensui 2006).

The Japanese government and the ESS/AC used two documents as the bases for drafting the legislation. One was a report prepared by an investigation team led by Corwin D. Edwards, who was an advisor for the US Department of State. The other was a draft dated August 1946 prepared by Posey T. Kime, an officer at ESS/AC with work experience at the Anti-Trust Division of US Department of Justice (Office of the History of Finance, Ministry of Finance 1982: 401–415).

Edwards's team, known as the 'Edwards Mission' or '*Zaibatsu* Mission' had a clear objective; the investigation of *Zaibatsu*, which were presumed to be a source of Japanese militarism. The mission's report proposed policies for dismantling the existing *Zaibatsu*. It also recommended the enactment of permanent and encompassing legislation to outlaw trusts and cartels. In order to deter the revival of *Zaibatsu* in the future, the report proposed a ban on holding companies, a restriction on the holding of other company's shares and of interlocking directories (Office of the History of Finance, Ministry of Finance 1982: 144–168).

Kime's draft codified the basic elements proposed by the Edwards Mission (Office of the History of Finance, Ministry of Finance 1982: 401–415). The draft was very comprehensive, covering all the spheres of three US Anti-Trust laws, namely, the Sherman Antitrust Act (1890), the Federal Trade Commission Act (1914), and the Clayton Act (1914). This shows the ambition of the drafting team. They wanted a powerful and comprehensive law, not a patchwork of bills.

The draft of the Antimonopoly Law prepared according to Kime's draft was submitted to the Diet on 22 March 1947. Without much debate, the draft passed through the Diet on 31 March and was promulgated on 14 April.

In effect, the Antimonopoly Law was meant to be a very powerful anti-cartel and anti-trust law. Despite multiple amendments, the law has retained its three basic principles (Misonou 1987: 20–21; Imamura 1993: 6). First, trusts were banned. Article 3 states that an enterprise must not effect private monopolisation or unreasonable restraint of trade. Second, the principle of banning cartels was introduced. The 'unreasonable restraint of trade', the latter part of the Article 3, meant that cartels *per se* were deemed illegal. Third, 'unfair trade practices' such as boycott, dumping, etc. were banned.

The definition of a cartel was simple and wide in scope. The law prohibited all kinds of cartels and restrictive practices without specifying any types and effects (the principle of '*per se* illegal'). Both vertical and horizontal cartels were banned. Regardless of the nature of the relationship (competitors or supplier-buyer; existing rivals or potential ones) or the level of formality (oral or written; binding or non-binding), all kinds of actions to control or restrain price, amounts, technology, investments, and any other aspects related to competition were prohibited. All types of business entities, including individuals, companies, and trade associations, were subject to these rules.

The law prohibited cartels and restrictive practices in general and listed few exceptions. The law was not applicable to those entities covered by the laws related to rights under the Copyrights, Patent Law, Utility Model Law, Design Law and Trademark Law. In addition, the laws related to partnership (including federation of partnership) that provided mutual support to small-scale enterprises or consumers (farmers' and consumers' cooperatives) received the same exemption; the critical issue was that the partners could voluntarily participate in, or withdraw from, such arrangements. It is important not to confuse the concept behind the original 'exceptions' with the reasons for 'exempted cartels' following the amendment of the act in 1953, and other special legislation. These are discussed later.

Dualism in policy organisation: FTC versus MITI

A remarkable dualism can be observed in the government organisation engaged in the competition policy in post-war Japan, especially through the mid-1990s. Falling short of the expectations of the 'trust-busters', the newly founded (Japanese) Fair Trade Commission (FTC) failed to 'monopolise' the competition policy, and it had to play constant power games with the associated ministries over the policy. Among these ministries, the Ministry of International Trade and Industry (MITI) was the most important. The FTC and MITI had distinctively different perceptions of the competition policy and the nature of the market; hence, their attitudes toward cartels were contradictory. Registered cartels in post-war Japan reflected the conflicts and compromises between these government organisations in each phase of economic development.

The FTC was founded in July 1947 as the main body for the administration of the Antimonopoly Law. It was born as an independent administrative commission directly reporting to the Prime Minister, and it was meant to be free from political pressures (Fair Trade Commission 1968: 75). The Antimonopoly Law stipulated the establishment and duties of the FTC.

The FTC was the gateway to the policy transfer from the US to Japan. During the early stage of its history, the members of the commission worked under the instruction of the ESS/AC. Even after the end of the occupation in April 1952, the FTC retained its original principles. When two types of cartels (recession cartels and rationalisation cartels) were introduced as legal exceptions, the FTC was reluctant to accept them (Misonou 1987: ch. 2).

The MITI had a long tradition. Although it was founded in 1949 via the transformation of the Ministry of Commerce and Industry, high-ranking MITI officials during the 1950s and 1960s had work experience at the ministry from before the war (Odaka and Ministry of International Trade and Industry 2013: 252–258). Most of them had knowledge of administration and policy during the age of rationalisation and the controlled wartime economy. Thus, they had little or no difficulty in getting accustomed to the introduction of government-monitored cartels and cartel registration. In addition, their concerns about the nation's economy had continuity with the pre-war era; the inferiority of the Japanese economy compared to that of Western countries, such as low productivity and the small scale of Japanese companies. Hence, their policy goals were to trim 'excessive competition' and improve competitiveness. The authorisation of cartels was perceived as not only acceptable but also desirable or even necessary. Until about the 1970s, the MITI regarded the Anti-Trust Law as an unnecessary impediment and perceived the FTC as a disagreeable counterpart (Misonou 1987: ch. 5).

The main determinants of the balance between FTC and various ministries were the political environment, the attitude of the Cabinet and the ruling party, and international pressure. Although the FTC's leverage was guaranteed by the law, the law-makers were the ones empowered to amend or abolish the law after all.

Typology of registered cartels (1953–1990s)

The rise and decline of registered cartels in post-war Japan can be analysed through the application of a typology. Authorised cartels can be classified into three types according to their legal basis. The first type is the registered cartel based on the amended Antimonopoly Law (Type A). The second is based on special legislation other than the Antimonopoly Law (Type B). Cartels based on these two categories are called 'exempted cartels' because they are legally exempted from the Antimonopoly Law. The third type is based on the so-called 'administrative guidance' received from the relevant ministries (Type C), and not on any of the other such laws.

Exempted cartels

Type A cartels were introduced by the amendment to the Antimonopoly Law in 1953. They had two sub-categories: recession cartels and rationalisation cartels (Fair Trade Commission 1968: 134–152). In the first, a group of producers and other economic actors in the recession formed a cartel according to the rules prescribed by the law. This type of cartel required the FTC's approval. The cartels' objectives could include control of price, the amount of production or shipment, or scale of capacity. The rationalisation cartel had similar objectives regarding capacity, technology and quality. A group of enterprises with special needs for 'rationalisation' applied for this category.

Type B cartels were also important. Defining specific aims and policy fields, the ministries passed a series of acts that explicitly permitted special types of cartels. These acts were regarded as a convenient tool for customising specific policy goals. The laws were usually for a specific duration (1–5 years), and any extension required the Diet's consent (the Statute Book of Japan, annual versions; Misonou 1987).

At the peak of this trend, there were over 30 laws that introduced a variety of 'exempted cartels' (Table 10.1). The top three laws that permitted the largest number of cartels were the Export and Import Transaction Law, the Law on Organisations of Small and Medium Sized Enterprises, and the Law on Proper Management in Environment- and Sanitary-Related Businesses. The first statute dealt with export and import associations, and other issues related to fair trade,

Table 10.1 Legal bases of 'exempted cartels' (Type B).

	Related laws	Industries applicable	Year of legislation	Year of abolition
1	Law concerning organisations of small and medium enterprises	SMEs	1957–1964	1997
2	Export and import trading law	Importer and exporter	1952–1961	Present
3	Law concerning provisional measures for the stabilisation of specified depressive industries	Specified industries	1978	1983 (→ no. 4)
4	Law on temporary measures for the structural improvement of specified industries (structural improvement law)	Specified industries	1983	1988
5	Law on temporary measures for the promotion of machinery industries	Machinery	1956	1971 (→ no. 7)
6	Law for temporary measures for the promotion of electronic industry	Electronics	1957	1971 (→ no. 7)
7	Law for temporary measures for the promotion of designated electric and machinery industries	Electronics and machinery	1971	1978
8	Temporary measures law for the ammonium sulfate industry rationalisation and export adjustment	Fertiliser industries	1954	1964 (→ no. 9)
9	Law on temporary measures for the stabilisation of fertilizer prices	Fertiliser industries	1964	1989
10	Sugar price stabilisation law	Sugar industry	1965	1997
11	Law on temporary measures for textile industry equipment	Textile	1956	1964 (→ no. 12)
12	Law on temporary measures for textile industry equipment and related equipment	Textile	1964	1970
13	Law on temporary measures for the structural improvement of specified textile industries	Spinning	1967	1972
14	Law on temporary measures for raw silk production equipment	Raw silk	1957	1959
15	Law concerning liquor business associations and measures for securing revenue from liquor tax	Brewery and liquor sale	1953	Present
16	Law on temporary measures for the rationalisation of coal mining industry	Coal mining	1955	1992
17	Law on temporary measures for the stabilisation of metal and mining related industries	Metal mining	1953	1968

Table 10.1 Continued.

	Related laws	Industries applicable	Year of legislation	Year of abolition
18	Fisheries production adjustment cooperatives law	Fisheries	1961	1997
19	Exporting fisheries development law	Fisheries	1954	1997
20	Law on special measures concerning the promotion of fruit-growing industry	Fruit-related production, process and sales	1961	1997
21	Law on temporary measures for pearl aquaculture adjustment	Pearl aquaculture	1969	1997
22	Law on special measures concerning fisheries reconstruction	Fisheries	1976	1997
23	Law on organisations of small and medium sized enterprises, and law on proper management in environment and sanitation related businesses[a]	Environment and sanitation-related industries	1957	Present
24	Copyright law (amendments of the copyright law in 1899 for the commercial secondary use of music records)		1970[c]	Present
25	Wholesale market law	Food wholesale	1971	1997
26	Port transportation business law	Port business	1951	1998
27	Road transportation law	Road transportation	1951[d]	Present
28	Civil aeronautics law	Aviation	1952[d]	Present
29	Law for small-sized shipping trade associations[b]	Domestic maritime industry	1957	Present
30	Marine transportation law	Maritime industry	1949[e]	Present
31	Law on non-life insurance rating organisation	Insurance	1948[e]	Present
32	Insurance business law	Insurance	1996	Present

This table contains only those laws for which the FTC has the numbers and contents of cartels. Laws related to cartel activities by cooperatives are excluded (which are subject to the Antimonopoly Law). Laws lacking obligations to report to or consult with the FTC are excluded. (In this case, the FTC does not seem to have information on the cartels, and often, there is no statistical data available from the FTC.)

[a] By the amendments in 2000, the law was renamed as Law Concerning Coordination and Improvement of Environmental Health Industry.

[b] By the amendments in 1964, the law was renamed Coastal Shipping Associations Law.

[c] There is no obligation to consult with and report to the FTC. The number of related cartels appears in the FTC's annual report.

[d] The law was amended in 1997, and consultation between the relevant Minister and the FTC was introduced. Since then, the number of related cartels have been included in the FTC's official statistics.

[e] The law was amended in 1999, whereby consultation between the relevant Minister and the FTC was introduced. Since then, the number of related cartels have been included in the FTC's official statistics.

such as rules about the place of origin. Export cartels were used to maintain product quality and 'orderly' exports. Import cartels were driven by the introduction of foreign patents. The Act on Organisations of Small and Medium Sized Enterprises opened a way for SME associations designed for collective business. The SME cartels were frequently a form of political compensation to firms whose upstream suppliers were often dominated by bigger companies that had authorised cartels. The last type of statues regulated restaurants, cafés, processed meat sales, hotels, barbers, public bath, cleaning, etc. The law allowed concerted action for improving sanitary conditions in the associated businesses.

Type A and Type B cartels had a number of processes and features. First, the relevant laws were based on compromises between the FTC and the ministries concerned. Second, the laws specified the scope of the target businesses (industries or type of business) and the types of actions and aims (types of cartels, concerted actions, or joint projects) that could be exempted from the general ban. Simultaneously, the necessary procedure (notification to or approval by the authority) was defined. Third, a group of businesses (trade associations, group of companies, or business units) applied for the law to apply to them. All information related to the 'exempted' actions by the individual applicants had to be reported to the authority (the FTC or relevant ministry) according to defined limits. Even in the case of Type B cartels where ministries, instead of the FTC were in charge, the respective ministries were obliged to report each application to the FTC. Two-thirds of the laws required ministries to get the FTC's consent for authorisation (Fair Trade Commission 1977: 765). In those cases, the FTC could order either modification or ban of the agreement, which the ministries had to respect. Thus, both ministries and the FTC were able to gather all the relevant information on legally authorised cartels.

Control of outsiders, the main reason for the authorisations under the pre-war cartel register, was no longer the general rule. Type A recession cartels and rationalisation cartels were explicitly prohibited from actions meant to eliminate outsiders. In contrast, half of the Act covering Type B cartels had clauses that enabled outsider controls. In the two fields of export cartels and cartels in the transportation sector, many laws stipulated a clause to control outsiders.

The publicity principle, a social tool to deter the abuse of (exempted) cartels, can be observed to some extent. In case of Type A cartels, the FTC disclosed information about the registered cartels in the Official Gazette or other media. The reason for authorisation and the particular cartel activities allowed (targeted products, type of action, how to control amount or other elements, and the authorised period) as well as the names of the individual companies applying for authorisation were often officially announced. The companies and people concerned, including 'outsiders', were allowed to file a complaint regarding the judgment. In such cases, the FTC organised public hearings. Hence, the procedures were publicly known and likely had announcement effects. It also aimed to deter secret cartels.

In contrast, in most of the cases of Type B cartels (where ministries are in charge, not the FTC), the principle of publicity was not stipulated by the law. Even so, it was relatively easy to identify the contents and membership of a cartel because the exercise of the exemption clause was often reported in the mass media.

Almost all trade associations, the most important basis of cartel activities, kept a list of their members, which was usually accessible to the public. Although the discretionary nature of the publicity policy made room for secretly authorised cartels, private businesses were aware that their actions could be disclosed to the public at any time.

Cartels by administrative guidance

Cartels in the third category (Type C) were authorised not by laws but by the so-called 'administrative guidance' (*Gyosei-Shido*) of the MITI. Administrative guidance is a general term for diverse forms of instructions by the government. It was widely used by ministries, and its use has been positioned as an important feature of Japanese industry policy. While some of the administrative guidances had clear legal foundations stipulated by the relevant laws, others lacked such foundations. The MITI's instructions on competition policy-related issues were based on a single sentence of the Ministry of International Trade and Industry Establishment Law, which defined the aim of the ministry. In addition, it had a serious conflict with the FTC's authority and the clauses of the Antimonopoly Law. Thus, some scholars and the media frequently questioned the legitimacy of its actions. The MITI, however, asserted and successfully defended its position, especially through 1970s (Misonou 1987: ch. 5).

The logic behind administratively exempting these cartels from general prohibition under the Antimonopoly Law was that they were *de jure* not a cartel, but a concerted action 'recommended' by the government. In most of the well-known cases, however, the business circle (companies and trade associations) initiated the request to the ministry to take action on their behalf. Intensive communication and feedback between the businesses and the government were the very conditions of this provision. Thus, this category can be clearly positioned as an 'authorised cartel'.

The dualism in policy organisation and the element of compulsory policy transfer were reflected in the different attitudes towards this policy (Misonou 1987: ch. 2). The MITI favoured this provision because they could mobilise it highly flexible and swiftly. For the FTC, such a provision involved the sheer denial of its authority and the spirit of the Antimonopoly Law. Thus, the FTC resisted the introduction of this policy. After a series of retreats and compromises in the 1950s, the FTC recovered the authority to be consulted before the implementation of this provision. The private business circle welcomed the speedy measures, although their attitude towards cartels was heterogeneous, and there was a sense of caution against too much state intervention.

These authorised cartels can also be regarded as a form of registered cartel. By its nature, this category lacks clear formality and standardised procedures, and there are few official documents that directly attest to the scope of the reporting. It is almost certain, however, that the authority had deep and extensive information about individual cases. First, in order to claim that the concerted action was not a private cartel but a state-led action, the MITI required sufficient data to convince other stakeholders, including the FTC. Second, the companies involved had a good reason to provide information. They wanted to control (potential) outsiders using this provision and they supplied comprehensive information to MITI for this purpose. Additionally, they wanted to ensure adequate cooperation with the MITI to safeguard themselves from prosecution initiated by the FTC. Third, the announcement effects to stabilise market conditions were an important reason for their concerted action. The mass media reported the details of individual cases regularly. Fourth, the official history of the MITI and the FTC contain detailed information about several cases that became open disputes or led to official prosecution because of the infringement of the law. They reveal that the MITI was informed in detail of those actions. Finally, the FTC maintained official documents about cases involving infringement by the cartels.

Rise and fall of post-war registered cartels

Japanisation and institutionalisation (1950s–1960s)

The first two decades after the end of the US occupation was the age of 'Japanisation'. During this period which has been described as the 'stagnation age of antimonopoly policy' (1952–1960), the rules defined by the Antimonopoly Law, as well as the existence of FTC, were under threat (Fair Trade Commission 1968: 121). As early as in February 1952, the first post-war authorised cartel (Type C) was implemented in the form of a MITI-led curtailment of production in the cotton spinning and chemical fibre industries. Subsequent amendments to the Antimonopoly Law in 1953 marked a major backlash against the strong anti-trust ideology initiated by the Americans, with the introduction of the two kinds of registered cartels (Type A). This amendment, however, did not decrease the number of cartels or concerted actions based on legally ambiguous administrative guidance (Type C). On the contrary, this practice mushroomed. The dotted bold line in Figure 10.1 shows this gap between the legal framework of the Antimonopoly Law and actual policy. Given the scarcity of foreign exchange and the authority to allocate it, the MITI could easily enforce the administrative sanctioned guidelines.

In 1953, the measures introduced to deter the possible re-establishment of *Zaibatu*, were also eased. Pure holding companies, however, were to remain forbidden for almost a half century, until 1997. Together with the partial easing of rules on the holding of shares by financial institutions, this change led to the formation of a new type of business group (*Kigyo Shudan*), which has a horizontal relationship centred on major banks (Shimotani 2010: 24–25). Thus, a competitive industrial structure appeared. In most of the key industries, a relatively large number of major players (around six to twelve) of similar size, competed with one another.

This period was also characterised by progressive institutionalisation. In parallel with the use of discretionary measures, the MITI expanded its authority by introducing a variety of 'exempted cartels' (Type B). Increasing numbers of SME policy cartels and export- and import-related cartels were the main contributors to

Policy transfer and its limits 185

the rise in the total number of registered cartels (Figure 10.2). From the mid-1950s, the legislation on manufacturing and mining industries followed the same approach, and the number of registered cartels in these fields increased during the 1960s.

The rapid growth of the economy from the mid-1950s to the early 1970s was an important element behind the rise in cartels and their authorisation. Despite cyclical recessions and losses in this phase, new entries continued and capacity grew because of the widely shared expectation of the long-term expansion of the market. The process industries were especially vulnerable to the cyclical recession and became a hotbed for cartels (Tilton 1996). For example, during the short depression in 1964, the petrochemical industry introduced a production capacity cartel for new investments in ethylene plants, guided by a shared expectation of future demand based on discussions between the government and the business leaders

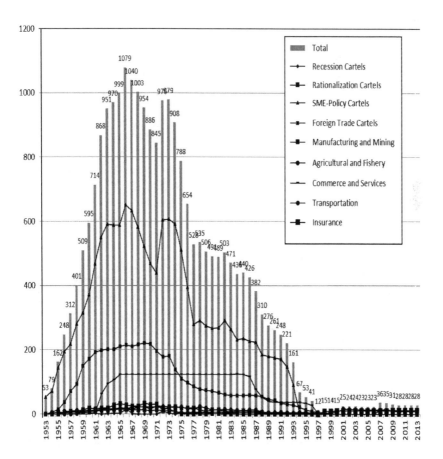

Figure 10.2 'Exempted cartels' in Japan (registered Type A and Type B cartels).

Note: The numbers in the graph show the total number of existing 'exempted cartels' (all of them are registered) at the end of March of each year.

Source: FTC Annual report 1954–2013.

(Hirano 2011). This state-led investment cartel model was also adopted by the pulp and ferro-alloy producers. In the case of the self-confident steel industry, the business leaders disliked state intervention and introduced a self-regulated capacity cartel with *ex-post* approval from the MITI. In all cases, the authorisation of the cartels stemmed from the notion of excessive competition and concerns about future over capacity.

In the 1960s, policy-makers focused on capital and trade liberalisation under the framework of the General Agreement on Tariffs and Trade (GATT) and the International Monetary Fund (IMF). Competition and industry policy were affected in three ways. First, the most powerful tool for the enforcement of Type C cartels, the control of foreign exchange, was removed from the government. Recognising the implications of this, the MITI compromised with the FTC in 1964. Henceforth, authorised Type C cartels were basically replaced by Type A cartels, which had greater transparency (Misonou 1987: 168–173; Fair Trade Commission 1997a: 8; Okazaki and Ministry of International Trade and Industry 2012: 231). This was a part of the institutionalisation process. Second, the MITI was deeply concerned about the competitiveness of Japanese industries and in 1962 tried to pass a law for state-led mergers and acquisitions. It was a typical strategic targeting policy and was touted as the 'new industrial order' with some resemblance to the wording used during the 1930s. This ambitious plan, however, faced strong opposition from private businesses. Big banks were already forming their horizontal business groups and did not wish to be disturbed. Many manufacturers were developing self-confidence in international markets and resented the revival of state intervention. Thus, the bill was scrapped. Third, this challenge demonstrated MITI's power and the fragility of the Antimonopoly Law. The FTC had to concede, and it became more lenient towards Type A and Type B cartels.

Transformation and inertia (1970s–mid-1980s)

The late 1960s and early 1970s were the turning point of the post-war cartel register system. The number of cartels peaked in 1966, though there was another spike during the early 1970s (Figure 10.2). Legislation on exempted cartels slowed. This period was marked by both transformation and inertia in policy.

The transformation is evident. First, a nationwide debate on the role of the Antimonopoly Law and competition policy took place for the first time. Against the backdrop of the MITI's pro-merger attitude and economic liberalisation, the re-merger of Fuji Steel with Yawata Steel to form Nippon Steel was announced in 1968 (Misonou 1987: 193–211). These two companies had their origins in the Japan Iron and Steel Corporation founded in 1934, which had been divided during the occupation. Almost simultaneously, another plan was disclosed to re-merge three successor companies of the pre-war monopolistic giant Oji Paper. The news triggered extensive debates among economists and met with some public resentment. The mass media reported this debate intensely. Suddenly the FTC was in the spotlight. While the merger in the steel industry was realised, the plan for the paper industry was dropped.

Five years later, the oil crisis led to a further re-evaluation of the FTC as well as changing perceptions about the lenient anti-cartel policy (Misonou 1987: ch. 5). Inflation, tactical buyouts by suppliers, and panic buying by consumers, as well as the disclosure of an illegal cartel of oil products, fuelled nationwide criticism of the existing policy. The FTC seized the opportunity and filed a criminal complaint against the oil refiners for violating the Antimonopoly Law. The MITI lost face and part of its authority because it emerged that the MITI itself had been involved in this secret and illegally formed cartel. Private companies were prosecuted, but the MITI and its officials were not. The public criticism was enormous. The ambiguous boundary between Type C, legally authorised cartels, and purely illegal cartels was a major point of discussion. The contradiction between the Antimonopoly Law and ministries' discretionary policy became obvious. After this case, informal authorisation and connivance related to illegal cartels gave way to more institutionalised processes.

The transformation in policy was rooted in the environment as well. The slowdown in growth delayed the implementation of the policy (Fair Trade Commission 1997b: 327). Authorised cartels tended to restrain exits from the market, contrary to the original policy goal. The prices of materials converged increasingly with international price levels following trade liberalisation. The domestic state-led or state-sanctioned cartels significantly lost their effectiveness. The transformation of the country's industrial structure was also decisive. The foundation of the Japanese economy shifted from capital-intensive process industries to knowledge-intensive assembly industries (e.g. electronics and automobile). In the latter, product differentiation was possible, and harsh international competition improved their position in the international market. Meanwhile, international pressure also increased. The trade frictions between Japan and the US became a serious national concern from the late 1960s through to the mid-1990s.

This period is also marked by a strong inertia in policy (Okazaki and Ministry of International Trade and Industry 2012: 227–277). First, a series of external shocks (the oil crises in 1973 and 1978, and waves of appreciation in the Japanese yen after 1971) and the unexpected slowdown of growth resulted in an unintended extension of the existing policy. Exempted cartels were mobilised through the early 1980s both as an emergency rescue measure and as a convenient tool to allow the 'soft landing' of declining industries (the so-called industry adjustment policy). The number of exempted SME cartels rose once again (Figure 10.2). Second, even after the official abolishment of Type C cartels in 1964 and the shift to a stricter attitude by the FTC against Type A cartels in the1970s, the MITI did not give up its role of 'guiding' the market. The ministry introduced the so-called 'guideline method' in 1975. According to this new scheme, the MITI announced its prediction of demand for specific products on a quarterly basis and prompted private companies to voluntarily reduce production. Compared to the previous approach to Type A cartels and the compulsory nature and feature of state-authorised cartels, this policy was weaker. However, this action could easily induce companies to undertake concerted action or create implicit cartels. Thus, the FTC intensified its surveillance in these areas.

Phase-out of authorised cartels (mid-1980s–mid-1990s)

The era since the mid-1980s was the final phase of authorised cartels and the cartel register in Japan. First, the international climate changed. The global shift towards stricter anti-cartel policies, increasing trade frictions with US and Europe, and trade surpluses against major trade partners played an important role. In the early 1990s, the MITI made its final step towards terminating the system. The MITI ceded its authority on competition policy to the FTC by shifting its activities to the newly defined field and requirements of industrial policy (Kurosawa 2009).

Second, since the 1980s, 'developmentalism' was criticised intensely in Japan. The cartel policy reflected these changes, and the MITI started to alter its views. The ministry recognised the system's limitations and sought an exit strategy from the policy. The debate on the amendment of the Depressed Industries Stabilisation Law (1978–1983) is an example. The law had previously been in place to authorise cartels to scrap excessive production capacities and to promote consolidation in specified industries that suffered 'structural' depression (Type B). On its expiry, a bill for a successor law was debated. Yamanaka, the Minister of MITI, made it clear that the new law, The Industry Structure Law [1983–1987] (Type B) should become the final one of this kind (Okazaki and Ministry of International Trade and Industry 2012: 248–257). In fact, in the second half of the 1980s, the number of manufacturing-related exempted cartels was halved. In the early 1990s, SME-related exempted cartels disappeared.

In the 1990s, this movement towards phase-out of registered cartels escalated for three reasons (Fair Trade Commission 1997b: 485–571; Okazaki and Ministry of International Trade and Industry 2012: 277–318). First, the FTC was always unenthusiastic in the authorisation of cartels. The registered cartels were a reluctant compromise. Riding on a fundamental change in the political and economic climate, the FTC took a bolder stance. Second, since the 1980s, international criticism about the 'lenient' cartel policy in Japan intensified. Japan–US trade friction peaked in the early 1990s, especially because of the huge trade surplus of Japan against US. Third, in the domestic policy, public opinion about the bureaucracy and the existing system became very harsh. In the field of competition policy, this resulted in a shift in the anti-trust and anti-cartel policies. On the one hand, the anti-trust policy was relaxed to facilitate M&As, and eventually, pure holding companies were legalised. On the other hand, the anti-cartel policy was intensified.

The phasing out process began with the most opaque of the registered cartels, namely, the ones based on administrative guidance (Type C). As an authorisation tool of cartels, it was abandoned in the mid-1960s, although the use of 'guidance' continued in various other fields of the MITI's policies. Ironically, the few remaining cartels in the late 1980s and early 1990s were the ones that maintained the import and export quotas imposed by the US; these were based on a series of 'voluntary' agreements.

For the Type A registered cartels, the 1980s also represented the final period of phase-out. The last 'rationalisation cartel' was implemented in 1982, followed by the last recession cartel in 1989. Eventually, in July 1999, the legal framework for the two oldest pillars of registered cartels was abolished following a fundamental amendment of the Antimonopoly Law.

Type B registered cartels were to be abolished in the 'Plan for Deregulation', which was approved by the Cabinet in March 1995. In July 1997, around 20 Acts related to exempted cartels were abolished or amended. The reduction continued even later. After the mid-1990s, only a few categories of exempted cartels remained. They were based on five laws in the following fields: insurance (around 8–9 cartels); shipping (5–10); road transportation (3); earthquake insurance (2); and domestic shipping (1). Almost all of them deal with services related to public goods, and they are often not considered cartels. The contents of these rules show significant homogeneity with the practices in the US and Europe.

Conclusion

The history of competition policy and cartel register in Japan is a remarkable example of policy transfer. During the first half of its history, the transfer took place through Japan's own initiative, although it was triggered by a strong sense of crisis under the threat of colonisation. The economic thoughts, legal system, and policy tools were imported, together with other elements of Western civilisation. As happened in Europe, feudal guilds were dismantled, and economic liberalism became the dominant economic perspective of the time. This development suggests a degree of affinity between the transferred elements and the needs of local society.

The policy to register cartels emerged in the mid-1920s, following the emergence of large corporations and modern cartels. Such laws mainly aimed at facilitating cartels, though the policy-makers eyed both authorisation and containment. Since the 1930s, new trends towards rationalisation and a controlled economy appeared. This was an effort to address local problems by adopting 'progressive' models from abroad.

The process of transfer had its limit. In almost all cases, selection and localisation were the norm. More importantly, home grown policies played a considerable role. The authorisation and register of local trade associations was a typical example. Parallel development (not transfer) in the same direction as that occurring in Western countries often explains the similarity.

The policy transfer under the US occupation was compulsory and had a profound impact. Coupled with the subsequent backlash, it resulted in very uncommon swings of policy, which is the most prominent feature of Japan's experience. Even when compared to the German experience, the passing of the relevant anti-cartel laws ten years earlier and the local reaction to it during the 1950s made the Japanese case unique.

The extensive cartel register system in post-war Japan was a reaction to address the gap between the previous historical trajectory on cartels and the transferred system. Two types of dualisms were at the root of the system. One was the dualism of the relevant policy organisations, namely, the FTC and the ministries, especially the MITI. The other was the dualism in policy implementation. While the core principle of *per se* illegality under the Antimonopoly Law was maintained, numerous statutes and administrative provisions were introduced to 'exempt' various practices from the principle.

This system had two functions. On the one hand, it authorised cartels and strengthened their function. On the other hand, it worked to control the cartels for public or national interests. The boundary between the industrial and the competition policies was not clear. Thus, it can be argued that the core of the transferred policy was challenged. Nevertheless, it is important to note that both the FTC and the Antimonopoly Law survived a series of challenges and eventually established the sole basis of the competition policy. In this respect, the Americanisation following the occupation had a long-lasting effect on the competition policy of Japan.

From a long-term perspective, the swings in policy from the late 1930s to the mid-1960s can be positioned as a deviation from a century-long historical trajectory. This is evident in any international comparison. It also opened the way for the highly institutionalised cartel register system in Japan. While the Japanese story is unique, the basic trends in the development of competition policy, the rise and decline of cartel register, and the reasons for these trends in Japan are similar to those in the other nations.

Acknowledgements

The authors would like to thank the participants of the session on 'Cartels' at the First World Business History Conference 2014 in Frankfurt and the session 'Regulating Anti-competitive Behavior in Historical Perspective' at the 18th annual meeting of European Business History Association 2014 in Utrecht. This research was partially supported by Grant-in-Aid for Scientific Research (A) 23243055.

Note

1 In his intensive study of US antitrust legislation and its impact, Wyatt Wells concluded that, 'If deconcentration and decartelization in West Germany rated as qualified success, then in Japan the program was as qualified failure' (Wells 2002: 186). This assessment has some validity. Germany had *Ordliberalism*, Ludwig Earhard and the integration in Europe, while Japan did not have their counterparts. This made the backlash in Japan look more impressive. This contrast should not be overemphasised, however. If the significance of the event is not measured by the gap between the goal and the results, but by that between the previous situation and long-term outcomes, the impact of policy transfer in Japan should be greater than that in Germany.

11 Cartel law and the cartel register in German twentieth-century history

Jan-Otmar Hesse and Eva-Maria Roelevink

Introduction

Today the German Federal Cartel Authority (*Bundeskartellamt*) is well known for its strict antitrust policy. As Andreas Mundt, the current president of the Federal Cartel Authority, points out, 'The competitive principle is the founding pillar of our economic and social order'[1] (Bundeskartellamt: Jahresbericht 2013: 3). To ensure that principle, the Cartel Authority today is approved to carry out a whole string of activities. Beyond the observation and the control of mergers one of the most important tasks of the administration is to reveal and sanction cartels. In 2013 the Cartel Authority completed work on several revealed cartels among them the famous 'Beer-Cartel'. Eleven brewers were convicted of illegal price agreements for bottled, as well as, draft beers. During the proceedings, the brewers were found guilty of having increased prices by one euro per crate; prices for draft beer had been arbitrarily increased. Ultimately, the Cartel Authority imposed fines of 338 million euros (ibid.: 36). The impressive volume of fines that run from record to record during the last few years may be understood, however, as both an indicator that cartels remain still quite active in Germany as well as the effectiveness of the Cartel Authority (Bundeskartellamt, Sektoruntersuchung Kraftstoffe – Abschlussbericht Mai 2011).

Nevertheless, the strict German antitrust policy of today is a quite young phenomenon. From the end of the nineteenth century until the Second World War, Germany did not pursue a policy that assessed cartels as having a negative impact on the economic order. On the contrary, Germany was known for its cartel friendly legal praxis. As famously expressed by the law professor Franz Böhm in1948, Germany used to be the 'typical country of cartels' (Böhm 1948: 212). In any case, the majority of cartels were of only minor importance for the economy, being related to small enterprises; especially during the Third Reich. Some of the cartels, however, gained nationwide and even international impact (e.g. the Coal Cartel, *Rheinisch-Westfälisches Kohlen-Syndikat*; hereafter *RWKS*) that was known as most powerful 'syndicate' of the economy.

Giving this legal and structural inheritance, Germany before 1945/47 is usually considered as a cartel-friendly country, where a powerful economic elite and highly concentrated industry succeeded in pushing the authorities towards an economic order that supported business interests. Indeed, it was only in 1947 that the Allies banned cartels and forced a general decartelisation. It was another ten years before the first general and legal ban on cartels was enacted in Germany; the Act against Restraints of Competition (*Gesetz gegen Wettbewerbsbeschränkungen*). The implementation of the market economy and the general ban of cartels in Germany after the Second World War have contributed to the impression that the end of the Second World War was the crossroads for German cartel policy and a fundamental shift toward antitrust policy. Nevertheless, this opinion has been sufficiently challenged by recent business history research that reveal that the seemingly 'powerful' economic actors of the German cartelisation prior to 1945/47 had been trapped in several internal conflicts. The cartel structure was actually neither stable nor had it suppressed internal competition among the cartel members (Roelevink 2015a; Schröter 2011; Reckendrees 2003). Such historical evidence reminds us, therefore that reality is not black and white; there is no such thing as a clearly defined legal order favouring the prohibition of cartels that causes predictable, 'perfectly competitive' economic outcomes and vice versa (Harding and Joshua 2003, esp. p. 265).

Following this particular strand of thought, our purpose here is to show how complex and highly volatile cartel legislation and the corresponding market order in Germany has been in the long run of the twentieth century. Additionally, the issue of how publicly cartels were announced and how in particular, the cartels were legally required to become public will be considered in detail. We start with an elaboration of cartel policy before 1945. The German debates on cartelisation until 1945 were characterised by a paradox. Whereas cartelisation was one of most discussed problems in newspapers, economic theory and among legal experts since the turn of the century, debates in the parliament, even though they were fierce, had no great effect on the cartel legislation. Other European countries observing the intense scientific debates therefore took legislative action earlier than Germany. This becomes evident especially in the issue of cartel registration. However, compared to other issues – such as the outsider problem of the Coal Cartel, the discussion on price effects and debates about the export dominance of cartelised German industries – the issue of registration was discussed in Germany only marginally (Binz 1952: 7–9). It was only in the mid-1920s that German cartel-legislation became general at all. Of course there was German cartel legislation before, but the essential parts of the cartel-legislation until 1923, when the Decree against the Abuse of Economic Power (*Verordnung gegen Missbrauch wirtschaftlicher Machtstellungen*) was enacted remained fragmentary and was elaborated on a case-by-case basis (Baums 1990). Even though between 1900 and the outbreak of the First World War the Reichstag adopted a proposal that suggested the establishment of a German Cartel Office (*Kartellamt*) three times, it was not realised before the enactment of the Act against Restraints of Competition (*Gesetz gegen Wettbewerbsbeschränkungen*) in 1957 (Blaich 1970). The incongruity between intensive public and scholarly debate on the one hand and reluctant legal action on the other hand also applies to the registration issue. So, to develop a greater understanding of the German cartel policy prior to 1945, it is essential to depict the legal praxis through the typical case-by-case handling process. This we will do by the examples of the Potash Cartel (*Kali-Kartell*) and the *RWKS* in the following section. The Act against Restraints of Competition of 1957 and its impact will be explored in the second section, where the claim of a comprehensive law is viewed in greater detail. The enactment of the 1957 Law is usually perceived as a deep rupture in the traditional German economic order initiated by the Allies' intervention and propelled by the Freiburg school of liberal economists, which increasingly won momentum during the 1950s (Freyer 2006; Gerber 1998, esp. pp. 232; Mierzejewski 2003; Nicholls 1994). There are, however, many reasons to object to such a characterisation and to consider the West German cartel legislation rather more as the transfer of the traditional cartel friendly and case-by-case process to the particular legal environment of the 1950s – thereby meeting the requirements of Allied control and international standards. At the very least the economy did not entirely switch to a cartel-free environment with perfect competition being the norm. Albrecht Ritschl (2005) linked arguments in favour of the continuity hypothesis together with the bold statement that West Germany's economic order originated from the Third Reich rather than marking a break. He used the cartel law as one of his most prominent examples. In the narrower field of cartel legislation, however, the initiating of a cartel register together with the law of 1957 does in fact mark an institutional rupture as we will show in the following.

The German cartel policy and the register issue before 1945

During the last third of the nineteenth century, when the first wave of cartel foundations penetrated the German economic order, the forms and types of cartels already varied greatly. Although we cannot go into detail here, we may broadly define a cartel as an association of independent enterprises from the same branches of industry, formed to eliminate 'unhealthy competition' (Cox 1981; Isay 1930: 3ff.). This general understanding covers cartels that were less strict and deep organised, such as loose 'price conventions', and the more elaborate 'syndicates', that organised the production-, price- and sales business of their cartel members (Tschierschky 1928). In addition to the problem of the great variety in the forms of cartels, one consequence of the lack of a registration obligation is that it is still challenging to quantify the general degree of cartelisation in the German economy. During the second half of the 1870s fewer than ten cartels were known in public. Since 1900 the number of cartels grew steadily. Before the outbreak of the First World War more than 600 cartels were officially known. During the interwar-period the number of cartels grew to more than 2500 cartels. Then, after 1925 the number of cartels declined (Berghoff 2004: 99, table). Even though especially the high number of known cartels in the 1920s was impressive one has to doubt whether their economic importance correlated with the number of known cartels. It is certain that the German cartels before the First World War were very powerful, while the interwar period was characterised by a greater number of cartels with less impact on the economy and policy. Yet, it is still almost impossible to quantify the importance of the German cartelisation in the economy. Even corporations that had not been members of cartels had to buy their material from cartelised suppliers, not even including the cartels in the German transportation sector. The effects and consequences of cartelisation went much further than historical research has so far revealed (Schröter 2013).

The cartelisation movement received additional support in 1897 when the German Supreme Court (*Reichsgericht*) confirmed the legitimacy of cartel contracts and gave priority to privately concluded cartel contracts. Cartel contracts were considered to be covered by the constitutional protection of the 'freedom of trade' (*Gewerbefreiheit*) (Schröter 1994: 462). In 1890 a German court had already determined that cartels did not contradict the principle of the freedom of trade (Blaich 1973: 44f.). With this watershed decision and the judgment of 1897, a cartel-friendly attitude was introduced into German cartel legislation. While other nations at that time, such as the United States of America, instigated general antitrust legislation, German legislation became characterised as having a favourable and friendly attitude towards cartels. Even though cartels and early forms of organised agreements had existed before, it was the judgments of 1890 and 1897 that opened up the great movement of cartelisation that would become responsible for the label 'typical country of cartels'.

Criticisms of various cartels increased, especially after the turn of the century, but the critics could not agree on one particular line of attack. Industry lobby organisations, mainly of the primary industry, removed the basis for comprehensive legislation, by emphasising the private character of their cartel-contracts and generally questioning the assumption of price effects throughout their cartel. Legal scholars debated on the cartel-question as well as the *Verein für Socialpolitik*. The scientific debate in Germany became particularly deep but had no impact on the legislation. A general cartel law was not passed at the federal level (Blaich 1970: 135–142). Instead the federal states introduced a series of laws that addressed special cartels. The variation within the cartel movement and the sophisticated discussions on cartels resulted in the introduction of a case-by-case approach handling cartels that quickly became acceptable.

Nevertheless, the number of petitions and applications directed to the Federal Parliament (*Reichstag*) increased. When in 1900 a shortage of coal was attributed to the Coal Cartel 'RWKS' and its price policy, there had to be a political reaction. Again, work began on a draft statute. Instead it was decided to arrange controversial hearings (*Kontradiktorische Verhandlungen*) at the Reichstag. Representatives of important cartels, trade organisations and consumer groups were heard. Academic scholars were invited as consultants. Apart from four Memoranda (*Denkschriften*) that were published between 1905 and 1908 the hearings of a total of twelve selected cartels had no great effects on the RWKS or the other cartels and eventually caused no general German cartel legislation (Blaich 1973: 249ff.). During the discussions, the introduction of public cartel registers had been suggested, being only a minor issue within the greater debate on the general treatment of cartels. Cartel representatives had opposed the idea during the hearings, expressing their organisations' economic importance and the need to conceal their actions, rather than betray secrets. After legislative proposals had been postponed several times, always with the scientific support of legal and economic experts, the project to introduce the register was dropped, together with all the other cartel law proposals (ibid.: 270ff.; Großfeld 1979, esp. p. 269).

The nation did not address general cartel legislation, which would have possibly integrated a registration obligation, until the inflationary year of 1923. By then, the most important and long lasting German cartels had already achieved the greatest possible influence and power. The *RWKS* was founded in 1893. Only four years later, the potash producers formed the *Kali-Kartell* that like the RWKS endured until the Second World War and was also considered one of the most influential German cartels. The *Kali-Kartell* was of special importance since Germany had a natural monopoly in potash, both locally and in the world market until 1914/18. The great importance of both the RWKS and the Potash Cartel was derived from their dominant influence on the domestic markets and their strong position in export markets.

In contrast to the RWKS, which was founded by private colliery owners from the Ruhr valley, the *Kali-Kartell* was founded by two state-owned enterprises that dominated the German potash industry (accounting for 77 per cent of the cartel quota in 1898). The *Kali-Kartell* became very successful in price setting and organising the sales-business of cartel members, despite not be able to prevent frequent market entries by cartel outsiders before the First World War. The price wars that were unleashed with every new producer ended with their painful and expensive integration into the *Kali-Kartell* (Tosdal 1913: 145ff.). This resulted in a slowly decreasing share of the cartel being controlled by the state-owned enterprises. The state-owned mines soon risked losing their dominance in the *Kali-Kartell*. Negotiations to settle new cartel-contracts became fiercer with every new entry. In 1909 negotiations failed completely. As a result the legislators drafted legislation to apply where a Compulsory Cartel (*Zwangskartell*) was threatened (Maetschke 2008). The proposal became the first legislative measure to reflect a change in German cartel policy: The state was now integrated into the cartelised German order and therefore was no longer interested in raising public attention to cartels by mandatory cartel registration. Instead the state supported a case-by-case handling of cartels and made use of this approach for its own interests. The cartel friendly and favourable handling approach was now supplemented with a strong support for cartels. Moreover, the state, was not only the legislator but also the economic actor in this situation, demonstrating its need for certain cartels and then using its power to stabilise them. By forcing the *Kali-Kartell* to renew agreements, the state supported its own interests and thereby changed its general attitude to produce a *pro*-cartel legislation. The proposed compulsory cartel statute was understood as signalling general support towards cartelisation in business as well as in public. However, the enactment also was postponed. Instead, in 1910, the state enacted the Potash Law (*Reichskaligesetz*). In future the *Kali-Kartell* would be forced to renew. Most important, the law secured the quotas to reduce the potential conflicts within the cartel. Instead of making the conflicts and functions of that cartel public – as would have occurred with a cartel register – the possibility of individual cartels protecting their secrets was secured (Moraht 1921/22: 58–62).

During the First World War the German state reconsidered its cartel policy, however under the circumstances of a highly managed economy. Since 1915 the state had changed to an even more ambitious cartel policy. Branches and industries of military importance were headed by War Corporations (*Kriegsgesellschaften*) organising the flow of raw material within the war economy (Roth 1997; van de Kerkhof 2010). The state also supported the already existing cartels to gain the greatest possible control of industry. The Ruhrcoal, by far the biggest coal industry in Germany, was an example where the state tried to control of coal-flows via the RWKS, while the War Corporation for Coal never exerted any real influence. At the outbreak of the war, the RWKS had been negotiating a renewal of the syndicate contract; a process that turned out to be ponderous and rather lengthy. The conflicts within the cartel were massive (Roelevink 2015a: ch. 3). During the spring of 1915 it became apparent that the RWKS would not renew on its own. This potential breakdown of the RWKS caused the state to intervene. The so-called *Bundesratsverordnung* that was announced in July 1915 de facto prevented the RWKS from dissolution and protected the cartelised organisation of the coal industry (Bundesratsverordnung 1915). Again, as before the war when the *Kali-Kartell* was not able to renew by itself, the state intervened to prevent a great cartel from breaking down and forcing its renewal. As with the intervention into the *Kali-Kartell*, the general terms of the *Bundesratsverordnung* remained fragmentary. By forcing the RWKS to renew, the state had already achieved its aim (Roelevink 2015b).

Wartime intervention by the state still had imperfect outcomes when the war came to an end in November 1918. In reaction to the revolution and the associated political upheaval, the state did not withdraw its interest from the RWKS but decided instead, to enhance its influence. Unless forced by political pressure from turmoil and socialisation threats the Weimar Republic only marginally changed German cartel legislation. The so-called Coal Industry Law (*Kohlenwirtschaftsgesetz*) of March 1919 enforced the cartelisation of the German coal economy. In contrast to the 1915 *Bundesratsverordnung,* which was for the purpose of preventing the breakdown of the RWKS, the coal industry law was directed at all German coal regions. Now other coal mining areas, such as those in the Aachen region were forced to organise coal cartels as well. Similar to the RWKS the *Kali-Kartell* had to face new attempts at regulation (*Regelung Kaliwirtschaft* 1919).

In 1923, and rather unexpectedly, the first national cartel legislation was launched, significantly as an administrative 'decree' rather than as a parliamentary law. Rapidly increasing inflation rates that were considered by the public to be the result of large cartels' pricing policies facilitated the initiative. In the Decree against the Abuse of Economic Power the legislator stuck with the principle introduced in 1897 that cartels were generally allowed and only the abuse of power was supposed to be controlled (*Kartellverordnung* 1923). The only new aspect was the introduction of a Cartel Court (*Kartellgericht*). The establishment of a public cartel register was discussed, although only marginally and thus did not become part of the decree (records of interrogation 1930: 358–366). The decree stipulated that in future, cartel contracts should be rescinded when they were not set out in writing. It was further declared that cartel contracts that did not acknowledge the competence of the new Cartel-Court, and later went to that court in case of conflict, were not acceptable. In practice, the decree only had a minor impact and was more a reaction to inflation and the general disintegration of the German economy than a serious attempt to strengthen cartel legislation. Since it was legally difficult to prove whether a cartel was guilty in misusing its power, the Cartel Court had no chance to reach greater relevance (Eggmann 1945: 11–17). For example, the RWKS adhered to its internal operation procedures in cases of conflict, and therefore successfully bypassed the Cartel Court. In the end, the RWKS was strengthened after the enactment of the misuse-decree, because it saved its organisational settings from increased state control (see the remark by Janus, RWKS board member, 1928). It was in 1926 that the Social Democrats suggested an extension of the Decree. By their reasoning, cartel abuses had not changed since 1923. By suggesting the establishment of a Cartel Office and a Cartel Register they hoped for an educational effect on the powerful cartels. The suggestion was easily argued against mainly by scholarly experts, who claimed a register would resulted in the transformation of cartel agreements into gentlemen's agreements. As cartels were still legal and therefore known in public, the idea of a register was not picked up, although the party renewed its suggestion in 1930 and even submitted a draft regulation in 1932 (Binz 1952: 14, 23ff.). While the number of cartels was rising, no great cartel law was enacted during the Weimar Republic.

In July 1933 the National Socialists announced their law concerning the creation of compulsory cartels (*Gesetz über die Errichtung von Zwangskartellen*, 1933). The law allowed the Minister of Economics to decree the establishment of a cartel and to extend cartels' powers. In contrast to the decree of 1923, where the private decision on entry and exit of cartel members had been strengthened, the Act of 1933 constrained the individual positions of the cartel members within a cartel. As in the First World War, the National Socialists had detected that cartels provided a useful tool for intervening in the economy. As Franklin D. Roosevelt commented in the German war economy: 'cartels were utilised by the Nazis as governmental instruments to achieve political ends' (cited in Schröter 2010: 528). By strengthening the cartels and at the same time limiting the power of individual members, the cartels should be used for the strategic purposes of the state. Three years later, in 1936, the obligation of a Cartel Register was introduced. The duties associated with disclosure were manageable; only nine questions were admitted to the questionnaire. Moreover, the register was never meant to be public (Binz 1952: 17f.). In 1938 the Cartel Court that had been introduced in 1923 was transferred to the *Reichswirtschaftsgericht*.[2]

The possibility to create compulsory cartels was meant to be applied in particular to industries and branches where a great number of small and middle-sized firms were at work (Ambrosius 1981: 187ff.). For the already cartelised and especially the greater cartels, as the *RWKS* and the *Kali-Kartell*, the National Socialists applied the special law tradition. In April 1933, before the law concerning the construction of compulsory cartels was enacted, the National Socialists enacted a law affecting changes in the coal economy (*Kohlenwirtschaftsgesetz*). The institutions of the coal industry that had been introduced in

1919 were dissolved. The Minister of Economy was free to replace the institutions or to re-install them. In addition, the state started work on restructuring and centralising the coal economy (Ziegler 2010). In the same year the National Socialists enacted a new law for the German potash industry (Kaliwirtschaftsgesetz 1933). The Kali-Kartell had to exist, if not, the Minister of Economics was authorised to create a cartel. More than in the previous laws, the Minister was entrusted with the power to intervene in the rules and obligations each cartel organised for its members. Import activities, and in particular export-activities, were solely the responsibility of the cartel. The *Kali-Kartell* became framed by a series of new institutions, such as an auditing agency. The overall control of the German potash industry was awarded to the Minister of Economics. We do not know much about the development of the cartels afterwards. Generally the history of cartels and their development during the Third Reich is an open field for research. Apparently, the politics of using the cartel structure of the German industry did not work. Ninety per cent of the cartels that were known to exist at the beginning of 1943 were dissolved by the end of 1943 (Newman 1948: 577).

Anti-Trust Policy in the Federal Republic of Germany since 1945

While the powerful cartels had been dissolved by the Allies after the war the state took an opaque attitude towards cartels. In contrast to the situation before the Second World War, the debate after the war departed from the case-by-case approach and tended toward national legislation, oscillating around the drafts for a federal ban of cartels. Positions about the institutional order relating to cartels was established a few years after the war. On the side of the German experts were still many of the Weimar economists, with the Freiburg 'Ordoliberals' and their intellectual head, Walter Eucken being the most influential school of thought (for their intellectual and institutional paths through the Third Reich, see Nicholls 1994; Haselbach 1991). The earliest German proposals for a cartel law had been drafted within the Administrative Office of the Economy (*Verwaltung für Wirtschaft*) in 1947 parallel to debates that had occurred in the Allied administrative bodies of the occupation zones. The cartel experts of the former Ministry of Economics were concerned with the drafts again and came together in different workgroups and councils. Among them were Paul Josten, former chief of the minister's cartel office, and Franz Böhm, formerly a research assistant to Josten and now professor of law at the University of Frankfurt. The so-called Josten commission launched the first drafts of the cartel law that strictly followed the principle of a general prohibition of cartels and therefore marked a deep rupture with the German cartel tradition (Robert 1976). The drafts (three 'Josten-drafts' were outlined between 1947 and 1949) triggered hefty critiques from German heavy industry representatives as well as from the German economic administration, especially because they suggested the dissolution of all forms of accumulated economic power. They were interpreted as a much too affirmative extension of the Allies' aim to remodel the German industry on the base of small and medium firms not able to economically threaten their neighbours.

While the Josten-drafts had been criticised, the West German state was founded in May 1949. The Allies had turned the responsibility for drafting and enacting a cartel law over to the German authorities in March 1949. They had intentionally restricted the task to a cartel-law, whereas the responsibility for the disentanglement of economic power was supposed to remain under Allied command (Murach-Brand 2004). Under these circumstances another strand of proposals were been drafted within the Ministry of Economics that followed much more closely the 'German tradition'. These did not prohibit cartels in general but aimed at carefully controlling the abuse of economic power. The first version of these drafts had been outlined by Eberhard Günther, who had previously been employed by the Nitrate Syndicate in Berlin and earned his PhD as a lawyer at the University of Freiburg. He would later become the first president of the Federal Cartel Authority that was finally erected with the enactment of Germany's first cartel law in 1957 (Berghahn 1985: 158; Nicholls 1994: 327). Though never being part of the 'Freiburg School' of economics and law, Günther followed the lines of the two most influential of the Freiburg representatives. In contrast to the claims of most of the English literature, there can be no doubt that Walter Eucken was in favour of a law that would not entirely ban cartels but only supervises abuses of economic power (Nicholls 1994; Gerber 1998; Mierzejewski 2003). Leonhard Miksch, one of his disciples, who worked at the minister of economics after the war, also strongly supported the 'abuse principle' of a cartel law, while challenging the 'prohibition principle' of the Josten drafts (Hesse 2015; Eucken 1949: 68; Miksch 1949). However, Miksch, as well as Eucken died short after the foundation of the West German state and Franz Böhm, who was a fervent fighter for the prohibition approach, was left as bearer of the 'Freiburg'-tradition in international literature. Until the final enactment of the law settled the matter, the debate oscillated between the 'abuse-principle' on the one hand and the 'prohibition-principle' on the other, both of which were increasingly modelled as extreme opposites. The question of publicity and registration that had gained some attention during the Weimar years completely disappeared during the rather zealous conducted debates of the early 1950s. German heavy industry especially tried to influence official drafts. Fritz Berg, chairmen of the Federation of German Industry (*Bundesverband der Deutschen Industrie*) pushed public opinion in favour of the 'abuse-principle' that, he argued would alone enable German companies to compete with the strong companies abroad, while the 'prohibition-principle' would severely threaten employment in West Germany. Only a strong and cartelised industry could resist international competition according to Berg; a perspective that was also shared by Chancellor Konrad Adenauer. When the Minster of Economics' draft for a cartel law was discussed in the cabinet in 1951, Adenauer summarised: 'It can be agreed that a prohibition of the abuse of economic power is necessary. But on the other hand it should be interfere into the procedures of economic life to the least possible extent' (Minutes of the 161st cabinet meeting 1951).

Business interests tried to push for a cartel law based on the 'abuse-principle' after parliamentary discussions left the cartel law unfinished in the first German parliament (1949–1953) and made necessary the launch of another draft in the second parliament (1953–1957). Nonetheless, the 'prohibition principle' reached consensus within the administration around 1952. The Allied High commanders had approved the drafts on that basis and in the cabinet meeting, when Adenauer made his comments, the officials of the Minister of Economics as well as the Minister of Finance spoke boldly in favour of the 'prohibition principle'. The only attack was by other departments such as the Minister of Agriculture and the Minister of Transport (ibid.).[3] Scholars like Franz Böhm, Fritz W. Meyer and Erwin von Beckerath, now representing the 'Freiburg School' of economics and law in public also supported the 'prohibition principle' (Robert 1976: 106ff.).

During the long years of debating and redrafting, however, the strict prohibition principle was highly perforated and the result was a cartel law that did not exactly promote 'perfect competition' in all parts of the German economy. The final draft prepared in the summer of 1952 had actually reached a final stage and had come close to the 1957 law. It proposed three different types of 'exemptions' from the general 'prohibition principle': general sector exemptions, cartels on a special permission, and resale price maintenance agreements (Tuchtfeld 1978; Hesse 2013). Since, in the final law registration only applied to most of the cartels exempted by these regulations, it is important to elaborate on them in greater detail.

1   Entire economic sectors were spared from the prohibition on cartels. This occurred mostly after intervention by the related departments during the debate on the law in the Federal Republics' cabinet meetings. Agriculture (§100), the financial sector (§102) as well as transportation (§99) managed to become protected from the cartel regulation as early as in 1950 (*Gesetz gegen Wettbewerbsbeschränkungen* 1957; Robert 1976: 140–149). Only the banking sector's exemption could have been justified at that time because it was subject to its own regulatory framework in connection with currency management and capital shortages (Ahrens and Wixforth 2010). In contrast, convincing economic arguments for a general exemption of agriculture and transport are much harder to find. Sectors, where public enterprises dominated, were also spared from the general cartel law, including postal services (§99), public banking (§101) and utilities, such as water-, electricity- and gas-supply (§103). While some of the branches could hardly have been completely exposed to free market competition by that time, it is astonishing how uncontroversial were the decisions to select sectors to receive exemptions from the general ban. In 1961, all these sectors together accounted for no fewer than 5.7 million employees, equalling one fourth of the total German workforce.[4] Heavy industry took their opportunity and was exempted from the law too. The *Ruhrcoal* that had formerly been under the control of the *RWKS* was able to re-organise parts of its former functions, for example, as sales-agencies. Until the beginning of the twenty-first century the Federal Cartel Authority was not responsible for the coal sector (Kurzlechner 2008: 67). This was also due to the fact that together with the Schuman plan and the foundation of the European Coal and Steel Community in 1951, the industry was transferred to international law and jurisdiction (Berghahn 1984; Goschler, Buchheim and Bührer 1989).

2   The exemption of entire branches and sectors is the more remarkable as even in the 'remainder' of the economy many exemptions from a strict prohibition of cartels were possible (§§2–7). Cartels contracted to improve export capacities of German industries and cartels to accelerate rationalisation of industries could, under certain conditions, receive special permission from the Federal Cartel Authority. A sudden decrease in consumer demand could justify the permission for a particular type of cartel. All these types of cartels had been mentioned as particular cases in the very earliest drafts in order to secure the support of the German industry that indeed had been fragile during the early fifties. Additional types of cartels though were added during the course of the fifties. No matter the fast recovering West German industry, cartel contracts dedicated to conditions of business and even discount cartels were granted (Nörr 1994: 202–207). For all these particular cartels a permission of the Cartel Authority had to be granted. During the parliamentary debates from 1955 to 1957 a further type of permission was added to the law: the Minster of Economics received the authority to grant special permissions to cartel contracts to which all described exemption rules would not apply but which he considered 'necessary for superordinate reasons of the overall economy and the common interest' – as paragraph 8 of the Act against Restraints of Competition holds (*Gesetz gegen Wettbewerbsbeschränkungen* 1957: 1083). Though the special permission was rarely used during the Federal Republic's history, generally cartel contracts could be confirmed basically everywhere in the economy by that instrument.

3   The third type of cartel that was eligible to receive special permission were related to all sorts of resale price maintenance agreements especially in retailing (§16). The paragraph targeted the strengthening of brand products and aimed at protecting small retailers that otherwise faced strong competition from large department stores. Apparently, it was due to the influence of Ludwig Erhard himself, who from earlier occupations in the 1930s kept contact with the brand manufacturer, that this third type of exemptions became part of the cartel law in a very early stage of the drafts (Beyenburg-Weidenfeld 1992: 216–221). From the perspective of competition theory, however, this type of exemption especially contradicted the ideal type of liberal market, because it directly affected the price mechanism.

The introduction of a cartel register with the 1957 cartel law

Academic economists in particular commented critically on the mushrooming number of exemptions. The famous Advisory Council to the Minister of Economics criticised especially the paragraphs on resale price maintenance, the exemption for agriculture and transport as well as the permission for cartels in times of economic crises and the sweeping clause for a minister's permission in the 1954 draft (Advisory Council 1954: 94). The experts under the chairmanship of Erwin von Beckerath, who had organised a group of liberal economists during the Nazi regime and who became the grey eminence of the Freiburg School after Eucken's death in 1950, also boldly supported a rather strict application of the law. They emphasised at the very end of their report that they were in favour of the enforcement of maximum publicity on the cartels as well as the use of the Federal Cartel Authority that in the end would grant the special permissions (ibid. no. 21: 96).

The claim for publicity of cartel contract resulted from the earlier initiatives and in particular from the debates of the late 1920s, where they however had been connected with the 'abuse-principle' of cartel regulation. It was considered then, that publicity would lend the cartel authority momentum to actually observe the accumulation of economic power (Binz 1952). In his post-war drafts for a powerful and independent national 'monopoly office', Walter Eucken had already emphasised publicity as an important feature of an abuse-legislation framework. In the 1952 government draft of a cartel law, however, officials objected to the idea of a cartel register because it would not allow cartels engaged in foreign trade or innovation to keep contract details secret after gaining permission of the Federal Cartel Authority (*Entwurf eines Gesetzes gegen Wettbewerbsbeschränkungen* 1952: 44). Since the public and parliamentary debates on the cartel law were mainly concerned with the question of an abuse or prohibition principle behind the law, the register issue never gained a prominent role. It seems to have been a pet of academic economists rather than being considered a serious and effective tool of economic policy. Nonetheless economists finally succeeded in bringing the idea back into the cartel law drafts.

The general idea that cartels should be forced to reveal maximum of transparency and that this in fact was an important aspect of cartel regulation was for the last parliamentary round of debate apparently raised by Walter Hoffmann, economist at the University of Muenster, in the meeting of the Economic Minister's Advisory committee in October 1954 (Minutes of the Advisory Council, 2 October 1954). A group of conservative Bavarian members of parliament raised the issue again in the parliamentary debates on the cartel law in 1955, suggesting that permissions given for cartel contracts should depend on a register entry (Höcherl/Stücklen/Seidl 1955). In an only somewhat relaxed form (the register entry was no longer a requirement for permission but a mandatory procedure after it), the register clause was integrated into the final draft without further parliamentary debate. Since it would apply only to the permitted cartels within the particular framework of the prohibition-principle with huge general exemptions, the publicity claim had lost most of its momentum for competition policy. Paragraph 9 of the 1957 cartel law required registration of all cartel contracts that had gained permission by the cartel authority based on paragraphs 2–8 of the law. Cartels in most of the exempted sectors as well as resale price maintenance agreements did not become subject to the obligation to register. Furthermore, registration was not a precondition for the legal enforcement of the cartel contract, similar to the early Norwegian legislation (see Chapter 8, this volume). Though the omission of registration could result in a fine, the register never gained the character of a powerful instrument for the suppression of cartels as it was supposed to become in the imagination of the architects of cartel legislation in Germany as well as other countries (Müller and Gries 1958: 72–75).

The form of the register was specified by decree on 15 January 1958. The Federal Cartel Authority was put in charge of the register that consisted of three divisions. Part A included all permitted cartels under paragraphs 2–8 of the cartel law; part B included the cartel contracts in the utilities' sector that only had to be brought to the attention of the Cartel Authority without needing permission and part C was dedicated to cartels that referred to technology and rationalisation rather than price setting (*Verordnung über die Anlegung und Führung des Kartellregisters* 1958: 1081, 68). All cartels had to indicate their name, the name and address of the owner or shareholder of the cartel, the legal form and address of the cartel, the 'basic content' of the cartel agreement as well as all possible restrictions that the Cartel Authority might have imposed on the cartel. Though the cartel register would not get published everybody was allowed to inspect the register (*Kartellgesetz*, §9). In a reduced form, cartels also had to be announced in the Federal Bulletin of Germany (*Kartellgesetz*, §10). After 1957, together with the annual reports of the Federal Cartel Authority that were also required by law, cartels and even cartel applications were largely regulated and treated publicly for the first time in Germany.

Given the controversial nature of public debates in the years before the enactment of the law, the comparatively smooth operation of the cartel authorities in the 1960s comes as a surprise. The expected flood of application for permission of existing or new cartels did not materialise. In its first year the Cartel Authority processed only 20 applications under the jurisdiction of §§2–7. Until 1974 a total of 448 applications had been submitted, of which 289 were actually granted. One third of the permitted cartels were related to exports and therefore did not affect the national market order (Report of the Cartel Authority 1974: 165). Contemporary observers, such as the American law professor Corwin Edwards saw the small number of permissions as a proof for a comparatively smooth implementation of policy by the German authorities, which also calmed down the former critics from industry after they got familiar with the new law. Public offenses against the law disappeared (Edwards 1966, cited in Harding and Joshua 2003: 104). Other authors blamed business for increasingly avoiding cartel legislation and the small number of permission was taken as an indicator for an increased number of illegal cartel agreements. The comparatively small number of successful fines against collusion also supports such a perspective: Between 1958 and 1974 the Federal Cartel Authority initiated 7385 suits against suspected collusion but no more than 621 (or 8.4 per cent) could successfully be proven and fines issued (Report of the Federal Cartel Authority 1974: 209). In sharp contrast, division B of the cartel register, that encompassed all cartel-like agreements in the field of public utilities and which had to be announced to the cartel office without any consequences, accounted for no fewer than 42,500 cases (Report of the Federal Cartel Authority 2009/10: 87).

The pure idea of 'perfect competition' as a benchmark for competition policy and cartel legislation also eroded internally in Germany during the 1960s as it did abroad. The erosion was propelled by the introduction of the idea of a 'workable competition' as articulated by James Maurice Clark in the US during the 1940s. The

German advisory council to the Minister of Economics used the idea as early as in its debates on the first amendment of the cartel law in 1961. The concept received greater attention after being transferred into German debates by the young economist Erhard Kantzenbach in 1967 (Hilger 2005: 235f.; Kantzenbach 1967). It was not, however, only the intellectual erosion of the perfect competition consensus that brought cartel legislation to the margin of public debate and decreased the meaning of the public cartel register as an instrument to secure a reduction in monopoly power. During the 1960s, accumulation of economic power in Germany, as well as abroad, increasingly took the form of corporate mergers. Mergers leading to a market share of more than 20 percent had to be announced to the Federal Cartel Authority according to the cartel law of 1957 but were not subject to prohibition. The number organisations using this type of accumulation of market power remained low in the first years of the cartel law when no more than an average of 26 mergers per year appeared. The figures increased dramatically by the end of the 1960, however, levelling at an average of 340 mergers per year between 1970 and 1973 and almost 600 between 1974 and 1977 (Lenel 1978).

Under these circumstances, the older idea of prospective merger control was revitalised and soon dominated public as well as scholarly debates. It had been discussed in post-war Germany as early as in the 1950s and was already part of the early drafts of the cartel law, representing mainly the closest connection with the US American antitrust-culture. The provisions were waived during the discussions in the German parliament and some scholars suspect industry pressure was behind this move (Nicholls 1994). On the occasion of the first amendment of the Cartel Law the issue was discussed again without success. Not before the third amendment of the Cartel Law in 1974, that also brought the abolition of the resale price maintenance paragraph, did prospective merger control became a part of the German cartel law.

Concluding remarks

As mentioned in the introduction we have problems with the suggestion that two clearly distinguished types of legislation existed in Germany; with the tendency to economic collusion in German being remodelled after the US anti-trust legislation after the Second World War. As early as the 1960s, scholars like the Swiss economist Edgar Salin considered such a perspective hard to apply not only to the German but also to the US American institutional order, in which some branches had been dominated by especially large companies rather than operating in 'perfect competition' (Salin 1963: 180; see also Berghahn 1985: 164). Cartel law has evolved in Germany prior and after the Second World War in interaction with industrial evolution, ideas of general economic order and politicians' aims rather than being a technical institutional structure that was engrafted on a passive economy. The great difference, which was subject to heated discussions prior and after the Second World War, was the main principle of cartel legislation. Whereas prior to 1945 the 'abuse principle' dominated – even though the principle was not shared by all institutions and scholars which was the reason for the fierce battles in the parliament, for example – the Act against Restraints of Competition introduced generally the 'prohibition principle'. Though the number of exemptions were criticised and the law was accused of tearing holes in that the 'prohibition principle', the basis for the cartel legislation now was no longer as a support for collusion but aimed at registering, controlling and even preventing cartels. At least in the legal framework we can discover a rupture in Germany's economic history. However, one was not translated into the actual economic outcome.

German cartel law changed its shape as well as its targets several times. The German cartel policy until 1945 had a generally cartel friendly attitude. Only in times of high economic and social pressure was cartel legislation enacted or changed. In general German cartel legislation followed a case-by-case approach that only in times of crises culminated in the establishment of a common and legal basis for all German cartels. In our opinion, this very nature of German cartel legislation explains the minor role of the cartel registration issue in public as well as in the scientific debates. Even the Decree against the Misuse of Economic Power in 1923 did not completely break from this tradition. In retrospect, the Decree proved to be a flash in the pan. The most important cartels, such as the RWKS did not go to the new introduced Cartel Court or give other responsibilities to the authority. Likewise, important cartels such as the *Kali-Kartell* and the RWKS were exposed to similar case-by-case cartel legislation. Here authorities as well as the majority in the parliament developed the handling of these cartels from initially being cartel-friendly to gradually supporting and then actually forcing cartel organisation. Whether this finding applies also to the uncountable number of small and medium sized cartels is difficult to decide given the current state of knowledge. The extent of cartelisation and the handling of cartels during the Nazi-period is still an open field in economic history. Launched from the ideas of the pre-Second World War debates and the cartel suspicions of the early 1950s, the cartel-movement of the post-war period turned out to be less intense and less dangerous than it was assumed. Corporate growth became the more threatening change in German industry as well as collusions of all kinds. The cartel authority, as it was established in 1957, therefore shifted its role from an office to grant permissions to cartels to the supervisory board of free market competition, dedicating most of its work to inquiries into the business practices of the country. Under these circumstances, however cartel registering never reached the role of an effective instrument in the application of competition policy in Germany.

Archival and printed sources

Ausschuss zur Untersuchung der Erzeugungs- und Absatzbedingungen der deutschen Wirtschaft. Verhandlungen und Berichte des Untersuchungsausschusses für allgemeine Wirtschaftsstruktur 1930, 3. Arbeitsgruppe: Wandlungen in den wirtschaftlichen Organisationsformen. Vierter Teil, Kartellpolitik, Berlin.

Draft of a Act against Restraints of Competition (Entwurf eines Gesetzes gegen Wettbewerbsbeschränkungen), 13.6.1952, Deutscher Bundestag 1. Wahlperiode 1949, Drucksache no. 3462: 44.

Höcherl/Stücklen/Seidel/Dollinger 1955 = Application of the members of parliament Höcherl, Stücklen, Seidl (Dorfen), Dr. Dollinger on the draft of an Act against Restraints of Competition, 11.5.1955, Deutscher Bundestag 2. Wahlperiode 1953, Drucksache Nr. 1253

Janus 1928 = Remarks Albert Janus (executive board RWKS), 8.03.1928, in: Stenographische Niederschrift über die Sitzung vom 8.03.1928, in: Bergbauarchiv im Montanhistorischen Dokumentationszentrum/Bergbau-Archiv beim Deutschen Bergbaumuseum Bochum [= BBA] 33 [= Rheinisch-Westfälisches Kohlen-Syndikat] /1006 [= record].

Minutes of the meeting of the advisory council of economic experts, 2.10.1954, Institut für Zeitgeschichte, Nachlass Hans Moeller, ED 150/36.

Report of the Federal Cartel Authority on its Activities in 1974 (Bericht des Bundeskartellamtes über die Tätigkeit im Jahr 1974), Bundestagsdrucksache 7/3791.

Report of the Federal Cartel Authority on its Activities in 2009/10 (Tätigkeitsbericht des Bundeskartellamtes), Drucksache des Deutschen Bundestages, Nr. 17/6640.

Statistisches Bundesamt Wiesbaden (ed.) 1972, Bevölkerung und Wirtschaft 1872–1972, Stuttgart.

Online

Minutes of the 161st cabinet meeting, 13.07.1951, TOP 2 ('Kabinettsprotokolle der Bundesregierung'. online: www.bundesarchiv.de/cocoon/barch/x/k/k1951k/kap1_2/kap2_55/para3_2.html).

Bundeskartellamt: Jahresbericht 2013: 3. [online: www.bundeskartellamt.de/Shared Docs/Publikation/DE/Jahresbericht/Jahresbericht_2013.html?nn=5311338.

Bundeskartellamt, Sektoruntersuchung Kraftstoffe – Abschlussbericht Mai 2011 [online: www.bundeskartellamt.de/SharedDocs/Publikation/DE/Sektoruntersuchungen/Sektorunt ersuchung%20Kraftstoffe%20-%20Abschlussbericht.pdf?__blob=publicationFile&v=5.

Laws

Announcement on the Establishment of Operating Companies in Coal Mining (*Bekanntmachung über die Errichtung von Betriebsgesellschaften für den Steinkohlen- und Braunkohlenbergbau*), 12.07.1915, Reichsgesetzblatt 1915: 427–430.

Decree against the Misuse of Economic Power (*Verordnung gegen Missbrauch wirtschaftlicher Machtstellungen*), 2.11.1923, Reichsgesetzblatt 1923: 1067–1071.

Decree on the Introduction and Conduct of a Cartel Register (*Verordnung über die Anlegung und Führung des Kartellregisters*) 15.01.1958, Bundesgesetzblatt I: 1081.

Kartellgericht, in Verordnung des Reichspräsidenten über Maßnahmen auf dem Gebiete der Rechtspflege und Verwaltung, vom 14.06.1932, Reichsgesetzblatt I, 1932: 285–296

Act against Restraints of Competition (*Gesetz gegen Wettbewerbsbeschränkungen*), 27.07.1957, Bundesgesetzblatt Nr. 41 1957: 1081–1103.

Law on the Potash Industry (*Kaliwirtschaftsgesetz*), vom 18. 12.1933, Reichsgesetzblatt II, 1933: 1027–1034.

Law on the Introduction of Compulsory Cartels (*Gesetz über die Errichtung von Zwangskartellen*), 15.07.1933, Reichsgesetzblatt I, 1933: 488f.

Law on the Change of Regulations in the Coal Industry (*Gesetz über die Änderung der kohlenwirtschaftlichen Bestimmungen*), 21.04.1933, Reichsgesetzblatt I, Jg. 1933: 203–205.

Law on the Regulation of the Potash Industry (*Gesetz über die Regelung der Kaliwirtschaft*), 24.04.1919, Reichsgesetzblatt 1919: 413–415.

Law on the Regulation of the Coal Industry (*Gesetz über die Regelung der Kohlenwirtschaft*), 23.03.1919, Reichsgesetzblatt 1919: 342–344.

Regulatory Statue concerning the Law on the Regulation of the Coal Industry (*Ausführbestimmungen zum Gesetz über die Regelung der Kohlenwirtschaft*), 21.08.1919, Reichsgesetzblatt 1919: 1449–1472.

Notes

1 The original German is 'Das Wettbewerbsprinzip ist ein tragender Pfeiler unserer [der deutschen, d.Vf.] Wirtschafts- und Gesellschaftsordnung.'
2 Minor changes on the Cartel Court were already enacted in 1932; see Kartellgericht, in Verordnung des Reichspräsidenten über Maßnahmen auf dem Gebiete der Rechtspflege und Verwaltung, vom 14.06.1932, in RGBl. I, 1932: 285–296, here 289ff.
3 Ludwig Erhard, the Minister of Economics, was not present at that meeting and was represented by Roland Risse and Walter Strauss. Their draft was supported by Franz Etzel (then High commissioner with the European Society for Coal and Steel) and Walter Hallstein (secretary of state for foreign affairs).
4 Accounted on the base of the official figures taken from: Statistisches Bundesamt Wiesbaden (ed.), *Bevölkerung und Wirtschaft 1872–1972*, Stuttgart 1972: 142, 167ff; 3.59 million employee in agriculture; 1.49 million in transport and information, 0.44 million in banking and insurance und 0.18 million in utilities = approx. 5.7 million of a total of 22 million.

12 Cartel registration in Sweden in the post-war period

Peter Sandberg

Introduction

Restrictive business practices were a widespread phenomenon during the interwar years. Cartels and other forms of business collusion were understood as a means to stabilise the economy and received wide support from the business community, interest groups and the political establishment. However, a new conception of competition issues emerged after the Second World War. This was, in many respects, a response to demands for increased international cross-border competition. Changes in competition policies took place in most European market economies and beyond, but with substantial differences in aim and scope. Sweden, a neutral country during the war, was surely influenced by these new conceptions.

As in many other Western European countries, a cartel register was established in Sweden after the war. The registration procedure was based on an anti-abuse principle and a business was only required to report a cartel when requested. From the authorities' perspective, the aim of the registrations was to map out the extent of restrictive business practices and to prevent abuses. By publishing the agreements (i.e. the cartels' understandings), the intention was that business itself would terminate the agreements. It is important to notice that cartels were not made illegal *per se*, and the set of rules became open to the authorities' own interpretation. Such indistinctness reflects the policy makers' ambivalence regarding competition matters.

Aims and issues

The main purpose of this survey is to examine the implementation of the Swedish cartel register as well as the evolution of Swedish competition policy during the post-war period. The aim is to present a broad picture of cartel registration as well as to make some general remarks concerning the contents of the register. Even though competition legislation tightened (but slowly) over time, it is unclear how the exercise of authority was carried out. Appreciating the authorities' response to, and interpretation of, the legislation is vital for understanding the implementation and outcome of the competition law. There are few comparative studies on competition policies before the formation and enlargement of the European Union.

Fortunately, there are exceptions. Putting Swedish cartelisation and decartelisation in a broader context, several scholars discuss the historical development of competition policies in the Western market economies during the post-war period (Edwards 1967; Schröter 1996, 2005; Wells 2002; Harding and Joshua 2003; Sandberg 2014). The present chapter contributes to understanding the implementation of competition policies in a national context and briefly discusses some of the basic aspects of the Swedish cartel register.

Perspectives and Problem Description

It has been suggested that the interwar period represented the peak of the cartel movement. The discourse on state regulations intensified during that period (Schröter 1996; Harding and Joshua 2003). Apart from Yugoslavia, the United States and some other non-European countries, the governments and businessmen in Europe became accustomed to businesses' collaborative behaviour. According to Harm Schröter, there were differences in the degree of cartelisation. Sweden, as classified in the figure below, was among the countries in Northern and Continental Europe that were generally positive in their acceptance of cartels.

The rise of liberal market regimes after the Second World War has partly been attributed to the growing influence of the United States (Edwards 1967; Wells 2002; Schröter 2005).

Pressure on a country's institutional arrangements, including its cartels and other restrictive business practices intensified. In accord with other efforts to open up the European economy to domestic and international competition, a process of decartelisation began after the war. According to one observation, 'active' competition legislation in the post-war period developed in Austria, Belgium, Denmark, Finland, France, Germany, Ireland, the Netherlands, Norway, Spain, Sweden, Switzerland and the UK (Harding and Joshua 2003). Most of these countries can be found in the upper box of Figure 12.1. Schröter's typology for the post-war period is thus in some respects different (see Figure 12.2).

I. Positive towards cartels: Austria, Belgium, Czechoslovakia, Finland, France, Germany, the Netherlands, Norway, Sweden, Switzerland
II. Ambivalent state intervention: Hungary, Italy, Japan, Poland, Spain
III. Generally ambivalent perception of cartelisation: Bulgaria, Canada, Denmark, South Africa, United Kingdom
IV. General prohibition of cartels: Argentina, Australia, New Zealand, United States of America, Yugoslavia

Figure 12.1 Cartelisation groups, 1920–1939.
Source: Schröter (1996: 141–142).

I. Decartelisation: EEC, the United Kingdom, Germany

II: Anti-abuse, strictly applied: Denmark, Ireland, the Netherlands, Sweden

III. Anti-abuse, cooperative tendencies: Austria, Belgium, Finland, France, Greece, Italy, Luxembourg, Norway, Portugal, Spain, Switzerland

Figure 12.2 Cartelisation groups, 1950–1990.
Source: Schröter (1996: 150).

Even though regulations of restrictive business practices differed in the European market economies, the 'anti-abuse' principle was similar in many respects:

> The norms generally focus on the effect of the conduct rather than on its characteristics, typically authorising government officials to control conduct where it has specified harmful effects. Sanctions are seldom attached to particular forms of conduct or specific 'arrangements' (such as cartels).
> (Harding and Joshua 2003: 98)

A hypothesis that has been put forward by Harm Schröter is that Sweden, along with the UK, was at the forefront of decartelisation in Europe:

> In Sweden one of the country's leading economists, Arthur Montgomery, won over official opinion with his insistence that open competition was of central importance for the country's welfare. From 1946 all Swedish cartels had to be registered. A governmental committee was set up to investigate the extent of cartelisation in the country, and published several reports at the beginning of the fifties. They were the background for a 1953 law prohibiting any abuse connected with cartelisation. These activities put Sweden along with the UK in the forefront of decartelisation in Europe.
> (Schröter 2005: 68)

This study of the Swedish cartel register challenges the picture of Sweden as a country at the forefront of the European decartelisation process. The evolution of the cartel legislation in a selection of Western European countries is discussed elsewhere in this book and can be used as a comparison with the Swedish case.

The Swedish case: the beginning

Cooperative business relationships that manifested themselves in trade organisations and cartels were well established before the First World War. According to early observers, cartels were a well-established and widespread phenomenon (Leifmann 1913). In the first decade of the twentieth century, inquiries into cartelisation and monopolisation in Swedish business started to occur. An example was the 1912 inquiry by the economist Adolf Ljunggren at the Business School in Stockholm. The cartel as a phenomenon was studied in the context of freedom of contract and freedom of association and as such was closely connected to the formation of the labour movement and trade associations in the latter part of the nineteenth century. The cartel was thus just another form of agreement between free citizens and a legitimate activity under the broader principle of freedom of contract. A cartel was understood as a monopolistic community of interests, formed by independent firms. On the other hand, a trust was seen as an organisation of fully integrated firms. Both types were characterised by exclusive forms of association and obstacles to free competition paving the way for increased business concentration (Ljunggren 1912).

One important outcome of Ljunggren's study was the implementation of a public inquiry by the Ministry of Finance focusing on the spreading of trusts and cartels (*Kartell- och trustutredningen* 1913). The final report was rather narrow and focused on the monopoly of the Swedish sugar industry and the taxation of sugar in Sweden, Denmark and Germany. Further enquiries began during the First World War. In some quarters of the Swedish Parliament the perceived negative outcomes of monopolies led, in the 1920s to proposals for further studies. The trust committee appointed in the same year concluded that some action was needed to prevent the negative effects of monopolistic behaviour. Temporary legalisation and a governmental trust commission with the authority to undertake special industrial investigations were established. Five years later the commission became permanent. On recommendations from the government, His Majesty the King could enforce special enquiries when it was considered that cartel agreements had negative effects on prices or distribution (SOU 1945: 12–20, 42).

A bigger topic

In 1927, the Swedish Cooperative Union and Wholesale Society (*Kooperativa förbundet*) proposed the supervision and registration of cartel agreements to the Swedish National Board of Trade (*Kommerskollegium;* LO *Propagandarådet* 1952: 5). The Cooperative Union had strengthened its position as a wholesaler and had become an important industrial force in its own right. The relationship between the Cooperative Union and private trade and industry (and their cartels) was characterised by tensions as the Cooperative Union had interests in public (i.e. open) cartel registration (Kylebäck 1974). The Swedish National Board of Trade and the Federation of Swedish Industries (*Industriförbundet*) opposed the proposal and no legal measures were taken at this time (SOU 1935: 65).

During the 1930s, the Federation of Swedish Industries started to show more interest in the debate on cartels and the problems related to restrictive business practices. The Federation had been part of the debate before and had become an important consultative organisation. When a government commission, Experts on Business Organisation (*1936 års Näringsorganisationssakkunniga*), began to investigate the extent of monopolies and cartels, the vice director of the Federation of Swedish Industries, Gustaf Settergren, became a member of the group of experts

(SOU 1940: 35). In an article in the Federation's periodical in 1936, he discussed the history and development of 'the policy of modern industrial cooperation', focusing on the legislation and cartelisation up until that time. In his concluding remarks, Settergren provided a reminder about the relatively liberal Swedish legislation and that the current attitude of the Swedish authorities was in most part 'non-interventionist'. In his opinion, there were then no signs of compulsive cartel registration in the near future. Settergren's and the Federation's view on the topic was clear – no further legislation was needed. The business community itself could handle the negative outcomes of monopolistic behaviour (*Industriförbundets meddelanden* no. 2 1936: 106–110).

It has been estimated that approximately 40 per cent of the total production in the Swedish home market was under cartel control in 1935, in privately owned business (SOU 1951: 27: 126). Such observations undoubtedly led to the appointment of a commission in the aftermath of the Great Depression. When the commission's report was published in the 1940s, some of the experts involved pointed to the need for some form of supervisory authority and a cartel register. The outbreak of the Second World War put any permanent legislation on hold until the circumstances stabilised. The report was in many respects a watershed in the Swedish official competition policy. From then on, there was a consensus on the need for some form of supervisory authority, but the scope remained unclear. The interpretation of what was meant by the concept 'restrictive business practices' was also blurred. According to the commission, the monopolistic behaviour of private business or cartel organisations had not reached any alarming levels. At the same time, however, there was a need for some kind of control. This was especially true in some specific markets and in sectors in which foreign competition was limited. Further information on business collaboration was needed, and a cartel registration authority seemed to be one of the most suitable options. Its assigned tasks were:

- To receive complaints concerning individual firms' or trade organisations' price and competition policies;
- To carry out inquiries when complaints were reported or on their own initiative if there were any suspicions of restrictive business practices;
- To negotiate with trade associations or individual firms when required;
- To publish parts of the results (the register);
- To propose public measures in each individual case;
- To propose revisions to the current legislation;
- To assist the Court of Justice and public prosecutors.

(SOU 1940: 35: 321–323; SOU 1945: 42: 18)

The 1936 commission began its inquiries before the outbreak of the Second World War and the special circumstances of the war economy made some of its conclusions obsolete. Nonetheless, the results became an important source when the legislative process continued after the war.

The early legislation

As mentioned in the introduction, American anti-trust policies influenced most of the European market economies following the Second World War. Sweden was no exception and a slow but steady legislative process antagonistic to cartels began immediately after the war. It is not true, however, to depict the situation as one where any kind of consensus had emerged on competition matters, since different interest groups and the political establishment had disparate agendas (Sandberg 2006). In 1945, the Commission for Post-war Economic Planning (*Kommisionen för ekonomisk efterkrigsplanering*) under the chairmanship of Gunnar Myrdal presented its report (SOU 1945: 42). Following the 1936 commission's recommendations, they too proposed the establishment of a cartel register. All the political parties in the Riksdag supported the proposal (Wallander 1952). The Federation of Swedish Industries argued that a cartel register could be an effective instrument for obtaining information on those restrictive business practices that had negative effects on competition. Their comments also pointed out some of the positive outcomes of business cooperation, especially regarding rationalisation benefits in production and distribution, standardisation, spreading technical knowledge and in creating more efficient transport systems (*Industriförbundets meddelanden* no. 8 1945: 500–510). From a social democratic (as well as labour movement) point of view, cartel registration was one step in the right direction to deal with widespread monopolistic tendencies. It is worth noting, however, that during the interwar years, the social democratic party had taken a much more pessimistic view of competition describing it as 'a waste of productive resources'. Uncontrolled and free competition was seen, especially during the economic crises in the 1930s, as a threat to economic stability which created further unemployment. On the other hand, the Cooperative Union was one of the driving forces in the legislation process during the same period (Brems 1951). Nonetheless, Richard Sterner, chief secretary of the labour movement's post-war programme, had confidence in the establishment of a registration authority, but feared that further measures were needed to prevent monopolistic behaviour (Sterner 1951). The labour movement became an important pressure group when further legislation eventuated.

In the summer of 1946, the Act of Probation on Restrictive Business Practices (*Lag om övervakning av konkurrensbegränsningar inom näringslivet*) was adopted and the Bureau of Monopoly Investigation (*Monopolutredningsbyrån*) was established under the authority of the Swedish National Board of Trade (*Kommerskollegium*). The chief initiator was the same economist Gunnar Myrdal, now Minister of Commerce in the social democratic government. Firms or trade associations were required on demand to give a full statement regarding any agreements that negatively affected prices, production, turnovers or distribution. These were thereafter officially published in the periodical *Kartellregistret*. The probation authority could also launch special inquiries into selected branches of industry. The results of these inquiries were also published in the periodical. When an agreement was declared closed by the participants involved, it was removed from the register and published in the periodical. The only exceptions were international agreements, unless they had a domestic scope. The financial sector and insurance companies were subject to the Bank Inspectorate and Insurance Inspectorate, respectively, and not subject to the cartel register (*Kartellregistret* 1947: 1).

At the end of 1951, approximately 500 agreements had been registered. Out of these, 200 agreements had also been deregistered. It was difficult for the authorities to interpret whether the deregistrations were an outcome of 'changes in mentality' of the representatives in different industrial sectors or whether these agreements had just become obsolete (Brems 1951). Another important issue was whether the deregistration actually meant cartels were going underground. It was impossible to determine whether a cartel had changed character from a formal to an informal contract (Sterner 1951). There was also a concern about the lack of coverage by the registration process. The fact that only certain branches or sectors had been subject to registration and inquiry made generalisations impossible. In other words, the uncertainty surrounding the extent of cartelisation in the economy was by this stage, significant. These limitations were acknowledged in the same year the cartel register was established. A governmental committee, the Experts of New Establishment (*Nyetableringssakkunniga*), was to investigate the private control of new establishments (SOU 1951: 27). Under the leadership of the Ministry of Commerce, the members of the committee were picked from a wide spectrum of businesses including large- and small-scale industry, handicrafts, agriculture, wholesale, retail trade, the labour movement and the Cooperative Union (Brems 1951). The appointment of the committee in 1951 marked the beginning of further legislation.

Towards a competition law

The debate on competition was very intense from the late 1940s until the mid-1950s. Several publications and ideological pamphlets were in circulation. A wide range of interest groups connected to different business organisations, the Cooperative Union, the labour movement and the spectra of the political parties, were involved in the debate. Most of these interest groups were also represented on the 1946 Committee and future commissions. It is problematic to provide a simple overview of these diverse interests and it is difficult to identify the main divisions in their attitudes to. At the risk of over simplification, we can observe a growing belief in the efficacy of further legislation on the part of the social democrats and the labour movement. From a business point of view, there was both a liberal and a more conservative perception of competition and restrictive business practices. Any consensus is hard to depict. Generally speaking, the business interests were suspicious of further legislation and believed that self-regulation was the best option to increase competition.

When the 1946 Committee was appointed, another economist and social democrat Karin Kock became chairman. She was later replaced by Richard Sterner, formerly at the Swedish Confederation of Trade Unions (*Landsorganisationen*). Sterner was one of the most prolific social democrats in the competition debate and published several reports and books on the subject. In 1946, his pamphlet, 'More Democracy in the Trade and Industry' discussed the important role of competition as a means to increase business efficiency and rationalisation (Sterner 1946). The idea was not new. In the 1930s, the social democratic Minister of Finance, Ernst Wigforss, had stated that cartelised structures in most industrial sectors were inefficient. In order to create more efficient business structures, the rationalisation of business organisation was a central aim (Wigforss 1938). From a social democratic perspective, not all forms of business collaboration were seen as obstacles to increased efficiency. On the contrary, some considered collaboration could speed up the rationalisation of business.[1] The most important goals were to reach full employment and keep consumer prices as low as possible. The Korean War was a threat to both employment and inflation. The price freeze that was implemented during the Second World War was still in place and had a great impact on price stability and business organisation (Sterner 1951). Yet another problem during the early post-war years was the 'gross price system', a phenomenon of vertical price-fixing and the private control of new establishments; as such it was under inquiry by the 1946 Committee (SOU 1951: 27–28).

When the Bureau of Monopoly Investigation started demanding registrations from businesses there was an emphasis on horizontal cartel agreements. It soon became apparent, however, that vertical agreements, such as the gross price system and the control of new establishments, were important. The gross price system was a complex hierarchical web of interrelations between manufacturers, wholesalers and retailers. Apart from ensuring manufacturers' control and fixing retail prices and distribution channels, the practices also cemented market structures (SOU 1951: 27: 302–316). Barriers to entry were very high and anti-competitive. Control of new establishments in some sectors prevented new entrepreneurs from entering certain markets, especially in the wholesale and retail sectors (SOU 1951: 27: 356).

The report of a group of experts in 1951 (mostly business representatives and academics), stated that cartel registration and the inquiries made by the 1946 Committee had provoked some reaction, either by business itself or by further legal proceedings. Legislation to prevent certain restrictive business practices was by its very nature perceived as negative, since it was impossible to enforce competition. It was, in other words, difficult to design competition legislation without hampering the freedom of contract (Brems 1951). Richard Sterner expressed the issue slightly differently. The important question, he stressed, was whether business itself had the ability to clean up the dozens of different horizontal and vertical cartel agreements in existence. The public publishing of the cartel register had forced businesses to take some measures, but in his view, not enough. Sterner pointed to the important initiative taken by business's own principal organisations (most notably the Federation of Swedish Industries) to negotiate with trade organisations and individual firms. This, he felt, was a step in the right direction. There was, however, a risk that these measures were mostly a response to legislative threats, and therefore it was important to actually adopt a law governing restrictive business practices (Sterner 1951).

The Federation of Swedish Industries established a cartel committee and an 'unofficial' cartel bureau in 1950. The purpose was to support and give guidance to members on questions concerning economic collaboration. For firms or trade organisations that were subject to cartel registration, the cartel bureau gave guidelines on legal matters and advice on how to change or close existing agreements. The Federation of Swedish Industries, together with the Swedish Federation of Wholesalers, Swedish Organisation of Handicraft and Small Business and the Swedish Retail Federation, established the Trade and Industry Competition Committee (*Näringslivets konkurrensnämnd*). All the parties had an interest in trying to persuade members in all business sectors to prevent restrictive competition practices. It was important for all the parties involved to reach consensus. If business itself could manage to halt competition-limiting agreements, there was a possibility of preventing further legislation (*Industriförbundets meddelanden* no. 3 1952: 107). In a pronouncement to the Ministry of Commerce, the Federation of Swedish Industries highlighted that since the establishment of the cartel register, business itself had managed to steer away from restrictive business practices. They also agreed that the Bureau of Monopoly Investigation was an important institution and further inquiries into different business sectors were needed. It was important that the Bureau could continue its work. In the Federation's opinion, there was no need for further competition legislation (*Industriförbundets meddelanden* 1952: 1: 41).

When the 1946 Governmental Committee (*Nyetableringssakkunniga*) presented its final report in 1951, it was accompanied by a proposed bill. The supervision of restrictive business practices was, by itself, insufficient to prevent practices that had 'harmful effects' on prices and efficiency, such as the introduction of new technologies (SOU 1951: 27: 530–535). From the Federation's point of view, it was the lack of definition in the report that was the weakest outcome. It argued that it was doubtful whether efficiency in production and distribution could be reached through legislation. Furthermore, it was deemed impossible to make sufficiently detailed inquiries to decide whether an agreement had negative effects on business efficiency (*Industriförbundets meddelanden* no. 1 1952: 41). From the Federation's point of view, it was clear that further legislation was not a satisfactory way to deal with restrictive business practices.

The Restrictive Trade Practices Act (*Konkurrensbegränsningslagen*) was passed in the autumn of 1953 and implemented in 1954. The 1946 Committee's report was the foundation for the design of the act, which focused on the gross price system (vertical price fixing) and the control of new establishments. There was no intention to make cartels or business collaboration illegal *per se*. The aim was to prevent certain types of restrictive business practices that had a negative impact on the determination of prices, business efficiency and the establishment of new enterprises. Two important institutions were established: the Ombudsman for Freedom of Commerce (*Näringsfrihetsombundsmannen*) and the Council for Freedom of Trade (*Näringsfrihetsrådet*). The former was appointed to prepare further measures dealing with restrictive trade practices, while the latter was constituted as a negotiating court. This consisted of members of various business interest groups, labour organisations as well as legal experts. In practice, when a restrictive practice was alleged a report was submitted by the referred firm or other appropriate juridical person to the Ombudsman, who decided whether a special enquiry was needed. The

Ombudsman also had the capacity to negotiate directly with individual firms or trade organisations (Martenius 1965). The Council for Freedom of Trade became a regulatory agency and functioned as a court of negotiation. In 1956, the Competition Act was sharpened and the Bureau of Monopoly was replaced by the National Rates and Cartel Board (*Statens pris- och kartellnämnd*). The cartel registration procedure continued as before under the new act, but with some important changes. First, the act explicitly prohibited two types of cartel agreements – tender cartels and vertical price fixing. These types of agreements were therefore no longer registered. Second, with the establishment of the Commissioner for Freedom of Commerce, it became possible for individual firms and private agents to report restrictive business practices to the authorities (Holmberg 1981).

In the opinion of the Federation of Swedish Industries, the Competition Act was too vague and unspecific. The efforts of the Bureau of Monopoly Investigation had made a great impact on business collaboration. By 1953, approximately a thousand agreements had been registered and a substantial number of these agreements had been declared closed and deregistered. According to the Federation of Swedish Industries, increasing the Bureau of Monopoly Investigation's resources appeared to be a far better way to reduce anti-competitive agreements than implementing competition laws (*Industriförbundets meddelanden* vol. 4 1953: 214–220).

No major changes – the period up until the 1980s

The Restrictive Trade Practices Acts of 1954 and 1956 were the guidelines for the competition authorities for decades to come. A 'triad' of the National Rates and Cartel Board, the Ombudsman for Freedom of Commerce and the Council for Freedom of Trade continued as the principle authorities regulating competition. They continued to take measures according to the legal framework. Principles of negotiation and anti-abuse permeated the actions taken by the authorities. The number of cartel reports to the Ombudsman showed an irregular but steady increase, while in contrast the number of verdicts passed by the Council for Freedom of Trade, from 1971 the Market Council (*Marknadsrådet*) and later the Market Court (*Marknadsdomstolen*), sharply decreased up until the mid-1970s. The total number of reports to the Ombudsman for Freedom of Commerce increased from 117 in 1954 to 309 in 1975. During the same period, the number of verdicts passed by the Council for Freedom of Trade (the Market Court) fell from 18 to 6 cases (Holmberg 1981: 74–76). The Restrictive Trade Practices Act was occasionally readjusted with minor changes to its aim and scope. The most important readjustment was the 1966 prohibition of the activity of refusal to deliver in (*Pris och Kartellfrågor* vols. 8–9 1965: 71–72). No other important changes in competition policies occurred until the late 1970s.

In 1978, a report by the Competition Inquiry (*Konkurrensutredningen*) suggested for a new or revised Restrictive Trade Practices Act (SOU 1978: 9) For the first time, a general prohibition on joint price fixing, market-sharing and quotation cartels was considered. The National Rates and Cartel Board pleaded for revised legislation, but was also anxious to emphasise the dangers facing any supervision required by more rigorous legislation. This was especially true considering the increase in business concentration that had occurred during the previous two decades (*Pris- och kartellfrågor* no. 6 1978: 5). The supervision of mergers and acquisitions had been on the agenda since the early 1960s, when it was decided to appoint a commission for Merger Investigation (*Koncentrationsutredningen*).[2] The National Rates and Cartel Board started to record mergers and acquisitions in coordination with the cartel register. This procedure was formalised in 1969 when a register of big business was set up by the National Rates and Cartel Board in cooperation with the Merger Investigation Commission. The main aim was to coordinate the big business and cartel registers and create a better understanding of the business concentration process and its socio-economic effects at both the macroeconomic and microeconomic level (*Pris och kartellfrågor* 1969: 7: 4–15).

The Competition Commission's (*Konkurrensutredningen*) 1978 report was clearly ambivalent between the pros and cons of increased competition versus business concentration. In many respects, the report encapsulates the official Swedish competition policy during the period (SOU 1978: 9: 82). According to the National Rates and Cartel Board's referral response in 1978, the competition policies needed to be put into a broad socio-economic context. Increased business concentration was in many respects the result of internationalisation of the economy in the preceding decades.[3] The need for large-scale production in certain sectors was necessary in order to remain competitive in the international market. To achieve these advantages, it was important to oversee the negative effects of business concentration. This meant keeping a close watch on firms' measures to promote efficiency in production and distribution and to prevent them engaging in restrictive business practices. Further price controls, supervision of cartels and other regulations on free competition enabled the prevention of the negative outcomes of business concentration (*Pris- och kartellfrågor* no. 6 1978: 5–9).

A new law, The Competition Act, was passed in 1983. There were no spectacular changes in the cartel registration procedure. The long-standing principles of anti-abuse and negotiation continued to guide the exercise of authority. The most important feature of the new act was merger control. The focus was on preventing mergers and acquisitions that fostered a dominate market position and eventually damaging prices and competition. The Ombudsman for Freedom of Commerce acted as a negotiator following legal probation by the Market Court. If an acquisition was considered seriously damaging by the court, a prohibition could be ordered by the Swedish Government (*Pris och konkurrens* no. 1 1983: 6–10).

Into a European legal framework

The National Rates and Cartel Board changed its name to the State Price and Competition Authority (*Statens pris- och konkurrensverk*) in 1988 and increased its scope on international matters relevant to competition and domestic price trends. The international dimension became generally more prominent in the late 1980s and the competition authorities published frequent reports on subjects concerning the practices of the European Court of Justice. At about the same time, a new commission was appointed. Its task was to conduct a survey of Swedish competition policies and propose changes to the legislation (*Pris och konkurrens* no. 2 1989). The commission pleaded for changes to the structure of the Market Court through the abolishment of representation from business interests and trade unions (Lundqvist 2003).

A merger of the State Price and Competition Authority and the Commissioner for Freedom of Commerce created the Swedish Competition Authority (*Konkurrensverket*) in 1992. In many respects, the changes in organisation, in this specific area, meant the end of the 'Swedish corporative model'; a structure fostered from the beginning of the twentieth century. The anti-abuse and negotiation principles, pragmatism and consensus seeking had been cornerstones of the competition policy up until the early 1990s. By replacing the representation of interested organisations in the Market Court with lawyers, the government authorities signalled the importance of new legislative principles in the field of competition policy.

The Swedish Confederation of Trade Unions supported the Commission's 1991 proposals for strengthened competition legislation but opposed the more formal juridical structure of the Market Court. The Trade Union feared that 'pragmatic views' would be replaced by the lawyers' interpretation of the law. In the opinion of the Federation of Swedish Industries, the formation of the Swedish Competition Authority was a step in the right direction to promote efficiency. Adaptation to the EEC's competition law was, however, not seen as a necessity and the Federation defended the corporative structures of the Market Court. Furthermore, the Federation opposed the Commission's proposal to prohibit horizontal price fixing and market segmentation. The anti-abuse principle on competition was, they argued, the only plausible solution to recognising the potential positive effects of business collaboration. In short, the Federation saw no reason to change the principles of the existing legislation (Lundqvist 2003).

The Commission's 1991 report marked an important shift in Swedish competition policy making. The anti-abuse principle was replaced by the prohibition principle; a principle in line with the European Court of Justice's legal framework (SOU 1991: 59). In many respects, the suggestions from the Commission were a step towards common European competition legislation. The new Competition Act was passed by the conservative/liberal government and implemented in 1993 (*Svensk författningssamling, konkurrenslag* 1993: 20). It tightened the rules on competition. Those violating the bans could face sanctions. By making cartel agreements illegal, cartel registration became obsolete and the process ceased to operate with the introduction of the new act in 1993 (Modin 1999c).

The Cartel Register – some observations

The cartel register under the authority of the Bureau of Monopoly Investigation operated from 1947 until 1993. The 1946 Act required individual firms or trade associations to give, on demand, a full statement regarding any agreement that could have harmful effects on prices, production, turnovers or distribution. It was

220 *Peter Sandberg*

up to the authority to decide which business sector became subject to investigation and the agreements were published in the *Kartellregistret*. One consequence of the authorities' special inquiries into selected branches was the amalgamation of specific lines of business, since a special investigation usually led to numerous registrations (Modin 1999a).

The registration process raises some issues for the interpretation of its contents. For example, a line of business that was under investigation tended to be prominent during a specific time span. This caused business clusters to appear in the register during specific periods. The pattern of initial registrations in 1947 suggests the authorities undertook investigations more or less randomly. The statistics represented in Figure 12.3 below reveal the major categories of agreements registered during the period 1947 to 1988. The figure shows a broad picture of each individual line of business that was most prominent during the whole period.

The wholesale and retail sector, (hereafter jointly called the distribution sector SNI 46 and 47), were the most prominent branches registered during the whole period. It is important to notice that the agreements from the distribution sector were 'integrated' with the manufacturing industry and thus present vertical agreements covering several different branches. Most agreements were vertical cartels

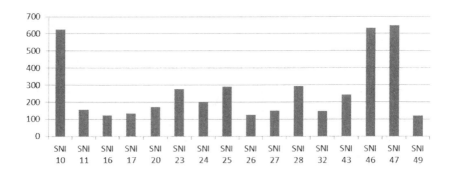

Figure 12.3 Lines of business with more than 100 cartel agreements registered in the Swedish cartel register, 1947–1988.

Note: SNI 10: manufacture of food; SNI 11: manufacture of beer, soft drinks, spirits and wine; SNI 16: manufacture of wood products and wooden articles; SNI 17: manufacture of pulp and other paper products; SNI 20: manufacture of chemical products; SNI 23: manufacture of glass, glassware, brickworks, cement and stone products, etc.; SNI 24: manufacture of iron, steel and other metals, also casting of iron, steel and other metals; SNI 25: engineering industry; SNI 26: manufacture of electric goods; SNI 27: manufacture of electric motors, generators, electric fitting, cables, electrical domestic appliances, etc. ; SNI 28: manufacture of different types of engines; SNI 32: manufacture of musical instruments, sport equipment, medical instruments, etc. ; SNI 43: building trade and adherent enterprise; SNI 46: wholesale trade; SNI 47: retail trade; SNI 49: transport.

Source: *Konkurrensverket*, *Kartellregistret* 1947–1988, D7: 1–339, the National Archives. Swedish Industrial Classification: SNI 2007, compatible with the industrial classification in the European Union and United Nations: Nace Rev 2.

integrated with other lines of business. The distribution sector's dominance was stronger until the mid-1950s and there is a possibility that the focus on the gross price system and the control of new establishments during this period explains the distribution sector's strong appearance. On the other hand, the food industry (SNI 10) was, until the early 1960s, by far the most dominant manufacturing group and continued to be prominent until the late 1980s. If the brewing industry (SNI 11) is included, the food industry is even more significant. The prominence of the distribution sector in combination with manufacturers implies the importance of vertical agreements. The importance of the distribution sector became less significant during the late 1950s, a possible outcome of the relatively early prohibition on vertical price fixing. The high numbers of agreements from the food industry up until the early 1960s were more or less expected, since it was the most cartelised sector during the interwar years (SOU 1951: 27: 126).

It is difficult to estimate the importance of changes in the legal framework on the cartel registration procedure. If one looks at Figure 12.4, the number of registrations rose for a short period in the mid-1950s. There may well be a correlation between the introduction of the Competition Act and the increase in agreements in 1953. At this stage, however, there is no evidence that the increases had anything to do with the possibilities for firms or individuals to notify restrictive business practices. The irregularities in the registration pattern over time can partially be explained by registration praxis, since each agreement was recorded separately and received its own registration number. The following case can serve as an example. In 1955, shortly after the Ombudsman for Freedom of Commerce was implemented, a number of small independent grocery shops notified the Swedish Retail Federation (*Köpmannaförbundet*) and its members of a refusal to supply (diaries) and controls being placed on new establishments (Holmberg 1981). It is difficult to estimate the importance of the reports from the grocers. It does, however, seem likely that the registration of 184 agreements by the Swedish Retail

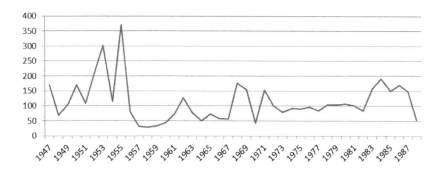

Figure 12.4 Number of new registrations in the Swedish cartel register, 1947–1988.
Source: Konkurrensverket, Kartellregistret 1947–1988, D7: 1–339, the National Archives.

Federation at the end of 1955 was initiated by the public reports to the Ombudsman. All the agreements had a regional focus, which also helps explain the high numbers of registrations (*Konkurrensverket, kartellregistret*, D7: 115–119, the National Archives).

The case above is rather extreme but can help illustrate the factors underlying irregularities in the registration patterns. When an industry was investigated, either on the initiation of the competition authority or on the request of the Ombudsman, the most common procedure was an investigation of the principal agent to the agreements. Until the mid-1960s, the agent was in a majority of cases (excluding ancillary agreements), usually a trade association or a former sub-division. Agreements could also be coordinated by so-called conventions or other more informal associations. In the horizontal agreements, the coordinating actors typically organised agreements in separate commodity groups. Such an approach was essential since most agreements required homogenous products. Commodity groups were in most cases registered separately, an approach that led to numerous registrations when an industrial sector was examined.

The contents of the agreements

According to Swedish legislation, a cartel is defined as a horizontal or vertical anticompetitive agreement between independent businesses (Grönfors 1969). It is thus *not* understood as an interest organisation. This is an important distinction for the understanding the registration procedure. Apart from tender cartels and vertical price fixing, registered agreements were not, according to the Swedish Restrictive Trade Practices Act, illegal and as the definition of 'competition restrictions' was uncertain, the authorities had no clear guidelines about what to register (Modin 1999a). The Ombudsman for Freedom of Commerce also often had difficulties in determining whether a registered agreement was in accordance with the law (Holmberg 1981). Such situations paved the way for the authorities' own interpretation and can be regarded as a legal vulnerability.

The authorities' approach to competition did not change dramatically over the time discussed here. Strictly speaking, the anti-abuse principle guided the exercise of authority and a registered agreement was not considered illegal. The 1966 Commission pleaded for more stringent registration procedures, whereby the effects of restrictive business practices were analysed in a broader macroeconomic context. The authorities opposed the Commission's proposal and pointed out, among other things, at the difficulties in estimating the significance of a cartelised sector in comparison with a non-cartelised sector. Apart from more detailed registration on purchase cooperation, the Commission's report signalled no radical change in the registration procedure (Modin 1999b).

There was great diversity in the agreements recorded in the cartel register, including a variety of restrictive business practices. Looking at Figure 12.5, it appears that price fixing and market divisions were the most common form of collaborations. Note too that an agreement could include more than one restrictive business practice. The figure above takes account of this, which explains the high

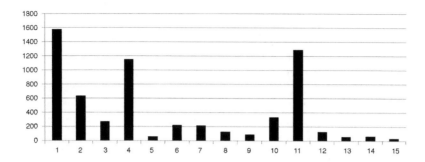

Figure 12.5 Types of contracts in the Swedish cartel register, 1947–1988.
Note: 1. clause on equal prices; 2. principles on discounts and terms of delivery; 3. allocation of production/sales quotas; 4. principles on market division; principles on protection of domestic markets; principles on sole rights on specific markets; 5. protection of trademarks; 6. clause on obligations to purchase; 7. clause on obligations on delivery; 8. cooperation in production; 9. cooperation in purchase; 10. marketing and sales cooperation; 11. ancillary agreements; 12. joint sales companies; 13. control of new establishments; 14. tender cartels; 15. agreements declared confidential by the authorities on request by the subject.
Source: Konkurrensverket, Kartellregistret 1947–1988, D7: 1–339, the National Archives.

number of agreements compared with the total number registered. The Swedish Wire Nail Manufacturers Association (*Sveriges Trådspiksfabrikanters Förening*) can serve as an example. Following an investigation by the Bureau of Monopoly Investigation, one agreement was registered in 1949. It stipulated price fixing, sales quotas as well as the control of new establishments. The agreement expired in 1957, and was replaced by a new agreement in 1960. The revised agreement was registered and received a new registration number.[4] Another case is the brewing industry. Between 1951 and 1955, a total of 65 agreements (including 98 participants) were registered. The agreements consisted mostly of market segmentation and sharing, but price fixing as well as sales quotas were included in some cases.[5] More complex examples exist which include both horizontal and vertical agreements.

There were some significant changes in the registration praxis. From 1947 until approximately the mid-1960s, the most common form of recorded agreement was price fixing and market division. Those are the types of agreements most commonly associated with cartels and restrictive business practices. There are, however, other forms of agreements registered in the cartel register that are not typically associated with cartels. In Figure 12.5 above, column 11 refers to ancillary agreements.[6] This form of restrictive business practice was the second-largest group of registered agreements during the whole period. Until 1954, only three such agreements were registered, while an additional 192 registrations followed between 1955 and 1965. Thereafter, it seems that the authorities began to observe ancillary agreements more closely. After 1956, approximately 1100 ancillary agreements were registered; approximately 43 per cent of the total number registrations between 1965 and 1988. This is of course an important finding and demands a critical analysis. While legally these agreements could not be described as cartels or even restrictive business practices according to the 1956 Competition Act, an ancillary agreement can be interpreted as a restrictive business practice where it obstructs or prevents an entrepreneur or firm from competing in specific markets.[7] Coordinating the cartel register with the merger register meant the competition authorities had an instrument to supervise the phenomenon more closely.

According to the Act of Supervision on Restrictive Business Practices, only cartels affecting the Swedish market were subject to registration (*Kartellregistret* 1947: 1). International cartels were out of reach, with one exception; international cartel activities in the domestic market. Three different types of geographical categorisation (the regional, the national and the international) can be identified. Cartels with a national scope, 59 per cent of the total, were the most common. The regional cartels amounted to 34 per cent while the international ones accounted for seven per cent of the total registrations between 1947 and 1988. Of the international cartels recorded, a majority had a Nordic scope and agreements between Swedish and Finnish businesses were the most frequent. The content varied from various forms of domestic market protection to other forms of market divisions and price fixing.[8]

The problem of estimating the sustainability of a cartel agreement (or a cartel organisation) is evident when one considers the imperfection of the recording procedure. What we obtain in the database is the time span starting with the latest ratified agreements. For example, when an agreement was recorded by the authority, it featured the latest ratification date. This makes determining the origin of the cartel difficult. Furthermore, it is impossible to tell whether a cartel (if understood as a public and formal agreement or an organisation) was dissolved when declared closed by the Price and Cartel Office. Another issue is reregistration. As in the case of the wire nail cartel, an agreement could be reregistered. This often involved changes in the contract either initiated by changes in the Competition Act or altered organisational forms. In other words, the reregistration procedure maked it difficult to trace an agreement over time or evaluate whether it was the same agreement. The only solution is to carry out case studies on a micro level, by studying either the individual firm or the individual business organisation. Such a research process thus becomes a matter of trial and error.

Concluding remarks

Cartels were a common feature in Sweden before and after the Second World War. Restrictive business practices and business collaboration were an accepted and widespread phenomenon from the early twentieth century and onwards. Prohibitions on cartels were not present before the Swedish membership of the EU was actualised. The long road to decartelisation was an outcome of the indistinctness in the legislative framework and the rather ambivalent position of policy makers and authorities. There was hardly any consensus on the pros and cons of business collaboration. Up to the early 1990s, the probation principle guided the legislative process. Furthermore, the participation of business interests and trade unions in the Council for Freedom of Trade and the Market Court of Trade made changes to the implementation of stricter competition policies slower. From such a perspective, the view of Sweden as a forerunner of decartelisation in Europe seems rather exaggerated. Up until the early 1990s, the decartelisation of the economy was an uncertain goal.

It is difficult to estimate the significance of the cartel register. It seems clear that the investigations and the registrations were an important tool for the authorities to acquire a better understanding of how cartels in certain sectors operated and what goals they wanted to achieve. It is important to stress the uncertainty of the approach, since firms and business organisations were only subject for registration on demand by the authorities. It was therefore not possible to estimate the true extent of the cartelisation. Since the competition law was vague it is difficult to determine what types of agreement were made in accordance with the law. Nonetheless, the cartel register created a better environment in which the authorities could monitor and, to a lesser extent, prevent abuse by restrictive business practises. The registration of cartels was a first step in a legal process which by the early 1990s made cartel agreements illegal under EU legislation.

Archival and printed sources

Statens pris- och kartellnämnd/Konkurrensverket, *Kartellregistret 1947–1989*, The National Archives (Riksarkivet).
Kartell- och Trustutredningen, 1913, *Kartell och trustutredningen. 1, Sockerindustri och sockerbeskattning i Sverige samt Danmark och Tyskland: utredning verkställd af inom Finansdepartementet tillkallade sakkunniga*. Stockholm.
LO Propagandarådet 1952, *Monopol och privatregleringar. Information och argument*, Stockholm.
'Kartellregistret', *Meddelanden från Kommerskollegii monopolutredningsbyrå*, Stockholm 1947.
Industriförbundets meddelanden (1933–1953), Stockholm.
Pris- och kartellfrågor (1965–1989), Stockholm.

Notes

1 Two of the leading social democratic economists, Gunnar Myrdal and Karin Kock, represented this view in the introduction to the Commission for Post-War Economic Planning (SOU 1945: 42: 8).
2 The Merger Investigation published five reports in the 1960s (see *Koncentrationsutredningen* 1968).
3 The annual number of mergers and acquisitions was as follows (average ten-year value): 1946–1955: 50, 1956–1965: 125, 1966–1975: 415, 1976–1985: 719 (Rydén 1971: 55; SOU 1990: 1: 16).
4 *Konkurrensverket, Kartellregistret*, register no. 242, D7: 25; register no. 1790, D7: 142, the National Archives.
5 *Konkurrensverket, Kartellregistret*, register no. 540–605, D7: 58–60, the National Archives.

6 Ancillary agreements: exclusive conditions. Restrictive business practices in combination with business acquisition or other property.
7 *Lag om motverkande i vissa fall av konkurrensbegränsning inom näringslivet* (Swedish Code of Statutes 1956: 244, §5).
8 *Konkurrensverket, Kartellregistret* 1947–1988, D7: 1–D7: 339, the National Archives.

13 The Dutch cartel collection in the twentieth century
Facts and figures

Lilian T. D. Petit

Introduction

Cartels were common in the Netherlands for the greatest part of the twentieth century. In Chapter 5 of this volume, Petit, van Sinderen and van Bergeijk discuss the Netherlands' competition policy and its drivers in the twentieth century. The present chapter studies the extent of cartelisation by providing data on the number of registered cartels in the Netherlands. By cartelisation we mean the presence of registered cartel agreements between firms, either submitted by firms themselves or identified by the government as such.

The Dutch have often characterised their country as a 'cartel paradise' (De Jong 1990; van Rooy 1992; van Gent 1997; Asbeek Brusse and Griffiths 1998). The introduction of the prohibition legislation in 1998, however, suggests an absolute turning point for the continued existence of that paradise. By studying the development of the registered agreements we examine whether the end of the Netherlands cartel paradise coincided with the introduction of the prohibition law of 1998. We will also provide a general overview of the content of the Dutch register.

Our information on cartels is drawn from several sources, however the Netherlands cartel register is the prime basis of information. This register existed from 1941 until 1998. In addition, two other sources complement the research findings. First, we can determine the extent of Dutch international cartelisation at the beginning of the twentieth century from a United Nations dataset (1947). Second, we can refer to the database of exemption requests, which were filed between 1998 and 2004 at the Netherlands Competition Authority (*Nederlandse Mededingingsautoriteit*, NMa).

We start with an overview of the formation of cartels prior to the introduction of the cartel register; international cartelisation during the inter-war period. Next, we study cartelisation through the cartel register. Third, we examine the exemption requests that were filed during the transition to the new Competition Law. We conclude by summarising our insights and assess whether the Netherlands cartel paradise was actually ended in 1998.

Before the cartel register

The Netherlands is a small open economy, implying that the country's economy is dependent on multiple international trade relations (Driehuis, van Heeringen and De Wolf 1975). International cartels were widespread at the beginning of the twentieth century. The worldwide crisis of the great depression, and resulting attitudes against wasteful competition caused a wave of international cartels (Fear 2006). Nussbaum (1986) estimates that cartels were involved in approximately 40 per cent of world trade between 1929 and 1937. In such an environment, firms inside a small open economy would also be expected to participate in cartels.

The League of Nations compiled a database of international cartels to 'assure the consumer of accurate knowledge so that he might not be misled through any misrepresentations by international industrial groups' (Klein 1928: 456; see also Chapter 3, this volume). The Netherlands-based firms participated in 22 (26 per cent) of the 86 registered cartels relating to industrial output and raw materials presented by League of Nations (see Table 13.1).

Of the purely international cartels, firms from the Netherlands took part in 17 (36 per cent) of 47, which appears high compared to the results from neighbouring countries. Germany had the highest cartel penetration ratio; German-based companies were active in 23 (49 per cent) international cartels. Other European countries, such as France, the UK and Belgium had companies that participated in respectively 14 (30 per cent), 13 (28 per cent) and seven (15 per cent) international cartels.

We observe that the Dutch firms' main allies were German companies; in ten of the 17 international cartels that included firms from the Netherlands, German companies were also present. Only four of the 17 international cartels with Dutch firms included industries from its neighbour, Belgium.

Of the 39 local cartels, Dutch firms took part in only five (13 per cent) of them. Besides its 13 international cartels, the UK was active in one local cartel, while German firms were active in 27 local cartels, France had companies in 13 local cartels and seven Belgium based cartels were local.

Beyond Europe's borders, Dutch firms appeared to be the only European cartel members involved in radio equipment with firms in the US, and with firms located in various Asian countries involved with tin (ore) and rubber. The purpose of cartelisation ranged from the preservation of markets (e.g. export regulation and maintenance of production) to price setting and disposing of surplus stocks (overcapacity). The Netherlands-based firms arranged prices in nine of the 22 cartels (41 per cent).

At the start of the twentieth century the Netherlands appeared to be linked to a relatively high number of registered cartels, from an international perspective. The following section presents the cartels in the Dutch cartel register in the second part of the twentieth century.

The cartel register

Overview of the register material

Under the legislation of 1941, (the Cartel Decree; *Kartelbesluit*), cartel agreements were required to be reported to the Ministry of Economic Affairs and this file was

Table 13.1 International cartels including the Netherlands during the interwar period.

Product	International (I) Local (L)	Participating countries	Start (exit)	Nature
Nitrogen I	I	UK, Germany, Norway, Belgium, France, Czechoslovakia, Netherlands, Italy, Poland, (separate agreement with) Chile	1930	Export regulation, import regulation, domestic reservation
Nitrogen II	I	UK, Germany, Norway, Belgium, France, Czechoslovakia, Netherlands, Italy, Poland, separate agreement with Chile (June 1934) and Japan (1936)	1931	Prices, import regulation
Diesel engines	I	Germany, Netherlands, US	1930	Market division
Radio equipment	I	Netherlands, US	1925	Export regulation, market division
High tension cables	I	Germany, Austria, Hungary, Czechoslovakia, Poland, Sweden, Norway, France, Spain, Netherlands, US	1930	Prices, production
Glass bottles	I	Netherlands, Germany, Czechoslovakia, Poland, Austria, Yugoslavia, Romania	1929	Export regulation
Cotton bale strips	I	Germany, Belgium, France, Netherlands		Prices, production
Cement	I	UK, Germany, France, Belgium, Denmark, Sweden, Norway, Yugoslavia (later: Netherlands)	1937	Prices
Moving picture recording and reproducing apparatus	I	Germany, Netherlands, US		Export regulation
Aluminium foils–Dutch market	L	Germany, Netherlands, Switzerland	1936	Sales
Aluminium foils–Belgian market	L	Germany, Netherlands, Switzerland, Belgium	1936	Sales

Table 13.1 International cartels including the Netherlands during the interwar period.

Product	International (I) Local (L)	Participating countries	Start (exit)	Nature
Aluminium foils– Scandinavian market	L	Germany, Netherlands, Switzerland, Belgium, Scandinavian countries	1936	Sales
Fittings– Dutch market	L	Germany, Netherlands	N.A.	Sales, prices
Door locks	L	Germany, Netherlands	N.A.	Prices
Linoleum	I	Germany, Sweden, France, Switzerland, Austria, Netherlands,	N.A.	Export prices, domestic reservation
Petroleum	I	Standard Oil, Shell, Anglo Persian	1928 (1933)	Maintain current production
Petroleum II	I	Standard Oil, Shell, Anglo Persian	1929 (1933)	Maintain current production
Petroleum III	I	Standard Oil, Shell, Anglo Persian, Romania	1932 (1933)	Maintain current production
Rubber thread	I	Germany, Italy, Hungary, Czechoslovakia, France, Netherlands, US	1931	Prices
Tin (ore) I	I	Malaya, Netherlands, East Indies	1921 (1925)	Surplus stocks
Tin (ore) II	I	Malaya, Nigeria, Netherlands, East Indies, Bolivia (later: Siam, French indo-china, Belgian Congo, Portugal, UK)	1931 (1942)	Prices, surplus stocks
Rubber	I	Malaya, Ceylon, India, Burma, Netherlands, East Indies, French Indo-China, North Borneo, Sarawak (later: Siam)	1934 (1944)	Prices, surplus stocks

Note: Seven other cartels include 'various European countries'. The participation of the Netherlands is not mentioned explicitly. These cartels do not appear in this table. Consequently, the involvement of the Netherlands might be underestimated.

Source: United Nations (1947).

archived in the cartel register. The 1958 Economic Competition Act (*Wet Economische Mededinging*; WEM), continued the use of the cartel register. In 1998 the register was brought to an end by the introduction of the Competition Law (*Mededingingswet*). Thereafter, the cartel register was redundant as the Competition Law prohibited cartels *per se*. Altogether, the register covers more than half of the twentieth century.

Registration of cartel agreements was not uncommon. Other countries (e.g. Sweden, Finland, Australia, the UK, Austria, Spain, Germany, Denmark and Japan) have kept a cartel register (Chapter 7, this volume). Most registers were closed before 1993 (the Finnish register was closed in 1992, and the Norwegian and Swedish register existed until 1993; see Chapters 6, 8 and 12, this volume). The Netherlands was the last country to close its register in 1998.

Asbeek Brusse and Griffiths (1997, 1998) set out the nation's cartel policy together with descriptive data, for the period up until 1985 using official ministry reports (see also Bouwens and Dankers 2012). Using the ministry reports, or secondary data, means their results may slightly differ compared to results based on the original cartel register and which are retained in the National Archives.

Accessing the original source material allows a more detailed study of registered cartels and, because the detailed ministry reports ceased in the early 1980s, can extend the period of analysis compared to previous investigations. This we will do for the period 1980 to 1998. Unlike the two studies that relied on parliamentary and ministry reports, re-examining the register means the material can be analysed, detached from any political interests that may have been important at the time of the minister's reports.[1] The present study examines the degree of registered cartelisation in the Netherlands from both a macro perspective and a sectorial perspective.

In the period 1941 to 1958, when the Cartel Decree operated, policies were affected more by the Second World War and the subsequent rebuilding process of the economy, than by competition policy (Verbond voor Nederlandse Werkgevers 1958).

To cover the period when the 1958 Economic Competition Act (WEM) operated, two other data-sources are used to throw light on cartelisation. The first is the annual reports of the Ministry of Economic Affairs, which included information from the cartel register from 1959 to 1981. The second is the primary data in the cartel register from 1980 until 1998. Thus for the last 18 years of the study we access the original cartel files.[2] We use the primary data after 1980 as detailed information was published in the annual reports only up until 1982. Using the secondary data runs the same risks as Asbeek Brusse and Griffiths's analyses (1997, 1998), they may differ from the primary data. Since two different data-sources are used, it is possible that the two time series are not perfectly comparable and there may be a structural break in the series in the early 1980s.

Content and scope

The content and scope of the cartel register must be clearly understood to draw accurate conclusions from the primary data. The following discussion explains the issues, opportunities and assumptions associated with the cartel register. First, we discuss how representative the register is. Second, we describe the duty to report.

The cartel register was, and still is, confidential. A non-public register was preferred to a public register since the latter would not be compatible with the idea of full registration. Confidentiality was expected to result in a higher reporting-rate. Nevertheless, several fruitless attempts were made to introduce a public cartel register, but they all failed because of political inconsistency (see Chapter 5, this volume).

Firms themselves saw the merits of an open dialogue between business and the government; a public register would frustrate this open dialogue (SER 1973). Driven by a fear of misunderstanding and resistance from third parties, cartelised firms supported the confidentiality of the register (ibid.). Nevertheless, under certain conditions the WEM provided for the publication of information (see Chapter 5, this volume).

The basic assumption of confidentiality should have led to a comprehensive administration of cartels. Nevertheless, threats and failed attempts to disclose the register as well as the fear of publicity under specified conditions might have reduced the incentive for firms to register their agreements at certain points in time.

The incentive to notify a cartel to the Ministry of Economic Affairs could also be subject to (intended) policy changes. If firms initiated an agreement and registered this accordingly just before 1998, the Netherlands Competition Authority (*Nederlandse Mededingingsautoteit*; NMa) might have investigated them as a result. As a prelude to the new competition law several policy changes were implemented. Specifically, these policies included: a general prohibition against vertical price agreements (1991); a prohibition of horizontal price agreements (1993); and a prohibition of market sharing agreements and tender agreements (1994). New agreements which would soon become prohibited in the 1990s might run the risk of non-notification or under-reporting in their official application.

The competition policy during the existence of the 'dormant' WEM from 1958 was labelled 'reactive' by Asbeek Brusse and Griffiths (1998). This contributed to firms' comprehensive lack of awareness of their duty to report their agreements. In 1973, 1984 and 1987/1988 inquiries were conducted by employees of the competition department of the Ministry of Economic Affairs with the objective of updating the cartel register. A considerable number of agreements were notified and outdated agreements were cleared. Moreover, De Jong (1990), a former employee of the Ministry of Economic Affairs, claims that a mere 50 per cent of the cartels were registered in the cartel register; a claim that remains unsubstantiated.

Nevertheless, under both the Cartel Decree (1941) and the WEM (1959) the duty to report was formalised into law. Deliberately ignoring the duty to report was considered an offence. A modest fine (less than 500 Dutch guilders) was imposed in various cases of non-notification under the Cartel Decree.[3] This duty to report was reinforced in the approach of the WEM. Under the WEM, in the case of non-notification, an agreement could lose its legal force and firms could risk a fine of up to 10,000 Dutch guilders or the business owner could receive a prison sentence of up to six months (WEM 1956, ss. 5, 49). In practice, parties were merely asked to make a notification, and sometimes this was combined with a minor fine (Barendregt 1991).

In summary, there are some limitations that impair the value of the cartel register as a definitive measure of actual cartelisation. On the other hand, several guarantees, such as the threat of fines in the case of non-notification and the confidentiality of the register strengthen the reliability of the register as a source of information. Overall, the register is, and remains, the most reliable and consistent means of assessing (registered) cartels in the Netherlands.

A competition agreement was considered an agreement or a civil contract that regulated economic competition between the owners of firms. Competition agreements (henceforth: agreements) were required to be reported to the Ministry of Economic Affairs within one month of the establishment of the agreement (WEM 1956 s. 2).

Agreements that regulated *non-economic* competition in the Netherlands were exempted from registration (WEM 1956 s. 4(1)). Also exemptions were granted for agreements that were applied abroad (i.e. export agreements or those that concerned international transport; Tweede Kamer 1960). Several exemptions for various sectors or agreements were implemented during the WEM. Free professionals or practitioners (such as notaries or medical specialists) were exempted from registration until 1987. Overall, from 1987 agreements were exempted that: were in operation less than one month, concerned regulated parts of the healthcare sector, joint purchase, individual vertical price maintenance, employees, international transport and export cartels.[4]

Measures of cartelisation

Both the ministry's annual reports and the primary data used in this study were based on the individual files of the cartel register. Within the files, the application form was the leading source of information.[5] Over time there were various types of application forms, although their questions remained relatively constant over time. As application forms were almost always found in the cartel files, they contained the information necessary to permit the study of the agreements and to make comparisons of cartel characteristics. In our study, the original files not containing an application form (approximately five per cent of cases) were omitted. It is unclear if these were reported in the ministry's annual reports. We included every submitted application form, even those with agreements that did not actually fall under the duty to report. On the basis of the responses to questions in the application form and the contents of the file we can assess the key features of registered cartels. Four elements are studied: the scope, persistency, nature and intensity of registered cartels.

The scope of cartelisation in the economy is ascertained by identifying the specific industries which were involved in cartels.

The persistency of cartelisation is calculated by identifying the recorded cartel entry and exit dates; the difference between those dates provides a measure of their duration. Cartel duration is considered to be an important measure of cartel success by Levenstein and Suslow (2006). In contrast to the annual reports, which used the date of notification, we tried to capture the actual starting date recorded in the primary data. This was based on the date of establishment of the agreement. This is either taken from the application form itself, or from the attached statutes or contracts. A cartel could be in existence for a significant time without being registered, either by mistake or on purpose. The exit date was the last date of added content in the file and does not necessarily coincide with the actual termination of the cartel. Ideally, one would use the actual termination date, but unfortunately this information is either unclear in the file or is not mentioned at all. In summary, the exit date implies the last visible visit in which content was added to a cartel file by the Ministry of Economic Affairs, regardless of the reason.

The content of the agreement has been classified in our study to draw conclusions about the nature of cartelisation. We used a classification of the agreements similar to Sandberg in Chapter 12 of this volume. Eleven types of agreements have been categorised: price agreements, division of markets, allocation of quotas, agreements on conditions, tender agreements, agreements on delivery and production, buy and/or sell combinations, marketing agreements, trademarks and protection of markets, and ancillary agreements.[6] The annual reports mention nine slightly different categories: price agreements, market sharing, tender agreements, exclusive dealing, financial agreements, production agreements, sales agreements, agreements on conditions and a remaining category 'other'.

As a measure of the intensity of cartelisation, three variables were examined in addition to those in the annual reports. First, the number of cartelised firms per agreement. Second the presence of an organising body. Such a body could support the coordination and stability of an agreement. Historically, high involvement by trade associations was thought typical for the Netherlands (Bouwens and Dankers 2012). Cartels with organisational and/or contractual solutions to problems of coordination, cheating and entry are expected to be the most successful in terms of duration (Levenstein and Suslow 2006). A third dimension of the intensity of a cartel is its internationalisation (i.e. the presence of foreign firms). De (2010), for example, suggests that global cartels had more chances to cease naturally than national or regional ones.

Cartelisation from a macro perspective

The foundations of the cartel register date back to the Cartel Decree, under which firms were obliged to report their cartel agreements to the Ministry of Economic Affairs. In 1948, 513 cartels were registered (Asbeek Brusse and Griffiths 1997). From 1951 to 1954, the number of domestic cartels increased by 100, 62, 116 and 198 respectively (Barendregt 1991). In 1955, 831 agreements were registered and in 1958 under the WEM 801 agreements were recorded in the cartel register (Tweede Kamer 1960). This section examines the agreements recorded in the Dutch register under the WEM between 1959 and 1998.

Cartels, entry and exit from the register

In this study we overlap the annual ministry reports from 1959 until 1985 with the original data files from 1980 until 1998 to compare directly the data from both sources for a period of five years. Figure 13.1 reveals a close match between both series.

As mentioned above, the annual reports indicate cartel entry based on the notification date whereas the primary data from 1980 onwards permit identification of the actual starting date. Since we are looking at cartelisation, rather than the registration of cartels, we focus on the actual starting date rather than the notification date. Identifying the termination date remains an intractable problem, since the actual date is unknown in most cases. Consequently, statements about termination and duration should be interpreted with caution.

Figure 13.1 shows the number of agreements and Figure 13.2 shows the entry and exit from the records. Examining only the total number of recorded agreements, it is notable that the two time series correspond exactly in 1983. Yet in 1980 and 1981, the primary data report more cartels than the annual reports and the opposite happens for 1985. In 1980 the annual report shows 72 (11 per cent) fewer agreements than the primary data. In 1985 the annual report shows 61 (13 per cent) more cartels than the primary data.

Once we study the entry and exit in these years, we find more discrepancies. The primary data reports 16 new agreements and seven terminations in 1980; the annual report on the other hand, reports 23 new agreements and four terminations. In 1985 the primary data reports 16 new agreements and 35 terminations, whereas the annual report reports seven new agreements and 18 terminations. The discrepancies can partly be explained by the use of the starting date, the primary data use the actual starting date instead of the registration date. Since the actual starting date is most often before the registration date, the primary data tend to report more agreements at a certain point in time. Yet, this does not explain the gap between the annual reports and the primary data in 1984 and 1985.[7] The outliers of cartel exit in 1974, 1984, 1987 and 1988, mark a reassessment of the register, and actually reflect that cancellation rarely took place. Appendix 1 provides an overview of the differences between the two data sources.

Overall, the number of agreements decreases between 1959, when it peaked at 875, and 1977. In the 1960s we notice a decreasing trend of new agreements in the Netherlands. In 1973 the ministry updated the content of the cartel register. This led to a considerable decrease in the number of registered agreements (Tweede Kamer 1975). Of the 654 agreements originally recorded, 111 appear to have been terminated (ibid.). The total stock of agreements reduced to 554 by the end of 1974. Terminations rarely occurred according to the ministry.

From 1977 an upward trend is visible; the number of agreements increases by approximately 20 a year until 1982. It is noteworthy that the number of agreements falls sharply, by more than 50 per cent, between 1986 and 1989. This again coincides with the reassessment of the cartel register in 1987 and 1988 by the ministry focussing on accuracy and completeness of the register (Tweede Kamer 1989). The 1987–1988 annual report states that many of the agreements in the register appeared outdated (ibid.).

From 1991, the number of agreements steadily decreased, with only a handful of new agreements notified after that date. This coincided with the 1991 announcement of the design of the Competition Law (*Mededingingswet*) that finally came into force in 1998 and the general prohibitions on vertical price agreements (1991),

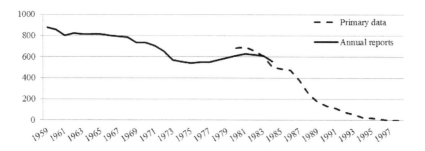

Figure 13.1 Number of active agreements reported in the cartel register.
Source: Cartel register (primary data), Tweede Kamer (1960–1982).

horizontal price fixing (1993) and market sharing and tenders (1994). On the one hand, the reduced number of new agreements may be attributable to greater restrictions on permitted agreements. It is also possible, however, that such agreements were initiated but not notified (see also Chapter 7, this volume). At the same time as the Netherlands was modifying its regulations, the European Union (EU) was established (in 1993). Its influence, together with less favourable public opinion towards cartels, means it is likely that more cartels terminated their agreements and fewer were initiated.

The annual reports from 1989 to 1992 provide aggregates of the number of agreements in the cartel register. They reveal respectively 293, 371, 455 and 468 registered agreements; significantly higher numbers than figures from the original files. Recall that the analysis based on the original files is using the last date of correspondence on the cartel, which is not implying that the cartel had actually been terminated. Once we ignore terminations, both series – the original data and annual report data – become rather similar (see Appendix 2). This underlines the effect of using the last date of correspondence in cartel register, but also illustrates that (after adjustment) both sources are relatively similar. At the same time, it might well be the case that the ministry's calculations from 1989 until 1992 did not pay attention to the cartels that were registered after the 1988 reassessment; ignoring both their activity or inactivity, and simply including them in the yearly reports.

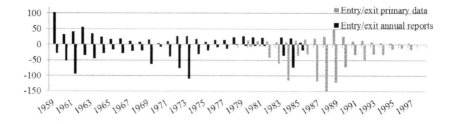

Figure 13.2 Entry and exit of agreements.
Source: Cartel register (primary data), Tweede Kamer (1960–1982).

Nature

Agreements may include various restrictions of competition (henceforth: sub-agreements) such as price, quantity and/or production aspects. On average, a single agreement comprised 1.7 sub-agreements from 1961 until 1998.[8] Figures 13.3 and 13.4 illustrate the total number of sub-agreements categorised by type, for the periods 1961–1981 and 1980–1998. In terms of the total number of sub-agreements, Figure 13.4 reveals more sub-agreements than Figure 13.3. This is partly explained by the difference in the number of categories used in the annual reports (9) compared to those applied to the primary data (11). Figure 13.3 reports slightly more price agreements and slightly fewer agreements on conditions than Figure 13.4. The discrepancy can also be explained by differences in definition. Discounts and bonuses are classified as price agreements in the annual reports, while the classification from 1980 views them as conditions. As a result, there are more agreements on conditions and fewer concerning price agreements from 1980 onwards. Appendix 1 provides an overview of the differences between the primary data and the annual reports for various categories.

Agreements on prices and conditions were the two most common types of restrictive elements from 1961 to 1998. In 1961, 244 agreements included sub-agreements on conditions although this decreased slightly over time. Approximately a third of the agreements dealt with conditions from 1961 until 1998.[9] Market sharing and the allocation of quotas were also common; both are direct instruments to increase profits.

In 1961 there were 692 sub-agreements on prices. Typically, this is one of the main interventions to exploit cartelisation optimally and increase profits. Horizontal price agreements were the most common types of price agreements; they appear in 45 per cent of cases in 1961 and 34 per cent in 1981 (Tweede Kamer 1982). Figure 13.3 shows that the number of price clauses reduced by 40 per cent between 1968 and 1973, where after it increased again from 1974. This fits the general decreasing trend in the total number of agreements (see Figure 13.1).

In the agreements after 1980, price clauses appear in 38 per cent of the compacts. On average an arrangement on prices comes with 1.34 other sub-agreements. Almost half (48 per cent) of the price arrangements are combined with agreements arranging conditions (e.g. selling conditions). The allocation of quotas was present in 22 per cent of price agreements. The division of markets occurred simultaneously with 21 per cent of cases with deals on prices.

After the reassessment in 1988 approximately 140 new agreements were established. The new pacts were less complex: they comprised on average 1.1 sub-agreements. Most of these arrangements approximately 40 per cent, concerned sub-agreements on trademarks (e.g. franchises). Price agreements, agreements on conditions and the protection of markets were present in approximately 12 per cent of these new compacts. The division of markets, the allocation of quotas, buy and/or sell combinations and clauses on delivery and production occurred in less than ten per cent of the agreements. Deals on vertical and horizontal prices were prohibited from 1991 and 1993 respectively. As of 1991 a mere six price agreements were submitted to the Ministry of Economic Affairs. Market sharing too was prohibited from 1994, and only three agreements were submitted that concerned the division of markets. Two of these concerned exclusive dealing.

Intensity

The primary data (1980–1998) permit us to study the intensity and persistency of agreements. We observe that the average annual number of cartel members was 231. This extremely high average might be explained by the high number of trade associations which tended to attract and facilitate more members and is therefore causing marked outliers. Also, the number of cartel members is measured as the maximum number of members mentioned in the cartel file. The median number, however, was 20, which points to a skewed distribution with marked outliers. Although comparing these data with those from other countries is highly speculative, Posner (1970) reports a mean of 29.1 participants in illegal cartels in the US. In the Swedish cartel register the mean number of members was 14.1 (median six) (Berg 2011) and in Germany the mean was 15 (Haucap, Heimeshoff and Schultz 2010). In new agreements, established after 1988, the mean and median number of members fell to 155 and ten respectively but from an international perspective, remained quite high.

The presence of an organising body was quite common; over half (52 per cent) of the agreements were controlled by a central organisation. Posner (1970), Hay and Kelley (1974), Fraas and Greer (1977) and Gallo *et al.* (2000), all using US data, find central organisations controlled respectively 44, 29, 36 and 23 per cent of the cartels they studied. Roughly one fourth of the new agreements after 1988 involved a central organisation, which is 50 per cent lower than over the period 1980–1998.

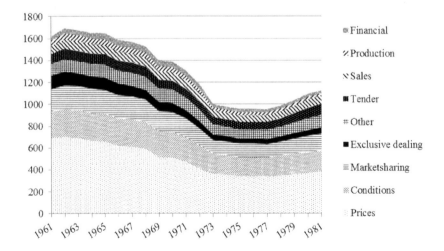

Figure 13.3 Frequency of restrictive elements by type, 1961–1981.
Source: Tweede Kamer (1962–1982).

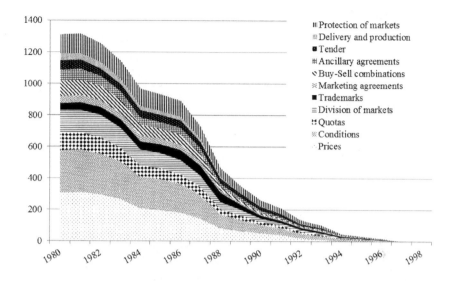

Figure 13.4 Frequency of restrictive elements by type, 1980–1998.

Note: In approximately six per cent of the agreements a restrictive element is absent due to there being either no description or a meaningless description in application form.

Source: Cartel register, primary data.

Various agreements involved foreign firms. We observe that 11 per cent of the agreements included at least one foreign participant. This might seem low for a small open economy such as the Netherlands. In Chapter 12 of this volume, Sandberg finds that seven per cent of the Swedish registrations between 1947 and 1988 were international cartels with activities in Sweden. For the new agreements from 1988 still 11 per cent included a foreign firm in the Netherlands.

Persistency of the agreements in the register

The average duration of agreements active after 1980 was 23 years; the median duration was 18 years. International comparisons of cartel persistency are particularly risky, but compared to other studies, the duration is fairly long: i.e. the average duration is 19.3 years (median 15.8) in Sweden (Berg 2011), 13 years in Finland (Hyytinen, Steen and Toivanen 2011), 13.4 years (median 11) in Germany (Haucap, Heimeshoff and Schultz 2010) and 7.2 years (median 5.5) in EU cartels (Connor and Helmers 2007).

The Netherlands duration might be overestimated due to the fact that firms often ignored the obligation to announce a termination, although other countries which had a cartel register may have suffered from similar biases. Yet, the duration measure might also be an underestimation because some cartel files were not officially closed and in those cases the last date of correspondence is used. It is unclear which effect dominates.

Cartelisation from a sectorial perspective

The Netherlands legislation followed the abuse principle, which meant that the WEM only prohibited cartels once it was clear that these ran counter to the public interest. It appears that the abuse legislation and the emerging competition policy provided a fruitful basis for cartel agreements. Van Muiswinkel, Vredevoogd and van der Wilde (1977: 158) claim that the products bought by the Dutch consumer were cartelised from A to Z. Meaning that each product was subject to cartelisation somewhere in the supply chain. This section describes the industries in the Dutch economy that were cartelised.

The period 1961–1981

Table 13.2 shows the average number of restrictive agreements between 1961 and 1981, the number of cartels in 1961, 1971 and 1981 and the two most popular sub-agreements per industry during the period 1961–1981.

Whereas traffic/transport and retail show a significant upward trend in the number of recorded agreements over the period, most of the manufacturing industries show a downward trend from 1961 until 1981. The vast majority are concerned with hard core restrictions such as prices, quotas and market sharing.[10] Agreements on conditions were also relatively popular. Tender agreements were relatively popular in the construction industry, the wood and furniture industry and mechanical engineering. Exclusive dealing was prevalent in the retail industry and in 'other metal' industries.

The period 1980–1998

Table 13.3 provides an overview of the total quantity of agreements in 1981, the number of agreements from 1980 onwards and the two most popular restrictions per NACE industry.

Taken together, the data show that in the Netherlands between 1961 and 1998, the wholesale, retail, construction, food, beverages and tobacco and non-metallic mineral (or: ceramics, glass and plaster) industries contained the greatest number of reported agreements, and are thus most represented in Tables 13.2 and 13.3. By contrast, in the second half of the twentieth century agriculture and the rubber and plastics industries tended to have fewer cartels in the Netherlands.[11]

We also find some overlap with the pattern of cartelisation in Finland and Sweden – both small and open economies such as the Netherlands – over the same period (Fellman and Shanahan 2011; Chapter 12, this volume); although reliable comparisons are difficult. In these countries, both the retail and wholesale sector were ranked first and second in terms of cartelisation. Transport, food production and the metal industry appear in the third, fifth and sixth place of the most heavily cartelised sectors in Finland (Fellman and Shanahan 2011). In Sweden food production, engineering industry and manufacture of engines are being ranked third, fourth and fifth (Chapter 12, this volume).

Compared to the cartelised industries in Germany, we notice that the building materials, as well as the construction industry were relatively cartelised (Haucap, Heimeshoff and Schultz 2010). Together these two sectors accounted for 30 and 43 per cent of the legal and illegal cartels (excluding wholesale and retail industries) in that country. We observe an aggregated rate of 18 per cent of the cartels active in the building materials and the construction industries after 1980 (including the wholesale and retail industries). Connor and Helmers (2007) find an aggregate rate of 14 per cent in those two industries in Europe. The Australian register, however, finds quite a low rate of agreement in the building materials industry; less than one per cent.

Table 13.2 Dutch registered cartels classified by industry (1961, 1971, 1981) and two most common restrictive elements.

Industry	1961	1971	1981	Most common restriction	Second most common restriction
Wholesale	152	126	102	P	C
Other metal	74	39	58	P	ED
Chemicals	72	55	29	P	MS
Ceramics, glass and plaster	65	49	36	MS	P
Foods and stimulants	54	48	39	P	MS
Graphics and publishing	45	45	20	P	C
Other industrial	43	37	29	P	MS
Textiles	32	11	10	P	C
Paper	29	31	16	P	C
Electro technical	27	12	7	P	C
Traffic/transport	26	53	48	P	MS
Construction	26	30	32	T	P
Handicrafts	26	21	25	P	O/C
Retail	24	26	55	P	ED
Mechanical engineering	21	20	19	P	T
Insurance	20	19	24	P	C
Wood and furniture	19	22	22	P	T
Banking	14	14	12	P	O
Shoes and clothing	8	9	5	P	C
Metal	7	6	4	P	C
Agriculture	6	8	14	MS	P
Leather and rubber	5	5	4	C	P
Other	4	14	15	P	C
Electricity, gas and water pipes	3	3	3	O	O

Note: Ranked by number of agreements in 1961. The top two restrictions are based on the average presence of these restrictions from 1961–1981. P = prices; C = conditions; ED = exclusive dealing; T = tender; MS = market sharing; O = other.

Source: Tweede Kamer (1962–1982).

The road motor vehicles industry in Australia, on the other hand, was ranked first with 17 per cent of all the recorded agreements (Fellman and Shanahan 2011). In Connor and Helmers (2007) the chemical intermediates contained most cartels; around 18 per cent of the sample. Despite international differences as regards the prevalence of cartels in various industries, we notice that cartelisation abroad prevailed in the entire economy. Obviously differences in the nature of the economies, as well as the legislation may contribute to differences in the degree of cartelisation recorded in various industries in each country.

Nature

When we look at the nature of the restrictive elements, we see that prices and conditions remained the most popular restrictions within most industries. Yet, prices were ranked as the most popular element in Table 13.2, whereas in Table 13.3 the popularity of conditions increased. We observe a slight shift away from hard core agreements after 1980. Typically, tender agreements in Table 3 occur in the same industries as in Table 13.2 (i.e. wood and cork, machinery and construction).

Intensity

The existence of a central organising body or association was relatively common in 'construction', 'pulp, paper, printing and publishing', 'wood and cork', 'textile', 'manufacturing not elsewhere classified (nec)', 'agriculture' and 'real estate activities'. Three out of four industries that arranged tender agreements were part of this group (i.e. 'wood and cork', 'machinery' and 'construction'). It is likely that tender agreements would require some form of central body as the coordinating agent for the interests of the participating parties. It might also suggest that these industries engaged a lot with one customer (i.e. the government) to build or construct public infrastructure or housing.

Agreements involved a relatively high number of foreign firms in the industries: 'chemicals and chemical products', 'pulp, paper, printing and publishing, 'financial intermediation', 'textiles, textile, leather and footwear' and 'mining and quarrying'. The number of participants differs between the industries. Manufacturing industries usually included fewer participants in their agreements, whereas agreements in 'real estate activities', 'sale, maintenance and repair of motor vehicles and motorcycles' and 'transport equipment' included many participants. The latter coincides with a relatively high degree of organisation. Industries involving a relatively high number of organising bodies, tend to include more members per agreement.

The Competition Law of 1998

The Netherlands Competition Authority (NMa) and its associated Competition Law came into effect in 1998, ending the cartel register. Figure 13.1 may suggest the number of cartels was reduced to zero in 1998. In fact, the correspondence

Table 13.3 Dutch registered cartels classified by NACE industry, 1980–1998.

Industry	1981	1980–1998	Most common restriction	Second most common restriction
Retail trade; repair of household goods	92	187	TM	P
Wholesale and commission trade	129	143	C	P
Other non-metallic mineral	84	98	P	Q
Construction	49	83	T	PRT
Transport and storage	68	81	P	MS
Food, beverages and tobacco	50	59	C	P
Financial intermediation	34	45	P	C
Metal	29	38	T	P
Renting of mandeq and other business activities	18	36	C	P
Chemicals and chemical products	33	35	P	C
Pulp, paper, printing and publishing	25	29	P	C
Other community, social and personal services	13	26	P	C
Machinery, nec	23	25	T	P
Wood and products of wood and cork	15	16	T	Q
Mining and quarrying	11	15	P	Q
Hotels and restaurants	8	15	TM	P/C/PRT
Textiles, leather and footwear	14	14	C	P
Manufacturing nec; recycling	13	13	C	P
Real-estate	9	12	P/C	
Sale, maintenance and repair of motor vehicles and motorcycles; retail sale of fuel	5	10	C/P	
Agriculture, hunting, forestry and fishing	7	9	D/Q/PRT	
Transport equipment	5	6	P/C	
Education	3	6	P	C/TM
Rubber and plastics	5	5	P	PRT/ PR_DL

Note: NACE industry classification refers to the statistical classification of economic activities in the European Community. Ranked by number of agreements from 1980 to 1998. Only industries containing 5 or more agreements are included. P = prices; C = conditions; Q = quotas; PRT = protection of markets; T = tender; MS = market sharing; TM = trademarks; PR_DL = production and delivery.

Source: Cartel register.

between the ministry and firms was closed in 1998 but actual cartelisation and the incentive to engage in anticompetitive behaviour was still present.

As a transition from the WEM to the Competition Law, firms could file a request for exemption for their cartel. From 1998 until 2004 the NMa assessed whether the applications were compatible with the new Competition Law. These exemption requests thus serve as an indirect measure of the intended continuing degree of cartelisation from 1998 to 2004.

A total of 315 exemption requests were filed over the six years, of which 276 were ruled ineligible, meaning that there was an intention to initiate or to continue with otherwise prohibited cartels. A mere 39 requests were granted. The healthcare industry filed the most requests – over 100. This outlier can be explained by a change of legislation in 2004, when the healthcare industry became subject to competition and this triggered a rush to claim exemption. Firms in the construction industry, for example filed 19 fruitless exemption requests and those in the manufacturing industries filed 25 exemption requests, of which only seven were granted. Comparing the exemption requests with the number of agreements from the register indicates that at least 18 per cent of the agreements recorded from 1980 to 1998 requested exemption. This implies that the degree of cartelisation was not actually zero in 1998, as suggested in Figure 13.1.

Connor and Helmers (2007) show the number of fines, the sum of the fines and the number of cartel recidivists in a number of European countries from 1990 until 2005. Although Germany has the highest number of cartel recidivists and sum of fines, the Netherlands still ranks relatively highly on these aspects and has the highest number of fines (14). Whether this is a result of an active and stringent competition authority, or a lack of awareness of the new legislation is unclear (see also van Sinderen and Kemp 2009).

Discussion

This chapter reveals an important era of registered cartelisation in the Netherlands that existed across the twentieth century. Measured by registered agreements, the degree of national cartelisation in the Netherlands was relatively high in the 1950s, 1960s and 1970s. Most of the Netherlands' cartels used a specific instrument to increase profits: price agreements. The cartels themselves appeared to be highly resilient and organised. A more stringent cartel policy that began in the late 1980s coincided with a reduced number of registered agreements (e.g. persistency), a reduced participant intensity and central organisation and less severe cartelisation. Compared to other studies, we observe that the duration, degree of organisation, international scope and number of participants was high in the period 1980–1998, and cartelisation was widespread through multiple sectors.

What was popularly regarded as a 'cartel paradise' through the second half of the twentieth century concluded as an anti-cartel regime by the end of the century – but with the real possibility that many cartels still operated. The question remains whether the cartel paradise was ended by the introduction of the prohibition legislation in 1998? The register, being a proxy for cartelisation, illustrates a smoothly fading paradise and not an absolute turning point in 1998.

One might assume that the intensity and incentive for firms to cartelise remains more or less the same over time. Should the Netherlands be classified as a cartel paradise up until 1998, we would expect to see no severe fluctuations in the number and characteristics of registered cartels. However, from late 1980s, the registered number of agreements reveals that fewer agreements were in operation or announced and they were less severe. Changing legislation and a changing attitude might explain the smooth disappearance of the paradise measured by registered cartelisation in the late 1980s (Chapter 5, this volume). Yet, the desire to cartelise remained intact, as illustrated by the high number of declined exemption requests after 1998. Hence, it is unlikely that the deeply rooted habit to cartelise disappeared in 1998. Perhaps the seemingly lost paradise was regained underground?

Archival and printed sources

Sociaal Economische Raad (1973), Advies inzake herziening van de Wet Economische Mededinging en versterking van het mededingingsbeleid uitgebracht aan de minister van Economische Zaken, no. 6, 15 June, 1973, Den Haag.

State Gazette (1975–1982), Wet economische mededinging, Jaarverslag. 1975 no.16; 1975 no.135; 1976 no. 204; 1977 no. 246; 1978 no. 179; 1980 no. 5; 1980 no. 197; 1981 no. 178; 1982 no. 122, The Hague.

Tweede Kamer (1960–1973), Verslag over de toepassing van de Wet economische mededinging. Nos. 5912;6348; 6689; 7157; 7623; 8038; 8558; 9082; 9563; 10,117; 10,642; 11,322; 11,883; 12,413, The Hague.

Tweede Kamer (1989), Rijksbegroting voor het jaar 1990 – Memorie van Toelichting – Appendix 11. Kamerstuk 21,300, chapter 13, no. 3, The Hague.

Tweede Kamer (1987), Rijksbegroting voor het jaar 1989 – Memorie van Toelichting – Appendix 10. Kamerstuk 20,200, chapter 13, no. 3, The Hague.

Tweede Kamer (1984), 1983–1984, 16,555, no. 11b

Tweede Kamer (1987), 1986–1987, 19,700 hfdst. XIII, no. 131

Appendix 1: Primary data compared with secondary data

	Primary data Original files	Secondary data Annual reports	Discrepancy (%)
Number of agreements 1980	682	610	−11
Number of agreements 1983	608	610	0
Number of agreements 1985	484	545	13
Number of new agreements 1980	16	23	44
Number of new agreements 1983	10	23	130
Number of new agreements 1985	16	7	−56
Number of terminated agreements 1980	7	4	−43
Number of terminated agreements 1983	61	36	−41
Number of terminated agreements 1985	35	18	−49
Number of price agreements 1980	311	371	16
Number of price agreements 1981	312	384	27
Prices	311	371	19
Conditions	265	187	−29
Market sharing, quotas and exclusive dealing	256	203	−21
Tender	59	93	58
Buy and sell combinations	96	101	−5
Other	323	139	−57

Source: Primary data, Cartel register; secondary data, Tweede Kamer (1960–1982).

Appendix 2: Comparison of the number of cartels adjusted for exit 1989–1992

Year	Cartels Primary data Original files	Exit Primary data Original files	Cartels not taking into account exit Primary data Original files	Cartels Secondary data Annual reports
1989	175	121	296	293
1990	132	71	367	371
1991	111	33	400	455
1992	73	52	452	468

Notes

1. The coding was done by professionally trained persons of the ACM who were familiar with competition policy. We used the digitalised original source material, identifying files which were not closed before 1980 such as reported by 'Centrale Archief Selectiedienst' (Central Archive Selectionservice – CAS). All the variables were checked, either by CAS and a trained person of the ACM or by trained persons of the ACM. Sample checks were performed and the final coding was compared with the original files.
2. The database was compiled from separate files of the 'Directoraat Mededinging, Ordening en Kartel van het Ministerie van Economische Zaken' (Directorate of Competition, Organization and Cartel of the Ministry of Economic Affairs – the Directorate). The total dataset contains over 4000 electronic scans. The CAS categorised the scans belonging to one cartel file. We count more than 2000 cartel files among these scans. The records that were still open after 1980 were analysed in detail.
3. Some areas fined for non-notification were: hairdressers (1952), painters (1953), hosier producers (1953), ropewalks (1954), evaporated milk (1954), milk producers and grocers (1958) and sauerkraut producers (1959).
4. Staatscourant 92, 1987.
5. In addition to the application form, the cartel files include: correspondence between the businesses and the ministry, statutes and contracts, background information such as newspaper-articles and reports of the Economic Surveillance Department (*Economische Controle Dienst*).
6. Sandberg defines exclusive conditions as ancillary agreements. Our definition of ancillary agreements includes subordinate aspects of cartel arrangements (i.e. not hardcore) such as arbitration and corresponding fines, credit control, employees, etc.
7. A possible explanation may be the reassessment of the cartel register in 1984. The reassessment led to many terminations. The ministry may have processed the terminations later in its administration than that the primary data treated them as terminations.
8. The figures for 1962–1982 are the average of the annual stock of registered cartels (i.e. the characteristics of a cartel is part of the analysis in each year it was registered), while after 1980 the figure refers to the average of unique cartels in the register (i.e. a cartel characteristic is taken into account only once).
9. The figures for 1962–1982 are the average of the annual stock of registered cartels, while after 1980 the figure refers to the average of unique cartels in the register.

10 Following OECD guidelines we define price fixing, bid-rigging, output restrictions and market division (sharing) to be hard core restrictions (OECD 1998).
11 Due to the classification of industries, there are some minor discrepancies in smaller industry sectors. Leather, for example, was classified as part of the textile industry in Table 13.3 whereas it was recorded as part of the rubber industry in Table 13.2.

14 Regulating competition of the Swedish insurance business

The role of the insurance cartel registry

Mats Larsson and Mikael Lönnborg

Introduction

Businesses that operate in the insurance market have long held contradictory attitudes to competition. The Swedish insurance industry provides a good example of these contradictions. On one hand, in the area of premiums and terms of insurance there are examples of fierce competition; on the other hand, there are also numerous examples of collusive organisations and formal and informal agreements that are far from the concept of 'free competition'. There are several reasons for these contradictions. For example, to establish reasonable premiums, experience-based information from a large number of companies is required; something, which is facilitated by collusion between companies. Moreover, the act of reinsurance means information about premiums and terms of insurance are spread among companies. As life insurance typically involves long contract periods the industry has argued that it is important to avoid 'unsound' competition that could hurt the reputation of the business at large. It has been considered essential for the legitimacy of the industry that individual corporations have not been forced to liquidate, since this might lead to a decrease in confidence which might have been devastating for the entire industry. Insurance companies have thus agreed on common formal rules of the game but also on informal honorary codes within the industry to maintain a 'sound' and 'fair' competition.

In a historical perspective, these measures of co-operation, which were supported by the government, have gained in importance as they served to stabilise the insurance market in an obvious way. This link with government has provided insurance with certain characteristics and given the industry a semi-official character. At the same time, there have been periods of extremely strong competition, for example, between different types of companies (mutual companies and joint-stock companies) or with the introduction of new products that have reduced the costs, or when there has been a change in market structure.

In this chapter, the focus of the analysis is co-operation within the Swedish insurance industry in the twentieth century, and in particular, the insurance cartel registry. The main objective of this chapter is to understand the extent of collusion in the market with help of the documentation of the registry. To understand the content of the insurance cartel register introduced in 1947 it is first necessary to explain how the insurance market emerged through self-regulation before this date, and how the legislation later affected the conduct of the market. The discussion will deal with how co-operation emerged in the mid-nineteenth century; what organisations were established to solve questions common to the industry and what some forms of co-operation actually looked like. In this chapter we will discuss both life and non-life insurance, while for an explicit analysis of cartels in the marine insurance sector see Petersson (2011).

What does co-operation mean and how should agreements that limit competition be interpreted? Agreements between competitors are most often called cartels, i.e. an agreement between companies about cooperating in one or several areas instead of competing. There are also different kinds of cartels, depending whether they focus on prices, conditions or division of the market. Price cartels are most often referred to when discussing cartels; parties that mutually agree on the price of a good or a service, irrespective of production costs (Scherer and Ross 1990).

The general attitude to competition and co-operation in the Swedish economy has long been incongruent (Lundqvist 2003; Jonung 1999). The legislation that has governed competition within the economy has, for this reason, changed over time. The current legislation (the Competition Law of 1993) gives insights into the current institutional framework for cartels and companies' attitudes to co-operation. According to this law, agreements between companies are prohibited if the aim is to prevent, limit or distort competition in any apparent way. The law prohibits agreements that directly or indirectly determine purchase or sales prices, but it also applies when production, markets, technical development or investments are limited or controlled. Furthermore, agreements that lead to a division of markets or sources of supply and agreements on different conditions for similar transactions where certain parties get a competitive disadvantage, are prohibited (Bernitz 1993). In theory, this gives a clear picture of the contents of agreements that limit competition, but the situation is considerably more complicated in practice.

Considering the special characteristics of insurance – the customer pays a fee in advance and expects possible compensation in the future – it is necessary that, in principle, all agents survive in the long run for the industry to keep the confidence of the general public. Thus, it is not very surprising that there have been different kinds of agreements to minimise the elimination of less competitive companies (Skogh 1991). The question is, however: can and should cartels and co-operation within the insurance industry be dealt with in the same way as within other lines of business? From a theoretical perspective, this is relatively simple; different kinds of collusion that entail a higher price for individual consumers are to be opposed since the price mechanism is then eliminated; something which might serve to distort the economy. But are there also factors that can serve to legitimise cartels and co-operation within the industry?

The chapter is organised as follows. First, we discuss the emergence of co-operation within the insurance industry since the establishment of the first joint-stock insurance companies in Sweden in the mid-nineteenth century. This is followed by an analysis of the different trade organisations, which have in various ways been important for creating uniform rules for the market. Then follows an analysis of how the political interventions from the 1930s onwards, deepened co-operation between companies but also created a close relationship between companies and the insurance supervisory authority. Then the centre of the chapter, analyses the formal agreements between companies that were reported to the so-called cartel register. This register makes it possible to scrutinise all of the 90 cartel agreements that were active in the Swedish market. In the conclusion we summarise why cartelisation was wound down, for instance by increasing competition; the oligopolisation of the market that occurred especially in the 1960s and the deregulation in the 1980s and 1990s that completely changed the rules of the game. In addition, we also draw some conclusion on how the cartel registry affected the insurance industry through collusion and competition in the market.

From informal co-operation to collusive organisations and standardisation

Attitudes toward cartels have changed considerably through time. In the latter part of the nineteenth century for example, cartels were allowed in Germany and the Scandinavian countries. Collusion between companies was considered to be part of the freedom of firms to make any kind of agreement. In the 1870s, various industrial cartels emerged and until the beginning of the twentieth century co-operation between companies was seen as a natural part of the Swedish economy. An important underlying reason was the absence of a strong government that could implement clear rules of the game for the agents. Since there was no legislation to supervise individual agents, agreements that limited competition were a way of overcoming uncertainty about the behaviour of one's competitors. Taking a co-operative approach enabled companies to avoid the threat of collapse caused by unfair methods of competition, or overcapacity could pose to a firm's survival (Lundqvist 2003; Schröter 1996; Ljunggren 1912).

Co-operation emerged as a natural part of the insurance industry at the same time as the establishment of Sweden's second joint-stock insurer Svea in 1866. The newly formed company asked for permission to access information from Skandia, which had operated its business for eleven years. This information, which was necessary for Svea to organise its own business, concerned for example the design of accounts and terms of insurance and premiums. As Skandia was located in Stockholm and Svea in Gothenburg, they did not compete directly against each other. On the contrary, Svea emphasised that co-operation would assist with covering the total insurance needs of the whole country and drive out foreign insurers that were then dominating the market (Fredrikson *et al.* 1972). Considering that commercial insurance was a new phenomenon, and that there existed no special insurance legislation, this co-operation could be considered a natural way of finding a mutual basis for pricing, marketing and distributing products as well as deciding on principles for reimbursement. Skandia and Svea were mixed companies, selling both life and non-life insurance. Gradually the insurers specialised, and sold only life or non-life insurance.

When the first 'pure' life insurance company Nordstjernan was established in 1871, it also received assistance from established companies to help it solve certain administrative questions. Thule, which was established two years later, however, introduced new principles to satisfy consumers' interests. This was strongly opposed by the other companies and Thule was initially excluded from any kind of co-operative agreement (Palme 1923).

In 1877, a formal agreement was concluded between Skandia, Svea and Nordstjernan that regulated a number of areas, including for example, higher premiums for people taking trips outside Europe; for certain professions that were particularly subjected to injuries (i.e. sailors and railroad personnel); and for health risks considered higher than normal. The agreement also contained regulated agent commissions, fees to doctors, commissions for reinsurance and a common policy for loans on life insurances. To guarantee that the agreement was observed, a clause was introduced that no major changes in the life insurance business were to be introduced without consulting the other companies. While this was a major agreement, it was of no great importance in practice, because it had already become obsolete by 1885. The key reason was the lack of an independent organisation that could supervise and punish transgressions against the agreement (Bergholm 1920).

The same agents had, however, already tried to formalise co-operation in the non-life sector by creating organisations that coordinated questions that were common for the industry, since this might serve to stabilise the market. In 1873, for example, the so-called Swedish Fire Tariff Committee was established. It coordinated the gathering of statistics to set 'reasonable' premiums on the basis of previous experience. The explicit objective of the Committee was to improve the insurance protection and make fire protection more efficient through correctly estimated premiums and well-adjusted insurance conditions. A basic premium was set by the Committee, which could be increased according to special tariffs for specific and more hazardous risks. If the policy holder undertook preventive measures, the premium could also be correspondingly reduced (Grenholm 1933).

The tariff Committee was clearly inspired by foreign role models; for example The Fire Offices Committee established in Britain 1858 and a similar organisation in Germany, established in 1871. In addition, the foreign companies in Sweden had formed so-called 'collegia' in both Stockholm and Gothenburg, to discuss insurance premiums and terms (Grenholm 1933: 6).[1] Given that the first Swedish insurance companies were influenced by foreign role models it is not particularly surprising that their interactions on foreign markets also followed the approaches used overseas. The work of the tariff Committee was also important for facilitating a clean-up of substandard risks. In order to obtain uniform premiums and mutual adjustments of premiums according to risk, it was necessary that all insurers had similar premiums. These were set on the cost structures of the least efficient company. Since not all agents were members of the tariff Committee, however, it was not possible to set monopoly prices.

The market was divided into two; one with companies belonging to tariff organisations and standard joint-stock insurers, and the other with mutual insurers that were referred to as non-tariff companies. In short, this meant that joint-stock insurers became members of the tariff organisations and followed instructions from the associations, while mutual insurers did not. As new lines of insurance emerged, different tariff Committees were created, such as minor insurance branches for personal accident insurance and burglary insurance. At the same time a division between tariff and non-tariff companies emerged. An association that facilitate the homogenisation of insurance routines was the Actuarial Society of Sweden, established in 1904. This ultimately led to a coordination of the mathematical estimates of premiums and risk of the individual companies regardless of ownership form (Sandström 2004).

Another co-operative organisation with a less direct objective of limiting competition was the Insurance Society founded 1875 in Stockholm. It changed its name to the Swedish Insurance Society in 1919, and is still active under that name. This organisation was initially devoted to create 'sound' conduct in the insurance market through education, information gathering and diffusion. The statutes of the association, however, also expressed the desire to increase co-operation by favouring common terms of insurance and premiums among companies. The association was important for standardising the definition of different insurance terms and increasing transparency within the industry. In addition to this society's efforts, industry information was distributed through, the *Journal of the Insurance Society*, which was first published in 1878 and which was later renamed in 1921, the *Scandinavian Insurance Quarterly* (Kleverman and Lönnborg 2000; see www.nft.nu).

The driving force behind the creation of the Swedish Insurance Society in the 1870s was, however, to advance special insurance legislation. There was a need to clean up the industry and eradicate less-serious companies, which were not solvent. The fact that the structure of several companies was not entirely favourable is shown by the bankruptcy of several smaller companies in the last few decades of the nineteenth century. A special insurance law was needed to not only contribute to the reinforcement of company finances, but to increase the legitimacy of the industry to existing and potential customers. This would also increase the possibility of driving foreign companies out of the market and recruiting customers who had not previously been insured. In 1886, a preliminary decree was introduced to supervise the industry (with the help of a part-time employed insurance inspector), but it was not until 1903 that a special insurance business law was introduced and the National Swedish Private Insurance Supervisory Service (hereafter the Swedish Insurance Inspectorate) was established (Larsson 1998; Boksjö and Lönnborg-Andersson 1994).

There were also obvious instances of competition in the insurance market. Skandia and Svea had been established with large insurance funds to protect their policy holders. Over time, however, it became apparent that the returns for life insurers were very high and less capital was required. As a consequence, pure companies with a considerably smaller capital stock were established. From the end of the 1880s until 1900, 13 mutual life insurance companies were established where policy holders themselves owned the firms. The first mutual company – later called Balder – was established in 1887 and was independent from the joint-stock companies. Allmänna Lifförsäkringsbolaget, which was established in the same year did, however, join the joint-stock companies' collusion when it came to premiums and insurance terms (Fredrikson *et al.* 1972; Englund 1982).

Towards the end of the nineteenth century, the antagonism between joint-stock companies with large capital reserves and the smaller mutual insurers with less-capitalisation became increasingly obvious. The criticisms mainly came from the large joint-stock companies that asserted that capital stock created confidence among the general public. The mutual companies with a small capital stock were thus jeopardising the legitimacy of the entire industry. The result increased uncertainty for policy holders in small capital stock mutual companies and certain smaller joint-stock insurance companies. In response several smaller mutual companies with economic problems merged with larger mutual companies. According to the mutual companies, the problem was not size. They considered that the joint-stock insurance companies tied too much capital into their own shares. The result was a yearly dividend that decreased the value of the capital of the policy holders. The debate between mutual companies and joint-stock companies was mainly pursued through the insurance journals but also using pamphlets and brochures. The argument came to be called the large 'battle of principles' and culminated in 1900–1902. The mutual antagonism was presented as a fight about how the insurance companies should be organised to best satisfy policy holders' interests. 'The combat of principles' was solved when an insurance business law was introduced in 1903 after decades of discussion (Bergander 1967; Larsson and Lönnborg 2015).

The legislation of 1903 was important because it created general confidence in the insurance industry. The government intervention also opened up further co-operation within the industry. The legislation was built on existing market norms and this meant that agreements that had previously existed between select companies could now constitute the basis for all agents in the market. The law thus contributed to the creation of unanimity between the companies. For example, it resulted in a standard approach to the mathematical calculations underpinning life insurance, the calculation of premiums, the calculation of profits and the distribution of profits to policy holders. The overall objective of the law, to create financial stability for the companies, led to a standardisation of the business, which in turn stimulated co-operation between the companies, not the least within areas where the law did not provide any clear guidelines. The stricter enforcement of the principle of publicity, the requirement that the financial position of the company be published for the general public, further improved standardisation of the market.

The legislation put the various organisational forms on the same level, which was particularly important for the mutual life insurance companies. This facilitated the organisation of a broad level of co-operation within the life insurance sector. After the big fight about principles, it was important to create a forum where mutual questions concerning life insurance could be discussed. In 1906, the Swedish Life Insurers Director Association was established, which consisted of representatives from both joint-stock companies and mutual companies. In 1936 the company changed names to The Swedish Life Insurance Companies' Association and over time, almost every life insurance company in Sweden came to join the association.[2]

Since the end of the 1880s, the existence of return commissions (i.e. when an agent gave part of his provision to the policy holders to attract new customers) had been strongly debated. This strategy created additional costs for the companies, because it encouraged individuals to take out amounts of insurance higher than they could really afford, and they were frequently forced to cancel their contracts. In 1890, Skandia, Svea, Nordstjernan, Thule and Allmänna Liv agreed to prohibit return commissions, but since there was no punishment system, the agreement had no effect in practice. The inability to enforce an agreement was a problem that was an early discussion in the Director Association as the same problem applied in situations where agents convinced policy holders to change insurers (disloyal competition). Another important question focused on the payment of commissions to doctors who examined potential policy holders and how, co-operation among the companies could mean avoiding those doctors who did not fulfil the companies' requirements (Bergander 1967).

Another feature of collaboration occurred in 1914, when life insurers (both joint-stock and mutual companies) jointly founded the reinsurance company Sweden Re. The company was partly created as a means of cleaning up the life reinsurance market because smaller insurers had signed treaties with foreign insurers that in the long run could jeopardise their survival and in turn hurt the confidence of the entire market. The creation of Sweden Re also meant that every life insurer used the same kind of reinsurance arrangements, which further enhanced collusion in the market (Larsson and Lönnborg 2014).

The insurance legislation was partly revised in 1917 resulting in stricter and more standardised accounting routines. An explicit prohibition against return commission was introduced and the companies also became responsible for the behaviour of their representatives. Even these changes, however, were not sufficient to solve the problem with the representatives in the industry. The law also led to a tightening of the rules for profit sharing to policy holders. The problem of return commission was not finally solved – as we will come back to – until the 1940s (Larsson *et al.* 2005).

The insurance business law of 1927 was yet another institutional change that further standardised insurance companies. This regulatory framework defined policy holders' obligations to provide information, while also standardising the terms of insurance among insurers. This increased comparability between companies but also decreased competition, since the companies, with a few exceptions, had the same life insurance premiums. The Insurance Inspectorate claimed, however, that the law mainly protected policy holders' interests and that it only had a limited impact on competition (Enskilt försäkringsväsen 1954).

Political intervention and increased collusion

During the 1930s, co-operation within the industry intensified. Several factors drove this trend, including, for example, a political debate on the nationalisation of the private insurance business and the low interest rate policy that limited the investment possibilities of the companies. The divided structure of an industry with a large number of insurance companies meant that, from a political point of view, the total administrative costs of the industry were considered to be excessive. The pursuit of the low interest rate policy meant the companies had large problems in getting a return on their investments in bonds. The sales organisations of the companies were dominated by a large number of representatives working in their spare time (so-called leisure agents, with generally limited knowledge about insurance and salaried through commission). The result was that many customers were enticed to sign relatively expensive agreements (which meant a higher commission for the agents) but which exceeded their ability to pay. This, combined with the poor economic conditions of the 1930s, in turn led to an increase in the number of cancellations. The higher rate of cancellations resulted in higher administrative costs, indicating the inefficiency of the entire industry. Altogether, there was a strong increase in the administrative costs of the private insurance companies in the 1930s, which increased criticism against the private insurance industry from the political left (Grip 1987; Kuuse and Olsson 2000).

In 1934 the head of the Insurance Inspectorate, O. A. Åkesson, was commissioned by the government to investigate if the increased cancellations and high administrative costs of the insurance companies could be reduced through governmental intervention. This triggered a debate about the risk of nationalisation of the private insurance business and how this could be avoided. The question was raised in the parliament in 1935, but was deflected with reference to the on-going studies within the insurance business by Åkesson (Grip 1987: 29–34).

In 1937 the Insurance Inspectorate concluded that it was necessary to increase the efficiency of the market using extensive mergers within the industry, to lower the number of companies. The Insurance Inspectorate was not in favour of nationalisation and urged the industry to rationalise and in particular, reorganise the sale organisations to avoid further political attention. The so-called monopoly committee was created by the insurance industry (one for life insurance and one for non-life insurance) to coordinate opposition to nationalisation. This committee was the driving force behind the 'clean-up' of the industry, but it was also active in undermining the arguments for nationalisation. The committees were transformed into a new organisation, the Swedish Insurers Federation in 1937 (today Insurance Sweden). The Federation, in close co-operation with the Insurance Inspectorate, urged individual companies to continue to rationalise their businesses thereby avoiding nationalisation (Grip 1987: 73f.). These measures, of course, increased the propensity for co-operation and collusion within the industry, and in part this was blessed by the monitoring governmental agency.

In 1937, parliament decided to create the suggested committee, using mostly people from the insurance industry, and with the head of the Insurance Inspectorate, Åkesson, as chairman. The work within this committee was halted by the outbreak of war but resumed in 1942 with largely the same representatives (Grip 1987).

The starting point for the legislative proposal that the committee presented in 1946 – and implemented as the 1948 law on insurance business – was to reduce the expenditures of the industry and thus decrease premiums for policy holders. To achieve this, a number of new principles were presented, several of which had consequences for market competition. Established companies' control was reinforced through the 'principle of need' criterion, which meant that a new company entering the market had to demonstrate to the Insurance Inspectorate that their services were not already provided by existing insurers. New companies were thus effectively prevented from entering the Swedish market and, sometimes, it could even be difficult for existing companies to enter into new areas (Law on Insurance 1948; SOU 1946:34; Larsson et al. 2005). This advantaged established and large companies and contributed to the already existing tendencies toward oligopoly. It also gave the government the power to effectively determine the structure of the market.

The introduction of the 'principle of equity' (fairness) – that aimed at reducing the premiums to a reasonable level relative to the insurance service provided – had indirect consequences for competition. The loose design of the principle meant an increase in the contacts between companies, via the various tariff Committees, to create the principles for estimating the information required by the Insurance Inspectorate. This made it possible for the companies to compare their cost trends and to adjust the interpretation of the regulatory frameworks to a level that suited the members of the associations. In contrast to the objective of the insurance committee, this served to reinforce the position of the tariff Committees (SOU 1946:25; Larsson et al. 2005: 66–69).

Even though the legislation did, in some cases, serve to undermine competition, it is difficult to draw a clear line between those rules that protected policy holders and those, which served only to lower competition.

Formal cartels – the cartel register

Co-operation in the insurance industry thus had both a formal and an informal character. It is clearly difficult to say anything definite about the importance of informal discussions and different 'gentlemen's agreements' among companies. Formal structures, including several different trade associations were established to solve mutual problems, to mutually interpret legislation and decide how to implement it in practice. Exactly ninety cartels were established within the industry. With the aid of the insurance cartel register it is possible to get a better perspective of these arrangements. The cartel register provides an overall picture of what kind of co-operation was established in the industry, the areas of interest and the participants.

After the outbreak of the Second World War, a number of regulatory measures were introduced to ensure provisions for the population. These principles continued in part after the war, but were supplemented by other government interventions, introduced with the aim of increasing state control of the Swedish economy. Among other things, by using legislation or the threat of legislation, the government tried to make the agents in the financial markets support economic policy. In the post-war program of the labour movement, there were suggestions of nationalising the insurance business in order to rationalise businesses and increase control over credit flows (Larsson et al. 2005; Jonung 1993). This eventually came to nothing, but the control of the private insurance sector was reinforced through other initiatives. The introduction of the cartel register was one such measure. The official cartel register was established by the Insurance Inspectorate in 1947 and was revised yearly until 1980. Behind this register was, for example, the Myrdal Commission, which at the end of the 1940s introduced a number of investigations to assess 'deficiencies in the competition' within different industries. Cartels were prohibited according to Swedish practice, but it was possible to obtain an exemption if the agreement was made public. The introduction of a cartel register solely for the insurance industry (this registry was totally separate from the cartel registry for the industrial sector; see Chapter 12 in this volume) also meant that older agreements entered the register. As a result the oldest cartel and number one in the register in 1947 was the foundation of the Fire Tariff Committee that started in 1873 (Sterner 1956; Boksjö and Lönnborg-Andersson 1994; Lewin 1992).

In the period 1947–1980, therefore, a total of 90 cartel agreements were registered in the public insurance cartel registry. Of these, about half ceased during the period but they were often replaced by new agreements which were similar to the old ones but with modifications. These agreements could be of two kinds, agreements or recommendations. The former were agreements that had been made between at least two parties and that built on mutual dependency. Recommendations, on the other hand, were often formal instructions connected to a co-operative organisation, for example the tariff Committees, and were often of a more binding form (Boksjö and Lönnborg-Andersson 1994: 147f.).

The majority of the registered cartels, about two thirds, concerned non-life insurance business while the remaining third had been created on the life insurance market. The more binding recommendations related to life insurance. This meant that non-life cartels were more common mainly because these were renewed more often, while life insurance cartels were more stable and with a binding character.

About half of all registered cartel agreements were made in the period 1946–1960 and the creation of cartels was particularly active in 1951–1955 (see Figure 14.1). Seen over the period beginning in the 1950s to the beginning of the 1980s, there was a decrease in the importance of these cartels – at least in the number of active agreements. This might partly be explained by the increased concentration of the insurance market, when a small number of companies and groups of companies increasingly came to dominate the industry. The starting point of the decreased importance of cartel agreements can be dated to 1967 when Skandia left the Swedish Insurance Rating Committee (the new name of the Fire Tariff Committee). The reason for leaving was that Skandia by then was a very large corporation into which almost every joint-stock insurer had merged, so the need for co-operation in the market had more or less vanished.

The emergence of cartels in the life insurance market was closely connected to institutional circumstances. The legislation was more detailed for these companies than for non-life insurance companies and this made it important to agree on how these new rules were to be interpreted.

The Swedish Consumer Cooperative's insurer, Folksam, held a special position in the co-operation within the industry. Officially, the company was critical to all kinds of co-operation and agreements since this were considered to increase costs and damage the interests of policy holders. This was expressed by the company in response to a report by the 1945 insurance committee:

> Our right to an independent pricing policy, when this is found to be justified, has been defended in the interest of the general public. By standing outside these associations of interested parties, which exist within the area of insurance, Folksam have also preserved their freedom in exercising this right.
> (Larsson *et al.* 2005: 182; authors' translation)

For this reason, Folksam did not sign any agreements, but in contrast – somewhat surprisingly – promised in writing to follow a third of all agreements. The motivation underlying this action is uncertain, but it is not farfetched to imagine that they chose to follow those agreements that, some way, decreased uncertainty in the market. As long as the motive of the cartel was not explicitly to set prices but rather, to clarify the rules of the game, Folksam followed the agreements, which is surprising considering their view on collusion.

The introduction of a new insurance business law in 1948 increased uncertainty in the market. New business principles were introduced and the Insurance Inspectorate controls changed. In this situation, the cartel agreements served as a practical interpretation of the legal texts and had a stabilising effect on the industry. This is confirmed by the large number of new cartel agreements in life insurance in the first half of the 1950s (see Figure 14.1).

Many agreements emerged in response to the regulatory framework. One example that emerged as a direct result of the regulations was agreement number F57. This required the company boards and managing directors of insurance businesses to be responsible for the sale of insurance, and ensure sales were conducted according to good insurance business practice. The agreement, among other things, served to control the qualifications of representatives (i.e. agents). A number of other agreements that emerged in the 1950s also created homogeneous conditions and premiums, supposed to make it easier for companies to control their agent network. This cartel agreement will be explored more in detail in the next section, because it gives insight into how cartel agreements interplayed with the regulations, supervision and informal codes of conduct of the insurance market.

In the 1960s, several agreements were introduced for group life insurance (where for instance an employer could insure all employees with one contract), creating a relatively new insurance product. In 1949 several insurers (both mutual and joint-stock companies) founded a joint-venture corporation called Förenade Liv ('United Life') to sell group insurance. The company itself was considered to be a cartel but many different cartel agreements were connected to the group insurance. Folksam, which was not a part owner of Förenade Liv, and sold group insurance under its own name, also joined the cartel agreement. Other examples of agreements that included group life insurance were: F 60 which was an agreement

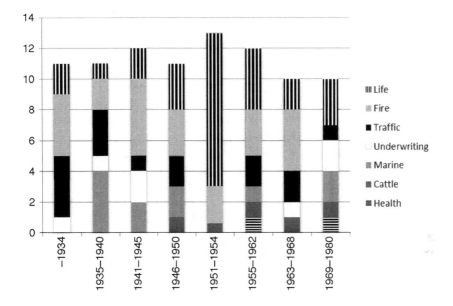

Figure 14.1 Swedish cartels by insurance type, 1873–1980.

Sources: Boksjö and Lönnborg-Andersson (1994: 152); the Swedish Insurance Inspectorates' registry of cartels.

between six companies about jointly pursuing group life insurance; F 66 in which seven companies jointly pursued sickness insurance; F 67 an agreement between nine companies on mutual insurance conditions for group insurance and F 68 which was an agreement between four companies on uniform premiums, balancing of risk of employment group life insurance. Both F 67 and F 58 were followed by Folksam. The emergence of group insurance was thus a phenomenon that reinforced collusion within the industry, while reducing the risks related to introducing a completely new insurance product. It is doubtful whether this was in line with the principles of free competition. Nonetheless considering that group insurance survived and has become a very important insurance product, the fundamental question is: what would have happened if the co-operation had not occurred to support this new line of insurance?[3]

The contents of the cartel agreements can be divided into five groups depending on their main objective: the geographical division of markets; standardisation of premiums; standardisation of terms of insurance; standardisation of insurance transactions and diversification of risk (see Figure 14.2). The objective of almost half of all cartels was to stabilise the premiums within a certain area, which had an indirect effect on the terms of insurance. From a competitive perspective, these agreements could be defined as 'real' cartels distorting the price mechanism. Those cartels where a standardisation of the terms of insurance was the main objective, there was seldom a direct effect on premiums, but these did, among other things, contain mutual definitions of risk, interpretations of new legislation and the establishment of common values. About a fourth of all cartels concerned these questions. Over time there was a decrease in the number of agreements that dealt with the standardisation of terms of insurance. This was likely the result of the legislation remaining relatively stable over time. Once the rules were interpreted and remained unchanged, the need for new agreements was limited. Since the 'principle of need' slowed down the entrance of new agents on the market, and the number of firms reduced through mergers, there was also a decrease in the incentive for the creation of new agreements.

Those cartels that served to diversify risks were often designed as insurance pools, where risks were systematically diversified between the member companies, and each member received a share depending on the company's size. Scandinavian insurance companies frequently cooperated through pool arrangements. In 1919, for example, the pool for aviation insurance was established, although it was only actually named in 1948 on entering the cartel register. Several other 'pools' between Swedish personal accident insurance companies were created at the end of the 1930s, and also later added to the register. Another example was the Swedish Atomic Insurance Pool that was created by several companies in 1956 in order to administer insurance and reinsurance of the risks associated with the production of

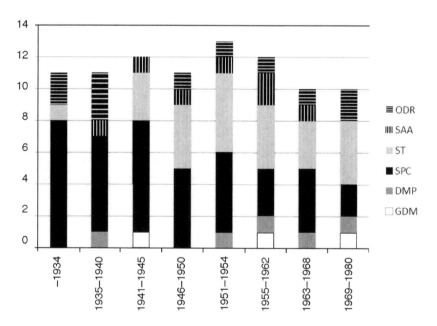

Figure 14.2 Cartel agreements by objectives and year of establishment.

Note: GDM = geographical division of markets; DMP = The division of markets by product; SPC = standardisation of premiums and conditions; ST = standardisation of terms; SAA = standardisation of acquisition activity; ODR = other distribution of risks.

Sources: Boksjö and Lönnborg-Andersson (1994: 153); The Swedish Insurance Inspectorates' registry of cartels.

nuclear energy. By definition, these pools were cartel agreements but it is doubtful that they did, in fact, have any effect on competition, because no single company would accept these risks. Within this type of cartel agreement, there were also syndicates for the financial support of common projects, such as group insurances, as for example the company Förenade Liv.

Cartels with different objectives had varying abilities to survive. Figure 14.3 clearly shows that the dominating objective was an agreement on prices and conditions. Price cartels were the most volatile and earlier agreements were frequently replaced by new agreements. Agreements that focused on insurance terms were similar. Cartel agreements that divided markets by geographical location and project were, in contrast, relatively few and unstable. Within the area of marketing (MK), there was only one agreement, which regulated insurance transactions, and this was renewed on several occasions (see below). This pattern is consistent with the general picture of cartel agreements in other industries. It has often been difficult to maintain long-term stability, particularly in regard to price agreements. As the products changed, it was also necessary to adjust the agreements.

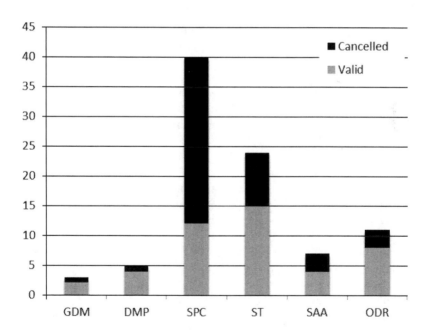

Figure 14.3 Cartel agreements by objective, valid and cancelled, 1947–1980.

Note: GDM = geographical division of markets; DMP = The division of markets by product; SPC = standardisation of premiums and conditions; ST = standardisation of terms; SAA = standardisation of acquisition activity; ODR = other distribution of risks.

Sources: Boksjö and Lönnborg-Andersson (1994: 153); The Swedish Insurance Inspectorates' registry of cartels.

The agreement on acquisition

In order to understand the importance and functioning of cartels, specific agreements must be studied and analysed in detail. From the registry analysed above we can discuss one of the cartel agreements in more detail. Below, we have chosen to describe how all the companies, via a cartel agreement, dealt with one of their major and enduring problems: the standardisation of acquisition (*anskaffningsöverenskommelsen*). This refers to how insurers' representatives should conduct themselves when selling insurance. In the 1930s debate on nationalisation, high administration costs were argued to be the result of organisations with a large share of leisure agents. Insurance companies had previously tackled this issue in the nineteenth century by attempting to establish common sales rules. These arrangements led to the establishment of the 'Royal Agreement' in 1907. The agreement was revised over the following decades to increase its efficiency. With the introduction of a new insurance business law in 1948, the agreement was renamed the agreement on acquisition, and in 1983, again renamed, the marketing agreement (Grip 1987; Strömbäck 1995).

From the beginning, the agreement aimed to reach a common view of the relationship between insurance representatives and customers, and control competition between the insurance representatives. Among other things, return commission, where the customer and the representative shared the commission was prohibited; but this rule was largely ignored. The agreement also contained a prohibition against moving existing insurance to a competing company. The agreement contained no sanctions, however, something that led to a tendency to dissolution. Accordingly, negotiations had to be resumed only a few years after the 'Royal Agreement' had been made. In order to create a new contract, similar to 1907, one company chose to go through the cooperative organisation 'The Swedish Life Insurers Directors Association (*Svenska Livförsäkringsbolags Direktörsförening*)'.

A new agreement was presented in 1910 and, besides a closer regulation of the agreement; it also contained a penalty system that would come into force if terms in the agreement were broken. The aim was mostly to increase control over the company's representatives. The people were, among other things, obliged to report to an industry-wide registration agency before they could start selling insurance. An arbitration board was also established to solve differences between the companies. The overall objective of the agreement was to contribute to a 'sound' competition, while at the same time removing less reliable representatives. The surviving representatives were offered training so that the agreement was to be distributed over the entire sales organisations (Lindström and Strömbäck 1983: 232f.).

While the insurance business law of 1927 contributed to the removal of some of the problems with acquisition, it also paved the way for controlling the acquisition of liability insurance. Until 1930, the 'Royal Agreement' only applied to life insurance, but in the middle of that decade, a similar agreement was introduced for non-life insurance. In the following years, there was an attempt to merge these two agreements into a single common agreement for the entire industry. This did not become a reality until the introduction of the new insurance business law in 1948. This agreement on insurance transactions was tied to the new law and became more important in controlling the business of company representatives. At the practical level, uniform requirements for training of the representatives were developed. An administrative board was established to ensure that the common rules of the game were followed and thus contributed to the creation of 'sound insurance practice' in the market. The sound insurance practice was described in the following general way:

> This general objective includes that in marketing, the rules of the game are to be respected, that dubious competitive methods should be refrained from, no derogatrory things should be said about one's competitors and truthful information should always be given.
> (Lindström and Strömbäck 1983: 235; authors' translation)

At the beginning of the 1980s, the agreement was reformed due to new marketing legislation and renamed 'the marketing agreement'. The rules of this agreement served to supplement laws and practice and set out how the agents should act in practice to fulfil existing expectations. A couple of overall rules for customer contact and relations to competitors constituted the basis for this. The aim was to reinforce confidence in the companies and increase the legitimacy of the entire industry (Skogh and Samuelsson 1985).

This cartelised outcome was an example of self-regulation producing common efforts to address a problem that could otherwise decrease the legitimacy of the industry. There were, however, other consequences. Among other things, the agreement led to the emergence of independent insurance brokers being counteracted (independent brokers were by law forbidden). It was, in fact, the companies' own representatives who carried out sales, as this guaranteed that the agreement would be met. These agreements (where only representatives from companies were allowed to sell insurance) can, of course, be questioned from a competitive perspective, but both individual companies and the Insurance Inspectorate considered market stability to be more important than competition through independent brokers.

The marketing agreement ceased to be valid in 1986. It was reorganised and transferred to Swedish Insurers Service, and finally dissolved in the mid-1990s. This deregulation, allowed for the first time in history, independent brokers to operate, making it impossible to continue the agreements, and thus increasing competition in the market. It was expected that the code of conduct in the industry would be maintained by the Insurance Inspectorate and the Swedish Insurance Federation with the assistance of the Swedish Insurance Society. The basic principles for acquisition of companies that had been established in the 1910s were still relevant when new distributional channels were established.

The last agreement in the insurance cartel registry was concluded in 1980 (and concerned insuring the Formula One race in Sweden). The documentation of the entire registry was originally kept at the Insurance Inspectorate (from 1991 the

Financial Inspectorate) but, s at the end of the 1990s it was transferred to the current location, the National Archives in Stockholm.

In sum, the cartel registry reveals that the majority of the cartel agreements within private insurance were some variety of price cartel, which led to the premiums being generally higher than if there had been 'free competition'. It is also clear that the design of many of the agreements mainly served to define the rules of the game for the agents and which, in the long run, served to protect policy holders. At the same time, the agreements facilitated company administration. Overall company self-interest dominated altruistic motives.

Concluding discussion

This description of co-operation within the insurance industry might create the picture that the industry was completely regulated by government legislation and cartel agreements and that competition was non-existent. This is not correct. In certain periods, competition was very serious for individual companies. This was largely due to the increase in market concentration, which completely changed the conditions for company conduct. In addition, competition became fierce within the non-life insurance sector (in particular in combined insurance) while life insurance continued to be protected. We will in this concluding remark summarise how and why this kind of market conduct was dissolved and competition restored.

Co-operation between insurance companies had already developed during the nineteenth century as a response to risks connected with the fast growing insurance market. When the co-operative agreements became more formal and were written down, the companies were increasingly motivated to follow their regulations. This also held for the establishment of the cartel register, which made the cartels even more officially accepted. Thus, the cartel register became a public means for the control and guidance of the insurance market.

In the middle of the 1940s competition intensified between mutual companies, and between mutual companies and joint-stock companies. This was due, particularly to the actions of the Consumers Cooperative's insurer, Folksam. The competition was confined, however, to non-life insurance and different combined insurance policies. Legislation continued to forbid any kind of price competition within the life insurance sector. In addition, from the 1940s almost every national insurer was selling both non-life and life insurance, but the latter had to be administrated through an 'independent' company. Each insurer had several daughter companies selling different insurance lines. Thanks to its well-consolidated business, and partly because of its close relationship to the trade union movement and Consumer Cooperative, Folksam was able to reduce its premiums considerably. This process was launched under the name 'take action' in 1946, when Folksam introduced more uniform tariffs, which in practice meant considerably lower premiums. The low-price policy turned out to be a successful strategy, which swiftly increased market share (Grip 2009; Blomberg 1964; Jüring 1978, 1983).

The increased concentration of businesses in the insurance market was of even greater importance, however, since it led to a questioning of the co-operation policy. During the nationalisation debate, concentrating the insurance business was emphasised by both companies and the Insurance Inspectorate as a way of making the industry more efficient. The expected scale advantages would lead to lower total costs and thus to lower premiums for individual policy holders. Large merger waves in the 1960s and 1970s were thus supported by both political and economic agents. But increased concentration within the industry not only served to create a potential for decreased premiums, it also contributed to an oligopolistic market with a small number of large companies. Most major joint-stock insurance companies were gathered into the Skandia group at the beginning of the 1960s. A few years later a large number of mainly national mutual companies a merged into what became the Trygg Hansa group in 1971. Together with a third group of companies, headed by cooperative Folksam, which was almost expanding by itself, these groups of companies did, at the beginning of the 1970s, collect almost two thirds of the premium incomes paid by Swedish companies (Englund 1982; Fredrikson et al. 1972).

Besides Trygg-Hansa and Folksam, there were mutual companies such as Vegete, Allmänna Brand, and Valand, which in the 1980s merged to create the group of companies Wasa with a market share of about 12 per cent. In the 1960s and at the beginning of the 1970s, regional and mutual county insurance companies began to grow swiftly and in the mid-1970s, these companies together had a market share amounting to almost 20 percent. These companies also carried out mergers, which resulted in 24 county insurance companies, jointly called Länsförsäkringar. At the end of the 1990s, there was also a merger between Länsförsäkringar and Wasa.

The emergence of a small number of dominating groups of companies in the insurance market was critical for the institutional reconstruction of that market. The deregulation of the Swedish financial market in the 1980s created an entirely new competitive environment in the insurance market and undermined self-regulation by the agents. The general attitude to competition in the Swedish economy also changed fundamentally from the 1980s. The insurance market gradually adapted to the European standard; a process that was closely related to the rapprochement with, and finally connection to, the European Community (later the European Union) (Hägg 1999; Larsson et al. 2005).

The changes in the market, deregulation and accession to EU were key reasons for that dissolution of the cartels; but what can explain the system's longevity? Co-operation within the insurance industry was an important part of the emergence of a stable market. From a competitive perspective, the question is whether this created a situation where customers paid a higher price than if the market had been free from cartels and collusion. This study has hopefully made it clear that such a question cannot be answered in any uniform way. On the one hand, co-operation most likely pressed the premium level upwards, especially considering that the cost of the least efficient companies was the basis for setting certain premiums. On the other hand, the co-operatives were important for creating a stable insurance market, where individual policy holders did not suffer financially because firms failed. It has thus been a question of choice between competition and stability, where the latter has dominated during the major part of the twentieth century.

Co-operation within the industry was developed in the twentieth century due to the emergence of co-operative organisations, trade associations and direct agreements. Of special concern was the role of legislation, which often supported co-operation within the industry. One example of this was the insurance business law from 1927 which resulted in the standardisation of the terms of insurance. Another key example was the insurance law from 1948 which was aiming for the homogenisation of establishment, insurance costs and official control between insurance companies of different types and sizes.

The importance of mergers has varied over time. Initially, collusion was the driving force for creating legitimacy in the insurance market, which is not surprising considering that insurance cannot work without the confidence of the general public. It can thus be claimed that the emergence of trade associations, as well as formal and informal agreements, was a way of defining the rules of the game for market agents. Initially, this was even a substitute for a special insurance legislation when co-operation became a reason for the industry to introduce self-regulation. Later, the agreements came to play the role of interpreting legislation and be an instrument for all agents to interpret the rules in the same way to avoid disloyal competition. Thus, it can be claimed that co-operation was partly a functional way of reinforcing and supporting the market economy. It is incorrect to interpret collusion as only being a means of avoiding price competition. The importance of co-operation within the industry was expressed by a representative of the industry in 1920:

> Not the least as concerns the once safely anchored and highly developed *co-operation*, the Swedish life insurance business does currently hold a particularly prominent and, in every right, distinguished position. No better desire can in fact be expressed for the continued successful trend of Swedish life insurance, than that the good co-operation within the same must henceforth remain and continue with the same high objectives that it has had so far, *the advantage of the policy holders and the benefit of society*.
> (Bergholm 1920: 40; authors' translation; italics in the original)

Cartel agreements and co-operation between companies were to continue, despite the fact that the legislation later come to regulate several of those questions previously dealt with in trade associations. This, together with rationalisations within the industry and political support for increased concentration, did in time give the insurance industry an oligopolistic structure. Government policy served to strengthen this trend.

In our view, it is incorrect to consider all kinds of co-operation as activities that serve to limit competition. Several agreements are instead examples of companies trying to establish mutual rules of the game in order to avoid crises that could emerge due to competition that had been driven too far. It is also from this starting point that the term 'disloyal' competition should be considered. This activity could, in the short run, increase the gains of individual companies, but in the long run undermine the confidence of the general public in the insurance business at large.

Folksam pursued a policy that was characterised by a mixture of competition and co-operation. Through a continuous desire to decrease the premiums, Folksam's put downward pressure on prices, although it also did informally follow a third of all cartel co-operative agreements.

How did then the cartel registry that was implemented in 1947 affect the insurance market? In short, the cartelisation that had started as early as the 1870s became part of the registry. In addition, the treaties in the registry revealed only part of the collusion in the market, where jointly founded corporations such as Sweden Re and Förenade Liv, and several trade associations, cooperated further. Through the cartel registry, however, it was possible for outsiders to overview formal agreements, even though in reality they were combined with gentlemen agreements and less visible and informal features of the intense collaboration on the insurance market.

It is, of course, impossible, to simply define and determine whether collusion in the insurance market was legitimate. In our view, the major part of the agreements did have a relatively high degree of legitimacy since they defined the rules of the game in various ways and partly protected the policy holders. Many agreements increased the price of the services, but the question is whether these control mechanisms of competition did not, at the same time, protect the stability of the insurance market. Collusion, for instance driven by the nationalisation debate, together with increased competition over time, facilitated a rationalisation of the market and made it more efficient. In short, the effects of cartels and co-operation on the market entailed both negative and positive out-comes.

Archival and printed sources

Swedish Insurance Inspectorates' registry of cartels. Swedish Insurance Inspectorate's archive, Registry of cartels (RC), Contracts on constraint competition division on valid and cancelled, D 1 BA, D 1 BB, D1 BC and D 1 BD. Swedish National Archives, Stockholm.

Notes

1 For discussion about similar committees in the UK, see Westall (1984); for Australia, see Keneley (2002); and for Spain, see Pons (2007).
2 The Consumer Cooperative's insurer Folksam, however, was only a member for a few years (Englund 1982: 65).
3 When Sweden entered the European Union and introduced a new competition law, the arrangement of joint ownership of 'United Life' was considered to be against the law and was dissolved. Today, the owner of the corporate brand 'United Life' is Folksam, the company that previously refused to participate in the joint-venture (Lönnborg 2009).

Part III
Conclusion

15 Conclusion

Susanna Fellman and Martin Shanahan

In 2014, Jean Tirole, was awarded the Nobel Prize for Economic Science for his 'analysis of market power and regulation'. In describing the significance of his contribution, the Nobel Committee wrote:

> If markets dominated by a small number of companies are left unregulated, society often suffers negative consequences. Prices can become unjustifiably high and new companies can be prevented from entering the market ... Jean Tirole has worked to develop a coherent theory ... showing that regulation should be adapted to suit specific conditions in each industry ...[1]

Registers of restrictive agreements are a form of regulatory instrument used by the authorities to better understand specific agreements between firms, and the specific conditions existing in their industry. Depending on the specific conditions existing in a country, the registers were used with a variety of aims: to reveal and expose; to identify and monitor; or to archive and record. They were used to address a variety of problems: inflationary pressure was one target, but so too was market manipulation, exclusive dealing, bid rigging and other forms of restrictive practices. The registers represent one example of a regulatory instrument that was aimed at specific conditions, in specific countries and specific industries. Although the registers emerged for a wide range of reasons and were used differently, there are also many similarities in how they were used. The view that publicity would deter anticompetitive behaviour was common to most (the exceptions were Australia and the Netherlands) and was something even the US authorities considered would help prevent detrimental behaviour. In many ways anti-competitive registers were a practical application of the principles later espoused by Tirole.

Nevertheless, registers of restrictive agreements fell from favour. Only a few now exist, despite their popularity in the 1950s and 1960s. One argument for their demise was the administrative burden of gathering detailed information on each potential restrictive agreement. Another was that they were relatively ineffective in punishing anti-competitive behaviour, with few significant court cases, or heavy fines. In the end, they were 'swept away' by international agreements that prohibited outright what many of the registers were monitoring and which the authorities were slowly rectifying.

It may come as a surprise therefore, that in several countries the registers are credited with playing a key role in changing business peoples' attitudes toward anticompetitive agreements. Processes which included notification and negotiation, rather than writ and prosecution not only shaped the behaviour of the parties involved, but that of their competitors and players in other markets. Why this was so remains difficult to explain. It may have been the threat of being caught, or the fear of being exposed, that finally persuaded some to change. This would not, however, explain why uninvolved firms in countries with secret registers similarly felt compelled to change their agreements with their competitors. More likely, the process of specific industry investigation and discussion helped firms identify what constituted restrictive trade practices in their fields of endeavour. Perhaps it was a realisation that attitudes were changing everywhere. Regardless of the reasons, the cartel registers can be viewed as one of the elements that helped open up national markets. By challenging the long-time practices of local businesses, and questioning comfortable arrangements whereby everyone 'in' the agreement benefited at the expense of everyone 'outside' the agreement, the regulators and their registers did much to advance competition, and subsequently international trade.

Business and economic history studies like the ones presented here have lessons for today. They highlight, for example, the importance of general business beliefs, in helping set the framework in which regulations are constructed. In the case of anti-competitive agreements, the differences between the beliefs established in America and Europe are testament to this. The power of vested interests and lobby groups is also well illustrated in a variety of ways: by the history of the League of Nations committees and the impact of business interests in shaping international debate; in the case of Norway, with a mixture of luck and political acumen that saw opportunities seized at critical moments; in the case of Holland, where the polder model of consensus slowed change for decades; in the case of Finland where interest groups' early influence helped shape debates for decades after. The form of the registers, and what they excluded, says much about lobbyists, but also about the major industries that dominated each country. Agricultural interests in Australia and Norway, for example were mostly successful in avoiding being captured in their registers, as were exporting industries in most countries. It is clear that what the legislation included in different countries was influenced by considerations of each nation's key industries and the need to safeguard particular sectors. By contrast, smaller manufacturers whose products were often sold directly to the public were mostly included in the registers. So, too, anti-competitive behaviour such as resale price maintenance, which directly impacted on consumers, was often made an offence.

Close inspection of the evidence as revealed in these studies also challenges the more simplistic interpretations of historical change. While American anti-trust laws and attitudes were influential, they did not simply replace policies and regulations in other countries. The fierce debates in Germany, and the rapid loosening of regulations in Japan after the initial 'harsh' regulations, reveal a much more nuanced story of gradual development as each nation interpreted regulations from their own perspective. The legal developments within individual European countries followed similar patterns so much that some scholars talk about a European competition policy model. On the other hand, within Europe the particular paths followed by individual countries were also quite distinct. For example the British and the German tradition varied considerably and emerged through quite different legal and cultural traditions. The records also show how many countries' regulators learnt from each other, often to a greater extent than from the US. The Finnish, for example, learnt from the Swedes, the Swedes from the Norwegians; the Australians from the British and Americans; South Korea borrowed elements from both the Japanese and the German legislation, while India and Pakistan followed the UK. Similarly, as countries observed the material success of the Americans, and the catastrophic outcomes of the Fascists, they sought to shift their economies towards those ideals consistent with rising living standards and enhanced competition. Such international 'spill-overs' serve as reminder as to the importance of example and experience in affecting neighbouring countries' regulatory frameworks.

Policy networks have been rightly identified as important for transnational learning. This book, however, also shows that transnational learning is a complex process, and that it is easy to over-emphasise individual policy-makers. What is learnt, how and to what extent it is adopted, is a result of the local economic and political situation, the significance of various pressure groups and their influence in policy making, and of a country's legal and cultural traditions. This book reveals that to understand 'European traditions' or 'European models' it is not enough to simply study Germany, France or the UK; something which has often been the case when discussing competition policy. The European experience is far more diverse than this. An international and transnational perspective requires a broader perspective, with attention given to specific countries, contexts and specific forms of learning. The cartel registers are one 'window' through which to study what was perceived as problematic; what was to be controlled and how such information could and should be used by local authorities. This book can only really scratch the surface of these issues.

Our emphasis on examining particular places and contexts also challenges the standard argument of the post-war Americanisation of competition policies. How much have their development been a process towards an 'American model' of anti-trust? In-depth studies of the roots of European Union competition policy reveal the extent of personal cooperation between European and US officials. The American pressure to implement a strong anti-trust policy after the war was both strong and direct in Germany and Japan, and these are usually cited as exemplars of American influence. The evidence shows, however, that shortly after new strict policies were implemented, their impact hampered recovery, and the policies were quickly, if quietly, adjusted. The competition policies that really worked in the post-war period then, were deep-rooted in the two countries' individual histories, political situations and economic structures.

Nonetheless, it is also clear, that internationally competition policy has converged. The debates on this issue have mostly concerned the gradual convergence of the EU member states' competition policy first through 'soft harmonisation' and later through more active demands for adopting common policies, but it has also occurred globally. To a large extent this is an obvious outcome of increasing contact and interaction in a world economy which includes elements of active harmonisation, gradual alignment and increasing market interactions. While it may be convenient to consider such change as a linear development towards more modern (and hence 'better') competition policy, as business historians we would caution against such a simplistic and potentially erroneous view.

The history of cartel registers also reminds us how far regulatory theory has progressed in the past century and a half. In the nineteenth century, the emergence of a new form of 'big' corporation; one that was large enough to dominate markets and impact on economies, initially left nation-states scrambling for the means to control and regulate them. While some countries like the US responded strongly against trusts and combines, others adopted more moderate policies. Smaller countries, and those with long traditions of family firms were more sanguine about the dangers posed by 'local' combinations and more concerned about external threats from international cartels. It took several decades of discussion, in both national and international fora, before individual countries began to adopt registers and other forms of business monitoring. In the process, administers, politicians as well as business men, learnt much about what constituted 'reasonable' and 'competitive' business behaviour. The boundaries of what government could, or should do, became clearer as policies were discussed, implemented and redrafted.

As regulations and attitudes changed, so did the opportunities presented by international trade. From a period of contraction in global trade between the wars, the coming of the registers also heralded the coming of more internationally open markets. This demanded a new level of supranational agreement and regulation. The lessons of the registers, however, remain. Businessmen, politicians, administrators and consumers now have a far better understanding of what constitutes 'acceptable' agreements and 'workable' competition today, compared with 50 years ago. Consumer advocacy groups, government administers and businesses have a far clearer understanding of what constitutes 'abuse' of market power and 'damage' to competitive processes. Governments, regulators and business people have a far better understanding of what 'works' in regulating firm behaviour, and distinguishing between what must be prohibited from what can be allowed to continue.

The content of the registers can also form a valuable source of information for studying cartel behaviour in specific industries, or how cartels and firms react to policy and regulatory changes. Indeed several chapters here have done exactly this. Research into the impact of anti-competitive behaviour on economic development; the interconnections of industries or the link between anti-competitive behaviour and sustainable business would all benefit from including information that remains under-explored in registers around the world. Although such material is never perfect, (as usual with historical sources), the registers are an under-utilised historical source for historians, economists and political scientists.

In the wake of the financial crisis, the recent calls for increased regulation and more pro-active state authorities are still to be fully played out. Simultaneously, new challenges emerge to test regulators. Whether the target is to require multinational businesses to pay the appropriate amounts of tax; or to ensure that firms abide by carbon emission standards, the need to design and apply appropriate regulations continues. The cartel registers and their history provide insightful and important lessons into the design and implementation of one form of business regulation that responded to a wide variety of firm and market forms.

Note

1   www.nobelprize.org/nobel_prizes/economic-sciences/laureates/2014/tirole-facts.html.

References

Aaltonen, E. 1953, *Kuluttajat yhteistyössä: Suomen osuuskauppaliikkeen vaiheet vuoteen 1917 ja katsaus edistysmielisen osuuskauppaliikkeen toimintaan sen jälkeen*, Kulutusosuuskuntien Keskusliitto, Helsinki.

Advisory Council to the Minister of Economics 1954, 'Report on Questions Concerning the Cartel Isssue', in *Advisory Council to the Minister of Economics, Reports from Dec. 1952 to Nov. 1954*, (ed.) Minister of Economics, Goettingen 1955.

Ahrens, R. and Wixforth, H. (eds) 2010, *Strukturwandel und Internationalisierung im Bankwesen seit den 1950er Jahren*, Steiner, Stuttgart.

Aldcroft, D. H. 1977, *From Versailles to Wall Street, 1919–1929*, Allen Lane, London.

Alfthan, F. 1921, 'Finländska karteller', *Ekonomiska Samfundets Tidskrift*, vol. VII, pp. 278–331.

Amacher, R., Sweeney, R. J. and Tollison, R. 1978, 'A Note on the Webb-Pomerene Law and the Webb-Cartels', *The Antitrust Bulletin*, vol. 23, no. 2, pp. 371–387.

Ambrosius, G. 1981, 'Die Entwicklung des Wettbewerbs als wirtschaftspolitisch relevante Norm und Ordnungsprinzip in Deutschland seit dem 19. Jahrhundert', *Jahrbuch für Sozialwissenschaft*, vol. 32, no. 2, pp. 154–201.

Andersen, K. 1937, *Rettens stilling til konkurransereguleringer*, Johan Grundt Tanum, Oslo.

Andersen, K. G. 2005, *Flaggskip i fremmed eie Hydro 1905–1945. Første bind av Hydros historie 1905–2005*, Pax, Oslo.

Annala V. 1953, 'Vähittäishintojen sidonnaisuus', *Kansantaloudellinen Aikakauskirja*, vol. 49 no. 1, pp. 19–30.

Asbeek Brusse, W. and Griffiths, R. 1997, 'Early Cartel Legislation and Cartel Policy in the Netherlands', *International Journal of Political Science*, vol. 32, no. 4, pp. 375–405.

Asbeek Brusse, W. and Griffiths, R. 1998, 'Paradise Lost or Paradise Regained', in *Competition Policies in Europe*, (ed.) S. Martin, Elsevier Science, Amsterdam, pp. 15–39.

Atiyah, P. S. 1985, *The Rise and Fall of Freedom of Contract*, Oxford University Press, Oxford.

Australian Treasury 2001, *Australia's Century since Federation at a Glance*, Economic Round-up, pp. 53–63.

Ballande, L. 1937, *Les Ententes économiques internationales: Étude monographique et statistique*, Librairie technique et économique, Paris.

Bannerman, R. 1985, 'Development of Trade Practices Law and Administration', *Australian Economic Review* vol. 3, no. 3, pp. 83–95.

Barbezat, D. 1989, 'Cooperation and Rivalry in the International Steel Cartel, 1926–1933', *The Journal of Economic History*, vol. 49, no. 2, pp. 435–447.

Barendregt, J. 1991, *Het mededingingsbeleid in Nederland: Konjunktuurgevoeligheid en effektiviteit*, Research Memorandum no. 17, Vrije Universiteit, Amsterdam.

Barjot, D. 1994, 'Introduction', in *International cartels revisited: Vues nouvelles sur les cartels internationaux, 1880–1980*, (ed.) D. Barjot, Editions du Lys, Caen, pp. 9–70.

Barjot, D. 2013, 'Les cartels, une voie vers l'intégration européenne? Le rôle de Louis Loucheur (1872–1931)', *Revue Economique*, vol. 64, no. 6, pp. 1043–1066.

Barros, P. P. and Mata, J. 1998, 'Competition Policy in Portugal', in *Competition Policies in Europe*, (ed.) S. Martin, Elsevier Science, Amsterdam, pp. 273–321.

Barton, A. D. 1963, 'The Proposed Legislation for the Control of Restrictive Trade Practices and Monopolies in Australia – an Appraisal', *Australian Economic Papers*, vol. 2, no. 2, pp. 125–150.

Barwick, G. 1963, 'Australian Proposals for the Control of Restrictive Trade Practices and Monopolies: Trade Practices in a Developing Economy', The G. L. Wood Memorial Lecture, University of Melbourne, 16 August.

Battarchajeya, A. 2012, 'India's New Antitrust Regime: The First Two Years of Enforcement', *The Antitrust Bulletin* vol. 57, no. 3, pp. 449–483.

Baums, T. H. 1990, *Kartellrecht in Preußen. Von der Reformära zur Gründerkrise*, Mohr Siebeck, Tübingen.

Beeman, M. L. 2002, *Public Policy and Economic Competition in Japan: Change and Continuity in Antitrust Policy, 1973–1995*, Routledge.

Beichmann, F. 1890, *Lov om handelsregistre, firma og prokura af 17de mai 1890 Utgivet med forklarende anmerkninger*, Fabritius, Kristiania.

Bennett, M. K. 1949, *International Commodity Stockpiling as an Economic Stabilizer*, Stanford University Press, New York.

Benni, A., Marlio, L., Lammers, C. and Meyer A. 1931a, *Etude sur les aspects économiques de différentes etentes industrielles internationales*, League of Nations, Geneva.

Benni, A., Marlio, L., Lammers, C. and Meyer A. 1931b, *Rapport Général sur les aspects économiques des ententes industrielles*, League of Nations, Geneva.

Berg, P. 2011, 'A Peak into the Swedish Cartel Register', Unpublished manuscript, Copenhagen Business School, Copenhagen.

Bergander, B. 1967, *Försäkringsväsendet i Sverige 1814–1914*, Lund.

Berger, F. 2000, 'La France, l'Allemagne et l'acier (1932–1952), De la stratégie des cartels à l'élaboration de la CECA', PhD thesis, Université Paris I Panthéon- Sorbonne.

Berger, F. 2006, 'Milieux économiques et États vis-à-vis des tentatives d'organisation des marchés européens dans les années trente', in *Europe organisée, Europe du Libre-échange, Fin XIXe siècle – Années 1960*, (eds) E. Bussière, M. Dumoulin and S. Schirmann, Peter Lang, Brussels, pp. 71–105.

Berghahn, V. 1984, 'Montanunion und Wettbewerb', *Geschichte und Gesellschaft*, special issue no. 10, pp. 247–270

Berghahn, V. 1985, *Unternehmer und Politik in der Bundesrepublik*, Suhrkamp, Frankfurt am Main.

Berghahn, V. 1986, *The Americanisation of West German Industry, 1945–1963*, Berg, New York.

Berghoff, H. 2004, *Moderne Unternehmensgeschichte: Eine themen- und theorieorientierte Einführung*, F. Schöningh, Paderborn.

Bergholm, P. 1920, 'Om utvecklingen av samarbete inom den svenska livförsäkringen åren 1866–1920', *Swedish Insurance Yearbook*, pp. 14–41.

Bernitz, U. 1969, *Marknadsrätt: en komparativ studie av marknadslagstiftningens utveckling och huvudlinjer*, Jurist- och samhällsvetareförbundet, Stockholm.

References 279

Bernitz, U. 1971, *Konkurrens och priser i Norden*, Jurist- och samhällsvetareförbundet, Stockholm.
Bernitz, U. 1993, *Den nya konkurrenslagen*, Juristförlaget, Stockholm.
Bertilorenzi, M. 2014, 'Business, Politics and Finance. The Rise and Fall of the International Aluminium Cartels', 1914–1945, *Business History*, vol. 56, no. 2, pp. 236–269.
Bervoets, J. A. A. 2000, M*ededingingsbeleid, PIVOT-rapport no. 93*, Rijksarchiefdienst PIVOT and Ministerie van Economische Zaken, The Hague.
Beyenburg-Weidenfeld, U. 1992, W*ettbewerbstheorie, Wirtschaftspolitik und Mittelstandsförderung 1948–1963: Die Mittelstandspolitik im Spannungsfeld zwischen wettbewerbstheoretischem Anspruch und wirtschaftspolitischem Pragmatismus*, Steiner, Stuttgart.
Binz, U. 1952, 'Kartellregister als Instrument der Kartellpolitik', PhD thesis, Bern.
Blachucki, M. 2013, 'Development and Goals of Competition Policy', *Ekonomia i Prawo*, vol. 12, no. 2, pp. 193–206.
Blaich, F. 1970, 'Die Anfänge der deutschen Antikartellpolitik zwischen 1897 und 1914', *Jahrbuch für Sozialwissenschaft*, vol. 21, no. 2, pp. 127–150.
Blaich, F. 1973, *Kartell- und Monopolpolitik im kaiserlichen Deutschland: Das Problem der Marktmacht im deutschen Reichstag zwischen 1879 und 1914*, Droste, Düsseldorf.
Bliss, M. 1973, 'Another Anti-trust Tradition: Canadian Anti-Combines Policy, 1889–1910', *Business History Review*, vol. 47, no. 2, pp. 177–188.
Blomberg, N. W. 1964, *Framsteg: Folksams uppkomst och utveckling*, Stockholm, Folksam.
Böhm, F. 1948, 'Das Reichsgericht und die Kartelle', Ordo. *Jahrbuch für die Ordnung von Wirtschaft und Gesellschaft*, vol. 1, pp. 212–245
Boje, P. and Kallestrup, M. 2004, *Marked, ervervsliv og stat Dansk konkurrencelovgivning og det store ervervsliv*, Aarhus Universitetsforlag, Aarhus.
Boksjö, A. and Lönnborg-Andersson, M. 1994, 'Competitive and Collusive Institutions in the Swedish Insurance Market', *Nordisk Försäkringstidskrift/Scandinavian Insurance Quarterly*, no. 2, pp. 139–159.
Borchardt, D. H. 1958, *Checklist of Royal Commissions, Select Committees of Parliament and Boards of Inquiry. Part I: Commonwealth of Australia 1900–1950*, Stone Copying Co, Cremorne, New South Wales.
Borchardt, D. H. 1970, *Checklist of Royal Commissions, Select Committees of Parliament and Boards of Inquiry. Part III. Victoria, 1856–1960*, Stone Copying Co., Cremorne, New South Wales.
Borrell, J. 1998, 'Spanish Competition Policy: A Case of Government's Response to Domestically Perceived Problems', *The Antitrust Bulletin*, vol. 43, no. 2, pp. 445–466.
Borrie, G. 1994, 'Restrictive Practices Control on the United Kingdom: Big Bangs and Lesser Detonations', in *Competition Law and Policy. Cases, Materials and Commentary*, (eds) T. Frazer and M. Waterson, Harvester Wheatsheaf, Hemel Hempstead, pp. 93–97.
Boserup, W. and Schlichtkrull, U. 1962, 'Alternative Approaches to the Control of Competition: An Outline of European Cartel Legislation and Its Administration', in *Competition, Cartels and their Regulation*, (ed.) J. P. Miller, North-Holland Publishing Company, Amsterdam.
Bouwens, B. and Dankers, J. 2012, *Tussen Concurrentie en Concentratie*, Boom, Amsterdam.
Brems, H. (ed.) 1951, *Konkurrens eller samverkan: ett diskussionsinlägg om kartell- och monopolproblemen*. SNS, Stockholm.
Brems, H. 1954, 'Scandinavia', in *Monopoly and their Competition and their Regulation*, (ed.) E. H. Chamberlain, Macmillan, London.

Brinch, L. W. 1935, *Oversikt over trust- og kartell-lovgivningen i fremmede land*, Fabritius og Sønners boktrykkeri, Kristiania (Oslo).
Brown, W. J. 1914, *Prevention and Control of Monopolies*, John Murray, London.
Bussière, E. 1994, 'La SDN, les cartels et l'organisation économique de l'Europe entre les deux guerres', in *International cartels revisited: Vues nouvelles sur les cartels internationaux, 1880–1980*, (ed.) D. Barjot, Editions du Lys, Caen, pp. 273–283.
Bussière, E. 1997, 'Les milieux économiques face à l'Europe au XXème siècle', *Journal of European Integration History*, vol. 3, no. 2, pp. 5–22.
Bussière, E. 2007, 'La Concurrence', in *La Commission européenne, 1958–1972*, (ed.) M. Dumoulin, European Community, Brussels, pp. 313–328.
Büthe, T. and Swank, G. 2007, *The Politics of Antitrust and Merger Review in the European Union: Institutional Change and Decisions from Messina to 2004*, Working Paper 142, Minda de Gunzburg Center for European Studies, Harvard University, Cambridge, MA.
Butlin, N. G., Barnard, A. and Pincus, J. J. 1982, *Government and Capitalism: Public and Private Choice in Twentieth Century Australia*, Allen and Unwin, Sydney.
Carlsson, K., Scheur, L. and Söderlind, E. 1995, *Konkurrenslagen*, Fritzes, Stockholm.
Cases, L. 1996, 'Competition Law and Policy in Spain: Implementation in an Interventionist Tradition', in *Regulating Europe*, (ed.) G. Majone, Routledge, London, pp. 180–201.
Cassel, G. 1927, *Les Tendances monopolisatrices dans l'industrie et le commerce au cours de ces dernières années: Caractères et causes de l'appauvrissement des nations*, League of Nations, Geneva.
Castberg, J. 1919, 'Trustkommisjonenen: To lovforslag', *Sociale Meddelelser*, pp. 33–47.
Cerretano, V. 2011, 'European Cartels and Technology Transfer: the Experience of the Rayon Industry, 1920 to 1940', *Zeitschrift für Unternehmensgeschichte*, vol. 56, no. 2, pp. 206–224
Cheffins, B 1989, 'The Development of Competition Policy, 1890–1940: A Re-Evaluation of a Canadian and American Tradition', *Osgoode Hall Law Journal*, vol. 27, no. 3, 1989, pp. 449–490.
Choi, Y. S. 2014, 'The Rule of Law in a Market Economy: Globalisation of Competition Law in Korea', *European Business Organization Law Review*, vol. 15, no. 3, pp. 419–437.
Christiansen, P. M., Nørgaard, A. S., Rommetvedt, H., Svensson, T., Thesen, G. and Öberg, P.-O. 2009, 'Varieties of Democracy: Interest Groups and Corporatist Committees' Scandinavian Policy Making', *Voluntas*, vol. 21, no. 1, pp. 22–40.
Cini, M. and McGowan, L. 2009, *Competition Policy in the European Union*, Palgrave Macmillan, Basingstoke.
Clavin, P. 2013, *Securing the World Economy: Reinventing the League of Nations 1920–1946*, Oxford University Press, Oxford.
Clavin, P. and Wessels, J. W. 2005, 'Transnationalism and the League of Nations: Understanding the Work of Its Economic and Financial Organisation', *Contemporary European History*, vol. 14, no. 4, pp. 465–492.
Clemensson, G. (ed.) 1948, *Svenska pappersbruksföreningen 1923–1948 Minnesskrift vid 50-årsjubileet*, Svenska pappersbruksföreningen, Stockholm.
Coates, A. 1987, *The Commerce in Rubber: The First 250 Years*. Oxford University Press, Oxford.
Collinge, J. 1969, *The Law Relating to the Control of Competition, Restrictive Trade Practices and Monopolies in New Zealand*, Sweet and Maxwell, Wellington.
Compston, H. 2003, 'Beyond Corporatism: A Configurational Theory of Policy Concertation', *European Policy of Political Research*, vol. 42, no. 3, pp. 787–809.

Connor, J. M. and Helmers, C. G. 2006, *Statistics on Modern and Private Cartels 1990–2005*, Working Paper no. 6–11, Purdue University, Indiana.

Conte, R. 1928, *Les Ententes Industrielles Internationales*, Rapport présenté à titre de documentation sur la demande du sous-comité des ententes industrielles internationales par la Chambre de Commerce Internationale, International Chamber of Commerce, Paris.

Cook, P. 1961, 'Trade Associations in South Australia', BEc(Hons) thesis, University of Adelaide

Coops, C. and Henrick, S. 2014, 'Australia: Overview', *Asia-Pacific Anti-trust Review*, http://globalcompetitionreview.com/reviews/60/sections/206/chapters/2329/australia-overview.

Cowen, D. V. 1950, 'A Survey of the Law Relating to the Control of Monopoly in South Africa', *The South African Journal of Economics*, vol. 18, no. 2, pp. 124–147.

Cox, H. 1981, 'Kartelle – Strukturanalyse, Wettbewerbswirkungen und wettbewerbspolitische Behandlung', in *Handbuch des Wettbewerbs: Wettbewerbstheorie, Wettbewerbspolitik, Wettbewerbsrecht*, (eds) H. Cox, U. Jens and K. Markert, Vahlen, Munich, pp. 225–269.

Cuff, R. D. 1973, *The War Industries Board: Business–Government Relations during World War I*, Johns Hopkins University Press, Baltimore.

Curli, B. 1990, 'L'Italia, la Società delle Nazioni e la discussione sugli accordi industriali internazionali, 1927–1931', *Rivista di Storia Economica*, vol. 7, no. 1, pp. 21–46.

Dabbah, M. 2011, *Competition Law and Policy in the Middle East*. Cambridge University Press, Cambridge.

D'Alessandro, M. 2007, 'Seeking Governance for World Markets: The League of Nations between Corporatism and Public Opinion, 1925–1929', paper presented at EBHA annual conference in Geneva.

Danielsen, R. 1984, *Borgerlig oppdemmingspolitikk: Høyres historie 1884–1984 Bind II*, Cappelen, Oslo.

Davis, J. S. 1946, 'Experience Under Intergovernmental Commodity Agreements, 1902–45', *The Journal of Political Economy*, vol. 54, no. 3., pp. 193–220.

De, O. 2010, 'Analysis of Cartel Duration: Evidence from EC Prosecuted Cartels', *International Journal of Economics and Business*, vol. 17, no. 1, pp. 33–65.

Decorzant, Y. 2011, *La Société des Nations et la naissance d'une conception de la régulation économique internationale*, Peter Lang, Brussels.

Decugis, H., Tschierschky, S. and Olds, R. E. 1930, *Etude sur le régime juridique des ententes industrielles*, League of Nations, Geneva.

De Jong, H. W. 1990, Nederland het kartelparadijs, *Economisch Statistische Berichten*, vol. 75, 3749, pp. 244–248.

Den Hoed, P., Buevink, J. and Keizer, A. G. 2007, *Op steenworp afstand, op de brug tussen wetenschap en politiek*, Amsterdam University Press, Amsterdam.

De Roos, W. A. A. M. 1969, *De economische machtspositie*, H. E. Stenfert Kroese N. V., Leiden.

De Rousiers, P. 1901, *Syndicats Industriels des producteurs en France et à l'étranger: Trusts, Cartells, Comptoirs*, Armand Collin, Paris.

De Rousiers, P. 1927, *Les Cartels et les trusts et leur évolution*, League of Nations, Geneva.

De Wolf, P. 1987, *Marktconcentratie en de gevolgen voor winstgevendheid en prijzen*, Eburon, Delft.

Dick, A. R. 1996, 'When Are Cartels Stable Contracts?', *Journal of Law and Economics*, vol. 39, no. 1, pp. 241–283.

Djelic, M.-L. 2002, 'Does Europe Mean Americanization? The Case for Competition', *Competition and Change*, vol. 6, no. 3, pp. 233–250.

Djelic, M.-L. 2005, 'From Local Legislation to Global Structuring Frame: the Story of Antitrust', *Global Social Policy*, vol. 5, no. 1, pp. 55–76.

Domeratzky, L. 1928, *The International Cartel Movement*, US Bureau of Commerce, Washington DC.

Don, H., Janssen, D., Schik M. and van Sinderen, J. 2013, 'De economie van het toezicht', *Economisch Statistische Berichten*, vol. 98, 4669, pp. 586–589.

Dore, R. 1986, *Flexible Rigidities: Industrial Policy and Structural Adjustment in the Japanese Economy 1970–1980*, Athlone Press, London.

Dowdle, M. 2013, The Regulatory Geography of Market Competition in Asia (and Beyond): A Preliminary Mapping', in *Asian Capitalism and the Regulation of Competition. Towards a Regulatory Geography of Global Competition Law*, (eds) M. Dowdle, J. Gillespie and I. Maher, Cambridge University Press, Cambridge.

Dowdle, M., Gillespie, J. and Maher, I. (eds) 2013, *Asian Capitalism and the Regulation of Competition: Towards a Regulatory Geography of Global Competition Law*. Cambridge University Press, Cambridge.

Driehuis, W., van Heeringen, A. and Wolff, P. de 1975, 'Price Formation and the Inflationary Process in a Small Open Economy (The Netherlands)', *The Economist*, vol. 123, no. 4, pp. 660–722.

Dullaart, M. H. J. 1984, *Regeling of vrijheid, Nederlands economisch denken tussen de wereldoorlogen*, Offsetdrukkerij Kanters B. V., Alblasserdam.

Dumez, H. and Jeunemître, A. 1996, 'The Convergence of Competition Policies in Europe: Internal Dynamics and External Imposition', in *National Diversity and Global Capitalism*, (eds) S. Berger and R. Dore, Cornell University Press, Ithaca, pp. 216–238.

Dyster, B. and Meredith, D. 1990, *Australia in the International Economy in the Twentieth Century*, Cambridge University Press, Cambridge,

Eatwell, J. and Taylor, L. 2000, *Global Finance Risk: The Case for International Regulation*, W. W. Norton, New York,

ECSC High Authority (Haute Autorité de la CECA) 1963, *La CECA, 1952–1962. Les dix premières années d'une intégration partielle*, European Communities, Luxembourg.

Eddy, A. J. 1912, *New Competition: An Examination of the Conditions Underlying the Radical Change that is Taking Place in the Commercial and Industrial World – the Change from a Competitive to a Cooperative Basis*, D. Appleton, New York.

Edwards, C. D. 1946, 'An Appraisal of the Antitrust Laws', *The American Economic Review*, vol. 36, no. 2, pp. 172–189.

Edwards, C. D. 1967, *Control of Cartels and Monopolies: An International Comparison*, Oceana Publications, New York.

Eggmann, E. 1945, *Der Staat und die Kartelle: Eine international vergleichende Untersuchung*, Ginsberger, Zürich.

Englund, K. 1982, *Försäkring och fusioner: Skandia, Skåne, Svea, Thule, Öresund 1855–1980*, Skandia, Stockholm.

Enskilt försäkringsväsen 1954, *Hur det vuxit fram och hur det övervakas*, Swedish Insurance Inspectorate, Stockholm.

Epland, G. S. 2012, 'Det norske kartellregisteret 1920–1939 og statens rolle i økonomien', MA thesis, University of Bergen, Bergen.

Espeli, H. 1990, 'Fra hest til hestekrefter', *Studier i politiske og økonomiske rammebetingelser for mekaniseringen av norsk jordbruk 1910–1960, Melding nr. 2* Institutt for økonomi og samfunnsfag Norges Landbrukshøgskole, Ås.

Espeli, H. 1993, *Fra Thagaard til Egil Bakke: Hovedlinjer i norsk konkurransepolitikk 1954–1990*, SNF-rapport 39/93, Bergen.

Espeli, H. 1995, *Private konkurransereguleringer innenfor forsikringsbransjen i Norge 1900–1985 og myndighetenes holdning til disse*, Norges Forskningsråd, Oslo.

Espeli, H. 2002, 'Perspectives on the Distinctiveness of Norwegian Price and Competition Policy in the XXth Century', *Journal of European Economic History*, vol. 31, no. 3, pp. 621–660.

Espeli, H. 2005, *Norsk telekommunikasjonshistorie bind 2: Det statsdominerte teleregimet (1920–1970)*, Gyldendal, Oslo.

Espeli, H. 2013, 'Economic Consequences of the German Occupation of Norway, 1940–1945', *Scandinavian Journal of History*, vol. 38, no. 4, pp. 502–524.

Espeli, H., Bergh, T. and Rønning, A. 2006, *Melkens pris - perspektiver på meierisamvirkets historie*, Tun forlag, Oslo.

Eucken, W. 1949, 'Die Wettbewerbsordnung und ihre Verwirklichung', *Ordo: Jahrbuch für die Ordnung von Wirtschaft und Gesellschaft*, vol. 2, pp. 1–99.

European Commission 1962, *Communication Relating to the Application of Article 85 of the Treaty to certain Exclusive Distribution Agreements*, OJ 113, 9 November, pp. 2627–2628.

European Commission 1987, *Sixteenth Report on Competition Policy*, European Communities, Luxembourg.

Evenett, S., Levenstein, M. and Suslow, V. 1997, 'International Cartel Enforcement: Lessons from the 1990s', *The World Economy*, vol. 20, no. 9, pp. 1221–1245.

Eyre, S. and Lodge, M. 2000, National Tunes and a European Melody? Competition Law Reform in the UK and Germany', *Journal of European Public Policy*, vol. 7, no. 1, pp. 63–79.

Fair Trade Commission (ed.) 1968, *The History of Antimonopoly Policy for Twenty Years*, Printing Bureau, Ministry of Finance, Tokyo [公正取引委員会編『独占禁止政策二十年史』大蔵省印刷局, 1968年]

Fair Trade Commission (ed.) 1977, *The History of Antimonopoly Policy for Thirty Years*, Fair Trade Commission, Tokyo [公正取引委員会編『独占禁止政策三十年史』公正取引委員会, 1977年]

Fair Trade Commission (ed.) 1997a, *A History of Antimonopoly Policy for Fifty Years*, Fair Trade Commission, Tokyo [公正取引委員会編『独占禁止政策50年の歩み』公正取引委員会, 1997年]

Fair Trade Commission (ed.) 1997b, *The History of Antimonopoly Policy for Fifty Years*, Printing Bureau, Ministry of Finance, Tokyo [公正取引委員会編『独占禁止政策五十年史』大蔵省印刷局, 1997年]

Fasting, K 1967, *Den norske papirindustris historie: 1893–1968*, Norske papirfabrikanters felleskontor, Oslo.

Fatima, S. 2012, 'Competition Law in Pakistan: Brief History, Aspirations and Characteristics', *Commonwealth Law Bulletin*, vol. 38, no. 1, pp. 42–62.

Fear, J. 1997, 'German Capitalism', in *Creating Modern Capitalism: How Entrepreneurs, Companies, and Countries Triumphed in Three Industrial Revolutions*, (ed.) T. K. McCraw, Harvard University Press, Cambridge, MA.

Fear, J. 2006, *Cartels and Competition: Neither Markets nor Hierarchies*, discussion paper 07-011, Harvard Business School, Cambridge, MA.

Fear, J. 2008, 'Cartels', in *Handbook of Business History*, (eds) G. Jones and J. Zeitlin, Oxford University Press, Oxford, pp. 268–292.

Fellman, S. 2008, 'Growth and Investment: Finnish Capitalism, 1850–2005', in *Creating Nordic Capitalism – The Development of a Competitive Periphery*, (eds) S. Fellman et al., Palgrave Macmillan, Basingstoke.

Fellman, S. 2010, 'Kilpailupolitiikka koordinoidussa markkinataloudessa – Kartelli- ja kilpailulainsäädäntö Suomessa 1958–1988 institutionaalistaloushistoriallisesta näkökulmasta', *Kansantaloudellinen Aikakauskirja*, vol. 106, no. 2, pp. 141–161.

Fellman, S. and Sandberg, P. 2015, 'Policy Concertation in Competition Policy in Two Corporatist Economies: The Case of Finland and Sweden, 1946–1992', unpublished manuscript.

Fellman, S. and Shanahan, M. 2011, 'A Comparison of Cartel Registers and Competition in Finland and Australia after World War II', Paper presented at Third European Congress on World and Global History, 14–17 April, London.

Folksams försäkringsutredningsbetänkande, 1962, *Folksams försäkringsutredningsbetänkande*, Folksam, Stockholm.

Fraas, A. G. and Greer, D. F. 1977, 'Market Structure and Price Collusion: An Empirical Analysis', *Journal of Industrial Economics*, vol. 26, no. 1, pp. 21–44.

Fraboulet, D. 2007, *Quand les patrons s'organisent: stratégies et pratiques de l'Union des industries métallurgiques et minières, 1901–1950*, Villeneuve-d'Ascq, Presses Universitaires du Septentrion.

Frazer, T. and Waterson, M. (eds) 1994, *Competition Law and Policy: Cases, Materials and Commentary*, Harvester Wheatsheaf, Hemel Hempstead.

Fredrikson, V., Hildebrand, K., Lundberg, F. and Odhnoff, W. 1972, *Framtiden Livförsäkringsaktiebolag: De Förenade, Framtiden, Victoria, Minnesskrift*, Trygg-Hansa, Stockholm.

Freyer, T. 1992, *Regulating Big Business Antitrust in Great Britain and America, 1880–1990*, Cambridge University Press, Cambridge.

Freyer, T. 2006, *Anti-trust and Global Capitalism, 1930–2000*, Cambridge University Press. Cambridge.

Fry, J. D. 2000, 'Struggling to Teethe: Japanese Antitrust Enforcement Regime Law and Policy', *International Business*, vol. 32, no. 4, pp. 825–857.

Fujita, T. 1988, 'Local Trade Associations (Dogyo Kumiai) in Prewar Japan', in *Trade Associations in Business History*, (eds) H. Yamazaki and M. Miyamoto, University of Tokyo Press, Tokyo.

Furnish, D. B. 1971, 'Chilean Antitrust Law', *The American Journal of Comparative Law*, vol. 19, no. 3, pp. 464–488.

Gallo, J. C., Craycraft, J. L., Dau-Schmidt, K. and Parker, C. A. 2000, 'Department of Justice Antitrust Enforcement, 1955–1997: An Empirical Study', *Review of Industrial Organization*, vol. 17, no. 1, pp. pp. 75–133.

Gao, B. 1997, *Economic Ideology and Japanese Industrial Policy: Developmentalism from 1931 to 1965*, Cambridge University Press, New York.

Geelhoed, L. A. 1996, '1995: conjunctuurherstel of economisch herstel?', *Economisch Statistische Berichten*, vol. 80, 3991, pp. 4–8.

Gentle, D. G. 1979, 'Australian Competition Policy 1900–1974: the Political Economy of the Public Interest', PhD thesis, University of Queensland.

Gerber, D. J. 1998, *Law and Competition in Twentieth Century Europe: Protecting Prometheus*, Oxford University Press, Oxford.

Gerber, D. J. 2007, 'Two Forms of Modernization in European Competition Law'. *Fordham International Law Journal*, vol. 31, no. 5, pp. 1235–1265.

Gerber, D. J. 2010, *Global Competition: Law, Markets and Globalization*, Oxford University Press, Oxford.

Godfrey, J. F. 1987, *Capitalism at War: Industrial Policy and Bureaucracy in France, 1914–1918*, Berg, New York.

Goldstein, E. E. 1963, *American Enterprise and Scandinavian Antitrust Law*, University of Texas Press, Austin.
Goodhart, C. A. E. 2008, 'The Regulatory Response to the Financial Crisis', *Journal of Financial Stability*, vol. 4, no. 4, pp. 351–358.
Goschler, C., Buchheim, C. H. and Bührer, W. 1989, 'Der Schumanplan als Instrument französischer Stahlpolitik: Zur historischen Wirkung eines falschen Kalküls', *Vierteljahrsheft für Zeitgeschichte*, vol. 37, no. 2, pp. 171–206.
Grabosky, P. and Braithwaite, J. 1986, *Of Manners Gentle: Enforcement Strategies of Australian Business Regulatory Agencies*, Oxford University Press, Melbourne.
Gradus, R. 1996, 'The Economic Effects of Extending Shop Opening Hours', *Journal of Economics*, vol. 64, no. 3, pp. 247–263.
Grenholm, Å. 1933, *Svenska Brandtariffföreningen: Några ord med anledning av dess 60-åriga tillvaro den 28 november 1933*, Norstedt, Stockholm.
Grip, G. 1987, *Vill du frihet eller tvång? Svensk försäkringspolitik 1935–1945*, Almqvist and Wiksell, Uppsala.
Grip, G. 2009, *Folksam 1908–2008: Försäkringsrörelsen, vol. 1*, Informationsförlaget, Stockholm.
Grönfors, K. 1969, *Lagstiftningen mot konkurrensbegränsning*, Akademiförlaget, Göteborg.
Großfeld, B. 1979, 'Zur Kartellrechtsdiskussion vor dem Ersten Weltkrieg', in *Wissenschaft und Kodifikation des Privatrechts im 19. Jahrhundert, Vol. IV: Eigentum und industrielle Entwicklung, Wettbewerbsordnung und Wettbewerbsrecht*, (eds) H. Coing and W. Wilhelm, Klostermann, Frankfurt am Main, pp. 255–291.
Gupta, B. 2005, 'Why did Collusion Fail? The Indian Jute Industry in the Inter-War Years', *Business History* vol. 47, no. 4, pp. 532–552.
Haaland, A. 1992, *Den norske trustloven 1913–1939: Trustlovens historie frem til 1926*, Working paper no. 6/1992, NHH, Bergen.
Haaland, A. 1994, *Fra konsesjonslov til 'midlertidig trustlov': norsk konkurransepolitikk 1905–1926*, SNF report no. 20/1994, NHH Bergen.
Hacker, J. S. 2002, *The Divided Welfare State: The Battle of Public and Private Social Benefits in the United States*, Cambridge University Press, New York.
Hadley, E. M. 1970, *Antitrust in Japan*, Princeton University Press, Princeton.
Hadley, E. M. and Kuwayama, P. H. 2002, *Memoir of a Trustbuster: A Lifelong Adventure with Japan*, University of Hawaii Press, Honolulu.
Haffner, R. C. G. and van Bergeijk, P. A. G. 1996, *Regulatory Reform in the Netherlands, Macroeconomic Consequences and Industry Effects*, Onderzoeksreeks directie Marktwerking, The Hague.
Hägg, P. G. T. 1999, *An Institutional Analysis of Insurance Regulation: The Case of Sweden*, Lund Economic Studies no. 75, Lund.
Haley, J. 2001, *Antitrust in Germany and Japan: The First Fifty Years, 1947–1998*, University of Washington Press, Washington DC.
Hambloch, S. 2009, *Europäische Integration und Wettbewerbspolitik: Die Frühphase der EWG*, Nomos, Baden-Baden.
Hannah, L. 1976, *The Rise of Corporate Economy: The British Experience*, Johns Hopkins University Press, Baltimore.
Hansen, P. H. 2014, 'From Finance Capitalism to Financialization: A Cultural and Narrative Perspective on 150 years of Financial History', *Enterprise and Society*, vol. 15, no. 4, pp. 605–642.
Hara, T. 1994, 'La conférence économique internationale de 1927 et ses effets sur la formation des cartels internationaux', in *International cartels revisited: Vues nouvelles*

sur les cartels internationaux, 1880–1980, (ed.) D. Barjot, Editions du Lys, Caen, pp. 265–272.

Harding, C. and Joshua, J. 2010, (2nd ed) *Regulating Cartels in Europe: A Study of Legal Control of Corporate Delinquency*, Oxford University Press, Oxford.

Harrison, B. 1893, *Public Papers and Addresses of Benjamin Harrison, Twenty-Third President of the United States*, Government Printing Office, Washington, DC.

Haselbach, D. 1991, *Autoritärer Liberalismus und soziale Marktwirtschaft: Gesellschaft und Politik im Ordoliberalismus*, Nomos, Baden-Baden.

Hashino, T. and Kurosawa, T. 2012, 'Beyond Marshallian Agglomeration Economies: The Roles of Trade Associations in Meiji Japan', *Business History Review*, vol. 7, Autumn, pp. 489–513.

Haucap, J., Heimeshoff, U. and Schultz, L. M. 2010, *Legal and Illegal Cartels in Germany between 1958 and 2004*, discussion paper no. 8, Dice, Dusseldorf.

Hawk, B. 1980, 'EEC and US Competition Policies: Contrast and Convergence', in *Enterprise Law of the 80s: European and American Perspectives on Competition and Industrial Organization*, (eds) F. Rowe *et al.*, American Bar Association, Chicago, pp. 39–62.

Hawk, B. 1995, 'System Failure: Vertical Restraints and EC Competition Law', *Common Market Law Review*, vol. 32, no. 4, pp. 973–989.

Hay, G. A. and Kelley, D. 1974, 'An Empirical Survey of Price Fixing Conspiracies', *Journal of Law and Economics*, vol. 17, no. 1, pp. 13–38.

Helander, V. 1979, 'Interest Representation in the Finnish Committee System in the Postwar Era', *Scandinavian Political Studies*, vol. 2, no. 3, pp. 221–237.

Hem, P. 2012, *Megleren: Paal Berg 1873–1968*, Aschehoug, Oslo.

Hesse, J. 2013, *Wirtschaftsgeschichte: Entstehung und Wandel der modernen Wirtschaft*, Campus, Frankfurt.

Hesse, J. 2015, 'Abkehr vom Kartelldenken? Das Gesetz gegen Wettbewerbsbeschränkungen als ordnungspolitische und wirtschaftstheoretische Zäsur der Ära Adenauer', in *Der Rheinische Kapitalismus und die Ära Adenauer: Rhöndorfer Gespräche Bd. 26*, (eds) H. G. Hockerts and G. Schulz, Bonn.

Hexner, E. 1946, *International Cartels*, North Carolina University Press, Chapel Hill.

Hilger, S. 2005, 'Zur Genese des "German Model": Die Bedeutung des Ordoliberalismus für die Ausgestaltung der bundesdeutschen Wettbewerbsordnung nach dem Zweiten Weltkrieg', in *Finanzmarkt-Kapitalismus: Analysen zum Wandel von Produktionsregimen*, (ed.) P. Windolf, Sonderheft 45 der Kölner Zeitschrift für Soziologie und Sozialpsychologie, Wiesbaden, pp. 222–241.

Hillman, J. 2010, *The International Tin Cartel*, Routledge, London.

Hilson, M. 2010, 'The Nordic Consumer Co-operative Movements in International Perspective, 1890–1939', in *Nordic Associations in a European Perspective*, (eds) R. Alapuro and H. Stenius, Nomos, Baden-Baden, pp. 215–240.

Hirano, S. 2011, 'Coordination of Plant Investment and Growing Overcapacity in the Petrochemical Industry Following the Recession Cartels (1972–1985)', *Socio-Economic History*, vol. 77, no. 1, Tokyo [平野創「石油化学工業における投資調整と設備過剰の深化」『社会経済史学』第77巻第1号, 2011年].

Hirsch, J. 1926, *National and International Monopolies from the Point of View and Labour: the Consuming Public and Rationalisation*, Preparatory Committee for the International Economic Conference, League of Nations, Geneva,.

Hirsch, J. 1927, *Monopoles Nationaux et Internationaux du point de vue des travailleurs, des consommateurs et de la rationalisation*, League of Nations, Geneva.

Hirschfeldt, J. 2008, *1766 års tryckfrihetsförordning och offentlighetsprincipens utveckling*, http://johanhirschfeldt.files.wordpress.com/2008/12/1766tf.pdf

Hodne, F. 1989, *God handel: Norges Handelsstands Forbund gjennom 100 år*, Norges Handelsstands Forbund, Oslo.

Hoerman, B. and Mavroidis, P. 2003, 'Economic Development, Competition Policy and the World Trade Organization', *Journal of World Trade*, vol. 37, no. 1, pp. 1–27.

Holmberg, S. 1981, *Mot monopolisering? NO:s verksamhet under 25 år*, Nordstedts, Stockholm.

Hovland, E. 1995, *Samhold mot avhold*, Bergen.

H. R. 1968, 'Vielä monopoleista', *Suomen Osuustoimintalehti*, vol. 58, no. 1, pp. 32–33.

Hunter, A. 1961, 'Restrictive Practices and Monopolies in Australia', *The Economic Record*, vol. 37, no. 77, pp. 25–49.

Hunter, A. 1963, 'Restrictions of Competition in New Zealand', *The Economic Record*, vol. 39, no. 86, pp. 131–141.

Hyytinen, A. and Toivanen, O. 2010, 'Kilpailunrajoitukset Suomessa 1958–1992', *Kansantaloudellinen Aikakauskirja*, vol. 106, no. 2, pp. 127–140.

Hyytinen, A., Steen, F. and Toivanen, O. 2011, *Cartels Uncovered*, working paper no. 08/11, Norwegian School of Economics and Business Administration.

Imamura, S. 1993, *Introduction to the Antimonopoly Law of Japan*, 4th edition, Yuhikaku, Tokyo [今村成和『独占禁止法入門〔第4版〕』有斐閣, 1993年]

International Chamber of Commerce 1926, *Rapport de la Commission des entraves au Commerce présenté au Comité Préparatoire de la conférence économique de la Société des Nations*, brochure no. 44, International Chamber of Commerce, Paris.

International Chamber of Commerce 1937, *Ententes Internationales – Congrès de Berlin – 1937*, document no. 4, International Chamber of Commerce, Paris.

Isay, R. 1930, 'Die Entwicklung der deutschen und ausländischen Kartellgesetzgebungen', *Zeitschrift für ausländisches und internationales Privatrecht*, vol. 4, no. 1, pp. 1–47.

Isopuro, A. 1964, 'Uusi kartellilakiehdotus', *Suomen Osuustoimintalehti*, vol. 54, no. 2, pp. 58–62.

Jaffe, J. 1967, 'Cartel Control in Israel', *Antitrust Bulletin*, vol. 12, no. 3, pp. 931- 948.

James, H. 2001, *The End of Globalisation: Lessons from the Great Depression*, Harvard University Press, Cambridge, MA.

Joelson, M. R. 2006, *An International Antitrust Primer: A Guide to the Operation of United States, European Union, and Other Key Competition Laws in the Global Economy*, Kluwer Law International, The Netherlands.

Johnson, A. M . 1959, 'Theodore Roosevelt and the Bureau of Corporations', *Mississippi Valley Historical Review*, vol. 45 no. 4, pp. 571–590.

Johnson, C. 1982, *MITI and the Japanese Miracle: The Growth of Industrial Policy, 1925–1975*, Stanford University Press, Stanford.

Jonung, L. 1993, 'Riksbankens penningpolitik 1945–1990', in *Från räntereglering till inflationsnorm*, (ed.) L. Werin, SNS, Stockholm, pp. 287–419.

Jonung, L. 1999, 'Med backspegeln som kompass – om stabiliseringspolitik som läroprocess', *Rapport till ESO – Expertgruppen för studier i offentlig ekonomi, Ds (1999:9)*, Stockholm.

Jüring, R. 1978, *Folksam: En berättelse om ett folkrörelseföretags roll i utvecklingen från ofärd till välfärd*, Folksam, Stockholm.

Jüring, R. 1983, *Det kooperativa alternativet i försäkring: Folksam 75 år 1908–1983*, Folksam, Stockholm.

Kantzenbach, E. 1967, *Die Funktionsfähigkeit des Wettbewerbs*, Vanderhoeck u. Ruprecht, Göttingen.

Karmel, P. H. and Brunt, M. 1963, *The Structure of the Australian Economy*, F. W. Cheshire, Melbourne.
Kelleher, G. W. 1960, 'The National "Antitrust" Laws of Europe', *Section of Antitrust Law: Proceedings at the annual meeting*, vol. 17, pp. 506–518.
Keneley, M. 2002, 'The Origins of Formal Collusion in Australian Fire Insurance, 1870–1920', *Australian Economic History Review*, vol. 42, no. 1, pp. 54–76.
Kenwood, A. G. 1995, *Australian Economic Institutions since Federation: An Introduction*, Oxford University Press, Melbourne.
Kessler, W. C. 1934, 'The New German Cartel Legislation: July 15, 1933', *American Economic Review*, vol. 24 no. 3, pp. 477–482.
Kessler, W. C. 1936, 'German Cartel Regulation under the Decree of 1923', *The Quarterly Journal of Economics*, vol. 50, no. 4, pp. 681–682.
Kestenbaum, L. 1973, 'Israel's Restrictive Trade Practices Law: Antitrust Misadventures in a Small Developing Country'. *Israel Law Review* vol. 8, iss. 3, pp. 411–465.
Kikkawa, T. 1994, 'The Relationship between the Government and Companies in Japan during and after World War II', in *World War II and the Transformation of Business Systems*, (eds) J. Sakudo and T. Shiba, University of Tokyo Press, Tokyo, pp. 59–80.
Kili, T. 1993, *Den borgerlige sosialisten: Wilhelm L. Thagaard 1917–1945*, Universitetet i Oslo, Oslo.
Klein, J. 1928, 'International Cartels', *Foreign Affairs*, vol. 6, no. 3, pp. 448–458.
Kleverman, A. and Lönnborg, M. 2000, 'Den svenska försäkringsföreningen – I det förgångna och i framtiden', in *Svensk försäkrings framtid: Svenska Försäkringsföreningen 125 år*, (eds) C. Bratt, A. Kleverman and E. Strömbäck, Swedish Insurance Society, Stockholm, pp. 157–167.
Knauth, O. 1914, *The Policy of the United States Towards Industrial Monopoly*, Columbia University, New York.
Knoph, R. 1926, *Trustloven av 1926 med kommentarer*, Norges Industriforbund, Oslo.
Koncentrationsutredningen 1968, *Vem äger makten: Fakta om makt och ägande ur koncentrationsutredningen*, Prisma, Stockholm.
Korah, V. 1982, *Competition Law of Britain and the Common Market*, Martinus Nijhoff Publishers, The Hague, pp. 284–5.
Korah, V. 1986, *An Introductory Guide to EEC Competition Law and Practice*, ESC, Oxford.
Korah, V. 1994, *An Introductory Guide to EEC Competition Law and Practice*, Sweet and Maxwell, London.
Kovacic, W. E. and Shapiro C. 2000, 'Antitrust Policy: A Century of Economic and Legal Thinking', *Journal of Economic Perspectives*, vol. 14, no. 1, pp. 43–60.
Kremers, J. J. M. 1991, Naar een sterkere binnenlandse groeidynamiek, *Economisch Statistische Berichten*, vol. 76, 3838, pp. 1228–1232.
Kudo, A. 1993, 'Introduction', in *International Cartels in Business History*, (eds) A. Kudo and T. Hara, Tokyo University Press, Tokyo, pp. 1–24 .
Kuin, P., Becker, H. M. and Admiraal, P. H. 1982, *Bij het scheiden van de markt: beschouwingen bij het academische afscheid van Prof. Drs. H. W. Lambers*, Stichting Maatschappij en Onderneming, The Hague.
Kuipers, S. K. 1991, *Marktwerking en werkloosheid in Nederland in de jaren dertig en tachtig*, Koninklijke Nederlandse Academie van de Wetenschappen, Amsterdam.
Kuisel, R. F. 1981, *Capitalism and the State in Modern France: Renovation and Economic Management in the Twentieth Century*, Cambridge University Press, London.

References 289

Kurosawa, T. 2009, 'Transformation of the Japanese Industrial Policy in the Age of Deregulation and Globalization', in *Neupositionierung regionaler Führungskrafte: Japan und Deutschland*, (eds) W. Klenner and H. Watanabe, Peter Lang, Frankfurt am Main.

Kurzlechner, W. 2008, *Fusionen, Kartelle, Skandale: Das Bundeskartellamt als Wettbewerbshüter und Verbraucheranwalt*, FinanzBuch Verlag, Münich.

Kuuse, J. and Olsson, K. 2000, *Ett sekel med Skandia*, Skandia, Stockholm.

Kylebäck, H. 1974, *Konsumentkooperation och industrikarteller*, Rabén and Sjögren, Stockholm.

Laakso, J. 1942, *Ajankohtaisia osuuskaupallisia talouspoliittisia kysymyksiä*, Kuluttajaosuuskuntien Keskusliitto, Helsinki.

Lamoreaux, N 1985, *The Great Merger Movement in American Business, 1895–1905*, Cambridge University Press, Cambridge.

Lapidus, J. 2013, 'Why Such a Permissive Attitude towards Monopolistic Associations? Social Democracy up to the First Swedish Law on Cartels in 1925', *Scandinavian Journal of History*, vol. 38, no. 1, pp. 65–88.

Larsson, M. 1998, *Staten och kapitalet: Det svenska finansiella systemet under 1990-talet*, SNS, Stockholm.

Larsson, M. and Lönnborg, M. 2010, 'The History of Insurance Companies in Sweden: 1855–2005', in *Encuentro Internacional sobre la Historia del Seguro*, (ed.) L. C. de las Cagigas, Fundació Mapfre, Madrid, pp. 197–237.

Larsson, M. and Lönnborg, M. 2014, *SCOR Sweden Re: 100 Years of Swedish (Re)Insurance History*, Dialogos, Stockholm.

Larsson, M. and Lönnborg, M. 2015, 'The Survival and Success of Swedish Mutual Insurers', in *Corporate Forms and Organisational Choice in International Insurance*, (eds) R. Pearson and T. Yoneyama, Oxford University Press, Oxford.

Larsson, M., Lönnborg, M. and Svärd, S. E. 2005, *Den svenska försäkringsmodellens uppgång och fall*, Swedish Insurance Society, Stockholm.

League of Nations 1927, *International Economic Conference: Resolutions Adopted by the Assembly*, September. 24. A. 117. 1927. II (B).

Leboutte, R. 2008, *Histoire économique et sociale de la construction européenne*, Peter Lang, Brussels.

Leifmann, R. 1913, *Karteller och truster*, Nordstedt, Stockholm.

Lenel, H. 1978, 'Konzentration', in *Handwörterbuch der Wirtschaftswissenschaft*, vol. 4, (eds) W. Albers et al., pp. 540–656.

Leucht, B. 2009, 'Transantlantic Policy Networks in the Creation of the First European Anti-Trust Law. Mediating between American Anti-trust and German Ordo-Liberalism', in *The History of European Union: The Origin of Trans- and Supranational Polity, 1950–72*, (eds) W. Kaiser, B. Leucht and M. Rasmussen, Routledge, Abingdon, pp. 56–73.

Leucht, B. 2010, 'Expertise and the Creation of a Constitutional Core Europe: Transatlantic Policy Networks in the Schuman Plan Negotiations', in *Transnational Networks in Regional Integration. Governing Europe, 1945–83*, (eds) M. Gehler, W. Kaiser and B. Leucht, Palgrave Macmillan, Basingstoke, pp. 18–37.

Levenstein, M. C. and Suslow, V. Y. 2006, 'What Determines Cartel Success?', *Journal of Economic Literature*, vol. 44, no. 1, pp. 43–95.

Levine, R. 2012, The Governance of Financial Regulation: Reform Lessons from the Recent Crisis, *International Review of Finance*, vol. 12, no. 1, pp. 39–56.

Lewin, L. 1992, *Samhället och de organiserade intressena*, Norstedts juridikförlag, Stockholm.

Liepmann, H. 1938, *Tariff Levels and the Economic Unity of Europe: An Examination of Tariff Policy, Export Movements and the Economic Integration of Europe, 1913–1931*, Allen and Unwin, London.

Linder B. J. and Sakar, A. 1971, 'Pakistan's Monopolies and Restrictive Practices Ordinance', *The Antitrust Bulletin*, vol. 16, no. 3, pp. 569–584.

Lindström, Y. and Strömbäck, E. 1983, 'Den nya marknadsföringsöverenskommelsen', *Nordisk Försäkringstidskrift/Scandinavian Insurance Quarterly*, no. 3, pp. 231–237.

Ljunggren, A. 1912, *Ekonomiska sammanslutningar av monopolistisk natur i Sverige*, Norstedt, Stockholm.

Löffler, B. 2002, *Soziale Marktwirtschaft und administrative Praxis*, Franz Steiner, Stuttgart.

Lönnborg, M. 2009, *Förenade Liv de första 60 åren*, Förenade Liv Gruppförsäkrings AB, Stockholm.

Lovasy, G. 1946, *International Cartels: A League of Nations Memorandum*, United Nations, Department of Economic Affairs, Lake Success and New York.

Lowe, P. 2009, 'Competition policy Institutions for the Twenty First Century: The Experience of the European Commission and the Directorate General for Competition', in *Competition Policy in the EU Fifty Years from the Treaty of Rome*, (ed.) X. Vives, Oxford University Press, Oxford, pp. 21–42.

Lundqvist, T. 2003, *Konkurrensvisionens framväxt: Konkurrenspolitik, intressen och politisk kultur*, Institutet för framtidsstudier: Stockholm.

MacGregor, D. H. 1927, *Les cartels internationaux*, League of Nations, Geneva.

Maclachan D. L. and Shaw, D. 1967, *Competition Policy in the European Community*, Oxford University Press, London.

Maddox, R. F. 2001, *The War Within World War II: The United States and International Cartels*, Praeger, Westport.

Mäenpää, O. 2008, *Julkisuusperiaate*, WSOY, Helsinki.

Maetschke, M. 2008, *Ursprünge der Zwangskartellgesetzgebung: Der Entwurf eines Gesetzes über den Absatz von Kalisalzen vom 12. Dezember 1909*, Nomos, Baden-Baden.

Maitland-Walker, J. (ed.) 1984, *International Anti-Trust Law, volume 1: A Review of National Laws*, ESC, Oxford.

Marlio, L. 1930, 'Les Ententes Industrielles', *Revue de Paris*, vol. 37, no. 1, pp. 829–852.

Martenius, Å. 1965, *Lagen om konkurrensbegränsning*, Stockholm, Nordstedts.

Mason, E. S. 1946, *Controlling World Trade: Cartels and Commodity Agreements*, McGraw-Hill, London.

Maurseth, P. 1987, *Gjennom kriser til makt: Bind 3 av Arbeiderbevegelsens Historie i Norge*, Tiden, Oslo.

McGowan, L. 2005, 'Europeanization Unleashed and Rebounding: Assessing the Modernization of EU Cartel Policy', *Journal of European Public Policy*, vol. 12, no. 6, pp. 986–1004.

McGowan, L. 2010, *The Antitrust Revolution in Europe: Exploring the European Commission's Cartel Policy*, Edward Elgar, Cheltenham.

Mercer, H. 1995, *Constructing a Competitive Order: The Hidden History of British Antitrust Policies*, Cambridge University Press, Cambridge.

Merrett, D. and Ville, S. 2000, 'The Development of Large Scale Enterprise in Australia, 1910–64', *Business History*, vol. 42, no. 3, pp. 13–46.

Merrett, D., Corones, S. and Round, D. 2007, 'The Introduction of Competition Policy in Australia: the Role of Ron Bannerman', *Australian Economic History Review*, vol. 47, no. 2, pp. 633–660.

Mierzejewski, A. C. 2003, 'America as Model? US Antitrust Policy and Ludwig Erhard's Struggle against Cartels in West Germany', in *The Impact of Nazism: New Perspectives on the Third Reich and Its Legacy*, (eds) A. E. Steinweis and D. Rogers, Lincoln, pp. 213–230.

Miksch, L 1949, 'Die Wirtschaftspolitik des Als-Ob', *Zeitschrift für die gesamte Staatswissenschaft*, vol. 105, no. 2, pp. 310–338.

Miller, M. (ed.) 2005, *Worlds of Capitalism: Institutions, Governance and Economic Change in the Era of Globalization*, Routledge, Abingdon.

Ministry of International Trade and Industry (ed.) 1961, *The History of Japanese Commerce and Industry Policy, vol. 9, Industrial Rationalisation*, Syoukouseisakushi-Kankoukai, Tokyo [通商産業省編『商工政策史 第9巻 産業合理化』商工政策史刊行会, 1961年]

Ministry of International Trade and Industry (ed.) 1964, *History of Japanese Commerce and Industry Policy, vol. 11, Industrial Control*, Shoukouseisakushi-Kankoukai, Tokyo [通商産業省編『商工政策史 第11巻 産業統制』商工政策史刊行会, 1964年]

Minobe, R. 1931, *Cartel, Trust and Konzern, volume 2*, Kaizousha, Tokyo [美濃部亮吉『カルテル・トラスト・コンツエルン（下）』改造社, 1931年].

Misonou, H. 1987, *The Antimonopoly Policy of Japan and the Industrial Organization*, Kawade-Shobo-Shinsha, Tokyo [御園生等『日本の独占禁止政策と産業組織』河出書房新社, 1987年]

Modin, M. 1999a, 'Från kartellregistrering till kartellförbud I', *Konkurrens*, no. 1, pp. 13–15.

Modin, M. 1999b, 'Från kartellregistrering till kartellförbud II', *Konkurrens*, no. 2, pp. 19–20.

Modin, M. 1999c, 'Från kartellregistrering till kartellförbud III', *Konkurrens*, no. 3, pp. 21–23.

Molina, O. and Rhodes, M. 2002, 'Corporatism: The Past, Present, and Future of a Concept', *Annual Review of Political Science*, vol. 5, no. 1, pp. 305–331.

Mond, A. 1927, 'International Cartels', *Journal of the Royal Institute of International Affairs*, vol. 6, no. 5, pp. 265–283.

Moraht, R. 1921/22, 'Die Entwicklung des internationalen Wettbewerbs auf dem Kalimarkt', *Weltwirtschaftliches Archiv*, vol. 17, pp. 51–67.

Moravcsik, A. 1998, *The Choice for Europe: Social Purpose and State Power from Messina to Maastricht*, Cornell University Press, Ithaca.

Morsel, H. 1997, 'Louis Marlio, Position idéologique et comportement politique d'un dirigeant d'une grande entreprise dans la première moitié du XXe s', in *Industralisation et sociétés en Europe occidentale de la fin du XIXe siècle à nos jours. L'Âge de l'aluminium*, (eds) I. Grinberg and F. Hachez-Leroy, Armand Collin, Paris, pp. 106–124.

Motta, M. 2004, *Competition Policy: Theory and Practice*, Cambridge University Press, Cambridge.

Müller, H. and Gries, G. 1958, *Kommentar zum Gesetz gegen Wettbewerbsbeschränkungen*, Frankfurt.

Munthe, P 1954, *Truster og trustlov: en oversikt over sammenslutninger og avtaler i norsk næringsliv og en analyse av den norske trustkontrollens virksomhet*, NHHs særtrykkserie, no. 9, Oslo.

Murach-Brand, L 2004, *Antitrust auf Deutsch: Der Einfluss der amerikanischen Alliierten auf das Gesetz gegen Wettbewerbsbeschränkungen (GWB) nach 1945*, Mohr Siebeck, Tübingen.

Myrvang, C. 1996, *Sosialistiske produksjonsidealer: 'dagen derpaa': Storskala og teknokrati i norsk sosialiseringsdebatt og -teori 1917–1924*, TMV Universitetet i Oslo, Oslo.

Newman, P. C. 1948, 'Key German Cartels under the Nazi Regime', *The Quarterly Journal of Economics*, vol. 62, no. 4, pp. 576–595.

Nicholls, A. J. 1994, *Freedom with Responsibility: The Social Market Economy in Germany, 1918–1963*, Oxford University Press, Oxford.

Nieuwenhuysen, J. P. (ed.) 1976, *Australian Trade Practices: Readings*, 2nd edition, Croom Helm, London.

Nieuwenhuysen, J. P. and Neville, R. N. 1976, *Australian Competition and Prices Policy*, Croom Helm, London.

Nishimura, N. and Sensui, F. 2006, 'Initiative, Compromises, and Discrepancies: Discovering the Origin of Japanese Antimonopoly Law', *Kobe Law Journal*, vol. 56, no. 2 ［西村暢史・泉水文雄「1947年独占禁止法の形成と成立」『神戸法学雑誌』第56号第2巻, 2006年9月］.

Nordvik, H. W. 1994, 'Conflict and Cooperation: Competitive Strategies and the Struggle for Control of the Norwegian Tobacco Market, 1905–1930', in *Crossing the Borders: Studies in Norwegian Business History*, (eds) R. P. Amdam, and E. Lange, Universitetsforlaget Oslo, Oslo, pp. 131–160.

Norman, N. 1994, 'Progress under Pressure: The Evolution of Anti-trust Policy in Australia', *Review of Industrial Organization* vol. 19, no. 9, pp. 527–545.

Nörr, K. W. 1994, *Die Leiden des Privatrechts: Kartelle in Deutschland von der Holzstoffkartellentscheidung zum Gesetz gegen Wettbewerbsbeschränkungen*, Mohr Siebeck, Tübingen.

Notz, W. 1918, 'Export Trade Problems and an American Foreign Trade Policy', *The Journal of Political Economy*, vol. 26, no. 2, pp. 105–124

Nussbaum, H. 1986, 'Market Organisation: International Cartels and Multinational Enterprises', in *Multinational Enterprise in International Perspective*, (eds) A. Teichova, M. Lévy-Leboyer and H. Nussbaum, Cambridge University Press, Cambridge.

Odaka, K. and Ministry of International Trade and Industry (eds), 2013, *The History of International Industrial Policy of Japan: 1980–2000, volume 1: Introduction*, Keizaisangyou-Chousakai, Tokyo ［通商産業政策史編纂委員会編, 尾高煌之助著『通商産業政策史1 総論 1980-200』経済産業調査会, 2013年］.

OECD 1964, *Restrictive Business Practices: Comparative Summary of Legislations in Europe and North America*. OECD, Paris.

OECD 1967–1975, *Guide to Legislation on Restrictive Business Practices*, OECD, Paris.

OECD 1971, *Restrictive Business Practices. Comparative Summary of Legislations in Europe and North America*. Paris

OECD 1974, *Guide to Legislation on Restrictive Business Practices*, OECD, Paris.

OECD 1978a, *Comparative summary of Legislation on Restrictive Business Practices*, OECD, Paris.

OECD 1978b, *Restrictive Business Practices: Comparative Summary of Legislations in Europe and North America*, OECD, Paris.

OECD 1991, *Competition Policy in OECD Countries 1989–1990*, OECD, Paris.

OECD 1993, *Competition Policy in OECD Countries 1990–1991*, OECD, Paris.

OECD 1995, *Competition Policy in OECD Countries 1992–1993*, OECD, Paris.

OECD 1997, *Competition Policy in OECD Countries 1993–1994*, OECD, Paris.

OECD 1998, *Recommendation of the Council concerning Effective Action against Hard Core Cartels*, C/M(98)7/PROV, March, OECD, Paris.

OECD 2007, *Competition Policy in OECD Countries 2006*, OECD, Paris.

Office of the History of Finance, Ministry of Finance (ed.) 1982, *The History of Finance in the Showa Period, volume 2: Antimonopoly*, Touyou-Keizai-Shinposha, Tokyo

[大蔵省財政史室編『昭和財政史 第2巻 独占禁止』東洋経済新報社, 1982年].
Ohde, T. 1961, 'Kartelli- ja monopolilainsäädäntö sekä maatalousosuustoiminta', *Suomen Osuustoimintalehti*, vol. 67, no. 1, pp. 204–211.
Okazaki, T. and Ministry of International Trade and Industry (eds) 2012, *A History of Japanese Trade and Industry Policy: 1980–2000, volume 3: Industrial Policy*, Keizaisangyou-Chousakai, Tokyo [通商産業政策史編纂委員会編, 岡崎哲司編著『通商産業政策史1980–2000年第3巻 産業政策』通商産業調査会, 2012年]
Olstad, F. 2010, *Med knyttet neve: LOs historie1899–1935 bind I*, Pax, Oslo.
Ottow, A. T. 2014, 'Erosion or Innovation? The Institutional Design of Competition Agencies – A Dutch Case Study', *Journal of Antitrust Enforcement*, vol. 2, no. 1, pp. 25–43.
Oualid, W. 1926, *Les Ententes Internationales et leurs conséquences sociales*, League of Nations, Geneva.
Oualid, W. 1938, *Les Ententes internationales de matières premières, préparé pour la Société de Nations*, Institut international de coopération intellectuelle, Paris.
Øvergaard, J. 1919, *Trust- og kartellovgivning i fremmede land*, Justisdepartementet, Kristiania (Oslo).
Palme, S. 1923, 'Thule under femtio år', in *Lifförsäkrings-Aktiebolaget Thule 1872–1922. Minnesskrift Del 1*, Stockholm, pp. 9–37.
Peeperkorn, L. 1987, 'Mededingingsbeleid op klompen', *Tijdschrift voor politieke ekonomie*, vol. 10, no. 4, pp. 57–75.
Peeperkorn, L. 1988, 'Openbaarheid van kartels', *Economisch Statistische Berichten*, vol. 74, 3645, pp. 212–214.
Pekkarinen J., Pohjola, M. and Rowthorn B. 1992, 'Social Corporatism and Economic Performance: Introduction and Conclusions', in *Social Corporatism: A Superior Economic System*, (eds) J. Pekkarinen *et al.*, Clarendon Press, London, pp. 1–23.
Peritz, R. J. R. 1996, *Competition Policy in America, 1888–1992: History, Rhetoric, Law*, Oxford University Press, New York.
Person, D. H. 1927, *L'Organisation scientifique du travail et les ententes*, League of Nations, Geneva.
Pettersson, G. J. 2011, 'Insurance and Cartels through Wars and Depressions: Swedish Marine Insurance and Reinsurance between the World Wars', PhD thesis, Umeå Studies in Economic History 44, Umeå.
Pitzer, F. 2009, *Interessen im Wettbewerb: Grundlagen und frühe Entwicklung der europäischen Wettbewerbspolitik, 1955–1966*, Franz Steiner, Stuttgart.
Poidevin, R and Spierenburg, D. 1993, *Histoire de la Haute Autorité de la CECA*, Bruylant, Brussels.
Polanyi, K. 1944, *The Great Transformation*, Ferrar and Rinehart, New York.
Pons, J. 2007, 'The Influence of Multinationals in the Organisation of the Spanish Insurance Market. Diversification and Cartelisation, 1880–1939', in *Internationalisation and Globalisation of the Insurance Industry in the 19th and 20th Centuries*, (eds) P. Borscheid and R. Pearson, Philipps-University, Marburg, pp. 49–65.
Portes, R. 1997, 'Users and Abusers of Economic Analysis', in *Economic Science and Practice*, (ed.) P. A. G. van Bergeijk, Edward Elgar Publishing, Cheltenham.
Posner, R. A. 1970, 'A Statistical Study of Antitrust Enforcement', *Journal of Law and Economics*, vol. 13, no. 2, pp. 365–419.
Prasad, M. 2006, *The Politics of Free Markets: The Rise of Neoliberal Economic Policies in Britain, France, Germany, and the United States*, Chicago University Press, Chicago.
Purasjoki, M. and Jokinen, J. 2001, 'Kilpailupolitiikan odotukset, saavutukset ja haasteet',

available from www.kilpailuvirasto.fi/cgi-bin/suomi.cgi?sivu=kilpailupolitiikan-odotukset.html

Ræstad, A. 1916, *Truster og karteller: en bok om privatmonopoler*, Cappelen, Kristiania (Oslo).

Rainio-Niemi, J. 2010, 'State Committees in Finland in Historical Comparative Perspective', in *Nordic Associations in a European Perspective*, (eds) R. Alapuro and H. Stenius, Nomos, Baden-Baden, pp. 241–267.

Ramírez, C. D. and Eigen-Zucchi, C. 2001, 'Understanding the Clayton Act of 1914: An Analysis of the Interest Group Hypothesis', *Public Choice*, vol. 106, no. 1–2, pp. 157–181.

Ramirez, S. 2008, 'La politique de la concurrence de la CEE et l'industrie: l'exemple des accords sur la distribution automobile (1972–1985)', *Histoire, économie et société*, vol. 27, no. 1, pp. 63–78.

Rampilla, N. R. 1989, 'A Developing Judicial Perspective to India's Monopolies and Restrictive Trade Practices Act of 1969', *The Antitrust Bulletin*, vol. 34, no. 3, pp. 655–682.

Rao, P. V. K. and Sastry, R. 1989, 'Restrictive Trade Practices in India', *The Journal of Industrial Economics*, vol. 37, no. 4, pp. 427–435.

Rathke, F. 2013, *Kartellregisteret: Et reguleringsinstrument 1945–1961*, Universitetet i Bergen, Bergen.

Reckendrees, A. 2003, 'Form Cartel Regulation to Monopolistic Control? The Founding of the German "Steel Trust" in 1926 and its Effect on Market Regulation', *Business History*, vol. 45, no. 3, pp. 22–51.

Ridgeway, G. L. 1938, *Merchants of Peace: Twenty Years of Business Diplomacy through the International Chamber of Commerce, 1919–1938*, McGraw-Hill, New York.

Riesenfeld, S. A. 1962, 'Antitrust Laws in the European Economic Community'. *California Law Review*, vol. 50, no. 3, pp. 459–481.

Rinne A. 1942, *Valtiojohtoisuus ja Osuuskauppaliike: Osuuskauppaliikkeen suhde muihin talouspiireihin ja valtioon*, Kulutusosuuskuntien Keskusliitto, Helsinki.

Rinne, A. 1948, *Monopolistiset yritysryhmät kuluttajain vaarana*, Kulutusosuuskuntien Keskusliitto, Helsinki.

Rissanen, K. 1978, *Kilpailu ja tavaramerkit: kilpailunrajoituslainsäädännön soveltaminen tavaramerkin yksilöimiin järjestelyihin*, Suomalaisen lakimiesyhdistyksen julkaisuja A 131, Helsinki.

Ritschl, A. 2005, 'Der späte Fluch des Dritten Reichs: Pfadabhängigkeiten in der Entstehung der bundesdeutschen Wirtschaftsordnung', *Perspektiven der Wirtschaftspolitik*, vol. 6, no. 2, pp. 151–170.

Robert, R. 1976, *Konzentrationspolitik in der Bundesrepublik: Das Beispiel der Entstehung des Gesetzes gegen Wettbewerbsbeschränkungen*, Berlin.

Roelevink, E. M. 2015a, *Organisierte Intransparenz: Das Kohlensyndikat und der niederländische Markt, 1915–1932*, C. H. Beck, Munich.

Roelevink, E. M. 2015b, 'Staatliche Intervention und kartellierte Logik: die Absatzgewinne des deutsch-niederländischen Kohlenhandels während des Ersten Weltkrieges', in *Jahrbuch für Wirtschaftsgeschichte*, no. 2, Verlag De Gruyter, Oldenbourg.

Rollings, N. 2007, *British Business in the Formative Years of European Integration, 1945–1973*, Cambridge University Press, Cambridge.

Roth, R. 1997, *Staat und Wirtschaft im Ersten Weltkrieg: Kriegsgesellschaften als kriegswirtschaftliche Steuerungselemente*, Duncker and Humblot, Berlin.

Rothstein, B. 1992, 'State Structure and Variations in Corporatism: The Swedish Case', *Scandinavian Political Studies*, vol. 14, no. 2, pp. 149–169.

Round, D. K. 2000, 'An Empirical Analysis of Price-Fixing Penalties in Australia from 1974 to 1999: Have Australia's Corporate Colluders been Corralled?', *Competition and Consumer Law Journal*, vol. 8, no. 1 pp. 83–124.
Round, D. K. and Hanna, L. M. 2005, 'Curbing Corporate Collusion in Australia: The Role of Section 45A of the Trade Practices Act', *Melbourne University Law Review*, vol. 29, no. 1, pp. 242–269.
Round, D. K. and Siegfried, J. J. 1994, 'Horizontal Price Agreements in Australian Antitrust: Combating Anti-Competitive Corporate Conspiracies of Complicity and Connivance', *Review of Industrial Organization*, vol. 9, October, pp. 569–606.
Round, D. K., Siegfried, J. J. and Baillie, A. J. 1996, 'Collusive Markets in Australia: An Assessment of Their Economic Characteristics and Judicial Penalties', *Australian Business Law Review*, vol. 24, August, pp. 292–312.
Round, K. A. and Shanahan, M. P. 2011, 'A Solution to the Perceived Crisis of Market Power: The Political, Social and Economic Background to the Australian Cartel Register', paper presented at European Business History Association Congress, Athens.
Round, K. A. and Shanahan, M. P. 2015, *From Protection to Competition: The Politics of Trade Practices Reform in Australia*, Federation Press, NSW.
Rousseau, G. 1998, *Étienne Clémentel (1864–1936). Entre idéalisme et réalisme, une vie politique: essai biographique*, Archives départementales du Puy-de-Dôme, Clermont-Ferrand.
Rydén, B. 1971, *Fusioner i Svensk industri*, Industriens utredningsinstitut, Stockholm.
Ryssdal, A. C. S. et al. (eds) 1991, *Konkurranse for effektiv ressursbruk*, NOU 1991: 27, Statens forvaltningstjeneste, Oslo.
Salin, E. 1963, 'Kartellverbot und Konzentration', *Kyklos*, vol. 15, no. 2, pp. 177–202.
Salonen, A. M. 1955, *Tutkimus taloudellisesta kilpailusta Suomen nykyisessä yhteiskuntaelämässä*, Kulutusosuuskuntien Keskusliitto, Helsinki.
Sandberg, P. 2006, 'Kartellen som sprängdes: Svensk bryggeriindustri under institutionell och strukturell omvandling 1945–1975', PhD thesis, Department of Economic History, Göteborg.
Sandberg, P. 2011, 'Decartelisation, Rationalisation and Amalgamation: Merger Control and Regulation of Business Concentration in Sweden in the Post-war Period', paper presented at European Historical Economics Society Conference, Dublin.
Sandberg, P. 2014, 'Den svenska kartellregistreringen', in *Organiserad samverkan: Svenska karteller under 1900-talet*, (ed.) B. Karlsson, Gidlunds, Möklinta.
Sandström, A. (ed.) 2004, *Svenska aktuarieföreningen 1904–2004*, Svenska aktuarieföreningen, Stockholm.
Sandvik, P. T. 2010, 'Såpekrigen 1930–31: Lilleborgsaken, venstrestaten og norsk økonomisk nasjonalisme', *Historisk tidsskrift*, vol. 89, no. 3, pp. 389–425.
Sandvik, P. T. and Storli, E. 2013, 'Big Business and Small States: Unilever and Norway in the Interwar Years', *Economic History Review*, vol. 66, no. 2, pp. 109–131.
Savoye, A. 1988, 'Paul de Rousiers, sociologue et praticien du syndicalisme', *Cahiers Georges Sorel*, no. 6, pp. 52–77.
Schaede, U. 2000, *Cooperative Capitalism: Self-regulation, Trade Associations, and the Antimonopoly Law in Japan*, Oxford University Press, Oxford.
Schedvin, B. 2008, 'Primary Phases of Australian Economic Development in the Twentieth Century', *Australian Economic Review*, vol. 41, no. 4, pp. 450–455.
Scherer, F. M. and Ross, D. 1990, *Industrial Market Structure and Economic Performance*, 3th edition, Houghton Mifflin, Boston, MA.

Schmitter, P. 1982, 'Still the Century of Corporatism?', in *Patterns of Corporatist Policy-Making*, (eds) G. Lehmbruch and P. C. Schmitter, Sage Modern Politics Series vol. 7, Sage Publications, CA.

Schröder, R. 1988, *Die Entwicklung des Kartellrechts und des kollektiven Arbeitsrechts durch die Rechtsprechung des Reichsgerichts vor 1914*, R. Greber, Ebelsbach.

Schröter, H. G. 1993, 'The International Dyestuffs Cartel, 1927–1939, with Special Reference to the Developing Areas of Europe and of Japan', in *International Cartels in Business History*, (eds) A. Kudo and T. Hara, Tokyo University Press, Tokyo, pp. 33–52.

Schröter, H. G. 1994, 'Kartellierung und Dekartellierung 1890–1990', *Vierteljahrschrift für Sozial- und Wirtschaftsgeschichte*, vol. 81, no. 4, pp. 457–493.

Schröter, H. G. 1996, 'Cartelization and Decartelization in Europe 1870–1995: Rise and Decline of an Economic Institution', *Journal of European Economic History*, vol. 25, no. 1, pp. 129–153.

Schröter, H. G. 2005, *Americanization of the European Economy: A Compact Survey of American Economic Influence in Europe since the 1880s*. Springer, Dordrecht.

Schröter, H. G. 2010, 'Loser in Power-Plays? Small States and International Cartelisation', *The Journal of European Economic History*, vol. 39, no. 3, pp. 527–555.

Schröter, H. G. 2011, 'Das Kartellverbot und andere Ungereimtheiten: Neue Ansätze in der internationalen Kartellforschung', in *Regulierte Märkte: Zünfte und Kartelle /Marchés régulés. Corporations et cartels*, (eds) M. Müller, H. R. Schmidt and L. Tissot, Chronos, Zurich, pp. 199–213.

Schröter, H. G. 2013, 'Cartels Revisited: An Overview on Fresh Questions, New Methods, and Surprising Results', *Revue Économique*, vol. 64, no. 6, pp. 989–1010.

Schulze, R. and Hoeren, T. (eds) 2000, *Dokumente zum europäischen Recht, vol. 3: Kartellrecht (bis 1957)*, Springer, Berlin.

Schumpeter, J. A. 1942, *Capitalism, Socialism and Democracy*, Harper, New York.

Scott, E. 1936, *Australia during the War: Official History of Australia in the War of 1914–1918*, vol. XI, Angus and Robertson, Sydney.

Seidel, K. 2010, *The Process of Politics in Europe: The Rise of European Elites and Supranational Institutions*, I. B. Tauris, London.

Shanahan, M. P. and Round, D. K. 2009, 'Serious Cartel Conduct: Criminalisation and Evidentiary Standards: Lessons from the Coal Vend Case of 1911 in Australia', *Business History*, vol. 51, no. 6, pp. 875–906.

Sheridan, K. 1974, *The Firm in Australia: A Theoretical and Empirical Study of Size, Growth and Profitability*, Thomas Nelson, Australia.

Shimotani, M. 2010, 'Thirty Years that Brought about the Huge Transformation', in *A Way toward an Economic Power: 1955–1985*, (eds) M. Shimotani and T. Suzuki, Minerva Shobou, Kyoto [下谷政弘「大変化をもたらした30年」下谷政弘・鈴木恒夫『「経済大国」への軌跡 1955～1985』ミネルヴァ書房, 2010年].

Shirato, S. 1981, 'Development of the Policy Organizing Fellow Traders', *Memories of the Graduate School of Meiji University, Commerce*, vol. 18, Tokyo [白戸伸一「同業者組織化政策の展開過程　産業資本確立期における動向を中心として」(『明治大学大学院紀要　商学篇』第18集, 1981年].

Skogh, G. 1991, *Vad skiljer försäkring från annan finansiell verksamhet?*, SNS Occasional Paper, no. 32, Stockholm.

Skogh, G. and Samuelsson, P. 1985, *Splittring och sammanhållning i svensk försäkring? En ekonomisk och rättslig analys av marknadsföringsöverenskommelsen*, Doxa, Lund.

Sleuwaegen, L. and van Cayseele, P. 1998, 'Competition Policy in Belgium', in *Competition Policies in Europe*, (ed.) S. Martin, Elsevier Science, Amsterdam, pp. 185–204.

Smith, A. [1776] 1995, *An Inquiry into the Nature and Causes of the Wealth of Nations*, book I, William Pickering, London.
Société des Nations 1933, *Exposé des travaux préliminaires, suivi d'un exposé sommaire des principaux travaux antérieurs de l'organisation économique et financière de la société des nations*, La Conférence Monétaire et Economique (Londres 1933), League of Nations, Geneva.
Société des Nations, Comité Economique 1929, *Rapport du Conseil sur les Travaux de la Trentiéme Session*, Geneva, 24 October–1 November, II. 47.
Sogner, K. 2013, *Andresens: En familie i norsk økonomi og samfunnnsliv gjennom to hundre år*, Pax, Oslo.
Souam, S. 1998, 'French Competition Policy', in *Competition Policies in Europe*, (ed.) S. Martin, Elsevier Science, Amsterdam, pp. 205–227.
South African Government 1977, *Report of the Commission of Inquiry into the Regulation of Monopolistic Conditions Act*, 1955 Government Printer, Pretoria.
Spier, H. and Grimwade, T. 1997, 'International Engagement in Competition Law Enforcement: The Future for Australia', *Trade Practices Law Journal*, vol. 5, December, pp. 232–241.
Spitzer, H. M. 1927, *La Rationalisation et les Cartels*, League of Nations, Geneva.
Staley, E. 1937, *Raw Materials in Peace and War*, Council of Foreign Relations, Washington DC.
Stalley, D. J. 1956, 'The Control of Monopoly: New South Wales', *University of Queensland Law Journal*, vol. 1956–59, no. 3, pp. 377–403.
Statens offentliga utredningar (SOU) 1935: 65, *Betänkande om folkförsörjning och arbetsfred*, Stockholm.
Statens offentliga utredningar (SOU) 1940: 35, *Organiserad samverkan inom svenskt näringsliv: Betänkande av 1936 års Näringsorganisationssakkunniga*, Stockholm.
Statens offentliga utredningar (SOU) 1945: 42, *Framställningar och utlåtanden från Kommissionen för efterkrigsplanering: Betänkande angående övervakning av konkurrensbegränsande företeelser inom näringslivet*, Stockholm.
Statens offentliga utredningar (SOU) 1946: 34, *Försäkringsutredningen: Förslag till lag om försäkringsrörelsen mm*, Del II, Motiv, Stockholm.
Statens offentliga utredningar (SOU) 1949: 25, *1945 års försäkringsutredning, I, Principbetänkande rörande försäkringsväsendet*, Stockholm.
Statens offentliga utredningar (SOU) 1951: 27, *Konkurrensbegränsning: Betänkande med förslag till lag om skydd mot samhällsskadlig konkurrensbegränsning angivet av Nyetableringssakkunniga*, Stockholm.
Statens offentliga utredningar (SOU) 1951: 28, *Konkurrensbegränsning: Betänkande med förslag till lag om skydd mot samhällsskadlig konkurrensbegränsning angivet av Nyetableringssakkunniga*, Stockholm.
Statens offentliga utredningar (SOU) 1978: 9, *Ny konkurrensbegränsningslag: Betänkande av Konkurrensutredningen*, Stockholm.
Statens offentliga utredningar (SOU) 1986: 55, *Försäkringsmäklare i Sverige: Delbetänkande av försäkringsverksamhetskommittén*, Stockholm.
Statens offentliga utredningar (SOU) 1990: 1, *Företagsförvärv i svenskt näringsliv: Betänkande från Ägarutredningen*, Stockholm.
Statens offentliga utredningar (SOU) 1991: 59, *Konkurrens för ökad välfärd: Betänkande av Konkurrenskommittéen*, Stockholm.
Sterner, R. 1946, *Mera demokrati i näringslivet: svar på PHM-propagandan*, Tiden, Stockholm.

Sterner, R. 1951, *Sätt fart på priskonkurrensen! En sammanfattning av Nyetabler ingssakkunniga program för kampen mot monopol och karteller*, KF, Stockholm.

Sterner, R. 1956, 'Konkurrens och konkurrensbegränsning inom försäkringsverksamheten: Några synpunkter', *Nordisk Försäkringstidskrift/Scandinavian Insurance Quarterly*, no. 1, pp. 1–23.

Stigler, G. 1964, 'A Theory of Oligopoly', *Journal of Political Economy*, vol. 72, no. 1, pp. 44–61.

Strömbäck, E. 1995, 'Rättskultur och försäkringsverksamhet', *Nordisk Försäkringstidskrift/ Scandinavian Insurance Quarterly*, no. 4, pp. 301–306.

Sturm R., 1996, 'The German Cartel Office in a Hostile Environment', in *Comparative Competition Policy: National Institutions in a Global Market*, (eds) B. G Doern and S. Wilks, Clarendon Press, Oxford.

Suortti, S. 1927, *Osuuskauppaliikkeen suhde yrittäjäryhmiin*, Kuluttajaosuuskuntien Keskusliitto, Helsinki.

Suslow, V. 2005, 'Cartel Contract Duration: Empirical Evidence from Inter-War International Cartels', *Industrial and Corporate Change*, vol. 14, no. 5, pp. 705–744.

Suslow, V. and Levenstein, M. 2006, 'What Determines Cartel Success?', *Journal of Economic Litterature*, vol. 44, no. 1, pp. 43–95.

Svennilson, I. 1954, *Growth and Stagnation in the European Economy*, United Nations, Geneva.

Symeonidis, G. 1998, 'The Evolution of UK Cartel Policy and Its Impact on Market Conduct and Structure', in *Competition Policies in Europe*, (ed.) S. Martin, Elsevier Science, Amsterdam, pp. 55–73.

Symeonidis, G. 2002, *The Effects of Competition: Cartel Policy and the Evolution of Strategy and Structure in British Industry*, MIT Press, Cambridge, MA.

Szokolóczy-Syllaba, A. 1975, *EFTA: Restrictive Business Practices*, Verlag Stämpfli and Cie AG, Bern.

Taylor, G. D. 1981, 'Debate in the United States Over the Control of International Cartels, 1942–1950', *The International History Review*, vol. 3, no. 3, pp. 385–398.

Teddennick, J. C. 1978, 'Webb Pomerene Act: a Reexamination of Export Cartels in World Trade', *Virginia Journal of International Law*, vol. 19, no. 1, pp. 151–182.

Teichova, A. 1974, *An Economic Background to Munich: International Business and Czechoslovakia 1918–1938*, Cambridge University Press, Cambridge.

Temple-Lang, J. 1980, 'EEC Competition Policies: A Status Report', in Enterprise Law of the 80s. European and American Perspectives on Competition and Industrial Organization, (eds). F.M. Rowe, F.M, F.G, Jacobs and M. R. Joelson, American Bar Association, Chicago, pp. 18–38.

Thiery, F. 1998, 'Construire l'Europe dans les années vingt: L'action de l'Union paneuropéenne sur la scène franco-allemande, 1924–1932', *Euryopa*, no. 7, p. 190.

Thorelli, H. B. 1954, *The Federal Antitrust Policy: Origination of an American Tradition*, Johns Hopkins University Press, Baltimore.

Thorelli, H. B. 1959, 'Antitrust in Europe: National Policies after 1945', *University of Chicago Law Review*, vol. 26, no. 2, pp. 222–236.

T Gilde, A. P. J. and Haank, D. J. 1985, De praktijk van de Wet economische mededinging, Stichting Wetenschappelijk Onderzoek Konsumentenaangelegenheden, onderzoeksrapport 37, The Hague.

Thue, L. 2006, *Nye forbindelser (1970–2005): Norsk telekommunikasjonshistorie bind 3*, Gyldendal, Oslo.

Tilton, M. 1996, *Restrained Trade: Cartels in Japan's Basic Material Industries*, Cornell University Press, Ithaca.

Timberg, S. 1953, 'Restrictive Business Practices: Comparative Legislation and the Problems That Lie Ahead', *The American Journal of Comparative Law*, vol. 2, no. 4, pp. 445–473.

Tosdal, H. R. 1913, 'The Kartell Movement in the German Potash Industry', *Quarterly Journal of Economics*, vol. 28, no. 1, pp. 140–190.

Trustkommisjonen (ed.) 1921, *Innstilling angående forholdsregler til motarbeidelse av trust- og kartellmisbruk fra den ved kgl: resolusjon av 29. februar 1916 opnevnte trustkommission*, Justisdepartementet, Oslo.

Tschierschky, S. 1911, *Kartell und Trust*, G. J. Göschen, Leipzig.

Tschierschky, S. 1927, *Zeitgemässe Kartellprobleme*, Berliner Buchdr., Berlin.

Tschierschky, S. 1928, *Kartell-Organisation*, Industrieverlag Spaeth und Linde, Berlin.

Tschierschky, S. 1930, *Kartellpolitik: Eine analytische untersuchung*, C. Heymann, Berlin.

Tschierschky, S. 1932, *Etude sur le nouveau régime juridique des ententes économiques (cartels, etc.) en Allemagne et en Hongrie*, League of Nations, Geneva.

Tuchtfeld, E. 1978, 'Kartelle', *Handwörterbuch der Wirtschaftswissenschaft*, vol. 4, pp. 445–462.

United Nations 1947, *International Cartels: A League of Nations Memorandum*, Lake Success, New York.

UNCTAD, 2009, *Handbook on Competition Legislation: Consolidated Report 2001–2009*, United Nations, New York.

van Bergeijk, P. A. G. 2002, Economisch onderzoek en marktwerkingsbeleid, in *Afscheid van de beleidseconomie?*, (eds) T. J. A. Roelandt and T. R. A. Grosfeld, Wolters-Noordhoff, Groningen, pp. 29–48.

van Bergeijk, P. A. G. 2005, 'Fouten maken', *Economisch Statistische Berichten*, vol. 90, 4473, p. 476.

van Bergeijk, P. A. G. 2008, 'On the Allegedly Invisible Dutch Construction Cector Cartel', *Journal of Competition Law and Economics*, vol. 4, no. 1, pp. 115–128.

van Bergeijk, P. A. G. and Dijk, M. A. van 1997, 'Resource Misallocation and Mark-up Ratios: An Alternative Estimation Technique for Harberger Triangles', *Economics Letters*, vol. 54, no. 2, pp. 165–167.

van Bergeijk, P. A. G. and Haffner, R. C. G. 1994, 'The Economic Consequences of Dutch Politics', *De Economist*, vol. 142, no. 4, pp. 497–505.

van Bergeijk, P. A. G. and Haffner, R. C. G. 1996, *Privatisation, Deregulation and the Macroeconomy*, Edward Elgar, Cheltenham.

van Bergeijk, P. A. G. and van Sinderen, J. 2000, 'Models and Macroeconomic Policy in the Netherlands', in *Empirical Models and Policy Making: Interactions and Institutions*, (eds) F. Den Butter and M. S. Morgan, Routledge, London, pp. 26–38.

van Bergeijk, P. A. G., Haffner, R. C. G. and Waasdorp, P. M. 1993, 'Measuring the Speed of the Invisible Hand: The Macroeconomic Costs of Price Rigidity', *Kyklos*, vol. 44, no. 4, pp. 529–544.

van Bergeijk, P. A. G., van Hagen, G. H. A., de Mooij, R. A. and van Sinderen, J. 1997, 'Endogenising Technological Progress: The MESEMET Model', *Economic Modelling*, vol. 14, no. 3, pp. 341–367.

van de Kerkhof, S. T. 2010, 'Public–Private Partnership im Ersten Weltkrieg? Kriegsgesellschaften in der schwerindustriellen Kriegswirtschaft des Deutschen Reiches', in *Wirtschaft im Zeitalter der Extreme: Beiträge zur Unternehmensgeschichte Deutschlands und Österreichs Im Gedenken an Gerald D. Feldman*, (eds) H. Berghoff, J. Kocka and D. Ziegler, C. H. Beck, Munich, pp. 106–133.

van Gent, C. 1997, 'New Dutch Competition Policy: A Revolution without Revolutionaries', in *Economic Science: An Art or an Asset, The Case of the Netherlands*, (eds) P. A. G. van Bergeijk, A. L. Bovenberg, E. E. C. van Damme and J. van Sinderen, OCFEB, Rotterdam, pp. 59–72.

van Muiswinkel, F. L., Vredevoogd, L. E. H. and van der Wilde, J. P. I. 1977, *De handelsonderneming*, Elsevier, Amsterdam.

van Rooy, Y. C. T. M. 1992, 'Het einde van het kartelparadijs', *Economisch Statistische Berichten*, vol. 75, 3878, pp. 908–912.

van Schaik, A. B. T. M. 1991, 'Marktruiming en inflatie', inaugural speech, University of Tilburg, available from https://pure.uvt.nl/portal/en/publications/marktruiming-en-inflatie(9612fbf6-eff3-41b0-85a8-f97665ed8b87).html.

van Sinderen, J. 1990, *Belastingheffing en economische groei*, Wolters-Noordhoff, Groningen.

van Sinderen, J. 2000, 'The Polder Model's Main Features and its Possible Role Model Function', in *The Netherland's Polder Model: Does it Offer any Clues for the Solutions of Europe's Socioeconomic Flaws?*, (eds) H. H. J. Labohm and C. G. A. Wijnker, Monetaire Monografieën no. 17, DNB, Amsterdam, pp. 21–28.

van Sinderen, J. and Kemp, R. G. M. 2008, 'The Economic Effects of Competition Law Enforcement: The Case of The Netherlands', *The Economist*, vol. 156, no. 4, pp. 365–385.

van Sinderen, J. and Kemp, R. G. M. 2009, 'Strategic Interactions in Competition Policy: Dutch Experiences', *European Competition Law Review*, vol. 5, no. 2, pp. 298–309.

van Sinderen, J., van Bergeijk, P. A. G., Haffner, R. C. G. and Waasdorp, P. M. 1994, 'De kosten van economische verstarring op macro-niveau', *Economisch Statistische Berichten*, vol. 79, 3954, pp. 274–279.

van Sinderen, J. and Kemp, R. 2008. 'The Economic Effects of Competition Law Enforcement: The Case of the Netherlands', *De Economist* 156: 365.

Verbond van Nederlandse Werkgevers 1958, *Wet Economische Mededinging: Tekst en Commentaar*, The Hague.

Ville, S. 1998, 'Business Development in Colonial Australia', *Australian Economic History Review*, vol. 38, no. 1, pp. 16–41.

Ville, S. and Fleming, G. 2000, 'Desperately Seeking Synergy: Interdisciplinary Research in Accounting and Business History', *Pacific Accounting Review*, vol. 11, no. 2, pp. 173–180.

Virkkunen, J. 2003, 'Kilpailulainsäädännän kehitys Suomessa', Master's thesis, University of Helsinki.

Vives, X. (ed) (2009) *Competition Policy in the EU: Fifty years on from the Treaty of Rome*, Oxford University Press, Oxford.

Walker, F. 1912, 'Policies of Germany, England, Canada and the United States towards combinations', *Annals of the American Academy of Political and Social Science*, vol. 42 (July), pp. 183–201.

Wallander, J. 1952, 'Kartellproblemet i Sverige', *Handelsvidenskapelig Tidskrift*, vol. 16, pp. 149–156.

Warlouzet, L. 2011, *Le Choix de la CEE par la France: L'Europe économique en débat de Mendès France à de Gaulle (1955–1969)*, Cheff, Paris.

Warlouzet, L. 2014, 'Towards a European Industrial Policy? The European Economic Community (EEC) Debates, 1957–1975', in *Industrial Policy in Europe after 1945*, (eds) C. Grabas and A. Nützenadel, Palgrave Macmillan, Basingstoke.

Warlouzet, L. 2016a, 'The Centralization of EU Competition Policy: Historical Institutionalist Dynamics from Cartel Monitoring to Merger Control (1956–91)', in *Journal of Common Market Studies* (forthcoming).

Warlouzet, L. 2016b, 'From Price Control to Competition Policy in France and in the UK: Europeanization and the Role of the German Model (1976–86)', in *Slowing Prices Down: Adaptation of States and European Economical Actors to the Inflationary Fever in the 1970s*, (eds) M. P. Chélini and L. Warlouzet, Presses de sciences-po, Paris (forthcoming).

Warlouzet, L. and Witschke, T. 2012, 'The Difficult Path to an Economic Rule of Law: European Competition Policy, 1950–1991', *Contemporary European History*, vol. 21, no. 3, pp. 437–455.

Watkins, M. W. 1926, 'The Federal Trade Commission: A Critical Survey', *Quarterly Journal of Economics*, vol. 40, no. 3, pp. 561–585.

Wells, W. 2002, *Antitrust and the Formation of the Post-War World*, Columbia University Press, New York.

Westall, O. M. 1984, 'David and Goliath: The Fire Offices', Committee and Non-Tariff Competition, 1898–1907', in *The Historian and the Business of Insurance*, (ed.) O. Westall, Manchester University Press, Manchester, pp. 130–154.

Whitwell, G. 1989, *Making the Market: The Rise of Consumer Society*, McPhee Gribble, Melbourne.

Wiedenfeld, K. 1927, *Les Cartels et les Trusts*, League of Nations, Geneva.

Wigforss, E. 1938, *Samarbete mellan staten och det enskilda näringslivet*, Tiden, Stockholm.

Wilks, S. 1996, 'The Prolonged Reform of United Kingdom Competition Policy', in *Comparative Competition Policy: National Institutions in a Global Market*, (eds) G. B. Doern and S. Wilks, Clarendon Press, Oxford, pp. 139–184.

Wilks, S. 2005, 'Agency Escape: Decentralization or Dominance of the European Commission in the Modernization of Competition Policy?', *Governance: An International Journal of Policy, Administration and Institutions*, vol. 18, no. 3, pp. 431–452.

Wilson, J. 2006, 'At the Crossroads: Making Competition Law Effective in Pakistan Symposium on Competition Law and Policy in Developing Countries', *Northwestern Journal of International Law and Business*, vol. 26, no. 3, pp. 565–596.

Wise, M. 1999, 'Review of Competition Policy and Law in the Netherlands', *OECD Journal of Competition Law and Policy*, vol. 1, no. 2, pp. 73–118.

Wise, M. 2000, 'Review of Competition Policy and Law in Spain', *OECD Journal of Competition Law and Policy*, vol. 2, no. 4, pp. 137–185.

Wise, M. 2003, 'Review of Competition Policy and Law in the UK', *OECD Journal of Competition Law and Policy*, vol. 5, no. 3, pp. 57–140.

Wise M. 2005, Review of Competition Policy and Law in Germany', *OECD Journal of Competition Law and Policy*, vol. 7, no. 2, pp. 7–66.

Witschke, T. 2009, *Gefahr für den Wettbewerb? Die Fusionkontrolle der europäischen Gemeinschaft für Kohle und Stahl und die 'Rekonzentration' der Ruhrstahlindustrie, 1950–1963*, Akademie Verlag, Berlin.

Wurm, C. 1988, *Business, Politics and International Relations: Steel, Cotton and International Cartels in British Politics, 1924–1939*, Cambridge University Press, London.

Yang, M. 1985, 'Cartel Regulations in Korea: Comparative and International Aspects', *Korean Journal of Comparative Law*, vol. 13, no. 1, pp. 123–135.

Yang, M. 2009, 'Competition Law and Policy of the Republic of Korea', *The Antitrust Bulletin*, vol. 54, no. 3, pp. 621–650.

Yoshino, S. 1935, *Japan's Industrial Policy*, Nippon-Hyouronsha, Tokyo [吉野信次『

日本工業政策』日本評論社, 1935年]
Yoshino, S. 1962, *Memoir of the Commerce and Industry Policy-making*, Shoukouseisakushi-Kankoukai, Tokyo [吉野信次『商工行政の思い出』商工政策史刊行会, 1962年]
Ziegler, D. 2010, 'Wider die "verhängnisvolle Planwirtschaft": Nationalsozialistische Neuordnungspläne für die Kohlewirtschaft 1933 bis 1937', in *Wirtschaft im Zeitalter der Extreme. Beiträge zur Unternehmensgeschichte Deutschlands und Österreichs: Im Gedenken an Gerald D. Feldman*, (eds) H. Berghoff, J. Kocka and D. Ziegler, C. H. Beck, Munich, pp. 253–274.
Zines, L. 1992, *The High Court and the Constitution*, 2nd edition, Butterworths, Sydney.

Index

abuse legislation 17, 19, 27–8, 51–3, 69; in Finland 92, 100, 105; in Germany 192, 196–7, 199, 202, 204; international comparison 113–14, 116, 119, 126; in Japan 174, 182; in Netherlands 82–3, 86, 240; in Norway 133–8; in Sweden 208, 210, 217–19, 222, 225
abuse system 21, 48, 52–3, 74–5, 83; in Australia 153; in Finland 94; international comparison 127, 131, 274; in Netherlands 87; in Norway 136–7, 144, 149
acquisition 19, 22, 45, 105, 113; international comparison 121–3; in Japan 175, 186; in Norway 144; in Sweden 218, 225–6, 262–3
Act of Probation on Restrictive Business Practices (Lag om övervakning konkurrensbegränsning inom näringslivet) 101, 117, 213
Actuarial Society of Sweden 252
Adelaide Steamship Co Ltd 154, 168
Administrative Office of the Economy (Verwaltung für Wirtschaft) 198
agricultural machinery trust 157, 159
Allmänna Brand 265
Allmänna Lifförsäkringsbolaget 252
Aluminium Association 33
American Tobacco Company 22
Andriessen, Frans 60
anti-competitive agreements 116, 125, 233
anti-trust 3, 5, 9, 11, 19; in Australia 158–9; in Finland 88; in Germany 198, 204; and ICC/LoN 33, 44; international comparison 115, 132, 272–3; in Japan 169, 176–7, 179, 184, 188; in Norway 138, 158–9; in Sweden 213
asbestos cartel 160, 163
Associated Northern Collieries 154–5, 168
Association for co-operative and price arranging organisations in the construction industry 79
Association of Finnish Businessmen (Suomen Liikemiesyhdistys) 89
Association for Social Policy (Verein für Socialpolitik) 194
Australia 7–8, 11, 68, 108, 152–68; Australian Industries Preservation Act 1906 152–3, 166; Commissioner of Trade Practices 163; Competition and Consumer Commission 165, 167–8; Constitution 156–8, 164, 167; High Court 155; international comparison 114, 117–21, 124–6, 128–9, 131, 271–3; and Netherlands 231, 241–2; Prices Adjustment Board 157; Restrictive Trade Practices Act 1965 152, 161, 164, 167; Restrictive Trade Practices Act 1971 164; Restrictive Trade Practices Act 1974 164; secret registers 152–67; and Sweden 267; War Precautions Act 1916 157
Austria 4, 7, 13, 67–8, 113–14; international comparison 116–17, 119, 121, 123–4, 129, 132; and Netherlands 229–31; and Norway 133, 137–8, 148; and Sweden 209

Balder 252
banks 38, 148, 153, 157, 159–60, 166, 184, 186
Bannerman, Ron 16, 161, 163
Barwick, Sir Garfield 158–9
Benni, Antonio Stefano 37–8, 42, 45
block exemptions 55–6
bone glue 38
bottles 38, 229
bread cartel 56, 159–60, 166
breweries cartel 145–6, 157, 159–60, 166
bricks cartel 153, 156, 165–6

British American Tobacco (Batco) 145
Brittan, Leon 60
Bundeskartellamt 51, 71, 75, 191
Bureau of Corporations 21–3, 25, 29, 40–1
Bureau d'information privé des Ententes Industrielles Internationales (BEII) 43, 47
Bureau of Monopoly Investigation – Sweden (Monopolutredningsbyrån) 213, 215–17, 219, 223

calcium carbide cartel 33
Campbell, Sir John 43
capitalism 1–13
cartel agreements 13, 17, 24, 35, 37; in Germany 203; international comparison 119, 122; in Japan 172; in Netherlands 70, 72, 74, 78, 84, 231; in Norway 142–6; in Sweden 211, 215, 220, 224, 250, 257–8, 261, 264
Cartel Office (Kartellamt) 37, 192
cartel paradise 10, 12, 66, 227, 244
cartel registers/registration 1–13, 26, 29, 52, 67; in Australia 152–67; in EEC 56; in Finland 88–109; in Germany 191–206; international comparison 111, 113–31, 271–5; in Japan 169–70, 175–6, 188–9; in Netherlands 70, 74, 77–8, 80, 84, 231–2, 234–5, 238–9, 246; in Norway 133–50; secrecy 152–67; in Sweden 208–25, 248–67; transparency 133–50
cartel tenders 72, 82, 113, 122–3, 131; in Australia 167; in Netherlands 232, 234, 236, 240–3, 245; in Norway 146–7; in Sweden 217, 222–3
cartelisation 18–19, 25, 31, 34–5, 37–8; in EEC 49–51, 63; in Finland 91–2, 97, 108; in Germany 192–6, 205; and ICC/LoN 41–3, 45; in Netherlands 66, 68, 70–2, 83, 87, 227–8, 231–5, 237, 240–5; in Norway 143–5, 148; in Sweden 209–10, 212, 214, 224–5, 240–5, 250, 267
cartels 1–13; in Australia 152–67; compulsory registration 48–64; early legislation 17–28; in EEC 48–63; in Finland 88–108; in Germany 191–205; and International Chamber of Commerce 30–46; international comparison 17–29, 113–31, 271–5; in Japan 169–90; laws 88–109, 191–206; and League of Nations 30–46; legislation 37, 93, 103, 137, 149, 176, 192, 195–7, 204–5, 210; legitimising 30–46; in Netherlands 66–85, 227–45; in Norway 133–50; in Sweden 208–25, 248–67
cases 22, 55–8, 63, 154–5, 168; Associated Northern Collieries case 1911 154–5, 168; Coal Vend case 154–5; Grundig-Consten case 55, 57–8, 63; Standard Oil case 1911 22
Castberg, Johan 136–7
cement cartel 144, 153, 159–60, 163, 166, 175, 220, 229
Central Association for the Consumer Cooperatives (Kulutusosuuskuntien Keskusliitto) 89, 91–5, 100, 103
Central Association of the Finnish Wood Processing Industry (Suomen Puuntjalostusteollisuuden Keskusliitto) 96–7
Central Union of Agricultural Producers and Forest Owners (Maataloustuottajien Keskusliitto) 95, 98–9, 103
La Chambre de Commerce Internationale 40
chemical cartel 33, 36–7, 58, 160, 162, 184–5, 220, 241–3
Chicago School 61
Clayton Anti-Trust Act 1914 17
Coal cartel (Rheinisch-Westfölisches Kohlen Syndikat) 191–7, 200, 205
Coal Industry Law (Kohlenwirtschaftsgesetz) 196–7
Coal Vend case 154–5
codes of conduct – Sweden 258, 263
collusion 12, 82, 108, 113, 122–3; in Australia 153–4, 156, 165–7; in Germany 203–5; international comparison 131; in Norway 135; in Sweden 208, 248–50, 253–5, 258–9, 265–7
Colson, Clément 37
combines 4, 10–11, 13, 17–18, 20, 22–3, 29, 132, 152–3, 156–7, 274
Comité des ententes industriels internationaux (CEII) 31, 35–45
Commission for Merger Investigation (Koncentrationsutredningen) 218, 225
Commission for Post-war Economic Planning (Kommisionen för ekonomisk efterkrigsplanering) 213
Commissioner of Trade Practices 163–4, 168
Commonwealth v The Associated Northern Collieries and Others 1911 154–5, 168

Competition Act (Konkurrenslagen) 217
Competition Commission/Inquiry (Konkurrensutredningen) 217–18
Competition and Consumer Act 2010
competition policy 50–1, 60–1, 89, 104, 219; in Australia 152–67; in EEC 48–63; in Finland 88–109; in Germany 191–205; and International Chamber of Commerce 30–46; international comparison 17–29, 113–31, 271–5; in Japan 169–90; law 217; and League of Nations 30–46; in Netherlands 7–8, 10, 12–13, 49–50, 66–88, 90, 107, 117–21, 123–6, 129, 133–4, 209, 227–46, 271; in Norway 133–50; role 1–13, 271–5; in Sweden 208–25, 248–67
concrete 163, 165–6
Confederazione Generale Fascista dell'Industria Italiana 37
confidential registers 7, 37, 40, 43, 70; in Australia 164; international comparison 126; in Netherlands 74, 77–8, 84, 231–3
consensus 7, 10, 66, 68, 72; in Finland 90; in Germany 200, 204; international comparison 272; in Netherlands 76, 84; in Sweden 212–14, 216, 219, 224
Consten SaRL and Grundig GmbH v Commission (1966) 55, 57–8, 63
Conte, Roger 34
cooperation 4, 7, 13, 17–19, 27; in Australia 167; in Finland 91–2, 96–7, 103; and ICC/LoN 30, 34, 47; international comparison 114, 118, 126, 273; in Japan 170, 184; in Netherlands 66–9, 71–2, 76; in Norway 135, 147; in Sweden 212–13, 218, 222–3, 248–59, 264–7
Copper cartel 33, 38, 160
Copper Exporters Incorporation 33
cotton/cotton bale strips 160, 172, 174, 184, 229
Council for Freedom of Trade (Näringsfrihetsrådet) 104–5, 216
crisis cartels 24–5, 71, 120

Davignon, Etienne 57–9
De Rousiers, Paul 34–5, 45
Deakin, Hon. Alfred 152
decartelisation 49–50, 108, 192, 209–10, 224–5
Decree against the Abuse of Economic Power (Verordnung gegen Missbrauch wirtschaftlicher Machtstellungen) 192
Decugis, Henry 37

Denmark 7, 13, 27, 114–18, 120–1; international comparison 123–5, 129; and Netherlands 229, 231; and Norway 133, 149; and Sweden 209, 211
deregulation 48, 60, 81, 189, 250, 263, 265
Deutsche Petroleum-Verkaufsgesellschaft 24
diesel engines 229
distribution agreements 53–4
Domeratzy, Louis 33–4
door locks cartel 230
Duchemin, René 40–1, 45
Dutch competition policy *see* competition policy
dyestuffs cartel 38

early cartel legislation 4, 6, 17–30, 89–90, 213–14
Economic Competition Act 1958 66, 71, 73, 75, 78, 82, 86, 117, 230–2, 234
economic drivers 6, 227
economic policy 51, 56, 66, 256
economic research 8–9, 11–12, 18, 31, 38; in Finland 88, 91; in Germany 192, 194, 198; and ICC/LoN 46; international comparison 114, 274; in Japan 170, 190; in Netherlands 67, 78–81, 227; in Norway 134–6, 144; in Sweden 224
ECSC 49–52, 71, 115
EEC 8, 10, 48–65; Commissioners for Competition 52–4, 57–60; competition policy 48–64; Court of Justice 58; Directorate General for Competition 52, 54–5, 58
efficiency 1, 7, 17, 21, 34; in EEC 50, 53–4, 56, 61–2; in Finland 102; international comparison 115–16, 118, 120, 126, 130–1; in Japan 175; in Netherlands 79–80; in Norway 135, 141; in Sweden 213, 215–16, 218–19, 251, 255, 262, 265, 267
Ehlermann, Claus-Dieter 60, 65
Elektrisk Bureau 147
employer organisations 40, 66, 69, 76–7, 86, 90, 104, 136, 138
enabling acts/laws 84, 133, 136, 139–40, 146–9
Entente International de l'Acier (EIA) 33, 36, 42–3
Erhard, Ludwig 51, 54, 201, 207
EU 48, 64, 79, 88, 208
European Coal and Steel Community *see* ECSC
European Commission 54–63, 79

European Court of Justice 58
European Economic Area Agreement 88, 129
European Free Trade Agreements 52–5, 57–9, 61–2, 64
European Free Trade Agreements Regulation 17/62 52–5, 57–9, 61–2, 64
European Free Trade Agreements Regulation 153/62 54
European Society for Coal and Steel 207
European Union *see* EU
exclusive dealing 60, 164, 234
exemption requests 227, 243
Experts on Business Organisation (1936 års Näringsorganisationssakkunniga) 211–12
Experts of New Establishment (Nyetableringssakkunniga) 214

Federal Cartel Authority – Germany (Bundeskartellamt) 51, 59, 71, 75, 191
Federal Parliament – Germany (Reichstag) 192, 194
Federal Trade Commission 22, 177
Federation of German Industries (Bundesverband der Deutschen Industrie) 199
Federation of Swedish Industries (Industriförbundet) 211–13, 215–17, 219
Finland 7, 10, 13, 68, 78–9; Act on the Control of Practices Restricting Economic Competition 1957 88–108; Act on the Control of Practices Restricting Economic Competition Law to Promote Economic Competition 1962 102; Act on the Control of Practices Restricting Economic Competition Law to Promote Economic Competition 1964 102–5; international comparison 273; Bureau for Freedom of Commerce (Elinkeinovapausvirasto – Näringsfrihetsverket) 104; Cartel Bureau (Kartellivirasto – Kartellbyrån) 101, 104; Central Chamber of Commerce 96–7, 99; Competition Authority (FCA) 105; Competition Council (Kilpailuneuvosto – Konkurrensråd) 90, 105; Competition Ombudsman (Kilpailuasiamies û Konkurrensombudsman) 105, 125; Confederation of Intellectual Workers (Henkisen Työn Keskusliitto – Unionen för Intellektuellt Arbete) 97–8;
Confederation of Trade Unions SAK (Suomen Ammatiliittojen Keskusjärjestö – Finlands Fackföreningars Centralorganisation) 97–8, 103–4; Council for Freedom of Commerce (Elinkeinovapausneuvosto – Nõringsfrihetsrådet) 104–5; Federation of Industries (Suomen Teollisuusliitto) 89, 97–100, 103; international comparison 114, 117–21, 123–5, 128–9, 272; Maastricht Treaty 1992 79; National Board of Trade and Consumer Interests (Elinkeinohallitus û Nõringsstyrelsen) 105; and Netherlands 87, 231, 236, 239–40; and Norway 133, 146; and pressure groups 88–109; and Sweden 209, 265, 267; Treaty on the Functioning of the European Union 64, 79; Wholesalers' Association (Suomen Tukkukauppiaden Liitto) 89, 97, 100
Folksam 258–9, 264–5, 267
Förenade Liv 258
France 33–4, 48–51, 53, 56–7, 63; competition policy 68, 71–2, 75, 209, 228–30, 273; Le Conseil de la Concurrence 1986 75; Le Décret du 9 Août 1953 49, 51–2, 71; Ordinance relative a la liberté des prix et de la concurrence 1986 75
freedom of information principle 9, 29, 101, 137, 140, 142–3, 148
freedom of trade (Gewerbefreiheit) 24, 194

GATT 49, 186
General Agreement on Tariffs and Trade *see* GATT
gentlemen's agreements 13, 17, 19, 25, 197, 256, 267
Germany 5, 7, 9, 12, 32–3; Bundesratsverordnung 1915 196; cartel laws 191–206; Coal Industry Law 1919 (Kohlenwirtschaftsgesetz) 196–7; competition policy 17–29, 191–207; Compulsory Cartel Law 1933 (Gesetz über die Errichtung von Zwangskartellen) 197; Decree against the Abuse of Economic Power 1923 (Verordnung gegen Missbrauch wirtschaftlicher Machtstellungen) 25, 29, 114, 149, 192, 196–7, 205; early legislation 17–28; and EEC 48–51, 53–4, 57, 63; Federal Cartel Authority (Bundeskartellamt) 51, 59, 71, 75, 191;

Gesetz gegen Wettbewerbsbeschränkungen 1933 71, 192, 200–2; gewerbefreiheit 24, 194; and ICC/LoN 41; international comparison 17–29, 113, 116–18, 120–1, 123, 129, 190–207, 272–3; and Japan 175–6; Kartell-Enquête 1902 25; Law against Restraints in Competition 1957 71, 192, 201; and Netherlands 68, 70–2, 75, 87, 228–31, 238–9, 241, 244; and Norway 133; Potash Law 1910 (Reichskaligesetz) 195; Potash Law 1933 (Kaliwirtschaftsgesetz) 198; Reichsgericht 24, 194; and Sweden 209, 211, 250–1
glass cartel 38, 159, 161, 229, 240–1
government intervention 2, 5, 11, 41–2, 61; in Australia 163–4; in Germany 193, 196, 200; in Japan 169, 175, 183, 186; in Netherlands 69, 72, 75–6, 84, 237; in Norway 133–5, 146–8, 150; in Sweden 212, 250, 253–6
Grundig-Consten case 55, 57–8, 63

Harrison, Benjamin 19
High Authority, ECSC 50
high tension cables cartel 229
Hirsch, Julius 13, 34
horizontal agreements 53, 61–2, 72, 77, 79; in Australia 154, 161–3, 165; in Finland 105; international comparison 113, 120, 122–3, 127, 132; in Japan 177, 184, 186; in Netherlands 82, 87, 232, 236–7; in Norway 150; in Sweden 215, 219, 222–3
Howard Smith Co Ltd 154
Huddart Parker and Co Pty Ltd 154
Hungary 4, 41, 115, 137, 148, 229–30

IG Farben 144
Imperial Chemical Industries (ICI) 36
industrial cartels 31, 42, 44, 250
industrial policy 56–7, 63
insurance 12, 95, 130, 140–1, 143; in Australia 154, 157, 159–60; companies 91, 153, 213–14; in Germany 207; inspectorate 214, 263; in Japan 181, 189; in Netherlands 241; Norway 148; in Sweden 248–67
Insurance Sweden 255
Inter-Parliamentary Union (IPU) 5, 115, 149
international aluminium cartels 33, 36, 38, 42–3

International Chamber of Commerce (ICC) 30–46
international drivers 6, 227
The International Industrial Cartel Committee (Comité des ententes industriels internationaux) 10, 31, 35–45
International Steel Cartel (ISC) 42–3
Isaacs, Attorney General 153
Israel Restrictive Trade Practices Act 7, 116–21, 123–4, 126–9

Japan 169–90; Important Export Products Trade Association Law 1925 174; Important Industries Control Act 1931 173; Iron and Steel Corporation 186; Rule on Trade Associations (Junsoku-Kumiai) 1884 172; Temporary Industrial Rationalisation Bureau 174
J.L. Tiedemanns Tobaksfabrik 145
joint-stock insurers 253

Kansa 91
Kartell-Denkschrift 25
Kartell-Enquête 25
Kartellamt 37, 192
The King and the Attorney-General of the Commonwealth v The Associated Northern Collieries and Others (1911) 154–5, 168
Knudsen, Gunnar 136
Kock, Karin 213
konsesjonslovene 26
Korah, Valentine 61

Lammers, Clemens 37–8, 40–4
Länsförsäkringar 265
Law against Restraints in Competition (Gesetz gegen Wettbewerbsbeschränkungen) 71, 192, 200–2
lead cartel 38
League of Nations (LoN) 10, 30–46, 175
legislation 2, 4–12, 17–29, 36–7, 41; in Australia 152–3, 156, 158–9, 164–7; in EEC 49, 59–60, 62; in Finland 88–108; in Germany 192–8, 202–5; international comparison 113–20, 122, 124–32, 272–3; in Japan 170–2, 174–81, 185–6, 190; in Netherlands 66–7, 70–3, 76, 78–9, 81, 86, 227–8, 240, 242, 244; in Norway 133–5, 137–8, 141, 149; in Sweden 208–10, 212–19, 222, 225, 249–50, 252–4, 256–7, 260, 263–4, 266

Index 307

Libbey-Owens 47
Liberal Party 27, 135, 159
linoleum cartel 38, 230
Loucheur, Louis 31–3
Lovasy, Gertrud 44
Lykke, Ivar 139

MacGregor, Donald H. 34
McIlwraith McEachern and Co Pty Ltd. 154
major cartels *see* cartels
margarine cartel 144, 160
Marjolin, Robert 57
Market Council – Sweden (Marknadsrådet) 217
Market Court – Sweden (Marknadsdomstolen) 217
marketing agreements 17, 103, 120, 157–9, 234, 250, 261–3
Marlio, Louis 36–8, 41–3, 45, 47
matches cartel 38, 91, 157, 160
mercury cartel 38
mergers 3, 13, 19, 21–2, 48–52; in Australia 164–5, 167; in EEC 60, 63; in Finland 105; in Germany 191, 204; international comparison 113, 121–3; in Japan 172, 174–5, 186; in Netherlands 80, 83–4; in Norway 144; in Sweden 218–19, 224–5, 255, 260, 265–6
Meyer, Aloys 36, 38, 43, 45
modernisation 66–86
Mond, Alfred 35–6, 38
Mond, Bruner and Co. 36
motor vehicles cartel 160, 242–3
motorcycles cartel 242–3
moving picture recording/reproducing apparatus cartel 229
Müller-Armack, Alfred 51, 54, 64
Murphy, Hon. Lionel 164
mutual insurers 153, 248, 250–4, 258–9, 264–5
Myrdal Commission: Commission for Post-war Economic Planning (Kommisionen für ekonomisk efterkrigsplanering) 213, 225, 257

nationalisation 254–6, 262, 265, 267
Netherlands 7–8, 10, 12–13, 49–50, 90; Association for co-operative and price arranging organisations in the construction industry (Vereniging van Samenwerkende en Prijsregelende Organisaties in de Bouwnijverheid) 79; Authority for Consumers and Markets (Autoriteit Consument en Markt) 83; Bureau for Economic Policy Analysis (Centraal Planbureau) 81; Business Agreements Act (Ondernemers-overeenkomstenwet) 1930 69–70; Cartel Decree (Kartelbesluit) 1941 70, 228–9; Committee for Economic Competition (Commissie Economische Mededinging) 73; Competition Authority (Nederlandse Mededingingsautoriteit) 83, 227, 232; Competition Law (Mededingingswet) 1993 235; Competition Law (Mededingingswet) 1998 83, 230; Economic Competition Act (Wet Economische Mededinging) 1958 71, 73, 86, 230; Establishment of Businesses Act (Vestigingswet) 81; facts/figures 227–46; and Finland 107; Industrial Organisation Act (Wet op de bedrijfsorganisatie) 1950 69; international comparison 117–21, 123–6, 129, 271; Ministry of Economic Affairs 69–70, 72–3, 76–7, 79–82, 86, 125, 228, 231–4, 237, 246; modernisation 66–85; and Norway 133–4; Price Law (Prijzenwet) 76; Shopping Hours Act (Winkelsluitingswet) 81; Suspension of Business Regulation Act (Wet Schorsing Bedrijfsregelingen) 1951 71; and Sweden 209; Wage Law (Wet op de loonvorming) 76
nitrogen fertilisers cartel 144, 229
Nordstjernan 251, 254
Norsk Hydro 144
Norway 4, 7, 9, 11, 13; Act on the Control of Restraints of Competition and Price Abuse 1926 11, 18, 26–7, 91, 114, 133, 135–6, 140–2, 146–9; Competition Act 1993 133, 150; concession laws 26, 136–8, 148; early legislation 17–28; Federation of Commerce – NFC (Norges Handelsstands forbund) 134; Federation of Industries – NFI (Norges Industriforbund) 134; and Finland 91, 99; international comparison 113–14, 116–17, 120–5, 129, 132, 272; and Japan 175; Labour Party 135, 138, 142; Minister/Ministry of Justice 26, 136–7, 142; Minister/Ministry of Provisions 139; and Netherlands 68, 87, 229; Price Act 1953 150; Price Directorate 133–4,

136–40, 142, 148–9; Price Regulation
  Act 1920 4, 113–14, 117, 133, 135,
  138–40, 149; Shipowners' Association
  135; and Sweden 209; transparency
  133–50; Trust Act (trustloven) 1926 11,
  18, 26–7, 91, 114, 133, 135–6, 140–2,
  146–9; Trust Commission 27, 134,
  136–8, 140–1, 143; Trust Control
  Council 134, 142–9; Trust Control
  Office 135, 144, 147–8, 150
notification systems 5, 10–11, 48, 50,
  52–5; in Australia 161; in EEC 59–63;
  in Finland 95, 97, 100–1, 103–7;
  international comparison 27, 115–16,
  120, 122, 124, 128, 130, 272; in Japan
  182; in Netherlands 86, 232–3, 235,
  246; in Norway 133–44, 147, 149–50

OEEC 49
Oldset, Robert E. 37
Olivetti, Gino
Ombudsman for Freedom of Commerce
  (Näringsfrihetsombundsmannen) 105,
  216–18, 221–2
Oualid, William 34, 43, 45

paper cartel 242–3
parliaments 5, 12, 25–7, 54, 77; in
  Australia 153, 156, 164; in Finland 96,
  98–101, 107; in Germany 192, 194,
  196, 199, 201–2, 204–5; international
  comparison 115; in Netherlands 82,
  231; in Norway 135–42, 144, 149; in
  Sweden 211, 255
Pellervo Society 95, 103
Petit, Lilian T.D. 66–86, 227–46
petroleum cartel 24, 38, 157, 159–60,
  165–6, 230
Phoebus (electric lamp) cartel 33
Polder Model 10, 76, 272
policy-holders 251–6, 258, 264–7
political inconsistency 77, 232
Potash Cartel (Kali-Kartell) 33, 38, 175,
  193, 195, 198
premiums 248, 250–6, 258–9, 264–5, 267
pressure groups, role 88–109
price agreements 77, 164, 167
price fixing 5, 56, 98–9, 104, 122; in
  Australia 156–7, 162–3, 165;
  international cpmparison 127, 132; in
  Netherlands 236, 247; in Sweden
  215–17, 219, 221–4
printing cartel 242–3
Privy Council 155, 168

Index 309

public institutions/organisations 3, 5, 7,
  32, 39–40; in EEC 48, 53, 56, 58; in
  Germany 197–8; and ICC/LoN 42–3,
  45; in Netherlands 67, 81; in Sweden
  216
public interests 3, 26, 73–4, 84, 115, 240
publicity 5, 8, 10, 77, 87; in Australia 164;
  in Finland 94, 100, 105, 107; in
  Germany 199, 202; international
  comparison 19, 21, 23, 28–9, 115, 119,
  271; in Japan 175, 182–3; in
  Netherlands 232; in Norway 138,
  148–9; in Sweden 253
publishing cartel 242–3
pulp cartel 24, 186, 242–3

quinine cartel 75

radio equipment cartel 229
rail materials cartel 38
rayon cartel 38
real estate cartel 242
Register of Trade Agreements 161
registration 1–13, 26, 29, 52, 54; in EEC
  56; in Finland 88, 106; in Germany
  196, 202–4; international comparison
  113–31; in Japan 169–70, 175–6,
  188–9; in Netherlands 70, 74, 77–8, 80,
  84, 231–2, 234–5, 238–9, 246; in
  Norway 133–50; in Sweden 208, 210,
  213–16, 218–25, 248, 250, 260, 264,
  267
regulating capitalism 1–13
Regulation 17/62 *see* EEC
regulatory change – Netherlands 79
Reichsgericht 24, 194
Reichsverband der deutschen Industrie 37
resale price maintenance 99, 104, 132, 164
Restauration économique 34
Restrictive Trade Practices Act – Sweden
  (Konkurrensbegränsningslagen) 26, 216
retail trade 92, 157, 214
Rheinisch-Westfälisches Kohlen-Syndikat
  (RWKS) 191, 193–7, 200, 205
Roemer, Karl 58
roof tiles 156–7, 159, 161, 166
Roosevelt, Theodore 21, 29
rubber cartel 42–3, 159, 161–2, 166, 228,
  230, 240–1, 243, 247
Ruhrcoal 196, 200
RWKS *see* Rheinisch-Westfälisches
  Kohlen Syndikat

Saxon Wood Pulp case 1897 24

Schlielder, Willy 59
Schmoller, Gustav 25
Schumpeter, Joseph Alois 30, 44
sclerosis 66–86
secret registers 152–67
Sherman Act 3, 17, 20–3, 26, 29, 49, 152, 177
Skandia 250–2, 254, 257, 265
social drivers 6, 227
SOFINA 38
South Korea 8; Monopoly Regulation and Fair Trade Act 117–19, 129
Spain 7, 9, 84, 117–21, 123; Court for the Protection of Competition 126; international comparison 129; and Netherlands 229, 231; and Norway 133; Service for the Protection of Competition 126; and Sweden 209, 267
Spinelli, Altiero 57
Standard Oil Case 1911 22, 24–5
Standard Oil Trust 19, 21, 24
Standard Telefon og Kabelfabrikk 147
standardisation 173, 183, 213, 250–4, 259–60, 262, 266
Steamship Owners' Association 154
steel pipes 166
Stoppani, Pietro 36, 42, 45
Streseman, Gustav 25
sugar cartel 166
Sutherland, Peter 60
Svea (Swedish joint-stock insurer) 250–2, 254
Sweden 7, 12–13, 27, 68, 79; Act on Probation on Restrictive Business Practices 1946 93, 101, 117, 210, 213, 219; Bureau of Monopoly Investigation (Monopolutredningsbyrån) 213, 215–17, 219, 223; Competition Authority (Konkurrensverket) 219, 222; Competition Commission (Konkurrensutredningen) 217–18; competition policy 248–67; Confederation of Trade Unions (Landsorganisationen) 214; Cooperative Union and Wholesale Society (Kooperativa förbundet) 91, 211; Council for Freedom of Trade (Näringsfrihetsrådet) 104, 216; Experts on Business Organisation (års Näringsorganisationssakkunniga) 211; Experts of New Establishment (Nyetableringssakkunniga) 214; Federation of Wholesalers 216; and Finland 88, 91, 93, 99, 101, 106; Fire Tariff Committee 251, 257; insurance cartels 248–67; Insurance Inspectorate 214, 252, 254–8, 263, 265; Insurance Rating Committee 256; Insurance Society 263; Insurers Federation 263; international comparison 114, 116–25, 129; Life Insurance Companies' Association 253; Life Insurers Directors Association (Svenska Livförsäkringsbolags Direktörsförening) 253–4, 262; Market Council (Marknadsrådet) 217; Market Court (Marknadsdomstolen) 217; Merger Investigation Committee 218; National Board of Trade (Kommerskollegium) 211, 213; National Private Insurance Supervisory Service (Swedish Insurance Inspectorate) 252; National Rates and Cartel Board (Statens pris- och kartellnämnd) 217; and Netherlands 87, 229–31, 239–40; and Norway 133, 135, 137, 146; Ombudsman for Freedom of Commerce (Näringsfrihetsombundsmannen) 216; Organisation of Handicraft and Small Business 216; post-war period 208–25; Retail Federation (Köpmannaförbundet) 221; State Price and Competition Authority (Statens pris- och konkurrensverk) 218; Trade and Industry Competition Committee (Näringslivets konkurrensnämnd) 216; Wire Nail Manufacturers Association (Sveriges Trådspiksfabrikanters Förening) 223

tariffs/tariff organisations 24, 28, 33–5, 49, 148, 152–3, 157, 186, 251–2, 256–7, 264
telephone equipment 147
terms of insurance 254
Thagaard, Wilhelm 134–6, 139, 143–6, 149–50
tin cartel 38
tobacco/tobacco trust 22, 145, 153, 157, 159, 161, 240, 243
trade associations 113, 130, 173, 219, 234, 238, 266
Trade Practices Commission 165
trade unions 6, 12, 66, 68, 70; in Finland 89, 97–8, 103–4; international comparison 21, 130; in Netherlands

76–7; in Norway 136, 138; in Sweden 214, 219, 225
transparency 133–50
transport and storage cartels 243
Treaty of Rome 1957 48–55, 71
Trust Control Council 134, 142–5, 149
trusts 3–5, 10, 34, 38, 40; in Australia 152–3, 156; in Finland 91–3, 95, 98; international comparison 17–23, 25–9, 115, 274; in Japan 177; in Norway 135, 137, 141, 149; in Sweden 211
Trygg Hansa 265
Tschierschky, Siegfried 37–8, 41, 45, 115, 193

UK 7–8, 13, 49, 51, 56; and Australia 158–9; competition policy 132; and EEC 61, 63; Fair Trading Act 1973 75; Fire Offices Committee 251; international comparison 113–14, 116–21, 123–5, 127–9, 132, 273; and Japan 175; and Netherlands 68, 71–2, 75, 84, 228–31; Office of Fair Trading 75; Restrictive Trade Practices Act 1976 75; and Sweden 209–10, 267
Unilever 145
Union des Industries de la Communauté Européenne (UNICE) 55
United Kingdom (UK) *see* UK
United Nations 44, 68, 132, 227
United States of America (US) *see* US
US 3–5, 9–11, 31–3, 37, 40; and Australia 153, 158; Bureau of Corporations 21–3, 25, 29; competition policy 22–3, 61; Department of Commerce and Labor 21, 33; early legislation 17–28; and EEC 49–50, 59, 62; Federal Trade Commission 22, 177; Federal Trade Commission Act 1914 177; and Germany 194, 203–4; international comparison 21–3, 25–6, 28, 115–16, 130, 132, 272–3; and Japan 169, 176, 184, 190; and Netherlands 230; and Norway 145; and Sweden 213; Webb-Pomerene Act 1918 4, 7, 32–3

Valand 265
Vegete 265
vertical agreements 53, 55, 61–3, 72, 82; in Australia 154, 161–3, 165; in Finland 98, 104; international comparison 113, 120–2; in Japan 177; in Netherlands 232–3, 235, 237; in Sweden 215–17, 220–3
vertragsfreiheit 23
Von der Groeben, Hans 52, 54–7
Vouel, Raymond 58–9

War Corporations (Kriegsgesellschaften) 196
Wasa 265
wheat and flour milling 157, 166
wholesale cartels 89, 91–2, 97, 100, 146; in Australia 161, 166; in Japan 181; in Netherlands 240–1, 243; in Sweden 211, 214–16, 220
wood 24, 96–7, 160, 240–3

zinc cartel 38

Taylor & Francis eBooks

Helping you to choose the right eBooks for your Library

Add Routledge titles to your library's digital collection today. Taylor and Francis ebooks contains over 50,000 titles in the Humanities, Social Sciences, Behavioural Sciences, Built Environment and Law.

Choose from a range of subject packages or create your own!

Benefits for you
- Free MARC records
- COUNTER-compliant usage statistics
- Flexible purchase and pricing options
- All titles DRM-free.

Benefits for your user
- Off-site, anytime access via Athens or referring URL
- Print or copy pages or chapters
- Full content search
- Bookmark, highlight and annotate text
- Access to thousands of pages of quality research at the click of a button.

REQUEST YOUR FREE INSTITUTIONAL TRIAL TODAY

Free Trials Available
We offer free trials to qualifying academic, corporate and government customers.

eCollections – Choose from over 30 subject eCollections, including:

Archaeology	Language Learning
Architecture	Law
Asian Studies	Literature
Business & Management	Media & Communication
Classical Studies	Middle East Studies
Construction	Music
Creative & Media Arts	Philosophy
Criminology & Criminal Justice	Planning
Economics	Politics
Education	Psychology & Mental Health
Energy	Religion
Engineering	Security
English Language & Linguistics	Social Work
Environment & Sustainability	Sociology
Geography	Sport
Health Studies	Theatre & Performance
History	Tourism, Hospitality & Events

For more information, pricing enquiries or to order a free trial, please contact your local sales team: www.tandfebooks.com/page/sales

The home of Routledge books

www.tandfebooks.com